Manual

Of

Housing Law

AUSTRALIA
Law Book Co.
Sydney

CANADA and USA
Carswell
Toronto

HONG KONG
Sweet & Maxwell Asia

NEW ZEALAND
Brookers
Wellington

SINGAPORE and MALAYSIA
Sweet & Maxwell Asia
Singapore and Kuala Lumpur

MANUAL

OF

HOUSING LAW

By

ANDREW ARDEN Q.C.
and
CAROLINE HUNTER

*Barrister, Senior Lecturer in Housing Law,
Sheffield Hallam University*

Seventh Edition

THOMSON

™

SWEET & MAXWELL

First Edition 1978 (HOUSING: Security and Rent Control)
Second Edition 1983
Reprinted 1983
Reprinted 1984
Third Edition 1986
Reprinted 1987
Reprinted 1988
Fourth Edition 1989
Fifth Edition 1992
Reprinted 1994
Sixth Edition 1997
Seventh Edition 2003

Published in 2003 by
Sweet & Maxwell Limited
100 Avenue Road
Swiss Cottage
London, NW3 3PF
Typeset by LBJ Typesetting Ltd of Kingsclere
Printed in England by Ashford Colour Press Ltd, Hants

British Library Cataloguing in Publication Data

A catalogue record
for this book is
available from
the British Library

ISBN 0–421–769 203

INTRODUCTION

Until the mid-1970s, the term "housing law" was in scant use: it was a term applied to a sub-division of planning law and on occasion merited a mention in landlord and tenant. The subject covered the powers and duties of local authorities, mainly in relation to slum clearance (by area or individual unit), the provision of public housing and such related matters as improvement grants. Housing law was confined to a study of the powers exercisable in the public interest in relation to what was statutorily identified as housing.

Reflecting the growth of legal aid, and the introduction of law centres, and the underlying social demand for "rights", housing law began to develop—largely through the pages of the Legal Action Group Bulletin (as Legal Action was then called) and subsequently through the *Encyclopedia of Housing Law*—with a somewhat wider focus on the law as it affected the use of property as a home, whether derived from private rights or from the public powers and duties conferred or imposed on local authorities, whether formally identified as housing or because they impacted on housing in practice.

The topics thus taken into the subject included the Rent Acts (governing private sector security and harassment/illegal eviction), leasehold enfranchisement and extension, matrimonial law so far as it affected the family home on domestic breakdown, environmental health (statutory nuisance and other provisions affecting housing), social security, rating, mobile homes, judicial review (enjoying its own period of unprecedented growth, itself in part a reflection of the same rise in rights awareness), as well as some planning law, compulsory purchase, conveyancing, contract and tort.

From these acorns have grown seven editions of this book (including the first, under the title *Housing: Security and Rent Control*).

The first edition coincided with the first homelessness Act. Since, we have seen the arrival (1980 Act) of security of tenure for public and quasi-public sector tenants, together with the right to buy, followed by the wholesale removal of housing associations into the private sector, and the concurrent diminution in their tenants' rights (1988 Act), only to see the "right to acquire" offered back to them (1996 Act), their identities changed by the same Act to "registered social landlords," and some sort of security parity reachieved by means of the so-called "probationary" or "starter" tenancy, in the form of introductory tenancies under Housing Act 1985 and shorthold tenancies under Housing Act 1988, the former entirely new with, and the latter substantially recast by, the 1996 Act.

Over the 1980s, we watched the fall from grace of the Rent Acts (1915–1988) and the rise in their place of the assured tenancy—the same class of security into which housing association tenants were moved. Full security was tempered by the shorthold, initially a landlord's option, more recently (1996 Act) the presumptive form of letting to which full security has become the exception.

Meanwhile, housing improvement grants, mandatory since 1959, have—with but a few exceptions—been reduced to a discretionary status and are now subsumed into a much broader discretionary system of "housing assistance" (Regulatory Reform (Housing Assistance) (England and Wales) Order 2002).

There have been many, many other changes, including the introduction of housing benefits followed by tight controls to prevent advantage being taken of their availability, and large-scale stock transfers (temporarily sub nom. the Tenant's Choice: in with the 1988 Act; out with 1996).

The 1996 Act also revised homelessness law, a cornerstone of housing law as it had defined itself. That reduction of rights has recently been reversed in part by the 2002 Act.

Fittingly, perhaps, from the perspective of this giddy review, that Act introduces a requirement for authorities to carry out homelessness reviews and formulate strategies for dealing with homelessness that is strongly reminiscent (at least for those with longer memories) of the function in s.91, Housing Act 1957—dating back to Housing, Town Planning, etc. Act 1919—of preparing plans for providing new housing (backing up the consideration of housing conditions and review of information which survived through to, and survives in, the 1985 Act).

Along the way, rates departed, poll-tax (individual-based) came and went, and the replacement council tax took local taxation back to a property base. General (rate) fund subsidy for council tenants was abolished and replaced with a requirement to budget to balance the Housing Revenue Account. Other changes to local government law also had an impact, with greater access to information and less access to money, a Chief Financial Officer and a Monitoring Officer to keep authorities on the straight-and-narrow, and cross-party committees to help take the politics out of local decision-making. That too changes gear—and direction—with the formal split between an authority's executive and their full authority.

Finally, we may note the Human Rights Act 1998 which has meant that decisions of public authorities are subject to ever closer scrutiny by the courts, a development which has already impacted on most housing issues and which may be considered the highest form yet of the rights-based movement with which we began.

It would be possible to continue to illustrate at length and we have not yet touched on Law Commission proposals for change to the mutliplicity of tenures under which housing is occupied and its replacement with two basic "types" of occupation agreement (*Renting Homes: (1) Status and Security* (CP162)). The point is clear: housing law is a subject in a state of constant evolution (if not revolution) and if this history is anything to go by, is probably destined so to remain.

That makes it difficult to keep up with. Furthermore, law is rarely retrospective (although the Law Commission may yet break the mould with its "big bang" proposal to introduce its new tenures in place of all existing tenures at one fell swoop—see CP162, para.14.45). Accordingly, one set of rules does not replace another, so much as two (or ten) sets co-exist for a period. And, as this is about where people live, that usually means decades rather than years.

This gives rise to difficult "policy" decisions as to what should be included in a book like this, without jeopardising its description as a Manual, and how to structure it to ensure that it reflects contemporary concerns.

In this edition, we have retained the basic format of the book— albeit revised to include the changes of the last five years, in the expectation—and hope—that a much more fundamental restructuring is just around the corner, if and when the Law Commission review of housing law is brought to fruition.

The most significant change is the introduction of an outline at the beginning of each Chapter, designed to allow the reader more choice about—as it were—which part of the forest to visit without being wholly dependent on we guides.

A number of topics continue not to be touched upon at all: conveyancing, house construction, planning law, compulsory purchase, mobile homes, council tax.

Other subjects are treated briefly, *e.g.* owner-occupation (including the rights to buy and acquire) and domestic breakdown will almost invariably require the assistance of a solicitor, and—so far as this book is of interest to law students—these are topics conventionally covered extensively in law courses.

Financial assistance, by way of housing benefit, is merely mentioned because the provisions and details change so frequently that what would be written here would almost certainly be out of date by the time it is read (and there are other, annual works which are available and accessible both to lawyers and to non-lawyers).

The underlying approach, however, has remained the same since the first edition, even if the structure and emphasis have changed with the times. That approach is to start with the task of identifying the principal housing "status" of tenants and other occupiers. The inherent thesis is that in almost every case it will be impossible to determine what are the respective rights and liability of a party to a housing arrangement without first determining what is the status of the occupier in law.

The first Chapter is therefore the child of the common law. Only once common law status has been determined does it become possible to turn to the work of Parliament and consider the many different categories of occupier which now exist by statute. The reader, then, is accordingly urged to bear with the first Chapter, largely devoid as it is of substantive rights and duties, for without it the remainder of the book will be of little practical value and the risk of its missapplication will be very real indeed.

It would be idle—and wrong—to ignore the fact that this book is but one in a set or series of which we are also the co-authors, from which it follows that we owe a debt of gratitude to those colleagues who work with us on other titles. The main text on which we constantly rely, and to which the reader is referred for enlargement of detail and for the other areas of housing law which have not been covered in this Manual, is Arden & Partington's *Housing Law* (Sweet & Maxwell, loose-leaf); for the source material, the reader may refer to the *Encylopedia of Housing Law*, and the *Housing Law Reports*, both also published by Sweet & Maxwell; Sweet & Maxwell likewise publish the *Journal of Housing Law* in which many issues are given a more detailed, and commonly more discursive, examination than is commonly available in the other titles. For a more detailed treatment of homelessness and allocations, the Legal Action Group is currently producing a 6th edition of our book devoted to the subject.

The law is stated as at September 30, 2002, save that we have taken into account statutory changes not yet in force at that time in relation to the Homelessness Act 2002. We have also mentioned, where relevant, the provisions of the Commonhold and Leasehold Reform Act 2002, which have yet to be brought into force.

Andrew Arden Q.C, M.C.I.H.,
Arden Chambers,
2, John St,
London, WC1N 2ES

Caroline Hunter,
Arden Chambers,
and
Sheffield Hallam
University

November 2002.

TABLE OF CONTENTS

11 DISREPAIR

12 HOUSING ACT—DISREPAIR AND IMPROVEMENT

13 DISREPAIR UNDER ENVIRONMENTAL LAW

TABLE OF CASES

TABLE OF STATUTES

TABLE OF STATUTORY INSTRUMENTS

Civil Procedure Rules

Rules of the Supreme Court

County Court Rules

ABBREVIATIONS

Statutes

Matrimonial Causes Act 1973	MCA 1973
Protection from Eviction Act 1977	PEA 1977
Criminal Law Act 1977	CLA 1977
Family Law Act 1996	FLA 1996
Protection from Harassment Act 1997	PHA 1997
Land Registration Act 2002	LRA 2002
Commonhold and Leasehold Reform Act 2002	CLRA 2002

Statutory Instruments

Civil Procedure Rules 1998	CPR 1998

Others

Anti-Social Behaviour Order	ASBO
Citizen's Advice Bureau	CAB
European Convention on Human Rights	ECHR
Houses in Multiple Occupation	HMO
Housing and Regeneration Community Association	HARCA
Large-Scale Voluntary Transfer	LSVT
Leasehold Valuation Tribunal	LVT
Notice of Proceedings	NOP
Notice of Seeking Possession	NSP
Registered Social Landlord	RSL
Rent Assessment Committee	RAC
Rent Assessment Panel Committee	RAPC
Retail Price Index	RPI
Right to Enfranchise	RTE
Right to Manage Company	RTM Company
Tenancy Relations Officer	TRO

CHAPTER ONE

The Classes of Occupation

Introduction

1.01 The Starting-point of Status. The starting-point of any study of housing law is the "status" of a person in premises, that is to say the "class" of occupation he enjoys. In turn, that involves two questions. First, there are classes of occupation rights—or means of identifying when they are absent—which have been developed over many years and are embodied in the common law. This gives us the existing legal concepts on which statutes bite. Moving on from there, the second part of the status issue is to identify within (or across) these common law classes of occupation those to whom the benefits of each body of statutory protection apply.

1.02 Law Commission. It is only when this exercise has been carried out that it is possible to say which substantive right—or duty—binds which occupiers and/or landlords. There is much scope for criticism of such a complex approach to housing rights and the Law Commission—the body charged with proposing major reforms to the law—has recently issued its proposals for a substantially simpler system of "Type 1" and "Type 2" rights of occupation, meaning those with full and those with only restricted security, which will do away with some, if not all, of this common law starting-point: see Renting Homes: 1 Status and Security—Law Commission Consultation Paper No.162.

1.03 Two Stages. Future editions of this book may, therefore, enjoy the benefit of an entirely new starting-point. Until that report is accepted, however, it remains necessary to approach status in the two stages described above. In this chapter, we are concerned (only) with the first stage—common law classes of occupation. In the next six chapters, we then consider these classes in the context of the numerous statutes which govern them.

1

1.04 Principal Occupation Classes. There are four principal ways in which a person can come to use premises as a residence:

Owner-occupation;

Trespass;

Licence; and

Tenancy.

1.05 Particular Arrangements. In addition, however, there are particular categories or combinations of circumstances, some of which must also be considered:

Tied accommodation;

Sub-tenants;

Joint tenants;

Tenants of mortgagors;

Assignees; and

Change of landlord.

1.06 Minor Arrangements. There is also a number of minor arrangements which do not fit comfortably or easily within either the classes of occupation considered in this chapter, or the specific classes of protection considered in the following chapters. For example, "shared ownership", where a person pays "rent" which is partly for use and occupation, and partly towards purchase. There are also "co-ownership" schemes, where member-tenants pay rent, but have an interest in the capital value of, usually, a block of flats. The complexity of such schemes, and the relatively few people affected, put the details of them beyond the scope of this book.

Outline

1.07 Owner-occupation

- Owner-occupiers may have a freehold, long-leasehold or (when the Commonhold and Leasehold Reform Act 2002 comes into force) commonhold interest;
- Owner-occupiers may mortgage their homes;
- Jointly owned property is held on trust;

- Trusts may also arise where a person contributes to the purchase, even though he is not the legal (named) owner;

- The courts have powers under the Trusts of Land and Appointment of Trustees Act 1996 to declare the extent of the trust and to order sale of the property.

1.08 Trespass

- Someone occupying a property without permission is a trespasser;

- Trespassers or "squatters" may be given permission to remain, in which case they become licencees;

- After 12 years, a trespasser may become entitled to ownership of the land through the law of adverse possession;

- A new class of trespass—"tolerated trespass"—has been recently identified by the courts in order to cope with those whose landlords have permitted them to remain in occupation after an order for possession has become effective, without re-acquiring their original rights;

- Trespass can sometimes be a criminal offence.

1.09 Licence

- A person with permission to occupy accommodation, but who does not have a tenancy will occupy under a licence;

- Licences may arise in a number of circumstances: family arrangements; sharing arrangements; long stay hotels; hostels; acts of kindness; and, genuine lodging arrangement;

- A tenancy rather than a licence will arise if the occupier has exclusive possession at a term for a rent;

- Even if an agreement is called a licence, it will be a tenancy if these elements are all present;

- Before a licensee can be evicted the licence must be properly brought to an end; if a fixed term contractual licence, the fixed term must expire; if a periodic contractual licence reasonable notice must be given.

1.10   Tenancy

- Tenancy is the normal arrangement by which one person occupies premises which are owned by another;

- There are four essential elements of tenancy: identifiable parties; identifiable premises; period of tenancy; and, exclusive possession;

- There are two common forms of tenancy: periodic and fixed term;

- A periodic tenancy is one which is granted to run from period to period, *e.g.* week to week;

- It can be terminated at common law by either the landlord or the tenant serving notice to quit;

- There are strict rules about the content and service of notices to quit;

- A fixed term tenancy is one which is granted for a specific period of time, *e.g.* six months;

- It is brought to an end by the period running out;

- Tenancies may also be brought to an end by the tenant surrendering the tenancy; but only if the landlord is willing to accept the surrender;

- A fixed term tenancy can also be terminated before the term has run out by the landlord obtaining forfeiture of the lease for breach of the agreement;

- Tenants may apply to the court for relief from forfeiture.

1.11   Other Circumstances

Tied accommodation

- An occupier of accommodation which is provided in the course of employment may be a service tenant or a service occupier;

- A person living in tied accommodation will be a service occupier if it is necessary for him to live in the premises in question in order to carry out the employment duties;

- A service occupier's licence is terminable on the cessation of employment without any requirement of notice.

Sub-tenancies

- Where a tenant's landlord is himself a tenant, the tenant will be a sub-tenant; the landlord is referred to as a mesne tenant;

- Particular difficulties arise for sub-tenants when the mesne tenancy is brought to an end;

- Provided the sub-tenancy is lawful, some statutory protection for sub-tenants is available;

- A sub-tenancy will be unlawful if there is a prohibition in the mesne tenancy on sub-letting; prohibitions may be absolute or qualified, *i.e.* it may require the consent of the head landlord;

- If the mesne tenancy includes a qualified prohibition on sub-letting the head landlord generally cannot withhold consent unreasonably.

Joint tenancies

- A joint tenancy arises where two or more persons share the tenancy;

- Service of a notice to quit by one joint tenant is sufficient to terminate the tenancy;

- Where accommodation is shared but there is only one named tenant, other occupiers will generally be his sub-tenants or licensees;

- Groups of sharers may occupy under "non-exclusive occupation agreements" which, if genuine, means that they will only be licensees.

Tenants of mortgagors

- Tenants of landlords who have mortgaged the property may be evicted by the mortgage company if the company repossesses the property on default of payment by the landlord and if the tenancy was created in breach of the mortgage deed.

Assignment

- Most tenancies include a prohibition on assignment;

- Where assignment is permitted certain formalities, including a written document, must be completed for it to be effective.

New landlords

- Where a landlord purchases a property with existing tenants, he takes it subject to those tenancies.

Owner-Occupation

1.12 Unmortgaged freehold. A person who owns the freehold of the house in which he lives, untrammelled by any mortgage, is the principal "model" for owner-occupation. Such a person has the fullest rights of occupation and protection of all. The right to occupy the house can only be interfered with in limited circumstances. For example, if a local authority or some other public body should purchase the house compulsorily, perhaps for some new development; or else, if the property falls into considerable disrepair, the local authority might place a closing order or demolition order on the house, as a result of which it will become illegal to live in it.

1.13 Another way in which such an owner-occupier might lose the right of occupation is if he goes into bankruptcy and the trustee in bankruptcy forces the sale of his home. Some of these incidents are outside the scope of this book: closing and demolition orders, and clearance by a local authority, are dealt with in Chapter 12. We shall consider one further way in which a freehold owner might come to lose the right to occupy his home, and that is as a result of a court order made in the course of a domestic breakup. This is dealt with in Chapter 9.

1.14 Mortgaged freehold. Many people who have a freehold interest in their homes, however, do so under mortgage. A mortgage is a loan against the security of property, *i.e.* a house or a flat. The money is usually borrowed in order to buy the property, although sometimes it may be needed for carrying out repairs or improvements. Sometimes people raise money by way of mortgage simply because they are in other financial difficulties. If a person falls into arrears with his mortgage repayments, eviction may follow: see Chapter 2.

1.15 Long leaseholders. A freehold interest is one which is unlimited in time: there is no "superior" interest or landlord who can claim the property in the future. The opposite of freehold is the term which is limited in time. Strictly, all such terms arc tenancies, whether they are on a lease for 999 years or a periodic weekly tenancy. In practice, however, to treat these last two occupiers in the same class of occupation would fly in the face of reality.

1.16 Accordingly, we include in "owner-occupation" those who do not have a freehold interest in their home, but who have a long leasehold interest, meaning one which is for a term of at least 21 years, which in normal circumstances will have been "bought" by a premium no different in quality (even if somewhat in quantity) than the purchase price paid for the acquisition of a freehold house. The first category of those are leaseholders who have been able to acquire their homes without a mortgage, who will pay what is usually a small, annual ground rent to a landlord, who is, at least in theory, entitled to reclaim the property at the end of the lease.

1.17 Termination. In practice, on the termination of the lease, most long-leasehold occupiers have rights of occupation similar to those enjoyed by other tenants and, in some circumstances, a leasehold occupier may be able to compel the landlord to sell him the freehold or extend the lease. These rights will also be considered in Chapter 2. If the leaseholder breaches the terms of the lease, however, the landlord may seek to repossess through the forfeiture procedure. This procedure is considered below (1.126–1.141).

1.18 Mortgaged leasehold. Leasehold interests may be held under mortgage, although usually it will not be possible to obtain a mortgage on a leasehold property unless there is at least a 30-year period to run on the lease. This is because mortgage companies need security for their loans, and must calculate what they can recover by resale of the property should the occupier fall into arrears on the mortgage at any given point in time. If the occupier falls into arrears in the last few years, the mortgage company will not have much to resell: but, then, there will not be much of a debt left on the property. If the occupier falls into arrears soon after the mortgage is granted, there will be time enough on the lease for the mortgage company to recoup its loan.

1.19 Leasehold by assignment. Many people do not acquire a leasehold interest directly from the freeholder who originally granted it. They acquire it instead from the existing leaseholder, commonly the existing occupier who is selling his interest. During the course of such a transaction, the freeholder will have little or nothing to do with the arrangements, save perhaps that his consent to them may be required (but will normally be easily available). Where a would-be occupier under leasehold purchases from an outgoing leaseholder, the transaction is called an assignment, but it is in all other respects much like a straightforward purchase. It does not matter how much time there is to run on the lease: the incoming occupier steps into the shoes of the outgoing occupier. It is the length of the interest itself, *i.e.* the lease, not the length of occupation left under it, which will determine the quality of the class of occupation.

1.20 Commonhold. The Commonhold and Leasehold Reform Act 2002 ("CLRA 2002") will introduce a new form of ownership for flats. At the time of writing (Summer 2002), CLRA 2002 had not been brought into force. Because of the need to have enforceable agreements about who is to maintain the common parts and provide common services, flats are usually sold on a leasehold basis, with a freeholder owning the common parts and remaining responsible for their upkeep and that of the block, subject to payment by the leaseholders. As noted above (1.18), however, this means that leaseholders have a "wasting asset" which may over time become unmortgageable.

1.21 Commonhold association. Under the commonhold system, however, all the common parts of the building will be owned by a "commonhold association." The association is a company whose members are the owners of the flats. The flats are then owned on the equivalent of a freehold basis (*i.e.* without any limitation of time), and may be mortgaged as such (1.14). The rights and obligations of the flat owners and the commonhold association are dealt with in a document called the "commonhold community statement". Commonhold, therefore, is a form of collective freehold, applicable to flats.

1.22 Trust. The common law doctrine of trust deals with the position which arises at law whenever property is held in the name of one person, but is intended for the benefit of another. Such property is held on trust and the ownership is no longer the untrammelled ownership of any other freeholder or leaseholder, but is subject to the trust, meaning the purposes of the trust and the interests of the beneficiaries. Property can be held on trust for the benefit of a number of individuals including one of the trustees himself. A person, for example, could buy a house, and put it on trust for the use of himself and his spouse and/or children. The person could not subsequently dispose of the property, unless all the beneficiaries consented to the proposed arrangements.

1.23 Trusts of land. Property is automatically considered to be held on trust whenever two or more people own land or premises jointly. Such a trust is now governed by the Trusts of Land and Appointment of Trustees Act 1996, which regulates all trusts of land.

1.24 The effect of a trust of land is that any of the joint owners (trustees) can apply to force the property to be sold, even against the wishes of the other party. This is a necessary provision, for the value of a half-share in a house will be non-existent if it is not possible to force a sale at will, nor as a matter of land policy would it be desirable to allow any kind of land—including housing—to be "locked" between parties in dispute. These rights are additional to the special provisions available to married partners, and will be of most relevance where people have been cohabiting without being married, or where non-cohabitants purchase property together.

1.25 Powers of the courts. Whenever property is held on trust, or is alleged to be held on trust, the High Court or the county court has power to declare whether or not it is held on trust, and in what proportions or for whose benefit, and can also make orders which affect what should happen to the property in question.

1.26 It is not only the parties who can apply to the High Court, but also someone else with an interest, *e.g.* a mortgagee (Trusts of Land and Appointment of Trustees Act 1996, s.14). In deciding what order to make (including whether the property should be sold), the court must take into account the following (s.15):

- The intention of the person or persons who created the trust;
- The purposes for which the property is held (*e.g.* is it as a family home);
- The welfare of any children living in the property; and,
- The interests of any mortgagee of the property.

1.27 How trusts arise. A trust sometimes arises under a formal deed. It may also arise if one person buys property, but for the benefit of another. It will also arise if one person buys property either wholly or in part with someone else's money. In the case of a house or flat, this might arise because, for example, a woman has made direct contributions such as putting up all or part of the purchase price of the property, or all or part of the deposit on a property purchased under mortgage, or has simply contributed to the mortgage repayments, or if she has contributed to maintenance or improvement of the property in such a way as to increase its value.

1.28 Where there is such a direct contribution, but it was made without any common intention—on the part both of owner and contributor—to share an interest in the property, the trust is known as a resulting trust (*Lloyds Bank Plc v Rosset*, 1991). Where the common intention was that the contribution would result on a share of the property, the trust is known as a constructive trust, even if there was no common intention as to the extent of the shares (*Drake v Whipp*, 1995). A common intention is one that is shared and expressed between the parties, as distinct from an intention which one or other party had in his or her own mind, but that was never communicated to the other (*Springette v Defoe*, 1992).

1.29 Declaration of trust. It follows that if a woman living with a man, whether or not married to him, has made such a direct contribution, the law has power to intervene at a time of break-up, and make an appropriate declaration: for example, that the house is held for the benefit of the woman, or that she has an interest in it—in the case of a resulting trust, proportionate to such direct contributions (*Pettitt v Pettitt*, 1991), and in the case of a constructive trust, proportionate not only to such direct contributions but to indirect contributions such as household expenses (*Gissing v Gissing*, 1971). Other evidence may, however, be available, to suggest that the parties intended shares to be in a proportion other than confined to (direct or indirect) contributions (*Midland Bank Plc v Cooke*, 1995).

Trespass

1.30 Absolute trespass. From those with the greatest rights of occupation to those with the least. A trespasser is one who occupies premises without any permission at all to do so. Permission given by anyone in a position to grant the authority will prevent someone being a trespasser.

1.31 Permission. For example, an owner may obviously give permission to occupy property, but so also may his agent, or a director of a company which owns property, or even someone who is himself no more than a tenant. A tenant is in a position to give permission because so long as his tenancy lasts, it is the tenant, rather than the landlord or the owner, who has possession of the premises. It follows, therefore, that an owner or a landlord could not give someone else permission to occupy premises if he has already let them to a tenant.

1.32 Squatting. Squatting is now a common term for occupying property as a trespasser. Sometimes people who enter as squatters are then given permission to remain. There is little popular distinction between those who squat without permission, and those who use short-life property with permission but there is considerable difference in law: those without permission are trespassers, those who have permission are "licensees" (*GLC v Jenkins*, 1975; see also *Camden LBC v Shortlife Community Housing*, 1992).

1.33 The term "squatter" is not therefore one which it is appropriate to use in discussion of housing law, although in one case in which it was used (*McPhail v Persons Unknown*, 1973) the description given was consistent with trespass, rather than licence. This does not mean that all squatters are trespassers, but simply that if the term is to be used in law, it must be confined to those who squat without permission. As far as possible, the term "squatter" will not be used further in this book.

1.34 Criminal law. Trespassers may be committing criminal offences. These are considered further in Chapter 7.

1.35 Adverse possession. An action to recover possession of land from a trespasser cannot be brought after the expiry of 12 years: Limitation Act 1980, s.15. For this purpose, the limitation period begins to run when the trespasser takes "adverse possession" of the land: 1980, s.15(6) and Sch.1. In order to be in adverse possession, a trespasser must have both factual possession of the land and an intention to possess it to the exclusion of the whole world, including the legal owner (*Pye v Graham*, 2002). The fact that, if asked to do so, the trespasser would have been willing to pay for his occupation of the land does not show an absence of the requisite intention (*Pye*).

1.36 It is not necessary for the same person or group of persons to be in adverse possession for the whole 12 years. As long as the period of adverse possession is continuous, the adverse possession of successive trespassers may be added together (*Asher v Whitlock*, 1865).

1.37 Once a trespasser has acquired 12 years adverse possession— of his own or by successive occupation—he is entitled to register ownership of the land, and the owner continues to hold the title to the land on trust for the trespasser.

1.38 Land Registration Act 2002. When LRA 2002 comes into force, new provisions will govern adverse possession. The provisions turn on whether land is "registered" or "unregistered" land (Land Registration Act 1925), a topic that is outside the scope of this book although it may be said that most, if not all, urban land is by now registered, and much rural land. The effect of the provisions will also depend on whether the trespasser had acquired his beneficial interest in the land (above, para.1.37) before they come into force.

1.39 Pre-commencement entitlement. If the trespasser had been in adverse possession for 12 years before commencement, the owner will already be holding title to the land on trust for him. On commencement day, that trust will be replaced by both a statutory right to be registered as the owner and a defence to any claim for possession (LRA 2002, Sch.12, para.18). The "issue" on any such claim to registration or possession will be the same as hitherto— had the trespasser accumulated 12 years of what is properly called adverse possession.

1.40 Post-commencement entitlement. The position will be harder after the Act comes into force. To acquire title by adverse possession, the trespasser must apply to be registered as owner, which, however, he may do after as little as 10 years adverse possession (LRA 2002, Sch.6, para.1). The owner then has the option (LRA 2002, Sch.6, para.3)—which he will normally take— of asking for the application to be dealt with under a special procedure (LRA 2002, Sch.6, para.5), pursuant to which the trespasser will have to show not only adverse possession but one of a limited number of circumstances (to be found in LRA 2002, Sch.6, para.4) amounting to additional reason as to why he should acquire the title, which are rarely likely to be fulfilled.

1.41 If successful in doing so, the trespasser will be entitled to registration. Even if unsuccessful, if left in occupation the trespasser can apply again after the full 12 years when he will not be required to show the additional circumstances. The difficulty is that, by reason of the initial application, the owner will have been put on notice of his occupation and enjoyed the opportunity to bring proceedings for possession.

1.42 Tolerated trespassers. In *Burrows v Brent LBC*, 1996, the House of Lords confronted the status of a former local authority tenant against whom a possession order had become effective, but whom the authority allowed to remain in occupation on terms. Such arrangements were—and are—common. Thus, when a tenant falls into arrears of rent, the court may make an order for possession, suspended so long as current rent plus an amount of the arrears is paid, to which terms the tenant may not adhere. In this case, the order will have become effective but a landlord—particularly a local authority or registered social landlord—may still want to give the tenant "another chance" by way of a new agreement designed to clear the arrears. Even where an outright order is made, the landlord may be willing to do this.

1.43 At common law, such a person could not be described as a trespasser: so long as he complied with the agreement, he had the landlord's express permission to be there. He would therefore be a licensee (1.45). The "policy" difficulty for the courts was that local authority security of tenure applies as much to licensees as tenants (3.19). Accordingly, the House of Lords came up with a new, rather contradictory, term—"tolerated trespass".

1.44 These are mentioned here because of the term used to described them. They are not trespassers in the conventional sense, and it would be misleading—however correct at common law—to continue to refer to them as licensees (in the discussion which follows). They are accordingly discussed further in context, at 3.159–3.162, below.

Licence

1.45 Permission. While the normal arrangement whereby one person rents, as a home, property belonging to another is that of tenancy (1.88–1.103), there is a number of arrangements of less formality which are known as licences. The term "licence" means "permission", whether used in connection with housing, driving a car, or selling alcohol (*Thomas v Sorrell*, 1673). In the housing context, it is used to describe one who is not a trespasser (because he has permission to occupy) but who is neither an owner-occupier nor a tenant. Were it not for "licences", there would be no term appropriate for such people as family, friends or casual guests.

1.46 Family. The most common example of licence is a person living in property which is either owned or rented by a member of the family, *e.g.* a parent. The non-owner, or non-tenant, is in this circumstance in law a licensee. Similarly, a cohabitant is a licensee of his partner, if it is the partner who owns or who is the tenant of the accommodation in which they live.

1.47 Technically, if one spouse is the owner or tenant of the matrimonial home, the other spouse is only his licensee, but it has been held that, both as a matter of practice and as a matter of good taste, it is inappropriate to consider one spouse as the licensee of another (*National Provincial Bank v Ainsworth*, 1965). The special position of both spouses and cohabitants will be considered in the context of break-up of a relationship in Chapter 9.

1.48 Sharing. Some people are quite obviously no more than licensees of another. Common sense dictates that a friend who comes to stay for a while is not to be considered a tenant, while at the same time he cannot be a trespasser because, of course, he is there by the host's invitation. This does not change simply because, for example, the guest is invited to stay for several weeks and even agrees to pay some sort of contribution towards the housekeeping expenses, or indeed, an amount of rent, although at this last stage the agreement is beginning to border on some sort of formal arrangement. Where two people move into accommodation, one named as tenant and the other not, it is likely that the latter will be viewed as no more than a sharer, and therefore licensee, of the other (*Monmouth BC v Marlog*, 1994).

1.49 Long-stay hotel occupation. There are other arrangements, however, where it is less immediately obvious whether a person is to be considered a licensee or a tenant. If someone goes to stay in a hotel for a few days, for example, it would not be considered that he had become a tenant of the hotel. But what if he had made his home over a number of years in the hotel? There are many who live for considerable periods of time in hotels, (more commonly cheaper, long-stay hotels), who have nowhere else to live and who regard the hotel as a home. In *Luganda v Service Hotels*, 1969 the Court of Appeal considered that, none the less, such an occupier was only a licensee and did not become a tenant. A similar view was reached in *Brillouet v Landless*, 1996.

1.50 Hostels. In the same way, the occupier of a hostel is usually considered a mere licensee, *e.g.* a YWCA hostel, as in *R. v South Middlesex Rent Tribunal Ex p. Beswick*, 1976; or one of the many hostels which exist not primarily to provide housing for people, but principally to help those who have had some sort of difficulty, such as drug addicts, mental patients, ex-prisoners, and only secondarily, in order to assist people to reach the point at which they can manage on their own, providing housing for some period or other: *Trustees of the Alcoholic Recovery Project v Farrell*, 1977.

1.51 The distinction which may be drawn between hostels and houses of bedsitting-rooms is that in a hostel there is normally a resident housekeeper or manager, and the occupier is bound to obey rules and regulations which interfere, far more than normal housing management rules do, with the occupier's way of life. See for example *Westminster City Council v Clarke*, 1992, where a hostel provided accommodation for vulnerable single homeless men.

1.52 Old people's home. *Abbeyfield (Harpenden) Society v Woods*, 1968 affords another example. The society ran an old people's home, consisting of single rooms for which the old people paid a weekly rent. The project could only exist satisfactorily so long as each of the occupiers was self-sufficient. Once an elderly person required constant care and attention, it was no longer possible for him to go on living there. There were no facilities for the provision of such assistance and, clearly, in a house containing nothing but the elderly, the consequences could be serious. It was held that the occupier was a lodger, *i.e.* a licensee, not a tenant.

1.53 Acts of kindness. Acts of kindness or generosity are not acts from which tenancies spring. In *Booker v Palmer*, 1942, a city family were provided with accommodation in the country during the war. They later suggested that they had become tenants of the property but the Court of Appeal applied what it termed a "golden rule" of interpretation of such matters: that the courts will not impute intention to enter into legal relations (including tenancy), where the spirit of the arrangement is family or friendly.

1.54 Holding over. This approach found some extension in the case of *Marcroft Wagons v Smith*, 1951. A woman had lived with her parents in a cottage for 50 years. Her father was the original tenant and, on his death, his wife was entitled by the law then in force to "succeed" to the tenancy. Only one such succession was, however, permitted and on the death of her mother the daughter faced eviction. She asked for the tenancy to be granted to her but the landlords refused, though they permitted her to remain in occupation while she found somewhere else to live, during which period they continued to charge her the same weekly rent as her mother had been paying. It was (with some hesitation) held, in effect, that there had similarly been no intention to create a new contract. The court emphasised that this could only be the result where the would-be tenant was already in occupation of the premises at the time at which the arrangement was made; if an arrangement on those lines was offered to someone not living in the premises, this could still constitute a tenancy.

1.55 New tenancy v statutory protection. The result of *Marcroft*, and a number of cases which followed it, has been that when a tenancy came to an end, but the occupier stayed on for a period of time paying a weekly sum of money, the courts have not necessarily assumed a new tenancy agreement. If the reason why the occupier had gone on paying, and the landlord accepting, rent was because there was a statutory right to remain in occupation, *i.e.* "protection", the courts would assume that what was intended by the payment and acceptance of rent was the exercise of the statutory right to remain, rather than a new contractual tenancy (*Clarke v Grant*, 1950), with whatever statutory consequences the particular legislation has in mind (see Chapters 3–5).

1.56 Tolerated Trespass. Where the statutory protection arises under the Housing Act 1985, however, the issues are somewhat different, as such protection attaches to both tenants and licensees (3.19). This was the genesis of the "tolerated trespasser" considered above (1.42), who would otherwise have been a licensee (because allowed to stay on) to whom security would have applied. This is discussed below (3.159–3.162).

1.57 Disputed right to remain. Even if there was a dispute between the parties as to whether or not the occupier was entitled to remain in occupation, then—even if the occupier continued to pay the rent and the landlord to accept it—the courts might not assume a new tenancy (*Longrigg, Burrough and Trounson v Smith*, 1979).

1.58 The position today is that while it is true that the normal inference to be drawn from payment and acceptance of rent is that there is a tenancy (*Lewis v MTC (Cars)*, 1975; see also *Street v Mountford*, 1986), if there is some particular or peculiar explanation or "special circumstance" why the landlord is leaving an occupier in his premises, and on that account accepting money, other than an agreement to enter into a new contract, the courts remain likely to uphold a finding that there is no tenancy, and consequently only a licence.

1.59 The operative word is "agreement". When a person stays on after the termination of a tenancy without a new tenancy, "rent" is properly called "mesne profits", and landlords frequently declare that money will only be accepted as such, although such a declaration is not decisive as to whether or not a new tenancy has been created. The fact that the payment is called "rent" will also not be decisive (*Westminster City Council v Basson*, 1990).

1.60 Bedsitting-rooms. Returning to cases where there has been no prior tenancy, in *Marchant v Charters*, 1977, there was a house of bedsitting-rooms: each of the occupiers had cooking facilities and equipment in his own room, the rooms were furnished and the occupiers lived wholly separate lives, that is to say there were no communal facilities. The house was expressed to be let, and was actually let, "to single men only," and there was a resident housekeeper with whom an arrangement could be made for the provision of evening meals, although this was not an obligatory part of the accommodation arrangement and was not something agreed to by the occupier in question. None of these circumstances would individually cause the arrangement to be considered only a licence. Indeed, many would have thought that even taken together there was nothing to distinguish the arrangement from a conventional bedsitting-room letting; such lettings have always been considered to constitute tenancies, rather than licences, and there is nothing exceptionable in the idea of a tenancy of a single room (*AG Securities v Vaughan*, 1988). Nonetheless, it was held that, in the individual circumstances of the case, the occupier was no more than a licensee.

1.61 The end of "intention". At the time, it was said that this was because the parties to the agreement would not have intended a tenancy, with all the formal consequences as to grant of separate possession (below) that this implied. This "intention" test was subsequently rejected by the House of Lords in the important decision of *Street v Mountford*, 1986, which caused a return to a much more traditional approach to the distinction between tenancy and licence, described as lying "in the grant of land"—including housing—"for a term at a rent with exclusive possession." In substance, the House of Lords was reiterating the proposition that "intention" did not mean the wishes or intentions of one or other—or even both—of the parties, but the intention that the law would impute to the parties on the basis of the nature of the arrangement they had actually made.

1.62   A term, a rent, exclusive possession. The important statement of principle in *Street* is:

> "In the case of residential accommodation there is no difficulty in deciding whether the grant confers exclusive possession. An occupier of residential accommodation at a rent for a term is either a lodger or a tenant. The occupier is a lodger if the landlord provides attendance or services which require the landlord or his servants to exercise unrestricted access to and use of the premises. A lodger is entitled to live in the premises but cannot call the place his own . . .
>
> If on the other hand residential accommodation is granted for a term at a rent with exclusive possession, the landlord providing neither attendance nor services, the grant is a tenancy; any express reservation to the landlord of limited rights to enter and view the state of the premises and to repair and maintain the premises only serves to emphasise the fact that the grantee is entitled to exclusive possession and is a tenant . . . There can be no tenancy unless the occupier enjoys exclusive possession; but an occupier who enjoys exclusive possession is not necessarily a tenant. He may be owner in fee simple, a trespasser, a mortgagee in possession, an object of charity or a service occupier. To constitute a tenancy the occupier must be granted exclusive possession for a fixed or periodic term certain in consideration of a premium or periodical payments. The grant may be express, or may be inferred where the owner accepts weekly or other periodical payments from the occupier."

1.63   Lodger or tenant? Attendance or services. The sort of attendances or services (see also 5.72–5.77, below) which would mean that the occupier was a lodger rather than a tenant might include daily room-cleaning, emptying of rubbish, changing sheets periodically, the provision of meals (see also 5.78) or other "housekeeping-type" activities (*Huwyler v Ruddy*, 1995).

1.64   Review of earlier decisions. The House of Lords in *Street* also analysed a number of the cases in which licence had been upheld, notwithstanding the grant of exclusive possession. It described *Booker v Palmer* (above) as a case only concerned with intention to create legal relations (rather than intention to create tenancy), and *Marcroft Wagons Ltd v Smith* (above) in the same way. *Abbeyfield (Harpenden) Society v Woods* and *Marchant v Charters* (above) were considered cases of "lodging."

> ". . . In order to ascertain the nature and quality of the occupancy and to see whether the occupier has or has not a stake in the room or only permission for himself personally to occupy, the court must decide whether upon its true construction the agreement confers on the occupier exclusive possession. If exclusive possession at a rent for a term does not constitute a tenancy then the distinction between a contractual tenancy and a contractual licence of land becomes wholly unidentifiable . . ."

1.65 The three hallmarks of tenancy. The House of Lords identified three hallmarks of tenancy: exclusive occupation of residential accommodation, payment and term (*i.e.* periods or length of tenancy).

> "Unless these three hallmarks are decisive, it really becomes impossible to distinguish a contractual tenancy from a contractual licence save by the professed intention of the parties or by the judge awarding marks for drafting . . . The only intention which is relevant is the intention demonstrated by the agreement to grant exclusive possession for a term at a rent. Sometimes it may be difficult to discover whether, on the true construction of an agreement, exclusive possession is conferred. Sometimes it may appear from the surrounding circumstances that there was no intention to create legal relationships. Sometimes it may appear from the surrounding circumstances that the right to exclusive possession is referable to a legal relationship other than a tenancy. Legal relationships to which the grant of exclusive possession might be referable and which would or might negate the grant of an estate or interest in the land include occupancy under a contract for the sale of the land, occupancy pursuant to a contract of employment or occupancy referable to the holding of an office. But where as in the present case the only circumstances are that residential accommodation is offered and accepted with exclusive possession for a term at a rent, the result is a tenancy . . ."

1.66 **A fork by any other name.** The question is determined not by what name the parties put on the agreement, but by what the agreement is considered to amount to in law:

> "It does not necessarily follow that a document described as a licence is, merely on that account, to be regarded as amounting only to a licence in law. The whole of the document must be looked at and if, after it has been examined, the right conclusion appears to be that, whatever label has been attached to it, it in fact conferred and imposed on the grantee in substance the rights and obligation of a landlord, then it must be given the appropriate effect, that is to say, it must be treated as a tenancy agreement as distinct from a mere licence . . . The important statement of principle is that the relationship is determined by the law, and not by the label the parties choose to put on it . . . It is simply a matter of ascertaining the true relationship of the parties . . ."

(Jenkins L.J. in *Addiscombe Garden Estates v Crabbe*, 1958).

1.67 Or, as it was put graphically in *Street*:

> "[t]he manufacture of a five-pronged implement for manual digging results in a fork even if the manufacturer, unfamiliar with the English language, insists that he intended to make and has made a spade."

1.68 **Paying arrangement.** In every case, one should ask whether the arrangement is the normal arrangement by which one person comes to occupy premises belonging to another for use as a home, customarily paying rent in money for the right. If it is, then this is likely to be a tenancy, however the parties have described it and whatever they may have said that their intentions were:

> "the courts must pay attention to the facts and surrounding circumstances and to what people do as well as to what people say" (*A.G. Securities v Vaughan*, 1988).

1.69 Once the occupier is paying for the accommodation, then there must be some overriding reason, such as those illustrated or referred to above or those considered below, which reduces the occupation to that of licence. Strictly, it is not even necessary to pay rent in order to establish that there is a tenancy (see most recently *Ashburn Anstalt v Arnold*, 1989), but the courts tend to look sceptically in this day and age at any arrangement purporting to be tenancy under which no rent is paid (*Heslop v Burns*, 1974) and will only be prepared to treat it as a tenancy if they can find some other consideration.

1.70 Evasion of protection. In addition to these questions, however, a person will be only a licensee if the rights which he has been given are not enough in law to amount to tenancy (*AG Securities v Vaughan*, 1988). The necessary elements of tenancy are considered below (1.90–1.103) and include the grant to the occupier of "exclusive possession" of the premises (1.98–1.103).

1.71 One device by which landlords sought to avoid the impact of Rent Act protection was the agreement which has come to be known as the "non-exclusive occupation agreement". This, too, is considered further below (1.209–1.215) although in practice such schemes have become less common, because it is less necessary for landlords to rely on them since the advent of the assured shorthold tenancy under the Housing Act 1988.

1.72 Another device was "rental purchase", whereby a person was allowed into occupation as a licensee, paying money towards purchase, but not enjoying the status of owner until the whole of the purchase price has been paid. Such schemes appear now to have fallen into almost total disuse and are therefore not considered.

1.73 Whatever the scheme, however, there is high authority (*AG Securities v Vaughan*, 1988, HL) for the proposition that the courts should lean against "pretences" designed to defeat statutory protection.

1.74 Trespassers, licensees and eviction. A person who is a trespasser but who is subsequently given permission, not amounting to tenancy, to remain on the premises becomes a licensee. A person whose licence is brought to an end becomes, technically, a trespasser. However, most of the recent laws relating to trespass do not affect those who entered as licensees but subsequently became trespassers.

1.75 Some licensees whose licences began before the commencement of Pt I of the Housing Act 1988 (January 15, 1989) are entitled to refer their contracts to the Rent Tribunal which has power to register a reasonable rent for the premises, and which means that a court, and in the case of some now long-standing licences, the Tribunal, has power to allow more time to leave premises occupied under licence. This is considered in greater detail in Chapter 6.

1.76 Eviction of licensees. Licensees may be termed "bare licensees", or may be termed "contractual licensees." One who is, by arrangement, paying a fixed sum of money for the right of occupation will be a contractual licensee. A friend, member of the family or cohabitant, even although he may be paying some amount by way of contribution to household expenses, will normally be considered a bare licensee.

1.77 This distinction may be relevant when the question of bringing a licence to an end arises. So long as the licence remains in existence, the licensee not only commits no offence by remaining on the premises but cannot be turned off them without the person who does so himself committing an offence: see Chapter 7. Once the licence comes to an end, however, the person who is immediately entitled to possession of the premises in question, which may be the owner of the premises, a landlord or may even be only a tenant of the premises, can reclaim possession from the former licensee, save in the case of a licence which attracts security of tenure under the Housing Act 1985 (3.19).

1.78 In most circumstances, it is necessary to obtain a court order before evicting the former licensee, and an offence is committed if this is not done; in other circumstances, it may not be necessary to obtain a court order: see Chapters 7 and 8. But unless the licence has been duly brought to an end, the person who seeks possession is not entitled to reclaim it, with or without court proceedings.

1.79 Fixed term licences. There are a few arrangements which may be described as "fixed-term" licences. That is to say, the period for which the right of occupation has been granted is fixed in advance. These arrangements require no notice to be given to bring them to an end because, in effect, the notice has been given at the outset of the arrangement.

1.80 Non-fixed term licences. Most licences, however, are not for a fixed period but exist from week to week, even from day to day, or perhaps as much as from month to month. In such cases, it is necessary to give notice in order to bring the arrangement to an end. It may be that some agreement about the length or form of notice has been reached while arranging the licence in the first place, *e.g.* one month's notice in writing. This is not a necessary element of a licence. If there is such an agreement, it would indicate that the licence was a contractual, not a bare licence. If there is such an agreement in force, then the licence cannot be determined except in accordance with it, for the law will not support a breach of contract (*Winter Garden Theatre (London) v Millenium Productions*, 1947).

1.81 Reasonable notice. Whether or not there is such agreement, however, the law additionally implies into every licence, whether bare or contractual, a term that it will not be brought to an end without "reasonable notice" being given. This means that a licence agreement which contractually provided for, *e.g.* one day's notice, would not be brought to an end in one day, unless the law considered one day a reasonable time (*Minister of Health v Belotti*, 1944).

1.82 Written notice. In the case of a periodic licence of a dwelling, other than in the case of what is called an "excluded licence" (8.20), the law now requires written notice of a minimum period of four weeks, which contains specified information. The information is the same as for a notice to quit for tenancies (see 1.119).

1.83 Reasonable time. What is a reasonable time is a question of fact. It will depend upon many circumstances: how long the licensee has been in occupation, how much furniture or property he has in the premises, size of family, what alternative arrangements have been or could be made, even the time of day or night could affect it. In addition, behaviour may affect what the law views as a reasonable time for determination of a licence. A violent licensee will not be given much time at all, *e.g.* a violent man who is cohabiting with the woman who is the tenant or owner-occupier cannot expect a matter of weeks in which to leave, even if he has lived in the property for years.

1.84 Alternative requirements. The rule may be shortly stated in this way: a licensee is entitled to a reasonable period of notice or a contractually agreed period of notice, or in the case of a periodic licence which is not an "excluded licence" (8.20) four weeks' notice, whichever is the longest. In most cases (other than excluded licences), court proceedings for eviction are required: see Chapter 8.

1.85   Alternative procedures. Court proceedings may be brought by ordinary possession action, or by a special, speedy form of procedure originally intended for trespassers, but also applicable to former licensees. This is a short application to the court still known under CPR Pt 55, and Sch.1 as Ord.24 in the county court, and Order 113 in the High Court. If these speedy proceedings are used, then the person seeking to evict the former licensee must establish that the licence had come to an end before the application was issued at the court (*GLC v Jenkins*, 1975). If normal proceedings are used, however, it is enough to show that the licence has expired by the time of the court hearing.

1.86   Licences and estoppel. In some cases, a rather different form of licence may be created which cannot be terminated but continues for the life of the occupier. This may occur where the occupier has incurred expenditure or otherwise acted to his detriment, in the belief that he had a right or interest in the property, and the owner of the land has encouraged that belief, so creating what is known as an estoppel. Thus, for example, an owner of a house may let a son into occupation, lead him to believe that the property will one day be transferred to him, and—in reliance on that belief—the son may expend money improving the property. In such circumstances, a trust will not arise because there is no intention to create an interest, nor a contribution to the purchase price (see 1.27). Instead, it is said that the father is "estopped" from denying the son's right to occupy.

1.87   Once the estoppel is established, it may be enforced by recognition of an irrevocable licence to occupy (*Inwards v Baker*, 1965, *Matharu v Matharu*, 1994). Where it becomes impossible for the licence for life to continue, *e.g.* because of an irretrievable breakdown in relations between the licensee and an owner with whom he is sharing the house, the courts adopt a flexible approach and seek the minimum equity to do justice (*Baker v Baker*, 1993).

Tenancy

1.88   The normal arrangement. Tenancy is the normal arrangement by which one person comes to occupy premises which are owned by another (see, generally, above paras 1.62–1.69, where the distinction between tenancy and licence is considered). It is customarily granted in exchange for a monetary payment, rent. It has been said (1.69) that this is not an essential element of tenancy but, except in the context of service tenancy (1.148–1.162), it is so likely that an arrangement under which no rent is paid will be considered a mere licence that this point will not be considered further here. Where someone has been a tenant, but stays on, whether this is because of a new tenancy or a mere licence will have to be considered (1.54).

1.89 Landlord's interest. A tenancy may be created even where the landlord does not himself have a tenancy of the land, but only a licence to occupy it, provided the hallmarks of a tenancy are present: *Bruton v London & Quadrant Housing Trust*, 1999. Thus in *Bruton*, the landlord only had a licence to occupy the land, and under the terms of the licence was not permitted to grant tenancies. The agreement entered into with the occupier had been said to be a licence. It was nonetheless held to be a tenancy because it gave exclusive possession of the premises to the occupier (1.98, below).

1. ESSENTIAL QUALITIES OF TENANCY

1.90 Four qualities. There are four essential qualities which will establish the existence of a tenancy. If one or more of them is missing, then the arrangement cannot be tenancy and for this reason will be that of licence (*AG Securities v Vaughan*, 1988). The four qualities are:

(i) *Identifiable parties*

1.91 A landlord and a tenant. There must be a landlord and a tenant. This does not mean that the tenant must know the identity of the landlord, for this is frequently unknown, where, for example, agents have granted the tenancy on behalf of the landlord. It means that a person cannot be a tenant either of himself, or of premises or land which have no owner (*Rye v Rye*, 1962).

1.92 A person can, however, be a tenant of a company of which he is a director, or an employee, or even the major shareholder, and a person can be a tenant of a partnership of which he is one of the partners. In such a situation, it would be wrong to refer to the tenant alone as the owner: he is only the owner when taken together with the other partners. The same applies to trustees or joint owners (*Rye*).

(ii) *Identifiable premises*

1.93 A tenancy of premises. There must be premises of which to constitute a tenancy. These premises can be as little as a single room, or as much as hundreds of acres of land. It is not, however, possible to be a tenant of part only of some premises, *e.g.* a shared room.

1.94 It is possible to be a joint tenant with another of premises (1.193–1.204) but if genuinely separate agreements have been independently reached with the landlord conferring a separate right to occupy on separate persons, *e.g.* a room, this cannot be tenancy because there is no identifiable part of the premises of which to have a tenancy. Even if the two—or more—individuals occupying were to divide up the room between themselves, they would still have to have access to the door in common.

1.95 In this connection it is important, however, to bear in mind the possibility that the arrangement may not be genuine, *i.e.* may be sham (1.209–1.215).

(iii)   *Period of tenancy*

1.96   Tenancy and time. One cannot have a tenancy in respect of which there is no period of time involved. That is exactly what tenancy is: a slice of time in the exclusive use of the premises belonging to another. There must be both an ascertainable date of commencement, and an ascertainable period for which it is to run, both of which must be capable of being established before the lease takes effect (*Prudential Assurance Co Ltd v London Residuary Body*, 1992).

1.97 The need to identify the period of the tenancy does not mean that a tenancy cannot in practice be granted for an indefinite time, which is normally what happens when a periodic tenancy is granted. In these cases, the period for which the tenancy has been granted is the time of the periodic tenancy, *e.g.* one week, but the tenancy is automatically renewed from week to week until determined by notice to quit (see 1.111, below). If not periodic, tenancies must be of a fixed term, *e.g.* 6 or 12 months or 5 years.

(iv)   *Exclusive possession*

1.98   The tenant's use. Exclusive possession means that the arrangement in fact conveys to the tenant the use to the exclusion of all others of the premises in question. Exclusive possession is the most important, and on occasion (albeit now only rarely) the hardest to establish of the four essential qualities of tenancy. It is hard to establish because even a licensee can have exclusive occupation of premises, and yet be considered no more than licensee, as in the circumstances described above (1.45–1.73).

1.99 Rights of entry. Exclusive use is not destroyed because the landlord retains some right to visit, for example, to inspect for disrepair, or to collect the rent, nor, for example because under the terms of the tenancy the landlord provides cleaning of the premises and a cleaner has occasional access to the premises to carry out his duties. Such functions are visits to the premises, or services performed to or in the premises, but they are not use of them. Indeed the express reservation of a right to enter for limited purposes emphasises that the occupier has exclusive possession: *Bruton v London & Quadrant Housing Trust,* above.

1.100 Unrestricted access. If, however, the extent of services is such that the access has to be unrestricted, *i.e.* not limited to particular times or occasions, the arrangement will be that of lodging, a form of licence (see 1.63).

1.101 The control test. It may be that in the normal management of a hotel or hostel, the landlord reserves the right to shift occupiers from room to room, as the occasion may demand. If so, the occupier cannot be described as having exclusive possession of the premises, even though he may have exclusive use of whatever room he is occupying for the time being. This is the "control" test: because the landlord controls even the internal use of the premises, the tenant cannot be described as having exclusive possession.

1.102 Sham. It is at this quality of tenancy that landlords have directed the most concerted attacks. The reservation of a right for the landlord himself to use the premises, not merely to visit them, or else a right to put some other person in to use them, would, if a genuine term of the arrangement, effectively destroy the idea of exclusive possession (*Somma v Hazelhurst,* 1978). Today, however, the courts are much quicker and more astute to appreciate that such terms may not be genuine but are a "sham" or "pretence" designed to avoid the protection that attaches to tenancies. In that case, the courts will not uphold the term (see 1.73).

1.103 Possession against all. If exclusive, possession is exclusive as against the whole world, including the person who granted the tenancy, so that even a landlord commits a wrong by contravening his tenant's exclusive possession without permission. Such a wrong is a trespass and is dealt with below (8.83–8.87).

2. PRINCIPAL TYPES OF TENANCY

1.104 Periodic and fixed term tenancy. There are two principal forms of tenancy: periodic tenancies and fixed-term tenancies. A periodic tenancy is one which is granted to run from period to period, *e.g.* week to week or month to month. A fixed-term tenancy is one which is granted for a specific period of time, *e.g.* three months, six months, or a year.

1.105 Need for writing. Neither sort of tenancy needs to be in writing, except for a fixed-term tenancy in excess of three years (Law of Property Act 1925, s.53).

3. IDENTITY OF LANDLORD

1.106 Weekly tenancy. A landlord under a weekly tenancy (but no other) is obliged to provide a rent book or similar document, and commits a criminal offence if he does not do so (Landlord and Tenant Act 1985, ss.4, 7). Under that Act, any tenant can, in writing, ask the person who last received rent under the tenancy for the full name and address of the landlord. If the person to whom the demand is made fails to reply, also in writing, within 21 days, he commits an offence. This may be important information if, for example, the tenant wants to commence proceedings against an absentee landlord and cannot do so without first establishing his identity. Both of these offences should be reported to the council's Tenancy Relations Officer: see Chapter 8.

1.107 All tenancies. Under the Landlord and Tenant Act 1987, s.48, all landlords of premises which are, or include, dwellings must provide the tenant by notice with an address in England or Wales at which tenants' notices may be served on him, until compliance with which duty rent is not due: the notice must be in writing, but may be by means of inclusion in a tenancy agreement, or in a rent book (*Rogan v Woodfield Building Services Ltd*, 1994).

4. TERMINATION OF TENANCIES

1.108 Termination of periodic tenancy. The normal way a periodic tenancy is brought to an end is by service of a valid notice to quit.

1.109 Notice to quit and periodic tenancies. Notice to quit a tenancy is a formal and technical document, to which old common law rules apply, as well as modern regulations introduced by legislation. Notice to quit can be given by either landlord or tenant, although it is uncommon for a tenant to give notice to quit with sufficient degree of accuracy for it to qualify as such.

1.110 Invalid notice. An invalid notice to quit may be treated as valid by the party who receives it, at least in so far as the technicalities of the common law are concerned, and a landlord who receives an invalid notice from the tenant may treat this as a surrender. If the tenant subsequently changes his mind about departing, whether after notice to quit or surrender, the landlord will still have to take court proceedings to evict him and might not be able to do so (5.152).

1.111 Requirements of notice to quit. All notices to quit residential tenancies, other than "excluded tenancies" which began on or after the commencement of Pt I of the Housing Act 1988 (January 15, 1989) must be in writing, must be of a minimum length of four weeks (Protection from Eviction Act 1977, s.5; *Hounslow LBC v Pilling*, 1993) and must expire on either the last day or the first day of a period of the tenancy. The meaning of "excluded tenancy" is considered in Chapter 8 (8.18).

1.112 The final condition—expiry on last or first day of tenancy—is derived from the common law, as is the provision that the notice must also be of at least one full period's length of tenancy, so that a four-week notice to quit a monthly tenancy would be invalid, as a month is longer than four weeks. However, only six months' notice is required to terminate a yearly periodic tenancy. The four weeks include day of service or day of expiry (*Schnabel v Allard*, 1967). The rent day is normally the first day of the tenancy, in the absence of evidence that it is another day.

1.113 Saving clauses. A notice to quit which is of insufficient length will not become valid at a later, correct time, but will be wholly invalid. Because of this need for accuracy, many notices to quit, especially those from landlords to tenants, add a saving clause, which will read something like this: ". . . on the 13th day of December 2001 or at the end of the period of your tenancy expiring next four weeks after service of this notice upon you."

1.114 Such a saving clause is valid and if December 13, 2001 was neither the first nor the last day of a period of the tenancy, the notice to quit would take effect on the next of those two possible days, four weeks after service.

1.115   Service of notice to quit. Service of a notice to quit has to be personal. Most service is effected by post, although some service is carried out by leaving it at the premises. It is not validly served until the tenant himself receives it, or it is left with a tenant's spouse or some other person who may be treated as the tenant's agent for this purpose, *i.e.* someone left by the tenant in possession or control of the premises (*Harrowby v Snelson*, 1951).

1.116   If the tenancy itself expressly requires service of a notice to quit in order to determine it, however, it will be sufficient if the notice is left at the last known place of abode of the tenant (Law of Property Act 1925, s.196; *Wandsworth LBC v Attwell*, 1995; *Enfield LBC v Devonish*, 1996). The Local Government Act 1972, s.233 which permits postal service of notices required or authorised to be given "by or under any enactment" does not apply to common law notices to quit (*Enfield*).

1.117   Contents of notice to quit. A notice to quit must identify the premises which are the subject of the tenancy, so that a notice given for the wrong address will be invalid. Minor defects in description, such as specifying a back garden that does not exist, are unlikely to invalidate the notice; and if a notice to quit identifies the wrong address, it may be validated by a covering letter sent to the right one. In one case, a notice to quit two rooms was held invalid where the tenant was tenant of only one (*Jankovitch v Petrovitch*, 1977).

1.118   The notice must be addressed to the tenant, although if only the first name is wrong this will not be enough to invalidate it. It may be enough to specify only one of two or more joint tenants (1.193–1.204) and it is certainly enough to serve one only of the joint tenants. The notice must also state that it is given by or on behalf of the landlord, unless it is given by an agent acting in the normal course of his business on the landlord's behalf when serving the notice.

1.119   Prescribed information. In addition, a notice to quit from a landlord to a tenant must contain certain specified information, also in writing. Without this information the notice is invalid. The information is as follows (by virtue of the Notices to Quit, etc. (Prescribed Information) Regulations 1988) although it does not have to be in the same form of words and will not be invalid if the different wording from earlier regulations is used (*Beckerman v Durling*, 1981; *Swansea CC v Hearn*, 1990):

(a) If the tenant or licensee does not leave the dwelling, the landlord or licensor must get an order for possession from the court before the tenant or licensee can lawfully be evicted. The landlord or licensor cannot apply for such an order before the notice to quit or notice to determine has run out.

(b) A tenant or licensee who does not know if he has any right to remain in possession after a notice to quit or a notice to determine runs out or is otherwise unsure of his rights, can obtain advice from a solicitor. Help with all or part of the cost of legal advice and assistance may be available under the Legal Aid Scheme. He should also be able to obtain information from a Citizen's Advice Bureau, a Housing Aid Centre, a rent officer or a Rent Tribunal Office.

1.120 Special procedures for Housing Act secure, assured, and introductory tenancies. Note that the termination of a Housing Act secure (public sector) tenancy (Chapter 3), of a Housing Act assured tenancy (Chapter 4), of an assured shorthold and of an introductory (public sector) tenancy (Chapter 6), are by their own special, and different, procedures. Termination is by the court, and different notice provisions apply.

1.121 Termination of fixed-term tenancy. The normal way a fixed-term tenancy comes to an end is because the time runs out.

1.122 Surrender. As well as notice to quit and expiry of fixed term, another common way of bringing a tenancy to an end is for the tenant to "surrender" it. It occurs, commonly, when a tenant wants to leave accommodation before the end of a fixed term and if so, will commonly conform to the legal requirement that a formal declaration of surrender be drawn up.

1.123 Surrender can, however, can also happen by operation of law, if the tenant performs some unequivocal act of surrender, such as returning the keys to the landlord, or removing from the premises all signs of occupation, including furniture, belongings and any family or friends—or animals—who were living with him (*Chamberlain v Scalley*, 1992). This may happen in the case of either a fixed-term or periodic tenancy, but it is most common in the latter case, when a periodic tenant wishes to quit without going through the formality of serving notice to quit.

1.124 In deciding whether there has been such an unequivocal act of surrender, the subjective intentions of the tenant (*e.g.* as to whether they intend to give up their rights to the tenancy) are irrelevant, it is the objective conduct which is crucial (*Zionmor v Islington LBC*, 1997).

1.125   Acceptance of act. It is an essential feature of surrender by operation of law that the landlord accepts the acts as acts of surrender. The landlord is not obliged to do so and can continue to consider the tenant liable for rent and other responsibilities in the premises. Abandonment of occupation may be considered a surrender (*R. v London Borough of Croydon Ex p. Toth*, 1988), but only where the landlord unequivocally accepts it as such (*Preston BC v Fairclough*, 1982). The landlord's conduct as a whole must be taken into account (*Brent LBC v Sharma*, 1992). The grant of a new tenancy to someone else will evidence acceptance of a surrender of the previous tenancy (*Tower Hamlets LBC v Ayinde*, 1994). There can even be surrender, by clear agreement, without quitting occupation (*Dibbs v Campbell*, 1988).

1.126   Forfeiture. The other common way of bringing a tenancy to an end, and one which is also normally only used in connection with fixed-term tenancies, is forfeiture. It may be used in cases of fairly short fixed terms, *e.g.* 12 months and also in cases of long leases (1.17, above).

1.127 There can be no forfeiture unless it is provided for in the tenancy agreement or lease. Forfeiture is commonly something the landlord can claim has occurred automatically once rent has been in arrears for a stated period of time, *e.g.* 14 days. It can also be part of an agreement that forfeiture will occur if some other breach of the tenancy takes place.

1.128   Re-entry. When there is a forfeiture in this way, the landlord claims to "re-enter" the premises, although he cannot in fact do so because of the rules governing eviction of tenants and it is therefore effected by proceedings for possession. A court has power to order "relief" from forfeiture, if the breach of the tenancy has been remedied, *e.g.* arrears of rent have been paid off.

1.129   Service charges. In the case of long leases, forfeiture is often invoked for the non-payment of service charges. Forfeiture in such cases is now prohibited unless the amount of the service charge has been agreed or admitted by the tenant or has been subject to a court or arbitration determination (Housing Act 1996, s.81).

1.130 Breach of other term. When the Commonhold and Leasehold Reform Act 2002, s.168 comes into force, landlords of long leaseholders (1.17) will also not be able to seek forfeiture unless the fact that there has been a breach of the lease has been determined by a court or tribunal. The landlord will be able to apply to the leasehold valuation tribunal for a determination.

1.131 Relief from forfeiture. All forfeitures of residential premises in which anyone is living must be by way of court proceedings (Protection from Eviction Act 1977). It is normally in the course of these proceedings that relief is sought.

1.132 Where the forfeiture is for a reason other than arrears of rent, a preliminary notice must be served, identifying the breach, calling for remedy (if the breach is remediable), and demanding compensation (where applicable) (Law of Property Act 1925, s.146).

1.133 The courts are chary of laying down general principles governing relief (*Hyman v Rose*, 1912), although remedying the breach will usually be necessary, and will invariably be so if the breach is non-payment of rent (*Barton, Thompson & Co v Stapling Machines Co*, 1966), though time will be allowed in which to do this. There can be no relief from forfeiture for breach of a covenant not to use premises for an immoral purpose (*British Petroleum Pension Trust Ltd v Behrendt*, 1986). Relief from forfeiture is not available to a Housing Act assured tenant (*Artesian Residential Developments Ltd v Beck* (1999): 4.73).

1.134 Waiver. There will be no entitlement to forfeit if the breach has been waived, *e.g.* waiver of illegal sub-letting (*Cornillie v Saha*, 1996; see 1.181).

1.135 Effect of relief. Relief may be granted in the High Court, if that is where the forfeiture proceedings are brought, but may also be granted in the county court. The effect of relief is to reinstate the lease as if there had been no forfeiture (*Hynes v Twinsectra Ltd*, 1995; *Rexhaven Ltd v Nurse*, 1995). Relief may be granted in relation to part only of the premises the subject of the lease (*GMS Syndicate v Elliott (Gary) Ltd*, 1982).

1.136 Arrears and relief. Where proceedings are brought in the county court, and the breach in question is non-payment of rent (including service charges explicitly reserved as rent in the lease—

Sinclair Gardens Investment (Kensington) Ltd v Walsh, 1995), there is automatic relief if all the arrears and the costs of the action are paid into court at least five days before the hearing; otherwise, the order for possession must provide at least four weeks before it takes effect, and there will again be automatic relief if all the rent and costs are paid into court. These provisions do not apply if the forfeiture is for, or also for, any other breach (County Courts Act 1984, ss.138–140).

1.137   If not obtained automatically, relief for arrears may still be available, as a matter of discretion, on an application made within six months of execution, *i.e.* even if afterwards (s.138). Unless s.138 is complied with, all other relief is barred.

1.138   While relief—including for non-payment of rent—may also be sought in the High Court (Supreme Court Act 1981, s.38), that procedure cannot be used to secure relief after execution, so as to circumvent the six month limitation (*Di Palma v Victoria Square Property Co Ltd*, 1985).

1.139   Relief—automatic or after execution—under s.138 may also be sought by a sub-lessee, who likewise cannot circumvent its provisions by seeking relief (outside the six month period) by application to the High Court (*United Dominions Trust v Shellpoint Trustees*, 1993).

1.140   Long leaseholders and arrears. The Commonhold and Leasehold Reform Act 2002, s.167 will, when in force, limit forfeiture of long leases (1.17) for arrears of rent, service or administration charges. If the amount of arrears is less than an amount to be specified by the Secretary of State—but not to exceed £500—or has been owed for less than a prescribed period of time, the landlord will not be permitted to exercise his right of re-entry or forfeiture.

1.141   Relief and disrepair. There is additional power to apply for relief from a s.146 notice which is concerned with an alleged failure to comply with a covenant requiring internal decorative repairs (Law of Property Act 1925, s.147). In the case of a lease of at least seven years, with at least three years left to run, the Leasehold Property (Repairs) Act 1938 prevents forfeiture for such a breach without the prior leave of the court (11.127).

5.   EVICTION OF TENANTS

1.142   Although at the end of a tenancy a tenant becomes in strict common law a trespasser, this is so untrue in practice as to be deceptive.

1.143 Housing Act secure and assured tenants. It has already been noted (1.120) that these tenancies cannot be terminated except by an order of the court, which will also govern the eviction itself.

1.144 Rent Act protected tenants. A tenant who is a Rent Act protected tenant becomes a statutory tenant on termination of the contractual tenancy and, in effect, can remain on in the premises indefinitely, or subject only to proof of one of a limited number of sets of circumstances, until a court orders him to leave: see Chapter 5.

1.145 Rent Act restricted tenants. A Rent Act restricted tenant is one who can refer his tenancy to the Rent Tribunal, in respect of rent registration, and who may also be able to secure some temporary relief from eviction, either from a court or from the Tribunal (6.64–6.94).

1.146 Other tenants. The general position of tenants who are neither Housing Act secure, Housing Act introductory, Housing Act assured, Rent Act protected, nor Rent Act restricted, is considered in Chapter 7. With the exception of "excluded tenants" (8.18) whose tenancies began on or after the commencement (January 15, 1989) of Pt I of the Housing Act 1988, all tenants, therefore including this residual class, are protected from eviction without due process of law, *i.e.* without a court decision which orders them to leave (Protection from Eviction Act 1977, ss.1–3, as amended): see Chapter 8.

Other circumstances

1.147 In addition to the main common law classes of occupation, there is a number of other circumstances which we must now consider. These are:

1. Tied accommodation;

2. Sub-tenants;

3. Joint tenants;

4. Tenants of mortgagors;

5. Assignees; and

6. Change of landlord.

1. TIED ACCOMMODATION

1.148 Job-related accommodation. Many people who live in premises they do not own are occupying accommodation which "goes with the job". Such people are not merely the obvious classes of service occupier or tenant, such as resident housekeepers, porters, au pairs, live-in help, caretakers, etc. but also people such as the managers of pubs and many who work in off-licences, and employees of some industries and of local authorities, who may, *e.g.* offer accommodation to key workers such as teachers and social workers as an inducement to work in particular areas. The accommodation is often job-related and the right to it customarily ends when the job itself is brought to an end.

1.149 This section is concerned only with accommodation which is job-related, and not with accommodation offered as an inducement, but which is not otherwise tied contractually to the employment.

1.150 An additional test. Job-related accommodation poses particular problems in terms of housing law. Clearly, occupiers are not trespassers, nor of course are they owner-occupiers, and so they must, of definition, be either tenants or licensees. There are, however, particular tests which apply to this distinction when job-related accommodation is in question, which are additional to those already discussed (1.45–1.146).

1.151 A person might appear to qualify as a tenant by application of one of the particular, job-related tests, and yet lack one of the four essential qualities of tenancy, or else be a licensee for some other reason, *e.g.* because on taking up new employment in a strange area, the employer offered to provide temporary accommodation as a pure favour. Unless, however, one of the prior tests applies, then the test which follows will determine whether occupation is by way of tenancy or licence.

1.152 A job-related occupier who is a licensee is called a "service occupier", while one who is a tenant is called a "service tenant".

1.153 A single arrangement. In all these circumstances, it is assumed that the employment and the housing arrangements were reached as part of an overall package and are connected. It is entirely possible that a tenant subsequently becomes his landlord's employee. The tenancy would not then normally become a service tenancy, any more than it would if someone subsequently rented accommodation from his employer.

1.154 It is possible, however, that a landlord who has become someone's employer will offer a new arrangement which, if accepted, could become one of licence (*Scrimgeour v Waller*, 1980). In deciding whether the new arrangement is valid, the courts will not take into account the inequality of bargaining power between the parties (*Mathew v Bobbins*, 1980), although they will recognise that a mere statement of intention is not binding, and may have been signed by the occupier because he had little choice (*AG Securities v Vaughan*, 1988).

1.155 A number of recent cases involving tied accommodation have concerned changes in circumstances, but these have been in the context of rights under the Housing Act 1985, which are available both to tenants and licensees, so that these cases do not address the fundamental, common law distinction (3.19).

1.156 The test of necessity. A person living in job-related accommodation will be a service occupier if it is necessary for him to live in the premises in question in order to carry out the employment duties (*Smith v Seghill Overseers*, 1875; *Street v Mountford*, 1986), or—at least—if it is a requirement of the contract of employment that he do so, and that requirement is imposed at the least for the better performance of employment duties (*Fox v Dalby*, 1874; *Glasgow Corp v Johnstone*, 1965), not merely as an arbitrary regulation, or whim, on the part of the employer (*Gray v Holmes*, 1949).

1.157 The fact that it is merely convenient for the employee to reside in the premises in question is not sufficient to make it for the better performance of his duties (*Ford v Langford*, 1949; *Chapman v Freeman*, 1978).

1.158 If neither of the factors above applies, then the occupier will normally be a service tenant.

1.159 Agricultural and forestry workers. Employees who occupy tied accommodation in agriculture and forestry occupy a peculiar position of privilege. Briefly, given certain qualifications— including length of employment in agriculture or forestry (but not necessarily with the same employer)—and despite the fact that they would normally qualify as service occupiers, they may come to enjoy full Housing Act 1988 security as if they had Housing Act assured tenancies (Chapter 4), or Rent Act protection as if they had tenancies (Chapter 5).

1.160 Tied accommodation and rent. One common problem which occurs in connection with occupiers of tied accommodation lies in establishing whether or not they are paying rent for their accommodation. Some will actually be doing so, *i.e.* they will be handing over a sum of money which will normally be entered as received in a rent book. Others may have an agreement as to how much rent they are paying for their accommodation, but this may be deducted from their wages at source. So long as the amount is quantified, they will still be treated as paying rent even if it is deducted at source (*Montagu v Browning*, 1954).

1.161 Others may not have any agreed quantification of rent, but receive lower wages than they would normally get for the job in question on account of the provision of accommodation. Whether rent is actually being paid or not should not affect whether they are considered tenants or licensees, contrary to the normal presumption that one who pays no rent is not a tenant (*Heslop v Burns*, 1974), but it may affect whether or not they can enjoy statutory protection (4.31, 5.80).

1.162 Tied accommodation and termination. A service licence which is expressly terminable on the cessation of employment comes to an end without any requirement of notice (*Ivory v Palmer*, 1975). Notice in accordance with the Protection from Eviction Act 1977 (1.119) is not, therefore, required (*Norris v Checksfield*, 1991).

2. SUB-TENANTS

1.163 Mesne tenants. It is entirely possible that a person's landlord is himself no more than a tenant of another. In such a case, the "middle" tenant is known as a "mesne" (pronounced "mean") tenant, and the "lower" tenant as the sub-tenant.

1.164 Many more people are sub-tenants than realise it. In strict law, the owner who holds only on a long lease is a tenant, although has been considered here as an owner-occupier (1.15–1.16). There are major property holdings still in existence in which the interests are all held on leasehold. Indeed, it is not only possible but common for there to be many "intervening" interests by way of superior leasehold between an actual occupier and the ultimate freeholder.

1.165 Continuation of mesne tenancy. So long as the mesne tenancy continues to exist, the sub-tenant is in no different a position than any other tenant. His landlord (the mesne tenant) must serve notice to quit in the normal way, and the sub-tenancy may fall into any of the classes of protection which will be discussed in Chapters 3–6. The position remains the same even when the mesne tenant is a Rent Act protected tenant (Chapter 5) and his contractual tenancy comes to an end. The mesne tenant becomes what is known as a statutory tenant, but the sub-tenant is in practice unaffected by this unless or until the mesne tenant's statutory tenancy is determined.

1.166 Termination of mesne tenancy. Difficulties arise once the mesne tenant's interest comes to an end. In such a case, the question to be decided is whether the sub-tenant has any right to remain in occupation as against the superior landlord. This will depend upon two main factors:

(a) Whether there is statutory protection afforded to the sub-tenant (Chapters 4 and 5); and

(b) Whether or not the sub-tenancy is a legal or illegal sub-tenancy.

1.167 Sub-tenants and statutory protection—(1) Housing Act 1988. In the case of a Housing Act assured tenancy (Chapter 4), it is unlikely that both mesne and sub-tenant will be Housing Act assured because they may both live in the same building (4.43–4.50). Otherwise, a Housing Act assured sub-tenant will become the tenant of a superior landlord if

(a) The mesne tenancy is determined, and

(b) At the time the mesne tenancy comes to an end the sub-tenancy is legal, even if the mesne tenancy was not Housing Act assured, unless

(c) The landlord is one whose tenants are not normally Housing Act assured (Housing Act 1988, s.18; 4.40).

1.168 Sub-tenants and statutory protection—(2) Rent Act 1977. In the case of a Rent Act protected tenant (Chapter 5), it may likewise be the case that the mesne tenant and sub-tenant live in the same building, so that the sub-tenant will not be Rent Act protected (5.44). If

(a) Both mesne tenant and sub-tenant are protected by the Rent Act, however, as can arise (*e.g.* in the case of an older letting—5.61), and

(b) At the time the mesne tenancy comes to an end, the sub-tenancy is legal, the sub-tenant will become the tenant of the landlord directly (Rent Act 1977, s.137).

1.169 A sub-tenant who is not a Rent Act protected sub-tenant (*Stanley v Compton*, 1951), or one who is an illegal sub-tenant, whether or not Rent Act protected, cannot take advantage of Rent Act 1977, s.137 in order to become the tenant of the landlord direct.

1.170 The fact that the mesne tenant is himself not a Rent Act protected tenant but, *e.g.* a Housing Act secure tenant (Chapter 3), does not affect the position as between mesne and sub-tenant (*Lewis v Morelli*, 1948; *Stratford v Syrett*, 1958) but does mean that the Rent Act 1977, s.137 cannot apply.

1.171 The tenancy will be on the same terms as from the mesne tenant, with the result that if the sub-tenancy was statutory as opposed to contractual (5.24), so it will remain (*Keepers & Governors of the Free Grammar School of John Lyon v Jordan*, 1995).

1.172 A Rent Act protected tenant who creates a lawful Rent Act protected sub-tenancy is obliged to notify the landlord of this in writing, within 14 days of creating the sub-tenancy, stating details of the sub-tenancy, including the name of the sub-tenant and the rent he is paying under the sub-tenancy (Rent Act 1977, s.139). Where the sub-tenant becomes tenant direct of the landlord by operation of s.137, then the landlord is entitled to disclaim responsibility for the provision of furniture, if he does so in writing within six weeks of the sub-tenant becoming his tenant (s.138).

1.173 Sub-tenants and statutory protection—(3) Housing Acts 1985 and 1996. No special provision is made to enhance the status of sub-tenants of secure tenants under the Housing Act 1985 (Chapter 3), or introductory tenants under the Housing Act 1996 (Chapter 6), for which reason the normal rule will usually prevail (1.191) that the sub-tenancy ends with the mesne tenancy.

1.174 Illegal sub-tenancy. There is only an illegal sub-tenancy if the terms of the mesne tenancy include a prohibition on sub-letting. Most written tenancies include such a term, and many weekly or monthly tenancies granted in the last few years and for which the terms are to be found in printed rent books provided by the landlord will also be subject to such a prohibition. Even a rent book issued for a period subsequent to the grant may be used as evidence of a prohibition (*RC Glaze v Alabdinboni*, 1992).

1.175 Some prohibitions on sub-letting are absolute, *i.e.* they simply state that it is not permitted. Some are qualified, *i.e.* they state that it is not permitted without the consent of the landlord. The law implies into a qualified covenant a condition that such consent will not unreasonably be withheld and if unreasonably withheld will treat the consent as given (*Balls Brothers Ltd v Sinclair*, 1931). This is, however, not so where the covenant is implied by Housing Act 1988, s.15, into a Housing Act assured tenancy (4.152).

1.176 Withholding of consent. There can only be an unreasonable withholding if there has been a request and a refusal before the sub-letting is granted (*Barrow v Isaacs*, 1891; *Eastern Telegraph Co v Dent*, 1899), which is extremely rare. It is withholding which is prohibited, however, so that if the tenant seeks consent, and the landlord fails to reply after a reasonable time, consent has been withheld (*Wilson v Fynn*, 1948).

1.177 The best tactic is to seek consent and, when it is withheld, seek a declaration from the court that the withholding is unreasonable (*Mills v Cannon Brewery Co.*, 1920).

1.178 Whether or not a withholding is reasonable will turn on the facts of each case (*Lee v K Carter (K) Ltd*, 1949) including the impact of statutory protection (*West Layton Ltd v Ford*, 1979). The reasonableness of withholding consent is not confined to questions about the proposed sub-tenant, but can include consideration of the landlord's own interests, provided they are interests which a reasonable landlord would have regard to (*Leeward Securities Ltd v Lilyheath Properties Ltd*, 1983), *e.g.* questions of good estate management, rather than an attempt to extract some benefit outside of the tenancy, such as unanticipated surrender (*Rayburn v Woolf*, 1985). The burden is on the tenant to show unreasonable withholding of consent (*Rayburn*).

1.179 Landlord and Tenant Act 1988. If the tenant seeks consent in writing, then the position is additionally affected by the

Landlord and Tenant Act 1988. This Act applies only where the covenant is a qualified covenant (1.175).

1.180 Where a written application is made, the landlord owes the tenant a duty to reply within a reasonable time, either consenting, or else giving written notice either of a refusal, in which case the reasons must be stated, or of a "conditional consent", in which case the conditions must be stated. An unreasonable condition is not permitted. Under this Act, the burden is on the landlord to show:

(a) That he replied within a reasonable time; and,

(b) That any condition attached is reasonable; and,

(c) That a refusal is reasonable.

1.181 Waiver of illegality. Even if an illegal sub-tenancy is created, it is possible that it will subsequently be "legalised". This can happen because the landlord learns of the illegal sub-letting and yet "waives" the breach of the term of the tenancy by continuing to accept rent from the mesne tenant as if nothing had happened.

1.182 Waiver requires that the landlord knew there had been an actual sub-letting, not, *e.g.* merely that a friend had come to live with the mesne tenant, and the act of waiver must be established, which normally means something more than a single rent payment accepted very shortly after the landlord found out when, perhaps, reaction to the sub-letting was still in process.

1.183 The knowledge of the landlord's employees, agents or officers is imputed to the landlord, so that if one such person knows of the illegal sub-letting and the landlord continues to accept rent there will have been waiver (*Metropolitan Properties Co v Cordery*, 1979). In one case, the issue of proceedings to gain access to the flat to inspect it, pursuant to the terms of the lease, was held to have waived an existing breach of the covenant not to sublet, of which the landlord was already aware (*Cornillie v Saha*, 1996).

1.184 Once waiver has occurred, the sub-tenant becomes a legal sub-tenant as if in the first place he had been allowed in lawfully.

1.185 No advantage of own wrong. A mesne tenant who lets illegally cannot himself subsequently take advantage of it (*Critchley* *v Clifford*, 1962) by claiming not to be bound by it. It is, after all, his wrong, or breach, not that of the sub-tenant. It is no ground for eviction of a sub-tenant by the mesne tenant that the letting was illegal.

1.186 Surrender by mesne tenant. There is one exception to all of these limits on when a sub-tenancy can survive the mesne tenant, which arises if the mesne tenant surrenders (1.122) to the landlord, and the landlord accepts the surrender (*Parker ⌐ Jones*, 1910). In this case, the sub-tenant becomes a tenant of the landlord regardless of whether or not the sub-tenancy is illegal, and regardless of class of protection.

1.187 This arises by operation of common law and may also be said to operate by way of waiver, *i.e.* of the illegality, although it is a waiver that takes place even although the landlord does not know of the existence of the sub-tenant. By accepting the surrender, the landlord is deemed to have waived any breaches by the tenant and to have taken over the tenant's liabilities, which include the sub-tenancy.

1.188 This will not happen if the mesne tenancy was within the Rent Act and already a statutory tenancy (5.24), however, because a statutory tenancy is not a tenancy at common law (*Solomon v Orwell*, 1954).

1.189 Sub-tenants and licensees. All of these provisions, however, depend on the sub-tenant being a tenant at all, not merely a licensee. Someone who is the licensee of a tenant will find that his licence comes to an end automatically, without the giving of any notice, on the determination of the tenancy, although it will still normally be necessary for court proceedings to be taken to evict him: see Chapter 8.

1.190 Whether or not a person is the licensee or sub-tenant of another will be a question of fact based on the normal considerations, but it is true to say that where the parties are living in the same premises, the court will look closely at the arrangement and, unless there is clear evidence of separate living, it is likely to be inclined to view another occupier as a sharer, or as a lodger, and therefore in either event a licensee, even though rent is paid, rather than as a sub-tenant (*Monmouth BC v Marlog*, 1994). Such clear evidence of separate living might be provided by a rent book, perhaps separate payment for gas and electricity, separate housekeeping, etc. This question, of whether a person is a licensee of, for example, someone he is sharing a flat with, is considered further under the next heading.

1.191 Sub-tenancy terminating with mesne tenancy. If the mesne and sub-tenancies are not both Rent Act protected, or if the sub-tenancy is not Housing Act assured, or if the sub-tenancy is illegal, so that neither Rent Act 1977, s.137, nor Housing Act 1988, s.18 applies (1.167–1.172) and if there is no surrender by the tenant (1.122), the sub-tenancy automatically determines, *i.e.* without notice or forfeiture, on the determination of the mesne tenancy (*Moore Properties (Ilford) v McKeon*, 1976).

1.192 Relief. A sub-tenant, even one who is an illegal sub-tenant, can apply for relief (1.131–1.141) from forfeiture (Law of Property Act 1925, s.146(4)).

3. JOINT TENANTS

1.193 Shared tenancy. A joint tenancy occurs wherever more than one person shares the tenancy. Joint tenants do not each have a different part of, for example, a flat or a house: they are all equally entitled to share possession of the whole of it.

1.194 Between them, they must establish the four essential qualities of tenancy (*AG Securities v Vaughan*, 1988); but need not establish them (and, in particular, exclusive possession) as against each other.

1.195 Rent liability. Joint tenants are, unless the agreement states to the contrary (*AG Securities v Vaughan*, 1988; *Demuren v Seal Estates*, 1978), each liable for the whole rent of the premises, so that if a landlord can only trace one of them, that one will be obliged to pay any and all rent outstanding, though he may subsequently be able to recover shares from any of the missing joint tenants. Where there is no joint liability for the rent this may prevent a joint tenancy arising, and the occupiers may only be licensees (*Mikeover Ltd v Brady*, 1989).

1.196 Acting in harmony. Married or cohabiting couples are frequently joint tenants, but so also are groups of friends. So long as they all remain together, acting, at least in relation to the landlord, in harmony, their position is exactly the same as that of a sole tenant.

1.197 If there is any application, *e.g.* for rent registration, then they must either all sign the application, or else one of them must sign as agent for the others (*Turley v Panton*, 1975; *R. v Rent Officer for Camden Ex p. Felix*, 1988).

1.198 Service of a notice to quit on one is good service (*Doe d. Aslin v Summersett*, 1830), although there is some doubt as to whether a notice to quit which identifies only one of the joint tenants as the tenant will be valid.

1.199 Termination by one of joint tenants. Problems arise when the joint tenants themselves wish to go their separate ways. If the tenancy is periodic, then one joint tenant can serve notice to quit and bring the contractual tenancy to an end (*Greenwich LBC v McGrady*, 1983; *Hammersmith & Fulham LBC v Monk*, 1991). The notice to quit must, however, be valid (1.111) if it is to have this effect (*Hounslow LBC v Pilling*, 1993), and cannot simply be "treated as valid" (1.110) by the landlord.

1.200 This is something only a joint periodic tenant can do. If the tenancy is fixed-term, one of the joint tenants cannot surrender it without the consent of all the others (*Leek and Moorlands Building Society v Clark, 1952*).

1.201 This technique is commonly used where a local authority want to re-house one of the joint tenants, together with the children, without leaving the other—usually the man—in accommodation now much larger than he needs (*Crawley BC v Ure*, 1995).

1.202 Interaction with family law. The right to serve a notice to quit is not affected by matrimonial homes and occupation rights under the Family Law Act 1996: *Harrow LBC v Johnstone*, 1997; 9.17, below. See also 9.13 on preventing service of a notice to quit in matrimonial cases.

1.203 Human Rights Act. It has recently been held in the Court of Appeal that, even after the notice to quit has expired, the property remains the man's "home" for the purposes of art.8 of the European Convention on Human Rights: *Quazi v Harrow LBC*, 2001. The effect of this is that where the eviction is sought by what is a "public authority" under the Human Rights Act 1998, s.6 (*i.e.* local authorities, and in some circumstances registered social landlords), the decision to evict must be proportionate and can be challenged in any possession proceedings. The case is due to be heard on appeal by the House of Lords.

1.204   Rent Act tenancies. If the tenancy is Rent Act protected (Chapter 5), termination by one joint tenant will not affect the right to security of tenure of the other(s) (*Lloyd v Sadler*, 1978). If one joint tenant simply departs, then the tenancy "devolves" on the remaining joint tenants (*Lloyd v Sadler*, 1978).

1.205   Joint tenancy v sole tenancy. It is possible, however, that people who assume that they are joint tenants are not so in law. For example, a group of friends take a flat together, but only one of them is named in, or signs the agreement, if any, or only one of them is named on the rent book. At first sight, the law would assume that the named occupier was the sole tenant, and that his sharers were either sub-tenants or licensees.

1.206   It is possible to upset this first impression with evidence that the entry of one name only was either an oversight or intentionally inaccurate, by showing that the landlord was contracting with the whole group, and that it was clearly intended, as between themselves and as between them and the landlord, that they should all have equal rights in the premises. This might be witnessed by the fact that they each pay the rent for the whole of the premises to the landlord in turn.

1.207   Although not impossible, it is none the less hard to upset the first impression created by a written indication that the tenancy belongs to only one of the sharers.

1.208   Sub-tenancy v sharers (licensees). Will the remaining occupiers then be licensees or sub-tenants? Again, the initial inference is that if a group of sharers are not joint tenants, there will be a sole tenant with a group of licensees (*Monmouth BC v Marlog*, 1994). There is some merit to this attitude, for as between the group of occupiers it is infrequently indeed that they will have intended the formality of landlord and tenant. More likely, they are all sharing the outgoings, perhaps even buying food together, and living as one household. This would all suggest licence, rather than sub-tenancy. Sub-tenancy could be established, however, if there was clear evidence of separate living, as suggested under the last heading (1.190).

1.209   Non-exclusive occupation. Another problem has been caused by the use of the evasive device of "non-exclusive occupation agreements." The technique of such arrangements is that the landlord enters into a series of separate contracts with each occupier, granting to the occupier the right to use the premises in question in common with others, but not to use a particular part of the premises. In this way, the landlord seeks to avoid a finding of tenancy of some part of the premises as against him, and—because the agreements are all separate—seeks also to avoid a finding of joint tenancy of the whole of the premises between himself and the group.

1.210 Such evasive devices often purport to retain for the landlord a right to come and live in the premises himself, or else to select new occupiers as and when one or other of the original group departs. Such arrangements could be genuine, *e.g.* if the landlord was effectively running a small-scale "hostel," and choosing the occupiers himself. An arrangement, if genuine, would create a series of individual licences, or, if specific rooms were allocated to individual occupiers, could create separate tenancies of the individual, specific rooms (*AG Securities v Vaughan*, 1988).

1.211 Genuine or sham. Sometimes, however, these arrangements are not genuine. With the availability of assured shorthold tenancies, landlords are less inclined to use such devices. Nonetheless, they are still sometimes used.

1.212 Sham arrangements. In *Street v Mountford* 1986, three cases in which the courts had upheld non-exclusive occupation agreements as genuine were said to have been wrongly decided, and to be obvious sham arrangements which the courts should have treated as tenancies. A "sham" (or "false label" as it is sometimes called) arises when a document claims one thing, but the reality or actuality is, and was intended to be, something quite different, *e.g.* creating the (false) impression that a group of occupiers are not joint tenants.

1.213 Pretences. The decision in *Street* did not, however, bring an end to litigation on such agreements. The matter was considered again by the House of Lords in *Antoniades v Villiers; AG Securities v Vaughan* 1988.

1.214 Save where the agreement was, unusually, a genuine arrangement between the landlord on one hand and separate individuals on the other, as in *Vaughan* itself, the House of Lords reiterated that "pretences" devised to get around statutory protection would not be upheld. The courts should look at all the circumstances, including the relationship between the occupiers before they approached the landlord, the negotiations and, so far as the written agreement is alleged to be a pretence or sham, even after they have taken up occupation. If the reality is that the occupiers are to use the premises as a home, together, paying a rent for it, then the arrangement must be construed as a (joint) tenancy no matter what documents have been drawn up.

1.215 Subsequent cases. There has been a number of subsequent Court of Appeal decisions which have sought to apply the principles laid down by the House of Lords. In two of them (*Stribling v Wickham*, 1989, and *Mikeover Ltd v Brady*, 1989), the court found that the arrangements were genuine licences, while in three others (*Nicolaou v Pitt*, 1989, *Aslan v Murphy*, 1989 and *Duke v Wynne*, 1989), the agreements were all found to be "pretences" and the occupiers held to be tenants.

1.216 Departing joint tenants. Once joint tenancy is established, there can still be problems. Commonly, in the course of time, one or more of the original occupiers will drift on to alternative accommodation. What, then, is the position of new occupiers, assuming that they are selected by the occupiers themselves and not by the landlord? If a new occupier is selected by the landlord, this will afford the landlord evidence that he is in overall possession of the premises and that there is therefore no tenancy at all.

1.217 New occupiers. If the landlord consents, a new occupier may become a joint tenant with the others. If he does not, then the existing occupiers cannot impose a new party to the tenancy on the landlord against his will. The new occupier must be either the subtenant or licensee of the existing and remaining joint tenants and, given the remarks which have already been made, is likely to be no more than licensee. In the course of time, it may be that all the original occupiers will have left and there will only be such licensees in occupation. The only defence left is if the existing occupiers, or some of them, can show that by the acceptance of rent or by some other conduct, the landlord has accepted them as tenants, or as joint tenants (1.54–1.55).

4.   TENANTS OF MORTGAGORS

1.218 Normal Position. A person is a tenant of a mortgagor when his landlord owns the property, whether freehold or leasehold, under a mortgage. If the landlord falls into arrears with mortgage repayments, the mortgage company may "foreclose" and, in effect, take the property over. It is in this situation that problems may arise for the tenant.

1.219 As long as the mortgagor remains in possession, the tenant's position is wholly unaffected by the existence of a mortgage on the property, even if the tenancy is granted in contravention of its terms (*Church of England Building Society v Piskor*, 1954). There are commonly such terms in a mortgage.

1.220 Prior tenancy. If a person owns property before taking a mortgage on it, then any tenancies existing at the date of the mortgage are unaffected by the deed (*Mornington Permanent Building Society v Kenway*, 1953), even where the tenant has consented to the mortgage (*Woolwich Building Society v Dickman*, 1996). In such a case, even if the deed prohibits the creation of tenancies, on foreclosure the tenant will become the tenant of the mortgage company.

1.221 Illegal tenants. Almost all mortgage deeds (except those specifically for "buy to let") prohibit the creation of tenancies, and as the majority of tenancies from mortgagors are in fact created after the mortgage, there are many tenants of mortgagors who are—in this sense—"illegal" tenants. This does not avail the mortgagor, or afford him any additional right to evict the tenant. If the mortgage company forecloses, however, then no matter whether the tenant is statutorily protected or not, he has no right of occupation as against the mortgage company, even though the mortgage company knew of the illegal tenancy, but continued to accept repayments (*Dudley and District Benefit Building Society v Emerson*, 1949; *Britannia Building Society v Earl*, 1989).

1.222 New tenancy? The only possibility is that, after foreclosure, the mortgage company either actively agrees to accept the continued presence of the tenant and takes on the tenancy, or does so by implication by taking rent from the tenant over such a long period that the only inference that can properly be drawn is that it is treating the tenancy as binding upon itself (*Taylor v Ellis*, 1960; *Stroud Building Society v Delamount*, 1960).

5. ASSIGNEES

1.223 Permitted or prohibited? The term "assignment" has been used before, to describe the purchase of a long lease from the existing leaseholder (1.19). The same may occur in connection with lesser forms of tenancy, that is to say that one tenant may assign the tenancy to another. An assignee steps into the shoes of the outgoing tenant, and occupies on exactly the same terms.

1.224   If there is nothing in the terms of the tenancy or statute (*e.g.* Housing Act 1988, s.15, prohibiting assignment of a Housing Act assured tenancy without the consent of the landlord; see 4.152) to prohibit this, then it is permissible. Most tenancy agreements and rent books do, however, include such prohibitions which, like sub-tenancies (1.175) may be absolute or qualified.

1.225   Statutory tenancy. Only a contractual tenancy can be assigned, *i.e.* not a Rent Act statutory tenancy (Chapter 5; *Jessamine Investment Co v Schwartz*, 1977).

1.226   Assignment by deed. Strictly, like a surrender, assignment should be by formal deed, but it can also operate if the transaction is in writing, in a document that sets out all the express terms and which is signed (Law of Property (Miscellaneous Provisions) Act 1989, s.2).

1.227   An assignment not by deed, though binding as between the two tenants, will not bind the landlord unless he accepts the assignment, *e.g.* by payment and acceptance of rent, in much the same way and to the same extent as if he were to be deemed to have created a new tenancy (1.54–1.55) or at least to the extent that the law must consider that he is estopped from denying the validity of the assignment, *i.e.* that it would be inequitable to allow him to do so (*Rodenhurst Estates v Barnes*, 1936).

1.228   A purported assignment that is neither by deed, nor in writing, signed and setting out the express terms, cannot be effective against the landlord. For the assignee to sustain the tenancy as his own, it will be necessary to demonstrate surrender by operation of law, accepted by the landlord, coupled to what the law will recognise as the grant by the landlord, by his conduct, of a new tenancy (1.55).

6. NEW LANDLORDS

1.229   Purchase subject to existing interests. When a person purchases property, he does so subject to existing interests in it. A tenancy is an interest in property as, indeed, is a sub-tenancy, and even an illegal sub-tenancy. Accordingly, a purchaser takes subject to existing tenancies. A licence is not an interest in property, it is a personal right, and it would appear to be the case that a licence does not bind a new purchaser, although there may be some doubt about this (*National Provincial Bank v Ainsworth*, 1965).

1.230 The new landlord takes subject to all the old landlord's rights, liabilities and duties. He also takes liable to any knowledge the old landlord had, *e.g.* such knowledge as would found a claim for waiver of an illegal sub-tenancy or assignment. A tenancy dates from its original grant and there is no new tenancy on change of ownership.

1.231 Notification. Before a tenant starts to pay rent to the new landlord, the old landlord should write to him, authorising the changeover, and will remain liable as landlord until either he or the new landlord does so (Landlord and Tenant Act 1985, s.3).

1.232 Change of ownership: special issues. There are special provisions relating to change of ownership which determine whether or not a tenant still has a resident landlord for the purposes of either the Housing Act 1988 (Chapter 4) or the Rent Act 1977 (Chapter 5). In addition, there are special provisions governing the transfer of ownership from local and other public authorities to Housing Action trusts, and in some cases into private ownership, which are considered in Chapter 3.

CHAPTER TWO

Owner-Occupation

Introduction

2.01 Owner-occupiers. In this Chapter, we shall examine in outline the rights of occupation of those who were described in Chapter 1 as owner-occupiers, *i.e.* freeholders, long leaseholders, and (once they come into effect) commonholders.

2.02 It has already been remarked that the fullest status that anyone can enjoy is that of freehold owner-occupation, unencumbered by mortgage (1.12). He has to pay neither rent nor mortgage repayments and has an absolute right of occupation which can only be interfered with in the sorts of circumstances indicated (1.12–1.13).

2.03 The position of the freeholder, the leaseholder and the commonholder as regards mortgage repayments is substantially the same, and will be considered under the general heading of mortgages (2.81–2.95). First, however, the position of the leaseholder, whether or not the property is mortgaged, at or before the end of the lease must be considered (2.06–2.20).

Outline

2.04 Leasehold Rights

- The Landlord and Tenant Act 1954 and the Local Government and Housing Act 1989 allow long leaseholders to continue to occupy after the end of the lease.

- The Leasehold Reform Act 1967 allows long leaseholders of houses the right to enfranchise, *i.e.* to compel the freeholder to sell the freehold to them, or to extend the lease for a further 50 years.

- Long leaseholders and other tenants of flats enjoy a right of first refusal under the Landlord and Tenant Act 1987, so that a freeholder who wishes to sell his interest must first offer it to the tenants.

- The Leasehold Reform, Housing and Urban Development Act 1993 introduced two important rights for long leaseholders:
  - The right to collective enfranchisement of the freehold interest in the block; and,
  - The individual right to acquire a new lease.

- Once the provisions of the Commonhold and Leasehold Reform Act 2002 are brought into force, long leaseholders and other tenants will enjoy a right to manage a building containing flats.

- The recovery of service charges from leaseholders is regulated by the Landlord and Tenant Act 1985.

2.05 Mortgages

- There are two main types of mortgages: capital repayment and endowment.

- Where other parties (*e.g.* a spouse or cohabitee) already have an interest in the home, they will not be bound by a later mortgage unless they agree to it.

- Where such agreement is given through undue influence, the mortgage may still not be binding on them unless the mortgage company has ensured that they have received independent advice.

- Where there are arrears in mortgage payments, there must be a formal demand for payment.

- The mortgage company may seek possession in the county court if the arrears are not paid off.

- The county court has power to suspend the order for possession if it is of the view that the arrears can be cleared within a "reasonable period".

Leasehold Rights

1.   LANDLORD AND TENANT ACT 1954; LOCAL GOVERNMENT AND HOUSING ACT 1989, SCH.10

2.06 Long leases. "Long leases" are those for more than 21 years (Landlord and Tenant Act 1954 ("1954"), s.2(4); Leasehold

Reform Act 1967 ("1967"), s.3(1); Landlord and Tenant Act 1987 ("1987"), s.59(3); Local Government and Housing Act 1989 ("1989"), Sch.10, para.2(3) (although in the last case only, the expression can include a lease under the "right to buy" provisions of the Housing Act 1985, even if it is for less than 21 years. This is extremely rare).

2.07 Although the lease must (normally) be for more than 21 years, that is not to say that the leaseholder must have been in occupation for that period, merely that the right under which he occupies is or was for that period, *i.e.* he may have taken an assignment (1.19).

2.08 Time runs from when the lease was originally granted (*Roberts v Church Commissioners for England*, 1972), and not from any earlier date to which it may have been backdated.

2.09 Premature termination. So long as a leasehold interest has not expired, an occupier has as full a right of occupation as a freeholder and this can only be interfered with in the same ways referred to above (1.12–1.13). For this purpose, however, it is assumed that the lease runs its full length: leases can be terminated prematurely, *e.g.* because of breach of a term of the lease, or non-payment of charges. In such a case, the lease is susceptible to forfeiture proceedings, just like any other fixed-term tenancy, with the possibility of relief discussed in Chapter 1 (see 1.131–1.141).

2.10 Statutory continuation. Assuming continuation of the lease, then so long as the occupier is using the premises, or part of them, as his home at the end of the lease, the lease will not come to an end and the occupier can remain in occupation indefinitely because it is automatically continued by statute (Landlord and Tenant Act 1954, Pt I; Local Government and Housing Act 1989, Sch.10). This is not so, however, if the landlord under the lease is one of the public landlords whose tenants cannot be Housing Act assured (4.40) or Rent Act protected (5.86).

2.11 Pre-April 1, 1990 leases. If the tenancy commenced before April 1, 1990, but terminated before January 15, 1999, the protection available is that of a statutory tenant (5.24–5.29) under the Rent Act 1977, save that:

    (i) There is an additional ground for possession, if the landlord can prove that he proposes to demolish or reconstruct the whole or a substantial part of the premises in question (1954, s.12); and,

(ii) While the other qualifying conditions (5.40) must be fulfilled, the fact that the tenancy is at a low rent is disregarded (1954, s.2(1), (5)).

2.12 Use as a home. The most essential element of protection under the 1954 Act is that at the end of the lease, the premises are being used by the tenant as his home, to the same extent as is necessary to sustain a Rent Act statutory tenancy (5.95–5.112). Protection may, however, extend to only part of the premises (1954, s.3(2)), *e.g.* if the tenant occupies only one part, and does not intend to resume possession of the remainder, perhaps a part which he has sublet (*Regalian Securities v Ramsden*, 1981).

2.13 Procedure. During the last year of a long lease, the landlord can take action in the county court to try to secure a predetermination of whether or not the tenant is going to enjoy protection (1954, s.2(2)).If he does not follow this procedure, then the tenancy will automatically continue, at the old—and usually low—rent, until brought to end by notice from the landlord (1954, s.3), indicating either that he intends to seek possession on one of the available grounds (2.11), or propose a statutory tenancy to commence at a specified date (1954, s.4), identifying the proposed terms of the statutory tenancy, and dealing with the question of "initial repairs" (1954, s.7; see below, 11.81–11.86).

2.14 Once the statutory tenancy has come into existence, it may later be determined in exactly the same way as one which arises under the Rent Act 1977 (5.118–5.172).

2.15 Termination post-January 15, 1999. For tenancies which are terminated under the 1954 Act after January 15, 1999, the tenancy will not become statutory, but will fall to be dealt with in the same way as those commencing after April 1, 1990 (1989, Sch.10, para.3(2)).

2.16 Post-April 1, 1990 leases. The protection available to these leaseholders (as well as to those which commenced earlier but terminated before January 15, 1999), is (by Local Government and Housing Act 1989) that of an assured tenancy under the Housing Act 1988.

2.17 Procedure. The 1989 Act continues the existing tenancy until the landlord serves a notice either proposing an assured monthly periodic tenancy or giving notice of seeking possession (1989, Sch.10, para.4(5)). A notice proposing a new tenancy must propose a new rent which must be sufficient to ensure that it is no longer at a "low rent," and must either state that it is to be on the same terms as the long tenancy or propose new terms (1989, Sch.10, para.4(5), (6)). The new rent may be above the level (£25000 per annum, 4.27) which will accordingly take the tenant outside protection (*R. (Morris) v London RAC*, 2002).

2.18 Where a notice of seeking possession is served, it must state the ground or grounds. The landlord may rely on some of the Housing Act 1988 grounds, *i.e.* ground 6 (4.97) and the discretionary grounds 9 to 15 (4.106–4.120). In addition, the landlord may also claim possession on the basis that he requires the premises for occupation for himself, any child over 18 or his parents or parents-in-law, provided his interest was not purchased after February 18, 1966, and that he can show that it is reasonable to grant possession. To rely on this ground, however, he must satisfy the "greater hardship" test (5.164: 1989, Sch.10, para.5).

2.19 The notice proposing a new tenancy or seeking possession must give the tenant the option either to elect to remain or to indicate a willingness to give up possession. Any application for possession must be made within two months of the tenant's election, or, if there is no reply, within four months of the landlord's notice (1989, Sch.10, para.13). The tenant may at any time, regardless of whether he has elected to remain, give one month's notice to terminate the tenancy (1989, Sch.10, para.13(4)).

2.20 An interim monthly rent may be proposed by the landlord, which the tenant may appeal to the rent assessment committee (1989, Sch.10, para.6). If the tenant wishes to dispute the proposed rent and terms of the new tenancy he must serve a notice on the landlord within two months making his own proposals. If no agreement can be reached the matter may be referred by either party to the rent assessment committee, which has similar powers as under the Housing Act 1988 (4.131: 1989, Sch.10, paras 11, 12).

2. LEASEHOLD REFORM ACT 1967

2.21 Enfranchisement and extension of long leases. Under the Leasehold Reform Act 1967, a person who is a long-leaseholder of a house, but not of a flat, can compel the landlord to extend the lease for a further 50 years beyond the date of its original termination, or may require the landlord to sell him the freehold (known as "enfranchisement").

2.22 These rights only apply to those houses which are not horizontally divided from any other premises, *i.e.* they do not, to any material extent, overlap or, as it were, underlap another property (1967, s.2). Material extent here means that—if it were to be enfranchised—it would prejudice the enjoyment of that which it over-, or under-laps (*Duke of Westminster v Birrane*, 1994).

2.23 The house need not, however, be free-standing: it may be in a row of terraced houses. The house can be sub-divided, and even sub-let. Thus, a house which is also a shop can qualify (*Tandon v Trustees of Spurgeons Homes*, 1982); the question is whether the building can reasonably be called a house (*Lake v Bennett*, 1970). A property divided into two maisonettes with separate entrances, but otherwise apparently a single residence, has been held to be a house for this purpose (*Malpas v St Ermin's Property Co Ltd*, 1992).

2.24 The Act formerly only applied to tenancies at a low rent, *i.e.* a rent which is not more than two-thirds of the rateable value or, if there is no rateable value, if the rent is less than £1,000 per annum in Greater London or £250 elsewhere. (1967, s.4). This requirement was abolished by the Commonhold and Leasehold Reform Act 2002. It still applies only to long leases (2.06).

2.25 Qualifying periods. A leaseholder must exercise these rights before the lease expires and within two months of the landlord serving a notice proposing a statutory tenancy (2.13) (Leasehold Reform Act 1967, s.1). The right may, however, be exercised after an extension to the lease has been granted. The leaseholder must have been occupying the house under a long tenancy for the last two years or for periods amounting two years in the last ten years.

2.26 Occupation as residence. The former requirement that the leaseholder occupied the premises as his residence was abolished by the Commonhold and Leasehold Reform Act 2002. There remains two exceptions: (a) where a house includes a flat let to a qualifying tenant for the purposes of the 1993 Act (2.58) and where the tenant occupies under a business tenancy. In both cases the tenant does not have the right to enfranchise unless he has been occupying the house or part of it as his only or main residence for the last two years or for periods amounting to two years in the last ten years.

2.27　It is enough to occupy only part of the premises, *e.g.* if the occupier has the lease on a whole house, lives in part, and lets out part, this will suffice (*Harris v Swick Securities*, 1969), provided, where necessary, he occupies at least part as his only or main, not just a residence (1967, s.1; *Poland v Earl Cadogan*, 1980).

2.28　Purchase price. Failing agreement between the parties, the purchase price can be fixed, by the leasehold valuation tribunal, and on appeal therefrom by the Lands Tribunal, but the procedure is complicated and anyone intending to use it should consult a lawyer or surveyor.

2.29　Extension does not cost anything, although a new ground rent (*i.e.* low rent) which is appropriate to the value of the house as at the date when the new lease is to start will take effect from that date (1967, s.15). Extension is provided mainly for those who cannot afford to enfranchise or who, perhaps being elderly and with no relatives to whom to leave any acquired interest, have no reason to do so. There are special grounds of opposition to enfranchisement or extension available to specified public landlords (1967, s.28).

2.30　Sooner is cheaper. Enfranchisement can be extremely cheap. All that is being bought back is the benefit of a very small ground rent and the fairly remote possibility that the landlord will ever get the property back at all. The longer there is to run on the lease at the time a notice indicating an intention to purchase is served, the cheaper the price will be, because the landlord's expectations are the most remote. It follows that once an occupier has fulfilled the residential qualification, he should exercise the power to enfranchise as soon as possible.

2.31　The price of enfranchisement bears no practical relation to current property values or even to the customarily lower than vacant possession value at which many sitting tenants are permitted to buy from their landlords. It may be a figure of less than £100, or not much more. The advice of a surveyor will count for much more than that of a lawyer where prices in enfranchisement and extension are concerned.

3.　LANDLORD AND TENANT ACT 1987

2.32　Additional rights. Long leaseholders also benefit from a range of rights contained in the Landlord and Tenant Act 1987,

Pts I, III and IV of which may most conveniently be considered in this chapter. Other tenants may also benefit from Pt I. (Pt II—the appointment of a manager—is considered in Chapter 11, below.)

(i) *Pt I—First refusal*

2.33 Right of first refusal. Pt I contains provisions designed to give the tenants (including long leaseholders) of blocks of flats a "right of first refusal" should the freeholder or a superior landlord wish to sell his interest in circumstances amounting to a "relevant disposal". The provisions apply only to flats, and there must be at least two flats in the building for them to operate. The block need not be purpose-built.

2.34 Exclusions. The provisions do not apply if the landlord is a resident landlord or an exempt landlord, or if less than 50 per cent of the flats are occupied by qualifying tenants, or if less than 50 per cent of the floor area of the building (excluding common parts) is not in (or intended for) residential use (1987, s.1).

2.35 Exempt landlords. "Exempt landlords" include local authorities, new town development corporations or the Commission for the New Towns, an urban development corporation, the Housing Corporation, charitable housing trusts, registered social landlords and Housing Action Trusts (1987, s.58).

2.36 Resident Landlord. "Resident landlord" is defined (1987, s.58) in terms very similar to the definition in the Housing Act 1988 (4.43–4.50). Accordingly, the mere fact that the landlord lives in a purpose-built block of flats will not prevent the right of first refusal arising. Where the resident landlord exemption does apply, however, *e.g.* in a converted house, the landlord need not have been in residence since the commencement of the tenancy, but only for a period of at least one year before the prospective disposal. The residential test is not "a" residence (as under the Rent Act 1977: 5.47–5.52), but "only or principal residence" (as under the Housing Act 1985: 3.32–3.35).

2.37 Qualifying tenants. All tenants, including Rent Act statutory tenants (5.21), are qualifying tenants, except shorthold tenants (6.09), assured tenants (Chapter 4), those to whom the business security of Pt II, Landlord and Tenant Act 1954 (3.39(n)) applies, and service tenants (1.148; 1987, s.3). If, however, a person has a lease of three flats in the building, *i.e.* someone who has *prima facie* acquired for sub-letting, or if a person is a sub-tenant whose landlord is himself a qualifying tenant, he cannot be a qualifying tenant, (1987, s.3).

2.38 Relevant disposal. The right of first refusal arises only in relation to a "relevant disposal." This means the disposal of any interest in the whole or part of the building other than a schedule of classes of disposal which includes:

   (i) The grant of a tenancy of a single flat;

   (ii) A disposal of an interest by way of mortgage;

  (iii) Disposal under Matrimonial Causes Act 1973, ss.23A, 24, or 24A (9.06);

  (iv) A disposal related to a compulsory purchase;

   (v) A disposal under the collective enfranchisement provisions of the Leasehold Reform, Housing and Urban Development Act 1993 (2.56);

  (vi) A disposal by way of gift to a member of the landlord's family or to a charity;

 (vii) A disposal by will;

(viii) A disposal to the Crown; and.

  (ix) A disposal to a company which has been "associated" (as defined) with the landlord company for two years (1987, s.4).

2.39 A contract to dispose is a relevant disposal (1987, s.4A). A disposal by a mortgage company falls within the provisions, even if it has taken the property back from the landlord under the mortgage.

2.40 Requisite majority. The provisions of Pt I are highly technical and are only described in outline. Where a relevant disposal is proposed, the landlord has to offer the tenants the right of first refusal, identifying what is on offer and its terms, including price. "Propose" here means a state of mind somewhere between mere consideration of a course of action, and a fixed or irrevocable determination to pursue it (*Mainwaring v Trustees of Henry Smith's Charity*, 1996).

2.41 The offer can only be accepted by a "requisite majority" of the qualifying tenants, within a period of not less than two months

(1987, s.5), "Requisite majority" means more than 50 per cent of the "available votes." "Available votes" means one vote for each flat involved (1987, s.18A). If the requisite majority accepts the offer, they have a further two months in which to identify a person to act on their behalf in the further transactions, and the landlord cannot sell to anyone else until the end of the "relevant period," which is defined to cover the designated procedure (1987, s.6).

2.42   One year restriction on disposal. If no one is nominated or the offer is not accepted, the landlord cannot dispose elsewhere for 12 months save on the same terms and at the same price (1987, s.7). (This is to prevent offers at an unnaturally high figure).

2.43   Nominated person. Once a person has been nominated, the landlord may not dispose of the property except to that person and must send out a contract within one month (1987, ss.8 and 8A). The nominated person then has two months in which to offer an exchange of contract (1987, s.8A).

2.44   Other Provisions. Other provisions deal with withdrawals and deemed withdrawals (in cases where time limits are not complied with) by both landlord and nominated purchaser and where the original proposed sale is by auction. There are also provisions to deal with a disposal which has not complied with the right of first refusal, which include the possibility of forcing the purchaser to resell to the tenants (1987, ss.11, 12A–12D; *Belvedere Court Management Ltd v Frogmore Development Ltd*, 1995).

2.45   Criminal offences. It is a criminal offence for a landlord, without reasonable excuse, to make a relevant disposal of property to which Pt I of the 1987 Act applies (1987, s.10A) with liability to a fine up to level 5 on the standard scale. Landlords under a duty to inform tenants of an assignment of the property (see 1.231) must also inform qualifying tenants of their rights under the 1987 Act (Landlord and Tenant Act 1985, s.3A). Failure to do so is a criminal offence.

(ii)   *Pt III—Compulsory acquisition*

2.46   Preconditions. Pt III of the 1987 Act permits a form of "compulsory purchase" by qualifying tenants. For this purpose a qualifying tenant must have a long lease (2.06). A "business tenant" cannot be a qualifying tenant, nor can a tenant whose lease comprises more than two flats, nor if his own landlord is a qualifying tenant (1987, s.26).

2.47 For the provisions to operate, a specified number of flats in a building must be occupied by qualifying tenants: if less than four flats, all of them; if four to ten, no less than all but one; if 10 or more, at least 90 per cent (1987, s.25).

2.48 Exclusions. As under Pt I (2.34), the provisions do not apply if more than 50 per cent of the building (excluding the common parts) is non-residential, nor if there is an exempt or resident landlord (2.35, 2.36).

2.49 Acquisition Order. The "acquisition order" can only be made by a court, which must be satisfied that the preconditions (above) apply and

(a) That one of two sets of further conditions applies, and

(b) That the conditions for making the order exist (1987, s.29).

2.50 Conditions. It is the conditions which define the purpose. The conditions are where the freeholder is (and is likely to remain) in breach of his obligations (in respect of repair, insurance, maintenance or management)—or would be if notice could be served on him—to such an extent that the appointment of a manager under Pt II (11.121) would not be a sufficient remedy, or else that there has been a Pt II manager for at least two years (1987, s.29).

2.51 Further provisions. Further provisions govern the terms of the acquisition and if the landlord cannot be found (1987, ss.30–33), but a landlord can apply for discharge of the order if the tenants do not proceed within a reasonable time, or if the number of tenants wishing to proceed falls below the requisite majority (1987, s.34).

2.52 Procedure. Before an application can be made to the court, a "requisite majority" of tenants (defined in the same terms as for Pt I: 2.40) must serve notice on the landlord of the intention to apply, identifying the grounds on which the application will be made, specifying what remedial steps might be taken to avert the application within a specified reasonable period, and containing such other information as might be prescribed by the Secretary of State (1987, s.27). The court can, however, waive the requirement of preliminary notice if it considers that it is not reasonably practicable to serve one. Unless the prior notice is waived by the court, no application can be made until the period specified for remedial action has expired (1987, s.28).

(iii) *Pt IV—Variation of leases*

2.53 Applications to vary. Finally, attention may be drawn to the provisions of Pt IV of the Act, which are again confined to long leaseholders (2.06). These provisions permit individual lease-holders to apply to court for a variation of the terms of a lease which fails to make satisfactory provisions governing repairs or maintenance of a flat or building or of facilities necessary to ensure that occupiers enjoy a reasonable standard of accommodation, insurance, repairs, the provision or maintenance or services, or the way service charges are computed (1987, s.35).

2.54 There is also provision for the variation of other leases within a building to ensure consistency (1987, s.36) and for "block applications" by a specified number of leaseholders in a building: two to eight flats, no less than all but one; nine or more flats, 75 per cent in support of the application, and the application is not opposed by more than 10 per cent.

4. LEASEHOLD REFORM, HOUSING AND URBAN DEVELOPMENT ACT 1993

2.55 Rights for leaseholders of flats. The rights of leaseholders of flats were further extended by the Leasehold Reform, Housing and Urban Development Act 1993, to compensate for their inability to enfranchise under Leasehold Reform Act 1967 (above), *i.e.* because their homes are flats not houses. Two rights were created by the 1993 Act:

(i) The right to collective enfranchisement of the freehold interest in a block of flats by qualifying tenants;

(ii) The individual right to a new lease of a flat.

(i) *Collective enfranchisement*

2.56 The right of collective enfranchisement is the right to have the freehold of the premises in which the flat is situated acquired on their behalf by persons appointed by them for the purpose (1993, s.1).

2.57 Qualifying premises. The building to be acquired must contain two or more flats owned by qualifying tenants (2.37), who must between them own at least two-thirds of the total number of flats in the building (1993, s.3). Where the building is not primarily in residential use or where there is a resident landlord in a building containing not more than four units, the right to collective enfranchisement is excluded (1993, s.4).

2.58 Qualifying tenants. Qualifying tenants have to have a long lease, broadly meaning one for more than 21 years (1993, s.7).

2.59 Excluded tenants. Certain tenants are excluded: business tenants; tenants of charitable housing trusts; and, those whose tenancies are illegal because granted by a mesne landlord in breach of a superior lease (1993, s.5).

2.60 Procedure. To make a purchase, qualifying tenants are entitled to information from their immediate landlord about those with superior interests (1993, s.11). Once the tenants decide to proceed they must serve an initial notice on the freeholder; this initial notice must be on behalf of tenants of not less than half of the total number of flats in the building (1993, s.13). Those qualifying tenants who are parties to the initial notice thereby become participating tenants.

2.61 The notice must state the name and address of a nominee purchaser, and also a proposed price, which must include not only the freehold price but also a price for any intermediate interests. The freeholder must serve a counter-notice either admitting or denying the right. The right may be denied on the basis that the freeholder intends to redevelop the premises (1993, s.21).

2.62 Nominee Purchaser. At the moment, the identity of the nominee purchaser is not specified, although in practice a company is often set up specially for the purpose. Once the relevant provisions of the CLRA 2002 come into force a specially constituted "RTE" (right to enfranchise) company will have to be used.

2.63 The price. If the price is not agreed, it is to be determined under statutory rules into which statutorily defined assumptions are built. The price has to comprise a number of elements: the freehold price; the price of any intermediate leasehold interest; the price of other interests to be acquired. The freeholder is entitled to compensation for any loss in value to any other property he owns, including loss of development value (1993, Sch.6). Disputes regarding price are referable to the leasehold valuation tribunal (1993, s.24).

2.64 Enforcement. The right may be enforced through application to the county court. Where there are disputes about the terms of the purchase, however, these may be referred to the leasehold valuation tribunal.

(ii) *New lease*

2.65 90-year lease. In addition, the 1993 Act gives individual tenants the right to acquire a new, 90–year lease. To exercise the right, there must be a qualifying tenant of a flat, *i.e.* one held on a long lease (2.58).

2.66 Procedure. The tenant proceeds by means of an initial notice, to which the landlord must respond with a counter-notice admitting or denying the right. The right can be denied on the basis that the landlord intends to redevelop (1993, s.45). Disputes regarding the terms and price may be referred to the leasehold valuation tribunal. Other disputes regarding progress may be referred to the county court. The tenant may withdraw (1993, s.52); in some circumstances of inaction by the tenant, withdrawal may be deemed to have taken place (1993, s.53).

2.67 Price and grant. If the price is not agreed, the dispute may be referred to the leasehold valuation tribunal. The price is determined according to statutory assumptions and includes compensation for the landlord (1993, Sch.13, 2.63). Once all the terms are agreed or determined, and the price being paid, the tenant is under an obligation to accept—in substitution for his present lease—a lease for a term which will amount to 90–years from what would have been the end of the current lease, at a peppercorn rent, (1993, s.56(1)). In addition, the tenant must clear any arrears of rent or service charges which have accrued (1993, s.56(3)). The new lease is, in general, to be on the same terms as the original (1993, s.57).

2.68 Future leases. Once a lease has been granted, there is nothing to prevent another such new lease being granted or indeed the right to collective enfranchisement being exercised. However, all rights to statutory security of tenure (2.17) are lost (1993, s.59).

5. COMMONHOLD AND LEASEHOLD REFORM ACT 2002

2.69 Right to manage. The right to manage, in cases of default by the freeholder, was introduced by the Landlord and Tenant Act

1987 and is considered in Chapter 11 (11.121). Once brought into force, CLRA 2002 ("2002") will offer qualifying tenants of qualifying premises a right to manage irrespective of fault.

2.70 Qualifying requirements. The same qualifying requirements as under the 1993 Act must be met as to premises and tenants (2002, s.72, 75: see 2.57, 2.58).

2.71 RTM company. In order to exercise the right, the tenants must first establish a right to manage company—"RTM Company"—which accords with the requirements of 2002, ss. 73 and 74. The RTM company then serves notice inviting participation by tenants in the company (2002, s.78). Provided membership of the RTM company includes qualifying tenants of at least half the number of flats in the building, notice claiming the right can be served on the landlord (2002, s.79). The landlord must respond with a counter notice admitting or denying the right (2002, s.84).

2.72 Procedure. If there is no dispute, the right to manage arises on the date set out in the initial notice, which must be at least four months after the date of the notice. If it is denied, the matter may be determined by the Leasehold Valuation Tribunal ("LVT"). If the LVT determines that there is an entitlement to the right, the right to manage will arise three months from the determination (2002, s.90).

2.73 Rights. Once it has acquired the right to manage, the RTM Company becomes responsible for management functions, *i.e.* those concerning services, repairs, maintenance, improvements, insurance and management (2002, s.96).

6. SERVICE CHARGES

2.74 Landlord and Tenant Act 1985. Many long leases and some shorter tenancies have provision for the landlord to levy service charges. Disputes commonly arise about the amount of service charges, and the quality of the work that the landlord carries out. The Landlord and Tenant Act 1985, ss.18–25 govern the levy and recovery of service charges.

2.75 Service charge. The Act applies to all charges payable for services, repairs, maintenance or insurance or the landlord's costs of management, which vary or may vary in accordance with their cost (1985, s.18). It does not apply to costs charged for improvements (*Sutton (Hastoe) Housing Association v Williams*, 1998). It will, however, be extended to charges for improvements, when the relevant provisions of CLRA 2002 are brought into force.

2.76 Reasonableness. Service charges can only be recovered so far as they are reasonably incurred and the works or services are to a reasonable standard (1985, s.19). Leasehold valuation tribunals have jurisdiction to determine whether charges are reasonable. When it comes into force, CLRA 2002, Sch.11, will add a reasonableness test for administration charges such as those for granting approvals and penalties for late payment of rent.

2.77 Exclusions. There are provisions for excluding—or seeking to have excluded—from service charges:

(i) Some costs that have been met with specified types of grant-aid;

(ii) Costs incurred more than 18 months before the demand for payment (and of which no notice was given within that time); and,

(iii) Landlords' costs in connection with a dispute (1985, ss.20A–20C).

2.78 Estimates and consultation. In the case of larger scale building works (*i.e.* those exceeding the greater of £1,000 or £50 multiplied by the number of dwellings), the landlord must provide the leaseholders with at least two estimates for the works and invite their comments (1985, s.20). There are additional provisions for consultation on the estimates where there is a recognised tenants' association. When CLRA 2002 comes into force, these limitations will also apply to other long term contracts (*e.g.* for cleaning services) and the details of the required consultation will be prescribed by the Secretary of State. Any or all of the consultation requirement may, however, be waived by a court where it is reasonable to do so, *e.g.* in cases of urgency (1985, s.20(9)).

2.79 Statements of costs. Under 1985, s.21 landlords must also provide a statement of relevant costs incurred during an account-ing period when requested to do so. This section will be amended by CLRA 2002 to require an annual statement of account, showing the charges, the costs and any balances held. A new s.21A will permit leaseholders to withhold the payment of service charges if the statement has not been provided or does not conform to the statutory requirements.

2.80 Separate accounts. At present, where landlords hold receive service charges they are deemed to be held on trust (Landlord and Tenant Act 1987, s.42). CLRA 2002 will add a new s.42A which will additionally require that any monies in the trust fund must be held in a separate designated account.

Mortgages

2.81 Nature of mortgages. Both freehold and leasehold (and, once available, commonhold—see 1.20) owner-occupation can, and frequently will, be subject to a mortgage. Mortgages are a form of loan against the security of the property in question. There are two principal sorts of mortgage: capital repayment and endowment.

2.82 Capital mortgage. A capital repayment mortgage is a loan which requires repayment in periodic amounts. Although it is not an essential part of a capital repayment mortgage, most mortgage companies insist that there is included in the package an element of insurance, called the mortgage protection policy. This provides insurance against the death of the owner-occupier, in which case the insurance will pay off any outstanding mortgage and so leave the property unencumbered for the next-of-kin.

2.83 Capital and interest. The two essential parts of the repayments are capital repayment and interest (commonly at a variable rate, though it can be fixed or, *e.g.* fixed for a period of time). Monthly payments are assessed at an amount slightly larger than the interest due on the original capital loan. This means that at the beginning of a mortgage repayment period, most of the payment is interest, and only a small amount of it is capital repayment. As the capital decreases, however, an decreasing proportion of the repayments goes to interest (still based on the original loan) and an increasing amount on capital.

2.84 Endowment. The monthly payment under an endowment mortgage is a sum assessed in two parts only: interest and life assurance premium. Subject to fluctuations in the mortgage interest rate, both these amounts remain the same. There is no capital repayment. Instead, the life assurance premium is calculated to produce a sum that either at the end of the period for which the mortgage has been taken out, or on the death of the mortgagor, will be sufficient to pay off the whole of the capital outstanding. There are other benefits which may be included in an endowment mortgage arrangement but they are decreasingly popular because the sums produced by the premium have in recent years proved insufficient to pay off the capital.

2.85 Repossession and arrears. Although all mortgage deeds contain a variety of terms (*e.g.* not to create tenancies—or tenancies other than of a particular type, *i.e.* without security—in the property without permission), it is usually only when an occupier falls into arrears with the repayments that the company has the right to take action to evict him, and to dispose of the property.

2.86 Absent agreement, either the mortgage company or the mortgagor may apply for an order for the property to be sold (under Law of Property Act 1925, s.91). Thus, if a mortgage company wishes instead to rent the property out until the market picks up, the mortgagor can apply to the court to force the mortgage company to sell in order to prevent interest continuing to accrue (*Palk v Mortgage Services Funding Plc*, 1992). Usually, an order for sale at the request of the mortgagor will be refused if the mortgage company can demonstrate a tangible benefit of which it will be deprived, but that will not include either its own policy considerations, or the power to conduct the sale through its own agents and solicitors (*Barrett v Halifax BS*, 1995).

2.87 Who is bound by the mortgage? The mortgage company will, however, have to be able to show that the mortgage is binding on those against whom it seeks possession. It will not be binding on someone with a prior interest, *e.g.* a tenant (1.220), or a spouse with a right of occupation under the Family Law Act 1996 (9.15), unless there has been an effective agreement to subordinate that right to the subsequent mortgagee (*Woolwich B.S. v Dickman*, 1996). Likewise, if there are joint owners on the face of the deeds, or as a result of a trust (1.27), all those who have an existing right must be shown to be bound by the mortgage before the company will be able to exercise its rights.

2.88 Securing someone else's loan. These issues commonly arise when a home is put up as security for a loan, which may not itself be for housing purposes but, *e.g.* a business purpose. Where one person puts up his own home as security, then the position is no different than in any other case where one individual borrows against the security of his house or flat. Problems arise where one person—who wants to borrow the money—needs the agreement of a joint owner or someone else with a prior right to use the property as security.

2.89 Undue influence. Where the agreement to the loan has been procured by a third party (such as a husband, cohabitee or employer) using undue influence, misrepresentation or another legal wrong, it may not be binding if the lender has notice of the wrong. In some relationships (*e.g.* parent/child, solicitor/client), undue influence will automatically be presumed (and therefore the lender would be on notice of it) in any transaction which was to the disadvantage to the borrower, unless it can be shown that he entered into it with "full, free and informed thought." This presumption does not, however, automatically apply to husbands and wives. To show undue influence in such cases, it is necessary to have evidence that the transaction was wrongful "in that it constituted an advantage taken of the person subjected to the influence which, failing proof to the contrary, was explicable only on the basis that undue influence had been exercised to procure it" (*National Westminster Bank plc v Morgan*, 1995; *Royal Bank of Scotland v Etridge*, 2001).

2.90 Effect on borrower. To avoid being bound by the wrong, the lender will therefore have to show that he had taken reasonable steps to satisfy himself that the other party has entered into the arrangement freely and in knowledge of the true facts, which will normally mean warning him or her—at a meeting not attended by the borrower—of the amount of the potential liability, and of the risks involved, and advising him or her to take independent legal advice (*Barclays Bank Plc v O'Brien*, 1993). Even if the lender does not meet with the borrower, the lender will be protected against the wrongdoing if he has confirmed with the wife that she has a solicitor acting for her, and has confirmation from the solicitor that the borrower has been appropriately advised (*Royal Bank of Scotland*, above).

2.91 Demand for arrears. Before legal proceedings are started, the mortgage company will normally make a written demand for any arrears of repayment. It is not obliged by law to do this, but in practice the court (which has discretionary powers which are described below) will not look kindly upon a mortgage company which has proceeded to exercise its full legal rights without warning the occupier and giving him a chance to redeem his position. If the arrears are paid off at that point, nothing further will normally happen. If an occupier has a bad history of arrears, however, the mortgage company may still decide to press on with the full legal procedure.

2.92 Demand for repayment. After any demand for the arrears, there will be a formal demand for repayment of the whole of the outstanding debt. This will be for all capital outstanding and any accumulated interest. At this point, an occupier can, if he is in a position to do so, buy off the mortgage company entirely, and retain possession of the property. There has to be such a formal demand, however, even if it is quite obvious that the occupier cannot comply with it.

2.93 Possession proceedings. The next step is for the mortgage company to issue possession proceedings in the county court. The company cannot evict the occupier without court proceedings. The court is not obliged to grant the possession order immediately. It has power to grant an order suspended on condition that the occupier continues to pay current instalments under the mortgage, and a fixed amount per payment off the arrears, or it may stay execution or postpone the date for giving up possession. Once an order has been executed, however, there are no further powers of stay, suspension or postponement, unless there are grounds on which to set aside the warrant for possession, or it is considered to be an abuse of the process of the court or oppressive to execute it (*Cheltenham & Gloucester BS v Obi*, 1994).

2.94 Suspended orders. The court will only exercise this discretion if it is of the view that the arrears can be cleared in a reasonable time (Administration of Justice Act 1970, s.36; *Town & Country Building Society v Julien*, 1991). If it does not think this can be done, then the order will be final, but will usually be suspended for at least 28 days to give the occupier time to start making alternative arrangements: see Chapter 10. While it has been said that an order may be deferred for a short period, *e.g.* three months, in order to enhance the prospects of sale by the occupier (*Target Home Loans Ltd v Clothier*, 1992), this is not a rule of law and if there is evidence that a sale could take place in a longer period, there is no reason why a court should not allow it (*National & Provincial BS v Lloyd*, 1995).

2.95 Reasonable time to clear arrears. There is no formal definition of reasonable time. Until recently, the courts had normally considered one year a reasonable time in which to clear the arrears (*Cheltenham & Gloucester BS v Grant*, 1994). It has now been said that a court should take as its starting-point the full period of the mortgage, and determine whether or not it would be possible for the mortgagor to maintain payment of the arrears by instalments over that period. This approach will call for more detailed analysis than had become customary, and amongst the

features the court will need to consider, will be how much the
borrower could reasonably afford to pay (currently and in the
future); if a difficulty is temporary how long it is likely to last;
what the reason was for the arrears; the remaining term; any
relevant contractual terms; the type of mortgage; over what period
it is reasonable to expect the lender to recoup arrears of interest,
and any other reasons affecting the security which should influence the length of the period (*Cheltenham & Gloucester BS v
Norgan*, 1995).

2.96   Consumer Credit Act 1974. Loans of less than £15,000,
which are not made by local authorities or building societies (and
certain other exempt organisations) are regulated by the Consumer
Credit Act 1974. Where the creditor is seeking repayment or
possession the court may make a "time order" to reschedule
payment of the debt (1974, s.129). The court must consider
whether it is just to make the order, and where possession
proceedings are involved this relates to the whole outstanding
balance under the mortgage (*Southern & District Finance v Barnes*,
1995). The court also has power to alter the rate of interest (1974,
s.136).

CHAPTER THREE

Housing Act Secure Tenancies

Introduction

3.01 Landlords whose tenants are secure. A range of "social landlords" provide "secure tenancies" within the Housing Act 1985, Pt III ("1985"). These are primarily local authorities and registered social landlords, but in the latter case only where the tenancy was granted on or before January 14, 1989 (at which time, those landlords were known as housing associations). Later tenancies are "assured" under Housing Act 1988 (see Chapter 4).

3.02 Other rights of secure tenants. Where tenants of social landlords are secure, they also gain a number of additional rights, including the right to buy.

3.03 Other tenants of social landlords. Tenants of social landlords who do not qualify as secure tenants under the Housing Act 1985 will normally qualify as assured tenants under the Housing Act 1988 and are considered in Chapter 4. The remaining tenants of social landlords, who do not qualify under either Act, will be considered in Chapter 7.

Outline

3.04 Social landlords

- Local authorities have specific powers to provide housing.

- Tenants of local authorities are secure.

- Certain other defined landlords can also grant secure tenancies.

- Registered social landlords formerly granted secure tenancies but have not been able to do so since January 15, 1989; their subsequent tenancies are assured (see Chapter 4).

3.05 Secure tenants. A secure tenant is one:

- To whom residential accommodation is let
  - As a separate dwelling,
  - Under a tenancy or licence,
  - Under which both the landlord condition and tenant condition are fulfilled.
- There is, however, a schedule of exceptions which may exclude someone who would otherwise be a secure tenant.
- On the death of the secure tenant, there is a right to one succession to a secure tenancy by a spouse or family member.
- A secure tenancy can only be repossessed by the landlord obtaining a court order, following service of a notice of seeking possession which sets out the statutory ground on which possession is sought.
- Some grounds require the court to be satisfied that it is reasonable to grant possession; others that suitable alternative accommodation is provided; and yet others that it is both reasonable and suitable alternative accommodation is provided.
- Anti-social behaviour provides a ground for possession or may be dealt with by way of injunction.

3.06 Additional rights and issues

- Secure tenants have a number of additional rights:
  - The right to buy;
  - Right to improve;
  - Rights to sublet and take in lodgers;
  - Right to exchange;
  - Right to repair;
  - Rights in relation to variation of terms of the tenancy; and
  - Rights to be consulted in matters of housing management.
- Local authorities are bound to charge "reasonable" rents; what is reasonable is largely a matter for the discretion of the local authority.
- Pre-1988 Act housing association tenancies (which are therefore normally secure) are subject to the fair rent regime of the Rent Act 1977.

- Management of the stock is largely a matter for the social landlord, although local authorities may enter into management agency agreements and their tenants may seek to set up their own tenant management organisation.

- Transfer of local authority housing has been a government policy for the last 20 years and a number of mechanisms exist to achieve this: these include voluntary transfer and Housing Action Trusts.

- Further financial protection and assistance is available to secure tenants.

Social landlords

3.07 Local housing authorities. Local authorities still remain the main providers of social rented housing, although current government policy is to seek to reduce the amount of rented stock they hold (see below for provisions governing transfer). Since 1980, most of their tenancies have been secure and continue to remain so.

3.08 Local authorities for housing purposes are: district councils; county and county borough councils (in Wales); London borough councils and the Common Council of the City of London; although county councils may, with the consent of the Secretary of State, also exercise housing powers. Unitary authorities will likewise be housing authorities.

3.09 Provision of housing. Under the 1985 Act, s.8, local housing authorities are bound to consider the housing needs of their areas. Pt II of that Act contains their powers to own, manage and dispose of their housing accommodation, although it should be noted that there is no absolute requirement that they should hold any stock of accommodation if they do not choose to do so (1985, s.9(5)).

3.10 Detailed provision is made as to who may be allocated local authority accommodation; this is considered in Chapter 10.

3.11 Other social landlords. New town commissions, urban development corporations and Housing Action Trusts all fulfil functions similar to those of local authorities and their tenants are likewise normally secure.

3.12 Registered social landlords. Housing associations, housing trusts and similar bodies—known under the Housing Act 1996

("1996") as "registered social landlords"—qualify for public funding for their activities. These are registered under Pt I of the 1996 Act with the Housing Corporation or with the Secretary of State in Wales.

3.13 Between 1980, registered housing associations and trusts were landlords whose tenants were normally secure. From 1989, by Pt I of the Housing Act 1988, however, their tenants were taken out of the Housing Act 1985 and placed into the same framework as private sector tenants, as assured tenants. That is the regime which governs all subsequent tenants of registered social landlords: see Chapter 4, below.

3.14 Pre- and post-January 15, 1989 registered social landlord tenants. In this chapter, accordingly, we are concerned with the tenants of registered social landlord only if the tenancy began before the commencement (January 15, 1989) of Pt I of the Housing Act 1988 ("1988").

3.15 Exceptions. A tenancy granted by a registered social landlord on or after that date cannot be secure unless either:

    (a) **Pre-Act contract.** It was entered into, pursuant to a contract for its grant which preceded that date; or

    (b) **New tenancy to former tenant.** It is the grant of a new tenancy (not necessarily of the same premises) to a person who was a former tenant of the same landlord, or one of a number of joint (1.94) such tenants; or

    (c) **Suitable alternative accommodation.** It is the grant of a tenancy resulting from an order for possession against a secure tenant, on the ground of suitable alternative accommodation (3.126, 3.127), and

        (i) The premises in question are those which the court has found suitable, and

        (ii) The court directs that the new tenancy should be a secure tenancy on the ground that an assured tenancy will not provide sufficient security; or

    (d) **New town corporation to housing association.** It falls within a small class of tenancy formerly held by a new town development corporation, and passed into housing association ownership before March 31, 1996; or

    (e) **Defective premises.** The tenancy is one granted under special provisions (Housing Act 1985, Pt XVI) dealing with buying back premises that have been designated as defective in their design (not covered in this book): 1988, s.34.

3.16 So far as this Chapter concerns housing association tenancies, it therefore applies mainly to tenancies already granted. Tenancies granted on or after the commencement of Pt I of the 1988 Act are, subject to its own schedule of exclusions, likely to be assured tenancies, and are considered in Chapter 4.

Secure Tenants

3.17 Let as a separate dwelling. A secure tenant is one to whom residential accommodation is let as a separate dwelling under a tenancy or licence (1985, s.79), under which both the landlord conditions and the tenant conditions are fulfilled, and which is not excluded from security under the schedule of exceptions (1985, Sch.1).

3.18 The term "let as a separate dwelling" is considered in relation to the Housing Act assured tenancies (4.16) and the Rent Act protected tenancies (5.40), as the greatest attention has been paid to it in connection with the private sector (but see also 3.20). Under those Acts, it refers to a letting by way of tenancy but not by way of licence (1.45).

3.19 Application to licensees. This is not so under the Housing Act 1985, which also applies to licences, whether or not granted for a monetary payment (1985, s.79(3)).

3.20 Licences within the 1985 Act are, however, only those which effectively grant the occupier exclusive possession (*cf.* 1.65). Where the landlord retains the right to move tenants to other rooms, the licence will not be within the Act (*Westminster CC v Clarke*, 1992).

3.21 Temporary licenses. The inclusion of licences does not extend to a licence granted as a temporary expedient to a person who entered the premises the subject of the licence, or other premises, as a trespasser (1985, s.79(4)): *i.e.* those who illegally entered unused public sector property awaiting demolition, but— to avoid unnecessarily leaving property empty—who were allowed to remain or else offered somewhere else temporarily (1.32).

3.22 Throughout this Chapter, save where a distinction is drawn, references to secure tenancy include licences brought into security by s.79.

3.23 Shared living accommodation. Another important distinction between private security under the 1988 and 1977 Acts and the 1985 Act is that, while the 1988 and 1977 Acts are specifically applied to those who share living accommodation (4.17, 5.71), there is no such provision in the 1985 Act.

3.24 The effect of this is that there cannot be a secure tenancy where living accommodation is shared, because there is no letting "as a separate dwelling": *Central YMCA HA Ltd v Saunders*, 1990; *Curl v Angelo*, 1948).

3.25 Living accommodation for these purposes means a living-room, rather than a bathroom or lavatory (*Cole v Harris*, 1945) or, probably, a kitchen unless it is big enough to eat in (*Neale v Del Soto*, 1945; *Central YMCA*; *Uratemp v Collins*, 2001. There remains some doubt about the position, where what is shared is a kitchen that is not big enough to sit and eat in). This exclusion tends to affect those in hostels and other shared accommodation.

3.26 For this purpose, it does not matter whether or not anyone else is actually sharing living accommodation at any particular time; it is sufficient if the terms of the letting are such that it is genuinely within contemplation—or there is a real prospect—that the occupier will have to share living accommodation with another at some future date (*Gray v Brown*, 1992).

3.27 Principal issues. Under this heading, we must consider:

- The landlord condition;
- The tenant condition;
- Exceptions;
- Succession;
- Loss of security.

1. THE LANDLORD CONDITION

3.28 Secure landlords. The landlord condition is that the landlord under the tenancy is:

- A local authority;
- A New Town corporation;

- A housing action trust;

- An urban development corporation or a housing co-operative as defined (1985, s.80(1)).

3.29 The section only applies to housing co-operatives set up under a housing management agreement (as defined in 1985, s.27B) (1985, s.80(4)).

3.30 Former secure landlords. A number of other landlords were formerly listed in 1985, s.80(1) until they were removed by the Housing Act 1988. They are:

- The Housing Corporation;

- A housing trust which is a charity;

- Registered housing associations (other than co-operative housing associations); and

- Unregistered housing associations which are co-operative associations (1985, s.80(1), (2), prior to amendment).

3.31 Tenants of such landlords whose tenancies were granted prior to commencement of Pt I of the 1988 Act (January 15, 1989) remain secure.

2. THE TENANT CONDITION

3.32 Occupation by individual as only or principal home. The tenant condition is that the tenant is an individual, as opposed to a corporate body, *e.g.* a company, and that the tenant occupies the dwelling-house as his only or principal home (1985, s.81).

3.33 This is a slightly different test (*Poland v Earl Cadogan*, 1980) from that of statutory residence under the Rent Act 1977 (5.96–5.110), and is, rather, closer to that to be found in relation to the Leasehold Reform Act 1967 (2.12).

3.34 Whether premises are occupied as a home at all, is, however, to be determined in the same way as the question whether they are occupied as a residence under the Rent Act 1977 (5.99).

3.35 Actual physical occupation may not be necessary (*Crawley BC v Sawyer*, 1987). Where the tenant is no longer in occupation, however, he is under the burden of establishing that he intends to return to the property, and must substantiate this through visible signs of that intention (*Ujima HA v Ansah*, 1997 and *Amoah v Baking & Dagenham LBC*, 2001).

3.36   Joint tenants. If the tenancy is a joint tenancy, then at least one of the joint tenants must be an individual as opposed to a corporate body, and at least one of the joint tenants must be in occupation as an only or principal home (1985, s.81).

3.37   A tenant does not necessarily lose security if he ceases to occupy as an only or principal home, so long as he is doing so when the tenancy purports to end (*Hussey v Camden LBC*, 1994), *i.e.* he may be able to resume sufficient occupation between service and expiry of notice to quit. (Note: a tenant who ceases to sustain sufficient occupation ceases to be secure; accordingly, the notice of seeking possession ("NSP") procedure considered below is inapplicable, and notice to quit in the ordinary way has to be served—see below, 3.65. As a notice to quit needs time to take effect, if the tenant does return, he becomes secure again and—because he is not a secure tenant—it is the notice to quit which has become inapplicable).

3.38   A tenant may acquire security if his own landlord surrenders (1.186) his tenancy, *e.g.* where an authority had let premises as a business (3.39(a)), part of which had been sublet residentially (*Basingstoke & Deane BC v Paice*, 1995).

3.   EXCEPTIONS

3.39   Exceptions from security. There are numerous exceptions from security (1985, Sch.1).

(a) **Long leases**. Long leases, *i.e.* leases for a period in excess of 21 years (para.1).

(b) **Introductory tenancies**. Tenancies which are granted under an introductory tenancy regime, and which have not moved into security pursuant to those provisions (para.1A; see Chapter 6).

(c) **Employee accommodation**. Premises occupied under a contract of employment which requires the tenant to occupy the dwelling-house for the better performance of his duties (1.156–1.158), and the tenant is an employee of the landlord, or of a local authority, a New Town development corporation, an urban development corporation or a

Housing Action Trust. (Note: this allows one public sector landlord to house the employee of another).

Also within this exclusion are premises provided to policemen free of rent and rates under the Police Act 1964, and premises rented to firemen in consequence of employment, where their contract of employment requires the fireman to live close to a particular station (para.2).

A requirement to occupy will not be implied, unless the occupation is in fact necessary for the tenant's employment duties to be carried out (*Hughes v Greenwich LBC*, 1993; *Surrey CC v Lamond*, 1998).

If occupation continues after employment ceases, it will be a question of fact whether the tenancy is still referable to the employment in question, or whether there has been an agreed or intended change in the nature or purpose of the occupation (*South Glamorgan CC v Griffiths*, 1992; *Elvidge v Coventry CC*, 1993; *Greenfield v Berkshire CC*, 1994).

(d) **Temporary use of employee accommodation**. Where premises have been occupied under the last exemption from security at any time in the previous three years, the landlord can let them out in other circumstances, without the occupier becoming secure, provided:

   (i) the landlord gives the occupier notice that this exception will apply; and

   (ii) (a) in the case of a local authority landlord, the landlord has not notified the tenant that he is to become secure, and

   (b) in the case of any other landlord, the tenancy, or tenancies, do not themselves extend more than three years beyond the last time when the premises were occupied under a para.2 exemption (para.2).

(e) **Development land**. Premises on land acquired for development, being used pending development for temporary housing accommodation, *i.e.* short-life user (para.3).

(f) **Homeless persons accommodation**. A tenancy granted to a person under Pt VII of the 1996 Act is not secure until the landlord notifies the tenant that he is to be a secure tenant (para.4).

(g) **Asylum-seeker accommodation**. A tenancy granted to someone being accommodation under the National

Asylum Support Service set up under the Immigration and Asylum Act 1999, Pt VI is not secure until the landlord notifies the tenant that it is to be (para.4A).

(h) **Job mobility accommodation.** Temporary accommodation granted to a person not hitherto resident in the same district or London borough as the premises, granted for the purposes of enabling the tenant to take up employment or an offer of employment within that district or London borough, or within an adjoining district or London borough, while looking for permanent accommodation.

Before the grant of the tenancy, the landlord must notify the tenant that this exception applies. In the case of a local authority landlord, the exemption lasts until the landlord notifies the tenant that he is to become secure. In the case of any other landlord who tenants are secure, the exception only applies for one year, or less if during that year the landlord notifies the tenant that he is to be a secure tenant (para.5).

(i) **Sub-leasing schemes.** Sub-lettings under leasing schemes are not secure. These are schemes under which the landlord takes a lease from a private sector landlord (*i.e.* one whose tenants would not be secure if granted a direct tenancy), which is either for a fixed-term or else granted on terms that the lease will come to an end when required by the landlord.

This scheme enables public landlords to take lettings of residential accommodation which would otherwise be left vacant by the private sector landlord, in order to lease it on to others (para.6).

(j) **Accommodation pending works for non-secure tenant.** Temporary accommodation provided to a tenant who is not a secure tenant, while works are executed to his usual home, is not secure (para.7).

(k) **Agricultural holdings.** Agricultural holdings within the Agricultural Holdings Act 1986 or farm business tenancies within the Agricultural Tenancies Act 1995 are not secure (para.8).

(l) **Licensed premises.** Tenancies are not secure if of premises which consist of or include premises licensed for the sale of intoxicating liquor for consumption on the premises (para.9).

(m) **Student lettings.** Student lettings are not secure if granted to enable the tenant to attend a designated course at an educational establishment and the landlord has, before the grant of the tenancy, notified the student that the exception applies.

A designated course is one designated by the Secretary of State for this purpose. This exception ceases at any time

   (a) In the case of a local authority landlord, if the landlord has notified the tenant that he is to become secure, and

   (b) In the case of any other landlord, until six months after he ceases to attend the educational establishment, or—if the tenant fails to take up his place on the course—six months after the grant of the tenancy (para.10), or if the landlord notifies the tenant that he is to be a secure tenant.

(n) **Business lettings.** Business tenancies within the Landlord and Tenant Act 1954, Pt II (see Chapter 6) are not secure (para.11).

It may be particularly difficult to decide whether this applies to those who occupy premises part of which consist of, for example, a shop or business. The following points may be noted:

   (i) It is not possible for a tenancy which was originally let for a business purpose to become a letting within the 1985 Act, for it will not have been let "as a dwelling" (*Webb v Barnet LBC*, 1988) unless there is an agreed change to residential use (*Russell v Booker*, 1982) but it is possible for a tenancy which was originally let as a dwelling under a secure tenancy to become a business letting and so move from 1985 Act protection into that of the Landlord and Tenant Act 1954, Pt II (1985, Sch.1, para.11), which is the main legislation concerned with business lettings.

   (ii) This move will happen if the predominant use of the premises is, or becomes, business use (*Cheryl Investments Ltd v Saldanha*, 1978), or if the business purpose can be said to be more than incidental to the residential occupation (*Wright v Mortimer*, 1996).

   (iii) This move will not necessarily happen merely because there has been some amount of of business use, perhaps ancillary to offices elsewhere (*Royal Life Saving Society v Page, 1978*), although it is not decisive (in favour of business use in the premises in question) that no business is carried out from elsewhere (*Wright*).

(iv) Merely taking in lodgers will not have this effect (*Lewis v Weldcrest*, 1978).

(v) The business activity must be part of the reason for, and the aim and object in, occupying the house, not merely an incidental hobby which made some money (*Gurton v Parrot*, 1990). It is always a question of fact and degree.

(o) **Almshouses.** Almshouses occupied under a licence from a charity are not secure (para.12).

4. SUCCESSION

3.40   Solitary succession. Under the Housing Act 1985, there can only be one statutory succession, which is to a surviving spouse or to a member of the deceased tenant's family (1985, s.87).

3.41   In some circumstances, there may be no succession at all. Thus, if the tenancy was originally a joint tenancy, but one of the joint tenants has died or otherwise surrendered his interest, there will be no further succession (1985, s.88).

3.42   Qualifying successor. Only a qualifying person can succeed. A person qualifies if, at the time of the death of the secure tenant,

(a) The would-be successor was occupying the dwelling-house as his only or principal home (3.32) and

(b) He was either

(i) The deceased tenant's spouse, or

(ii) Another member of the deceased tenant's family (1985, s.87).

3.43   In the case of anyone other than a spouse, it is also necessary to show that the would-be successor had been residing with the deceased tenant for at least 12 months before his death.

3.44   Residing with. "Residing with" means more than "living or staying at" the premises, although does not necessarily require so much as permanent or indefinite residence: *Swanbrae v Elliott* 1987; *Hildebrand v Moon*, 1989.

3.45 A period of absence does not necessarily break the continuity of residence. It depends on the nature and extent of the continuing connection with the premises throughout the period of absence and the quality of the intention to return (*Camden LBC v Goldenburg*, 1996).

3.46 The qualification of 12 months' residence with the deceased tenant, applicable to would-be successors other than a spouse, does not have to have been at the property to which succession is being sought: *Waltham Forest LBC v Thomas*, 1992. Thus, if the tenant came to stay with, say, a child in that child's home, but—less than 12 months before the end of the tenant's life—parent and child moved back into the parent's home, the child will still be able to succeed.

3.47 Choice of successor. There can be no joint succession. Where there is a number of potential qualifying successors, the deceased tenant's spouse takes precedence, but otherwise the qualifying persons must agree amongst themselves who is to take over the tenancy. If they cannot do so, the landlord is entitled to choose. There is, however, no obligation to notify the landlord on the agreed successor (*General Management v Locke*, 1980).

3.48 Member of family. Members of the family are defined (1985, s.113) as: spouses, parents, grandparents, children, grandchildren, siblings, uncles, aunts, nephews and nieces; including step-relation, half-relation and illegitimate children and persons living together as husband and wife.

3.49 "[L]iving together as husband and wife" means more than merely living together in the same household (*City of Westminster v Peart*, 1991).

3.50 A homosexual couple cannot be considered to be living together as husband and wife: *Harrogate BC v Simpson*, 1984; *Fitzpatrick v Sterling HA*, 1999.

3.51 The list is exhaustive. It is not considered that its limitations discriminate against excluded family members in such a way as to breach Arts 8 (right to family life and respect for home) or 14 (non-discrimination) of the European Convention on Human Rights: *Wandsworth LBC v Michalak*, 2002.

3.52 No qualifying successor. If there is no one qualified to succeed on the death of the tenant under the statutory rules, the tenancy may yet remain secure if a court orders its transfer under one of a number of family statutes governing both partners and children, *e.g.* where a court makes such an order in favour of a person who did not fulfil the residential requirements, or in favour of a former spouse (likewise not residing with the deceased tenant).

3.53 Otherwise, the tenancy will cease to be secure once it has vested—pursuant to the rules applicable to the devolution of property (including tenancies) on death—and it is known that the vesting is not pursuant to one of those statutes (1985, ss.89, 90). In the interregnum, it therefore remains secure.

5.   LOSS OF SECURITY

3.54 Ways of losing security. Leaving aside for the moment an order for possession made by the court (3.143–3.156), there are several circumstances in which security can be lost.

3.55 First of all, security will be lost if there is a change of landlord, and the new landlord does not fulfil the landlord condition (3.28–3.29; see also transfer of public housing, below).

3.56 Secondly, security will be lost if the tenant ceases to occupy the premises as his only or principal home (3.32).

3.57 Loss of security by assignment. In addition, any assignment (1.223) of a secure tenancy causes security to be lost, unless either:

  (a) The assignment is pursuant to an order of the court under one of a number of family provisions (Chapter 9), governing both partners and children, or

  (b) It is to someone who qualifies as a successor (3.42–3.46), or

  (c) It is pursuant to the "right to exchange" (1985, s.91) (below, 3.214).

3.58 If the secure tenant sublets the whole of the premises, either at one go or piecemeal, security is also lost, even if the subletting is to a person who qualifies as a successor (1985, s.93).

3.59 A mere licence arrangement, however, will not cause the loss of security (*Hussey v Camden LBC*, 1994).

3.60 In any of these cases, once security is lost it cannot be regained (1985, ss.91, 93), *e.g.* by evicting a sub-tenant or by reassignment. Security will not now normally be lost by bankruptcy.

Security of Tenure

3.61 Contractual security. If a secure tenancy is a periodic tenancy (1.97), the landlord cannot bring it to an end at all: only the court can do so (1985, s.82(1)), only on specified grounds and only after the landlord has followed the appropriate preliminary procedure.

3.62 If the tenancy is a fixed-term tenancy (1.97), it can only be forfeited by court order, and even if it expires by effluxion of time, there will come into its place an automatic periodic tenancy, on the same terms as the preceding fixed-term tenancy, and of which the periods are the same as those for which rent was paid under the preceding fixed-term tenancy (1985, s.86).

3.63 The only exceptions to this latter proposition are:

(a) If the landlord and the tenant agree a new fixed-term tenancy to follow the first fixed-term tenancy; and

(b) If the court orders possession to be given up at the end of the fixed-term, *i.e.* in forfeiture proceedings. (Note: on proceedings to forfeit (1.126–1.130) a fixed-term secure tenancy, the court has a choice of orders: it may determine the fixed-term, but not order the tenant out, in which case the periodic (and Housing Act secure) tenancy will follow (1985, s.86(1)); or, it may grant a possession order).

1. TERMINATION OF TENANCY

3.64 Continuation until possession. In the case of a periodic tenancy, whether originally periodic or following a fixed-term, the tenancy itself continues until the date the court orders the tenant to give up possession (1985, s.82).

3.65 Notice of seeking possession (NSP). The court can only make an order for possession on specified grounds, and only if either:

(a) The landlord has followed the proper procedure, or

(b) The court considers it just and equitable to dispense with the requirement for a notice (1985, s.83).

3.66 This procedure is in place of notice to quit, and is commonly known as a "notice of seeking possession" or NSP. Whether or not it is just and equitable to dispense with the NSP depends on all of the facts and circumstances both in which there was an omission to serve the notice and otherwise affecting landlord and tenant (*Bradshaw v Balwin-Wiseman*, 1985; *Kelsey Housing Association v King*, 1995).

3.67 Effectiveness of NSP. The NSP must normally specify a date after which legal proceedings may be issued (1985, s.83(4)(a)). The NSP then remains in force for one year following that date (1985, s.83(4)(b)).

3.68 The specified date must not be earlier than the date when the tenancy could have been brought to an end by notice to quit (1.111–1.112) (1985, s.83(5)).

3.69 There are special provisions which apply when reliance is placed—in whole or part—on Ground 2, Nuisance and Annoyance (3.101). In these cases, the notice must state that proceedings for possession may be commenced immediately, and must specify a date by which the landlord wants the tenant to give up possession (1985, s.83(3)). Again, that date must not be earlier than when the tenancy could have been brought to an end by notice to quit (1985, s.83(5)). The difference allows the landlord to start proceedings under Ground 2 earlier than in other cases. (See also Anti-Social Behaviour, below).

3.70 NSP—Further conditions. The court cannot entertain proceedings for possession in a case to which Ground 2 is relevant unless the NSP is still in force at the time the proceedings are begun (1985, s.83A(1)), which means one year after the date specified as that by which the landlord wants the tenant to give up possession (1985, s.83(3)).

3.71 In any other case, the court cannot entertain proceedings for possession unless the proceedings are commenced after the specified date (1985, s.83A(2)), and the NSP is still in force at the time the proceedings are begun, which is for one year from that date (1985, s.83(4)).

3.72 Domestic violence. Ground 2A allows recovery of property where there has been domestic violence leading to the departure of one of a couple (married or who have been living together as husband and wife) one of whom is, or both of whom are, a tenant of it (3.109).

3.73 If this Ground is to be used, the court is not to entertain proceedings for possession unless satisfied that the landlord has served—or has taken all reasonable steps to serve—a copy of the NSP on the partner who has left (1985, s.83A(3)).

3.74 If the case is one in which Ground 2 (above) is also specified, the court may dispense with this service requirement, however, if just and equitable to do so (1985, s.83A(5)).

3.75 Contents of notice. The NSP must be in the form prescribed by the Secretary of State, or substantially to the same effect, and it must specify the grounds on which the court will be asked to terminate the tenancy and make a possession order (1985, s.83(2)).

3.76 The particulars must be sufficient to enable the tenant to know what he has to do in order to put matters right, *e.g.* they must specify an amount of arrears (*Torridge DC v Jones*, 1985; *Mountain v Hastings*, 1993, cf. *Marath v MacGillivray* 1995). In cases where Ground 2A (domestic violence—3.109) is being relied on, the incidents of violence should be particularised: *Camden LBC v Mallett* (2001).

3.77 An error in the particulars will not, however, invalidate the notice, provided it sets out what the landlord intends in good faith to prove (*Dudley MBC v Bailey*, 1990).

3.78 There is power (1985, s.84(3)) for the court to allow additional grounds to be specified, or the grounds to be altered, which imports power to alter or add to the particulars (*Camden LBC v Oppong*, 1996).

3.79 Domestic violence and service. If the new grounds include Ground 2A (domestic violence—3.109), the court has to be satisfied that the landlord has served a notice on the partner who has left, or has taken all reasonable steps to do so (1985, s.83A(4)). Again, the court may dispense with this requirement, however, if just and equitable to do so and if Ground 2 is also specified (1985, s.83A(5)).

3.80 Fixed-term tenancies. An NSP must also be served before possession can be sought of a fixed term tenancy. The NSP has effect with respect to any periodic tenancy arising on the termination of the fixed term by virtue of 1985, s.86 (3.62) (1985, s.83(6)) The specific provisions for notices in relation to Ground 2 (3.69) do not apply to notices served on fixed term tenants (1985, s.83(6)).

2. GROUNDS FOR POSSESSION

3.81 The most significant element in security law is the grounds for possession. These fall into three classes (1985, s.84(2):

  (i) Ground plus reasonableness;

 (ii) Ground plus suitable alternative accommodation; and

(iii) Ground plus suitable alternative accommodation plus reasonableness.

3.82 The Grounds for possession are set out in 1985, Sch.2.

(i) *Ground plus reasonableness*

3.83 Reasonableness—additional requirement. In relation to this class of ground for possession, the landlord must satisfy the court:

  (a) That the ground is itself made out; and

  (b) That it is reasonable to make the order sought (1985, s.84)).

3.84 It is important always to bear in mind that this requirement is additional and must be considered in every case (*Peachey Property Corp v Robinson*, 1967).

3.85 Reasonableness—general principles. "Reasonable" has to be determined having regard to both the interests of the parties and also to the interests of the public: *Cresswell v Hodgson* (1951; *Battlespring v Gates*, 1983. There is no general restriction, save relevance, as to what the court can take into account under this heading (*Cresswell*), which is to be considered as at the date of the hearing: *Rhodes v Cornford*, 1947.

3.86 Reasonableness—arrears. Even where arrears are of charges owed to a third party, such as water rates, it may nonetheless be reasonable to make an order for possession, and a judge should not limit himself to doing so only in "exceptional circumstances": *Lambeth LBC v Thomas*, 1997.

3.87 In *Lal v Nakum*, 1982, a tenant withheld rent on account of an alleged breach of repairing obligation by the landlord (Chapter 11), which allegation he did not sustain in court. He had, however, saved the withheld rent and could have paid it all at once: none the less, the court made an outright order for possession. The Court of Appeal set this aside.

3.88 Where, however, a tenant lost a counterclaim for disrepair and was unable to make any provision to pay off the arrears in *Haringey LBC v Stewart*, 1991, the Court of Appeal upheld the outright order for possession.

3.89 In *Woodspring DC v Taylor*, 1982, a couple had lived in their house for 24 years. The man lost his employment and suffered a heavy tax demand; the woman had diabetes and was attending a blood specialist. The Department of Health and Social Security took over their rent payments, and were paying £1 per week off the arrears. Until the recent difficulties, the Taylors had always been good tenants. The county court judge made an order for possession, but the Court of Appeal had "difficulty in understanding how anyone could have made an order turning them out of their home."

3.90 Reasonableness—anti-social behaviour. In cases under Ground 2 (nuisance and criminal behaviour—3.101), the court must always take into account the interests of the neighbours: *Woking BC v Bistram*, 1993; *Kensington & Chelsea RLBC v Simmonds*, 1996; *Darlington BC v Sterling*, 1996; *Newcastle CC v Morrison*, 2000; and *West Kent HA v Davies*, 1998.

3.91 The fact that the nuisance behaviour was carried out by someone other than the tenant does not mean it is not reasonable to grant possession: *Simmonds, Sterling; Camden LBC v Gilsenan*, 1998; *Portsmouth CC v Bryant*, 2000. This is so even where there are alternative remedies, such as an injunction (3.167), available against the perpetrator: *Morrison*.

3.92 In severe cases, such as drug dealing from the premises or racial harassment, it will only be in exceptional circumstances that it is not reasonable to make an order: *Bristol CC v Mousah*, 1997; *Davies*.

3.93 Reasonableness—impact of homelessness. While it is right for a judge to consider the effect of a possession order in rendering a tenant homeless, it is wrong for the judge to consider the possible outcome of any application made by the tenant as a homeless person (*e.g.* that the tenant may be intentionally homeless (10.45): *Mousah; Sterling; Shrewsbury & Atcham BC v Evans*, 1997; *Lewisham LBC v Akinsola*, 1999; *Watford BC v Simpson*, 2000; *cf. Croydon LBC v Moody*, 1999.

3.94 Reasonableness—impact of ECHR, Art.8. In *Lambeth LBC v Howard* (2001), the Court of Appeal considered the impact of Art.8 of the European Convention on Human Rights (respect for home) on the discretionary grounds for possession. It concluded that Art.8 would not lead the courts to reach substantially different decisions from those which they had been reaching for years when applying the test of reasonableness.

3.95 Rent unpaid. The first ground is Ground 1: rent due from the tenant has not been paid, or an obligation of the tenancy has been broken or not performed.

3.96 There will be no arrears if the tenant has exercised the right to set-off an amount against the landlord's breach of his repairing obligations (11.102–11.112), although it has already been noted that if the tenant does so wrongly there will be a ground for possession (whether or not it is then likely that it will be reasonable to make the order depending on whether or not the tenant has the money to pay the arrears—3.87–3.88).

3.97 It will usually be unreasonable to make the order if the tenant has paid off the arrears by the date of hearing (*Hayman v Rowlands*, 1957), although in some circumstances, *e.g.* a long history of non-payment, it may still be possible (*Bird v Hildage*, 1948).

3.98 Breach of term. There will be no breach of a term of the tenancy if there has been a waiver (1.81) of the breach.

3.99 It is only breach of a term of the tenancy which gives rise to the claim, not breach of some additional, ancillary agreement, *e.g.* a personal undertaking (*RMR Housing Society v Combs*, 1951).

3.100 In *Heglibiston Establishments v Heyman*, 1977, it was held that cohabitation did not amount to a breach of a covenant prohibiting immoral user. In *Sheffield CC v Jepson*, 1993 and *Green v Sheffield CC*, 1993, orders were made or upheld for breaches of terms prohibiting the keeping of pets in blocks of flats.

3.101 Nuisance and annoyance. Ground 2 (as amended by the Housing Act 1996) permits eviction—where reasonable to make the order—if the tenant or any person residing in or visiting the dwelling-house has been guilty of conduct causing or likely to cause a nuisance or annoyance to others residing, visiting or otherwise engaging in a lawful activity in the locality.

3.102 Nuisance here does not necessarily mean nuisance in a technical legal sense, but in a natural sense; in any event, annoyance is a term with a wider meaning, although it must be such as would annoy an ordinary occupier (rather than especially sensitive): *Tod-Heatly v Benham*, 1885; *Harlow DC v Sewell*, 2000.

3.103 Where the allegation is one of nuisance by members of the family or visitors, there need not be any personal fault on the part of the tenant (*Davies, Bryant*), although the extent of personal fault will be relevant to the question of "reasonableness" (3.91).

3.104 In *Manchester CC v Lawler*, 1998, the Court of Appeal held that locality may be part of, or the whole of an estate. In each case, it is a question of fact for the judge whether the place in which the conduct occurred is or is not within the locality of the dwelling. It would seem, though, that there must be a link between the behaviour and the fact that the family lived in the area; the link is the legitimate interest which the landlord authority have in requiring their tenants to respect the neighbourhood for the benefit of the authority's other tenants: *Northampton BC v Lovatt*, 1997.

3.105 Immoral and illegal use. Ground 2 also applies where the tenant or any person residing in or visiting the dwelling-house has been convicted either of using the dwelling-house or allowing it to be used for immoral or illegal purposes, or of an arrestable offence in, or in the locality (see last para.) of the dwelling.

3.106 Immoral use will normally lead to an order for possession, though not invariably (*Yates v Morris*, 1950).

3.107 "Arrestable offence" means (Police and Criminal Evidence Act 1984, s.24):

(i) Any offence which bears a fixed penalty (*e.g.* murder);

(ii) Any offence for which a first offender of 21 or more could be sent to prison for five or more years; and,

(iii) Any offence specifically identified as such.

3.108 Illegal use only applies when the use of the premises has something to do with the conviction, even if the offence was not one which as a matter of law necessarily involved the use of premises. Nonetheless, the use of the premises must have been part of the facts leading to the conviction, rather than only incidentally the site of the commission of the offence (*S. Schneider and Sons v Abrahams*, 1925). (Note: a conviction for possession of cannabis at the premises will be unlikely to lead to an order, especially as it will mean the imposition of a double penalty—*Abrahams v Wilson*, 1971).

3.109   Domestic violence. Ground 2A applies where:

(a) The property was occupied—whether on their own, or together with others—by a married couple or a couple living together as husband and wife;

(b) One of whom is, or both of whom are, a tenant of it;

(c) One of whom has left because of violence or threats of violence towards (usually) her or a member of her family who was residing with her immediately before she left the other;

(d) The court is satisfied that the partner who has left (*i.e.* the victim of the violence) is unlikely to return. (See also the added requirements for notice: above, 3.73).

3.110   Deterioration of premises or furniture. Grounds 3 and 4 concern deterioration of the premises or common parts, or of any furniture provided by the landlord in the premises or common parts, attributable to the acts, neglect or default of the tenant, or of someone living with him.

3.111 No order will be made on either of these grounds if the default was that of a sub-tenant or lodger and before the hearing the tenant has taken such steps as are available in order to evict him.

3.112   Deception. Ground 5 is that the tenant is the person, or one of the persons, to whom the tenancy was granted, and the landlord was induced to grant the tenancy by a false statement knowingly or recklessly made by the tenant or by a person acting at the tenant's instigation, *i.e.* obtaining a tenancy by deception.

3.113 As such an allegation is of a quasi-criminal nature (and if the tenancy was granted under Pt VI, an actually criminal nature, *cf.* 10.223), it will accordingly require a high standard of proof. Once proved, however, the judge may, in deciding whether it is reasonable to grant possession, take into account the need to discourage dishonest applications generally: *Rushcliffe BC v Watson*, 1991 and see also *Shrewsbury & Atcham BC v Evans*, 1997; *Lewisham LBC v Akinsola*, 1999.

3.114 If the tenancy was granted to two persons, *e.g.* cohabitants, spouses, one of whom has departed, the ground is only available against the remaining tenant if he was guilty of the false statement or had instigated the deception by the departed tenant.

3.115 Premium on exchange. Ground 6 relates to the "right to exchange" (3.214): it arises if the tenancy arose by exchange, to which either the tenant, or a member of his family from whom he has taken over the tenancy, was a party (3.40), and a premium (*i.e.* money or other pecuniary consideration, *e.g.* goods) was paid in connection with the exchange (whether to, or by the tenant or member of his family). In the case of a member of the family, he must still be living in the property with the tenant.

3.116 Conflict with other purposes. Ground 7 governs employment-related accommodation (not excluded from security, *cf.* 3.39), and arises where:

(a) The premises are part of, or in the grounds of, a building held by the landlord for non-housing purposes; and

(b) The letting was in consequence of employment; and,

(c) The tenant or someone residing in the property has been guilty of conduct such that, having regard to the purposes for which the main building is held, it would not be right for the tenant to remain in occupation.

3.117 Accommodation pending works. Ground 8 arises where the secure tenant of one set of premises is asked to move to another set of premises while works are carried out. The ground may be compared to Sch.1, para.7 (1985) of the exceptions to security

(3.39(j)), excluding from security tenants who have similarly been moved, but from an insecure tenancy.

3.118 Ground 8 is only available if the terms of the move included an undertaking that the tenant would move back once works were completed, and the works are now completed and the original property ready for reoccupation.

3.119 The requirement of reasonableness allows the tenant to argue, *e.g.* that the works have not been done as agreed, or that they have taken so long that he has now set down new roots in the alternative property and ought not to have to move back again.

(ii) *Ground plus suitable alternative accommodation*

3.120 Suitable accommodation. Under this category of ground for possession, it is not necessary to show reasonableness in addition to the ground, but instead it is necessary to show that suitable alternative accommodation is available. In effect, these are estate management grounds.

3.121 Once satisfied on both points—ground and suitable alternative accommodation—the court has, accordingly, no discretion whether or not to make the order.

3.122 If the landlord is not the local authority, the certificate of the local authority that suitable accommodation will be provided by that authority will be conclusive evidence that alternative accommodation so provided is suitable (1985, Sch.2, Pt IV, para.4).

3.123 Otherwise, alternative accommodation will only be suitable if it is of premises to be let as a separate dwelling under a Housing Act secure tenancy, or under a Housing Act assured or a Rent Act protected tenancy, other than one subject to any of the mandatory grounds for possession (4.87–4.96; 5.123–5.142) including short-hold (Chapter 6; 1985, Sch.2, Pt IV, para.1).

3.124 The accommodation must, in the opinion of the court, be reasonably suitable to the needs of the tenant and his family. The must, on this, have regard to:

(a) The nature of the accommodation usually provided by the landlord to persons with similar needs;

(b) Distance from the place of work or education of the tenant or members of his family;

(c) Distance from the home of the family or any member of
the tenant's own family (*e.g.* relatives who require or
provide support), if proximity is necessary to the well-
being of either relative or tenant;

(d) The needs (as regards extent of accommodation, which can
in an appropriate case include a garden: *Enfield LBC v
French*, 1984) and means of tenant and his family;

(e) The terms of the accommodation; and,

(f) If furniture has hitherto been provided, whether furniture
is to be provided in the alternative accommodation, and its
nature (1985, Sch.2, Pt IV, paras 1 and 2).

3.125 This schedule of matters to which regard is to be paid is
not exhaustive; the weight to be given to each is a matter of degree
in each case (*Enfield LBC*).

3.126 Overcrowded accommodation. The first ground under
this class is Ground 9, and arises when the dwelling currently
occupied is overcrowded within the meaning of Pt X of the
Housing Act 1985, in such circumstances as to render the occupier
guilty of an offence (14.09–14.17). In relation to this ground only,
it should be noted that alternative accommodation is not to be
deemed unsuitable solely because it offends the space standard
described in Chapter 14 (14.10(b); 1985, Sch.2, Pt IV, para.3).

3.127 Redevelopment. Ground 10 is available when the landlord
intends, within a reasonable time of seeking possession, either:

(a) To demolish or reconstruct the building, or part of the
building which includes the dwelling in question; or

(b) To carry out work on the building, or on land let together
with the building, and

(c) In either case, cannot reasonably do so without obtaining
possession.

3.128 The landlord has to be able to show an established, settled
and clearly defined intention to do the works, and that it needs
possession in order to execute the works (*Wansbeck DC v Marley*,
1987).

3.129 Approved development area. Ground 10A was added in
1986, and applies when the landlord, within a reasonable period of

obtaining possession, intends to sell with vacant possession, but it applies if, and only if, the property is in an "approved development area" (that is to say, approved by the Secretary of State or, in the case of a registered social landlord, by the Housing Corporation). There is provision for a dwelling which falls partly within, and partly outside of, such an area.

3.130   Conflict with charitable purposes. Ground 11 is available only to a landlord which is a charity within the meaning of the Charities Act 1993, and the tenant's continued occupation of the dwelling would conflict with the objects of the charity, *i.e.* where the charity has a specific purpose, such as the assistance of single parents, or the disabled, and neither the tenant nor anyone living with him any longer qualifies for such a description.

(iii) *Ground plus suitable alternative accommodation plus reasonableness*

3.131   Suitable and reasonable. In this class, the landlord must prove:

(a) That the ground is available and applicable; and

(b) That suitable alternative accommodation (as defined, 3.122–3.125), is available; and

(c) That it is reasonable to make the order sought, thus importing the court's discretion considered above (3.85–3.94).

3.132   Non-housing property required for employee, disabled persons accommodation. Ground 12 applies where:

(a) The property forms part of, or is in the grounds of, a non-housing building, or in the grounds of a cemetery; and

(b) Was let in consequence of employment (3.39); and

(c) The property is now reasonably required for a new employee.

3.133   This Ground is similar to Case 8 under the Rent Act 1977 (5.158).

3.134   Adapted housing. Ground 13 applies to dwellings which have features which are substantially different from ordinary houses, designed to make the house suitable for the occupation of a physically disabled person.

3.135 The ground is only available if there is no longer a physically disabled person of the class for whom it was provided in occupation (which need not be the tenant, but could be a member of his family), and the landlord requires it for occupation of one such disabled person.

3.136 Required for person with special needs. Ground 14 is available only to housing associations or housing trusts engaged in letting property to specific categories of persons who, for reasons other than poverty, have particular difficulty satisfying their housing needs, *e.g.* ethnic groups, battered women, young people, the mentally handicapped.

3.137 This ground is only available when either there is no longer such a person in occupation (whether as tenant or not), or the local authority are offering the tenant a secure tenancy elsewhere, and in either case the landlord requires the dwelling for occupation by a person of the class they are engaged in assisting.

3.138 Sheltered accommodation. Ground 15 applies to "sheltered accommodation," *i.e.* houses or flats in a group which are in practice let to people with special needs, and in close proximity to which a social service or other special facility is provided, *e.g.* for elderly people, or the disabled.

3.139 As under the last two grounds, the ground is only available when there is no longer a person of the designated class in occupation, and the premises are required for occupation by such a person.

3.140 Underoccupation. Ground 16 is only available when the tenant has succeeded to the secure tenancy on the death of a previous tenant (3.40–3.51).

3.141 It is never available when the tenant is the spouse of the deceased secure tenant.

3.142 It is only available when the accommodation afforded by the dwelling is more extensive than is reasonably required by the successor, and notice of seeking possession (3.65) was served both no earlier than six months after the death of the previous tenant and no later than 12 months after his death.

3. ORDERS FOR POSSESSION

3.143 Once the court is satisfied that a ground for possession has been proved and, as necessary, that it is reasonable to make an order for possession and/or that suitable alternative accommodation is available, it must make an order for possession.

3.144   There are two types of order: outright and suspended.

3.145   Outright orders. An outright order grants possession to the landlord after some finite period of delay, usually two weeks but on occasion, in extreme hardship, sometimes stretched to a maximum of six (1980, s.89).

3.146   Once the period of delay granted by the court has run out, the landlord can issue a bailiff's warrant and there may be a further period of delay before any actual eviction.

3.147   Suspended orders. An order may be suspended where possession is sought on any of the grounds where the court must be satisfied that it is reasonable to make an order (Grounds 1–8—3.95–3.119 and Grounds 12–16, 3.131–3.142) (1985, s.85(1)).

3.148   The order may be suspended for a finite period longer than two to six weeks, or indefinitely, but on conditions (1985, s.85(2), (3)). The court also has power to stay an order for possession, or to adjourn proceedings, or to postpone the date for possession (s.85).

3.149   These powers may not only be exercised for the benefit of the tenant, but also for his spouse or ex-spouse (Chapter 9) (1985, s.85(5), (6)).

3.150   Suspended orders—rent arrears. In cases of rent arrears, it is usual for the possession order to be suspended on conditions. A court should not make an order producing an indefinite suspension, disappearing into the "mists of time" (*Vandermolen v Toma*, 1981; *Taj v Ali (No. 1)*, 2001), although in *Lambeth LBC v Henry*, 2000 a suspension period of 23 years was upheld by the Court of Appeal.

3.151   Suspended orders—anti-social behaviour. In cases under Ground 2 (3.101), it may be appropriate to suspend the order: *Kensington & Chelsea RLBC v Simmonds*, 1996; *Greenwich LBC v Grogan*, 2001 *Portsmouth CC v Bryant*, 2000; *Castlevale Housing Action Trust v Gallagher*, 2001. In considering whether suspension is appropriate, the judge must consider future conduct. There is, however, no point suspending an order if the inevitable outcome will be future breaches: *Canterbury CC v Lowe*, 2001.

3.152 Warrant for possession. The powers to suspend or postpone can be exercised at any time before execution of the warrant for possession, but not thereafter unless either the circumstances are such that there are grounds to set aside the original order, *e.g.* if the tenant had no notice of the proceedings, or if it was an abuse of the process or oppressive to proceed with the warrant (*Governors of Peabody Donation Fund v Hay*, 1986; *Leicester CC v Aldwinckle*, 1991; *Hammersmith & Fulham LBC v Hill*, 1994; *Barking & Dagenham LBC v Saint*, 1999; *Southwark LBC v Sarfo*, 1999; *Hammersmith & Fulham LBC v Lemeh*, 2001; *Lambeth LBC v Hughes*, 2001.

3.153 Oppression in the execution of a warrant requires unfair use of the court's procedures, or action by a person which is open to criticism as unfair use: *Jephson Homes HA v Moisejevs* 2001.

3.154 Application to suspend warrant. Where a tenant applies to suspend a warrant for possession, it is open to the landlord to adduce evidence of a ground—or grounds—of possession different to those relied upon at the original hearing, even if those grounds had existed when the original order was made: *Sheffield CC v Hopkins*, 2001 (original order made on the grounds of rent arrears, evidence of nuisance adduced at application to suspend warrant). Where the new ground was already available at the time of the original possession action, the landlord will only be allowed to raise the matter if the tenant was warned that the landlord was only going to bother proceeding on the one ground, so that he will have been aware that the other could also still subsequently be used to give rise to eviction.

3.155 Conditions. Conditions may be imposed on any adjournment, stay, suspension or postponement. In all cases, however, unless it will cause exceptional hardship to the tenant, or would otherwise be unreasonable, the court will order payments of rent and of any arrears that there may be (1985, s.85(3)).

3.156 If conditions are complied with, *e.g.* to clear arrears, it is worthwhile applying for discharge, rather than leaving on the court file an order which might later be activated erroneously and with inadequate warning to the tenant.

3.157 Orders and security. If an order for possession is made, it may be suspended by agreement with the landlord, usually on terms, or on terms ordered by the court: in either event, the tenant may cease to comply with the terms.

3.158 If the order is suspended by the court, on terms with which the tenant ceases to comply, the breach terminates the tenancy and entitles the landlord to obtain a warrant for possession (*Thompson v Elmbridge BC*, 1987; *Greenwich LBC v Regan*, 1996).

3.159 Tolerated trespassers. If the landlord waives the subsequent breach, the tenant will be able to remain in occupation, and the question will be whether or not he does so on the basis of the existing tenancy and still under the terms of the order for possession, or by an agreement to a new tenancy (*Regan*).

3.160 If the landlord does not waive the breach, but does not seek to evict, the tenant will occupy as what is known as a tolerated trespasser: *Regan; Marshall v Bradford CC* 2001.

3.161 If the landlord obtains an outright order, but agrees to suspend it, a new tenancy or licence will only be created if this is the intention of the parties. If there is no such intention then the former tenant is likewise a mere tolerated trespasser, although the former tenancy can be revived by an application to the court by either party to vary the possession order (*Burrows v Brent LBC*, 1996).

3.162 A tenancy will not automatically revive simply because arrears have been paid off in full; an application must be made under 1985, s.85(2): *Marshall.*

Anti-Social Behaviour

3.163 Policies on anti-social behaviour. During the mid-1990s, there was an upsurge of concern about anti-social activity on local authority estates, particularly intimidation of residents by gangs, usually of youths, but also involving the use and sale of drugs, and other criminal activity.

3.164 In the absence of sufficient support from the criminal justice system, a number of local authorities used their powers as such, or as landlord or landowner, to seek injunctive relief from the civil courts.

3.165 In turn, this led to three sets of provisions contained in Pt V of the Housing Act 1996. One of these provisions was the introduction of a broader ground for possession for nuisance and annoyance (3.101) and speedier proceedings where it is relied on

(3.69). Secondly, introductory tenancies were introduced to allow authorities a period in which to assess individual tenant conduct (see Chapter 6). Finally, there was the introduction of a statutory basis for injunctive relief.

3.166 Further provision for anti-social behaviour was made by the introduction of anti-social behaviour orders under the Crime and Disorder Act 1998 (Chapter 8).

3.167 Injunctions against anti-social behaviour. A local authority landlord can seek an injunction either from the county court or from the High Court to prohibit a person from engaging in, or threatening to engage in, conduct causing or like to cause a nuisance or annoyance to a person residing in, visiting, or otherwise engaging in a lawful activity in property held under secure (or introductory: see Chapter 6) tenancies held from the authority, or in accommodation provided to the homeless by the authority under Pt VII (see Chapter 10) (1996, s.152(1), (2)).

3.168 Likewise, an injunction can prevent the use of, or threat of the use of, such premises for immoral or illegal purposes.

3.169 The injunction can prevent the person entering such premises, or being in the locality of them (see above, para.3.104).

3.170 The injunction can only be granted if the person against whom it is sought has used or threatened violence against one of those (above, 3.167) intended to be protected, and there is a significant risk of harm to that person, or other similar people, if it is not granted (1996, s.152(3)).

3.171 There must be a link between the person whom the injunction is intended to protect and residential premises: *Enfield LBC v B*, 1999, where the threats of violence were against social services staff in an office located near a local authority estate, not against any residents of the estate, and therefore did not qualify.

3.172 The injunction can relate to particular acts or conduct, and/or types of conduct, or particular premises or a particular locality, and can either be for a specific period or generally until the court varies or discharges it (1996, s.152(4)).

3.173 Powers of arrest. A power of arrest can be attached to the injunction. A power of arrest allows a police officer to arrest, without warrant, any person whom he suspects is in breach of the order. The power can be attached where the person against whom the injunction is sought has used or threatened violence to a person residing, visiting or otherwise engaged in lawful activity in the particular locality and there is a significant risk of harm to that person, or a person of a similar description, if the power of arrest is not attached (1996, s.152(6)).

3.174 The power of arrest can be attached for the purpose of securing a medical report on the person against whom the injunction is made (1996, s.156).

3.175 The power of arrest need not relate to the whole of the terms of an injunction, and need not be for the same period as the injunction (1996, ss.152(6), 157).

3.176 *Ex parte* **orders**. Though normally the person must be given notice of the application for an injunction, the court may make an order *ex parte* (without notice)—*e.g.* where there is concern for the safety of victims or a fear that residents of estates will not co-operate and give evidence until an injunction is in place.

3.177 Considerations relevant to the grant of an order *ex parte* include whether it is likely that the applicant will be prevented or deterred from seeking the power of arrest, and whether the person against whom it is sought is evading service (1996, s.154).

3.178 If the court uses this power, it must as soon as just and convenient afford the person against whom it is made an opportunity to be heard (1996, s.152(7)).

3.179 **Discharge or variation**. The person against whom an order is made, or who is subject to a power of arrest under the terms of an order, may apply for the order, or the power of arrest, to be discharged or varied (1996, ss.152(5), (7), 157).

3.180 **Powers of arrest and other injunctions**. Landlords— whether local authorities or otherwise—can also seek injunctions against tenants, including, where appropriate, in respect of anti-social behaviour, pursuant to the terms of a tenancy, *i.e.* in respect of an actual or threatened breach.

3.181 Where a local housing authority, housing action trust, registered social landlord or charitable housing trust uses these powers in respect of a breach of the terms of the tenancy which consists of nuisance or annoyance, immoral or illegal user, by the tenant, one of them, or a sub-tenant, lodger or other occupier of, or visitor to, the premises, the court can also attach a power of arrest to the order (1996, s.153).

3.182 The provisions described above governing powers of arrest apply to such an order.

Additional Rights of Secure Tenants

1. RIGHT TO BUY

3.183 Entitlement. The best-known additional right of a secure tenant is the "right to buy."

3.184 The right to buy arises only after a tenant has spent two years as a secure tenant, although not necessarily in the same premises nor necessarily continuously (1985, s.119).

3.185 The tenant has to be secure both when applying to buy, and throughout the process (*Sutton LBC v Swann*, 1985; *Jennings v Epping Forest DC*, 1992; *Muir Group HA v Thornley*, 1992; *Bradford City MBC v McMahon*, 1993).

3.186 Once matters in relation to the purchase have been agreed or determined, the tenant may obtain an order to require the landlord to transfer the property to him, under 1985, s.138.

3.187 If, however, the landlord is at the same time seeking to evict the tenant, *e.g.* because of anti-social behaviour, it is up to the court in which order it hears the two, conflicting applications—to compel the sale and for possession: *Bristol CC v Lovell*, 1998. The sequence of events and the seriousness of the allegations made by the landlord will be relevant to how the court exercises its discretion: *Tandridge BC v Bickers*, 1998.

3.188 Family members. The right may be exercised together with other members of the family whom the tenant identifies for this purpose (1985, s.123). If the tenant died after establishing the s.123 right, such other members of the family would be entitled to pursue the purchase, even if not otherwise entitled to succeed to the tenancy (3.40; *Harrow LBC v Tonge*, 1992).

3.189 Freehold or leasehold. If the dwelling is a house, and the landlord owns the freehold, the right to buy is a right to the freehold (1.12). Otherwise (*i.e.* if the property is a flat, or if the landlord only has a lease), the right is to a lease of, normally, 125 years, although it may be less if the landlord's own interest is itself not that long (1985, Sch.6).

3.190 Other matters. There are detailed provisions governing the definition of "house" and "flat" (1985, s.183), and the exercise of these rights by joint tenants (1985, s.118). Where the tenant is unable to secure a mortgage to purchase the property he will be entitled instead to opt to acquire on rent to mortgage terms, provided that he is not entitled to housing benefits (1985, ss.143–153B).

3.191 Exemptions. Some property is exempt from the right to buy (1985, Sch.5), including property belonging to a housing trust which is a charity, sheltered accommodation (*cf.* 3.138) and accommodation adapted for the physically disabled (*cf.* 3.134).

3.192 Discount. The right is to buy at a discount (1985, s.129), amounting to:

 (a) (In the case of a house) 33 per cent for up to three years as a secure tenant, plus one per cent per year thereafter, to a maximum of 60 per cent, or

 (b) (In the case of a flat), 44 per cent for up to three years, plus two per cent. per year thereafter to a maximum of 70 per cent.

3.193 There are also maximum discounts set by the Secretary of State, under 1985, s.131, which vary depending on the area in which the property is situated.

3.194 A discount will normally to be repaid if the house or flat is subsequently sold within three years (1985, s.155).

3.195 Non-compliance with time-limits. If the landlord fails to comply with the statutory time provision for handling the right to buy, would-be purchasers will be able to serve notices, the effect of which will be to "penalise" the landlord by treating rent payments during the periods of delay as deductions from the purchase price (1985, s.153A, 153B).

3.196 Preserved right to buy. On a transfer of stock to the private sector (see further below), a secure tenant's right to buy is "preserved": 1985, ss.171A–171H. Where transfer is, as is most common, to a registered social landlord, it is the right to buy which is preserved, rather than the right to acquire given to assured tenants (4.155).

3.197 The preserved right to buy will be inapplicable if the right to buy as against the former landlord was unavailable because of paras 1–3, Sch.5, 1985 Act (charities and certain housing associations), or in such other cases as may be excepted by order of the Secretary of State: 1985, s.171A(3).

3.198 The right to buy is only preserved so long as the tenant occupies the premises as his only or principal home (3.32).

3.199 The right may be exercised by the tenant, or a qualifying successor, as defined, and may extend from the original premises to other premises to which the tenant has moved and which are rented from the same landlord (or if a company, a connected company): 1985, s.171B.

3.200 By section 171F, a court is not to make an order for possession against a tenant or qualifying successor on the ground of suitable alternative accommodation without ensuring that the right to buy will be preserved (or that the tenant will be Housing Act secure as against the new landlord).

3.201 A subsequent disposal by the (new) landlord does not terminate the preserved right to buy, unless either the new landlord is a landlord whose tenants are Housing Act secure (so that there will be a new right to buy in any event), or the original landlord has failed to register the right as a notice on the register of land in accordance with 1985, Sch.9A. If the tenant loses the right due to a failure to register, he may recover compensation for breach of the statutory duty under 1985, Sch.9A.

3.202 The preserved right to buy may also be determined on the termination of the landlord's interest by a superior landlord, other than by merger, but where this occurs because of the intermediate landlord's act or omission, there is a right to compensation: s.171E.

3.203 Section 171C empowers the Secretary of State by regulation to modify Pt V of the 1985 Act for the purposes of the preserved right to buy, which he has done (SI 1993/2241, as amended), principally in order to exclude the right to acquire on rent to mortgage terms (above, 3.190).

2. IMPROVEMENTS

3.204 Right to improve. Secure tenants also enjoy a "right to improve". It is a term of all secure tenancies that the tenant will not make any improvement, without the written consent of the landlord, which consent is not unreasonably to be withheld (1985, ss.79–99). Although cast in a negative frame, the term substantively confers a positive entitlement to improve, where consent has been granted. A refusal of consent can be challenged in the county court (1985, s.110).

3.204A For these purposes, improvement includes addition or alteration to a dwelling, and external decorations (1985, s.97). If the landlord does refuse consent, he is obliged to provide a written statement of reasons, and in the course of any subsequent challenge by the tenant, the burden lies on the landlord to show that the refusal was reasonable, which it may do, amongst other ways, by showing that the improvement would make the dwelling, or neighbouring premises, less safe, or that it would cause him to incur additional expenditure, or that it would reduce the value of the house (1985, s.98).

3.205 Financial matters. Secure tenants may be entitled to compensation for certain improvements (1985, s.99A), their rent is not to be increased on account of improvements they execute (1985, s.101), and the landlord has power to reimburse the tenant for the cost of any improvements carried out, on the tenant's departure (1985, s.100).

3. SUBLETTING AND LODGERS

3.206 Rights to let. Secure tenants have an absolute right to take in lodgers, and a qualified right to sublet part of their premises (1985, s.93).

3.207 The right to sublet is expressed as a negative obligation: the secure tenant shall not sublet part without the written consent of the landlord (1985, s.93(1)(a)). This consent, however, is not unreasonably to be withheld, and if unreasonably withheld is to be treated as given. Accordingly, the right is in substance a positive entitlement to sublet with consent (1985, s.94).

3.208 Consent. The exercise of a qualified right to sublet has been considered above (1.175–1.178) but it is worth restating that, no matter how well-founded may be anticipation of refusal, a tenant will not be able to claim unreasonable withholding without first making the request (*Barrow v Isaacs*, 1891).

3.209 If the landlord fails to reply within a reasonable time, consent is deemed to have been withheld (1985, s.94(6)), but if the landlord does refuse, then a written statement of reasons for refusal must be provided (1985, s.94(6)).

3.210 Consent may, however, be sought after the subletting, and if given will then validate it (1985, s.94(4)).

3.211 No conditions may be attached to a consent (1985, s.94(5)).

3.212 When considering the reasonableness of a refusal, over-crowding will be relevant (14.09–14.15) as will any proposals for works which the landlord may have and which would affect the accommodation likely to be used by the sub-tenant (1985, s.94(3)).

3.213 The burden of proof lies always on the landlord to show that the withholding is reasonable (1985, s.94(2)), and the tenant may apply to the county court for a declaration that a withholding is unreasonable (1985, s.110).

4. EXCHANGE

3.214 Right to exchange. All secure tenants have the right to exchange their properties with another secure tenant, whether of the same landlord or not (1985, s.92(1)).

3.215 The right extends to include Housing Act assured tenants of the Housing Corporation, a registered housing association, or housing trust which is a charity, *i.e.* those landlords formerly within the 1985 Act (3.30: 1985, s.92(2A)).

3.216 There can even be three-way exchanges, provided all are Housing Act secure tenants or have a relevant assured tenancy, and the landlord of each has consented in writing (1985, s.92(2)).

3.217 Consent. A landlord has 42 days in which to consent, and can only refuse consent on one of a specified schedule of grounds (1985, s.92(4), (5)). The landlord loses the right to reply on any of the grounds unless he replies within 42 days.

3.218 If the landlord refuses consent on another ground, consent is to be treated as given.

3.219 This does not, however, mean that the exchange can necessarily take place. The landlord is entitled to attach one condition to any consent: if there are rent arrears, or there is another breach of a term of the tenancy, the landlord can require the arrears to be cleared, or the breach to be remedied (1985, s.92(5)).

3.220 The landlord may not, however, attach any other conditions to the consent, and any that are attached may be disregarded (1985, s.92(6)).

3.221 The grounds for refusing consent are (1985, Sch.3):

(a) The tenant or proposed assignee already is under a court order to give up possession;

(b) Proceedings for possession have commenced, or NSP has been served (3.65), on any of the grounds for possession which require only that it is reasonable to make the order (3.83–3.119);

(c) The accommodation would be too large for the prospective assignee or otherwise not reasonably suitable to his needs;

(d) The premises were let in consequence of employment, and form part of, or are in the grounds of, a non-housing building or a cemetery (3.39, 3.132);

(e) The landlord is a charity and the proposed assignee's occupation would conflict with its objects (3.130);

(f) The property is designed for a physically disabled person, and if the proposed assignee moved in, there would be no such person in occupation (3.134);

(g) The landlord is a special needs housing association or trust, and if the proposed assignee moved in there would be no one with the relevant need in occupation (3.136);

(h) The accommodation is sheltered and, as above, if the proposed assignee moved in, there would be no one with the relevant needs in occupation (3.138).

5. REPAIR

3.222 Right to repair. The "right to repair" (1985, s.96) permits secure tenants to require local authority landlords to appoint a contractor when repairs are not carried out on time, and if there are further delays to receive compensation: the provisions are governed by regulations—see the Secure Tenants of Local Authorities (Right to Repair) Regulations 1994 (SI 1994/133).

6. HEATING CHARGES

3.223 **Right to information.** In addition, there is power for the government to introduce provisions which would entitle secure tenants to find out how their landlords have calculated heating charges included in the rent (1985, s.108). This power has not yet been brought into use.

Related Provisions

1. VARIATION OF TERMS

3.224 A landlord may vary the terms of a secure tenancy by notice to take effect no sooner than the landlord could have served notice to quit (1.111–1.114). Before that date, the tenant may respond with notice to quit, in which case the variation will not take effect before the tenant's departure (1985, ss.102, 103).

3.225 Before any such notice is served, the landlord must serve a preliminary notice, outlining the intended variation, explaining its effect and inviting the tenant's comments.

3.226 This is not necessary, however, if the variation relates to the rent payable, or any amount in respect of rates, services or facilities provided by the landlord.

3.227 A notice of variation cannot vary the extent of the premises let under the tenancy.

2. CONSULTATION

3.228 **Housing Management.** Where more general changes to housing management arrangements are intended, whether or not amounting to a variation of the terms of tenancies, local authorities and some other landlords under secure tenancies may be obliged to consult with their tenants (1985, s.105).

3.229 "Housing management" includes new programmes of maintenance, improvement or demolition, and changes in practice or policy, likely to affect the secure tenants of the landlord as a whole or a group of them (1985, s.105(3)), but excludes questions of rent, payments for services or facilities provided by the landlord (1985, s.105(2)).

3.230　All landlords bound by these consultation provisions (1985, s.114) must make and maintain consultation machinery or arrangements for notifying their tenants of proposed changes in matters of housing management, and ascertaining their views. They must publish details of these arrangements (1985, s.105(5)).

3.231　When the landlord seeks approval of an area for the purposes of a "redevelopment scheme," in connection with Ground 10A (3.129), however, different consultation provisions apply; similarly, a disposal by a Housing Action Trust of a property subject to a secure tenancy (3.258) carries with it its own, alternative consultation provisions.

3.　INFORMATION

3.232　**Information about terms**. Landlords under secure tenancies must publish information which explains the effect of the express terms of their secure tenancies, the security provisions of the 1985 Act and other provisions considered in this chapter, the right to buy, and the provisions of the Landlord and Tenant Act 1985, s.11, (11.47–11.79; 1985, s.104).

3.233　Copies of this publication must be provided to secure tenants. Where the landlord is a local authority, the information regarding the right to buy and repairing obligations must be provided annually.

Rents

1.　LOCAL AUTHORITY RENTS

3.234　**Reasonable rents**. Local authorities are bound to charge reasonable rents and to review their rent levels from time to time; in setting their rent levels, they are bound to have regard to the principle that rents of property of one class or description should bear broadly the same proportion to private sector rents as the rents of houses of any other class or description (1985, s.24).

3.235　**Ring-fencing**. Local authorities have a long history of discretion in relation to their decisions as to what comprises a "reasonable" rent. The provisions of the Local Government and Housing Act 1989 have, however, severely limited the theoretical freedom which local authorities enjoy over rent levels, by requiring an authority's Housing Revenue Account to be balanced (1989, s.76), and limiting what can be credited and debited to it (so as to exclude any contribution from an authority's general fund, *i.e.* by the body of local taxpayers generally: this is the policy known as "ring-fencing of the account"; see 1989, s.75 and Sch.4).

3.236 Challenging local authority rents. There has been a number of attempts to challenge local authority rent levels in the courts (both by those who think they are too high, and by those who think they are too low), most of which have failed.

2. HOUSING ASSOCIATION RENTS

3.237 Fair rents. Tenancies which began before the commencement (January 15, 1989) of Pt I of the 1988 Act (3.05), from housing associations, housing trusts and the Housing Corporation, were excluded from Rent Act protection by ss.15 and 16 of the Rent Act 1977 (5.86). They were and are, however, subject to the same fair rent structure as those private sector tenants (Rent Act 1977, Pt V1).

3.238 The same is true of housing association tenancies which, although granted after that date will, for one of the reasons set out in 3.15 above, not become Housing Act assured tenancies but remain within all or part of an earlier regime of protection.

3.239 Register. Although there is a separate part of the register for housing associations and other such bodies (1977, s.87), the same general principles will apply (*Palmer v Peabody Trust*, 1975) on the determination of their fair rents as other Rent Act protected tenants (5.175–5.189).

3.240 Increase without termination of tenancy. Provision is made to allow housing associations to increase these rent without the need to go through the process of determining the tenancy and granting a new one at the higher rent. This they may do by serving notice of variation, similar to that already considered in relation to Housing Act secure tenants generally (3.224) (1977, s.93).

3.241 Operation of provisions. It is not necessary to consider the operation of the fair rent system in relation to housing association tenancies, for the system is largely the same as that to be considered in relation to the private sector, and variations in detail are relatively minor. It may, however, be noted that a registered rent forms the rent limit for a housing association tenancy (5.213; 1977, s.88).

3.242 Other housing association tenants. Housing association, etc. tenancies which are within the Housing Act 1988—*i.e.* as assured tenancies (Chapter 4)—are subject to the same rent provisions as those applicable to other, private sector assured tenants.

Local Authority Housing Management

3.243 Management powers. *Prima facie*, all housing management powers and duties are vested in the landlord authority and must be exercised by them.

3.244 Under ss.27–27AB, 1985 Act, however, local authorities may, after consultation with their tenants, be authorised by the Secretary of State to enter into management agency agreements with another body—*e.g.* a registered social landlord—and may be obliged to enter into such agreements with a "tenant management organisation," *i.e.* a body formed by the tenants, complying with regulations (the Housing (Right to Manage) Regulations 1994, SI 1994/627).

3.245 Best Value. Under the provisions of the Local Government Act 1999, Pt I, local authorities are obliged to secure continuous improvement in the delivery of their service, including housing management. This has, to date, been achieved through a regime of "best value" reviews and performance plans.

3.246 The achievement of best value is secured by an inspection framework. Inspections are carried out through the Housing Inspectorate—an arm of the Audit Commission. For registered social landlords, a similar regime on inspection of their housing management functions, is carried out by the Housing Corporation.

Transfer of Public Housing

3.247 Transfer policy. As mentioned above (3.07), government policy is to try to reduce the size of the housing stock held by local authorities.

3.248 Two mechanisms to achieve this were introduced by the Housing Act 1988, but one of them—"Tenants' Choice"—under 1988, Pt IV, was repealed by the 1996 Act. The other is considered briefly below under its own heading (Housing Action Trusts).

3.249 In addition, local authorities may engage in voluntary stock transfer (1985, s.32). If part of a programme of 500 or more dwellings, such transfers will qualify as a Large-Scale Voluntary Transfer ("LSVT") under Leasehold Reform, Housing and Urban Development Act 1993, s.135.

3.250 Like any other disposal of local authority housing stock, such a transfer requires the consent of the Secretary of State. In the case of LSVT, this may lead to the payment of a "levy" under 1993, s.136, designed to reimburse the Government, out of the receipts for past housing subsidy paid on the property. The vast majority of transfers of stock have taken place through this voluntary means.

3.251 Consultation. Before any transfer (other than to another landlord whose tenants will be secure), a local authority must consult all their affected secure and introductory (6.29) tenants: 1985, s.106A and Sch.3A. The Secretary of State's consent will, again, be needed (1985, s.32) but, if it appears to him that a majority of the tenants do not wish the proposal to proceed, he cannot give it (1985, Sch.3A, para.5).

3.252 Housing action trusts. Only six Housing Action trusts have ever been declared and it is not anticipated that there will be any more. For that reason, only a brief outline is included here.

3.253 Housing Action Trusts were intended not only to take over housing stock but also, in their designated areas, a number of other housing-related powers and duties (many of which are referred to in Chapters 12–14, below), either together with the local authority, or instead. The proposals were intended to deal with parts of a local authority's area, not the whole of the area of each local authority.

3.254 The Secretary of State has power to transfer to a Housing Action Trust: (a) certain housing powers under the Housing Act 1985 (1988, s.65), certain planning powers (1988, ss.66–67); certain public health powers (1988, s.68); certain powers in respect of highways (1988, s.69); and (b) land and housing belonging to a local authority in its area (1988, ss.74–76).

3.255 The Secretary of State could not designate a Housing Action Trust without first carrying (or having carried) out a ballot or poll, and if a majority of the tenants who responded to the ballot or poll were opposed to it, he had to abandon the proposals (1988, s.61).

3.256 Among the considerations which could influence the Secretary of State when deciding whether or not (subject to ballot) to designate a Housing Action Trust were the extent of local authority housing in an area, its physical state and design, the need for repair of accommodation in the area generally, the way in which the local authority housing was being managed, living conditions in the area, social conditions and the environment (1988, s.60).

3.257 The principal objects of the Housing Action Trust were to secure repair or improvement of the accommodation it took over, and its proper and effective management and use, and to encourage diversity in the ways in which people occupy accommodation (tenancy—public or private, owner-occupation), as well as generally to secure or facilitate the improvement of living conditions in the area, and social conditions and the general environment (1988, s.63).

3.258 The purpose, was not for the Housing Action Trust to replace the local authority indefinitely; it was intended to achieve its objects and wind itself up as soon as practicable (1988, s.88). Its purpose, rather, was to transfer the housing to others, whether owner-occupiers or landlords, (to both of whom a Trust may give financial assistance: 1988, s.71).

3.259 Transferee landlords had to be approved for the purpose by the Housing Corporation: 1988, s.79. The Housing Corporation could not approve a public sector landlord, or a county council, or any body which it thought would be under the control or influence of the public sector landlord, county council or its officers or members (1988, s.79). For this purpose, public sector landlord means any local housing authority or a new town corporation. Although the primary function of a housing action trust was to transfer the housing to others, tenants nonetheless have the option in certain circumstances of transferring back to the local authority (1988, s.84A).

3.260 Because of the role of the Housing Corporation in approving landlords, it has power to provide legal assistance to a tenant transferred from a Housing Action Trust to a private landlord (1988, s.82). The power only applies to someone who was a Housing Act secure tenant at the time of the transfer, or his surviving spouse.

Further Financial Protection and Assistance

3.261 There are other forms of financial protection or assistance which may be applicable.

3.262 Premiums and deposits. Premiums and deposits are not specifically prohibited under the Housing Act 1985: *cf.* 5.216–5.227.

3.263 Accommodation agency charges. Accommodation agency charge provisions (4.159) are unlikely to be relevant as matters of practice.

3.264 Utility charges. The provisions governing the resale of utilities, *i.e.* gas and electricity (4.162) are also not likely to be relevant (but *cf.* para.3.223).

3.265 Housing benefits. Under the Social Security Contributions and Benefits Act 1992 rent rebates and allowances, together with council tax rebates, are available to assist those on income support and others with low incomes with their housing costs. The details of these support schemes are so commonly varied that it is impracticable to consider them here. There is a number of annual publications which contain current provisions.

CHAPTER FOUR

Housing Act Assured Tenancies

Introduction

4.01 New Status. The assured tenancy was introduced in 1988, by the Housing Act of that year ("1988"), to replace:

(a) The Rent Act 1977 protected tenancy in the private sector (Chapter 5), and

(b) The Housing Act 1985 secure tenancy in relation to housing association tenancies (Chapter 3).

4.02 Commencement. These provisions applied from the commencement of Pt I of the 1988 Act, January 15, 1989.

4.03 Transitional Cases. There is a small number of circumstances in which a letting commencing on or after January 15, 1989 may still fall within either the Rent Act 1977 (5.08), and or the Housing Act 1985 (3.15).

4.04 Assured shorthold tenancies. Following the model of the "protected shorthold" tenancy under Rent Act 1977 (6.99), the 1988 Act also included a class of assured tenancy known as the assured shorthold (1988, s.20), with considerably less security of tenure than fully assured tenants.

4.05 Initially, this was the legal exception rather than the norm, in the sense that there was a fully assured tenancy unless a notice was given before the tenancy began that it was to be shorthold.

4.06 In the fully private sector, however, shorthold rapidly became the most common form of letting and, with changes in policy towards the homeless (see Chapter 10), shorthold lettings became, from February 28, 1997, the universal default form of letting, *i.e.* subject to a number of exceptions (4.57), all assured tenancies were to be assured shortholds unless and until notified that the tenancy was to be fully assured.

4.07 Despite this, most assured tenants of registered social landlords ("RSLs") are in fact notified that their tenancies will be fully assured before, immediately on, or within a fairly short period of time from, the commencement of their tenancies. RSLs are engaged in the long-term function of providing rented accommodation, and do not seek to operate on the basis of being able to evict for anything other than the sort of good reason embodied in grounds for possession, whereas a fully private landlord may well wish to retain the freedom to evict for other reasons, *e.g.* to sell when the market moves in favour of owner-occupation.

4.08 Structure of Chapters. Notwithstanding the shift to a presumptive shorthold, however, in view of:

(a) The almost complete absence of security of tenure enjoyed by the assured shorthold tenant, and

(b) The fact that most RSL tenants are not shorthold,

this Chapter will therefore, as with earlier editions, continue to describe full assured security, leaving shorthold security to be dealt with in Chapter 6, along with other forms of letting which enjoy only limited security.

Outline

4.09 Assured tenants

- An assured tenant is one to whom residential accommodation is let as a separate dwelling under a tenancy (not a licence), which the tenant occupies as his only or principal home, and which is not excluded from security under the schedule of exceptions.

- A form of assured tenancy was introduced in 1980 and there are transitional provisions which apply to such tenancies.

- There are particular provisions which apply to agricultural and forestry workers.

- All new assured tenancies created on or since February 28, 1997 are automatically assured shorthold unless either:

- The landlord indicates through notice or the tenancy agreement that the tenancy is to be fully assured or
- It arises out of an existing tenancy in one of a number of specified circumstances.

- There are limits on the grant of fully assured tenancies where the grant is of temporary accommodation to a homeless person.

4.10   Security of Tenure

- There is provision for one statutory succession to an assured tenancy, but only by a "spouse".

- An assured tenancy can only be repossessed by the landlord by obtaining a court order, following service of a notice of seeking possession which sets out the statutory ground on which possession is sought.

- Where an assured tenancy is for a fixed term which terminates, the tenant will be entitled to remain in occupation, under the same terms, as a statutory periodic tenant.

- Some grounds require the court to be satisfied that it is reasonable to grant possession, others are mandatory.

4.11   Rent and other terms

- Where the tenancy agreement does not contain its own rent review clause, the 1988 Act provides a mechanism for rents of periodic assured tenancies to be varied on an annual basis.

- Variations under this procedure may be referred to the Rent Assessment Committee to determine the open market rent.

- Terms as to access, to carry out works, are automatically implied into the tenancy.

- Terms as to assignment and subletting may be implied into periodic assured tenancies.

4.12   Further Financial Protection and Assistance

- Some assured tenants of registered social landlords have the "right to acquire" their homes.

- There are provisions as to accommodation agency charges, resale of utilities and welfare benefits which are relevant to assured tenants.

Assured tenants

4.13 Principal issues. The Housing Act 1988 assumes that all tenants to whom property is let as a separate dwelling (on or after the commencement of 1988, Pt I: January 15, 1989) are assured tenants if they fulfil the qualifying conditions, and unless there is some factor which takes them out of Housing Act assured protection (1988, s.1).

4.14 There is a number of issues:

(a) There must be a qualifying letting as a separate dwelling, which is not within any exclusion.

(b) 1980 Act assured tenancies.

(c) Agricultural and forestry workers.

(d) Assured or Assured Shorthold.

(e) Temporary accommodation for the homeless.

1. QUALIFYING LETTING

4.15 Tenancy. For there to be an assured tenancy, there must be a tenancy (1.90), *i.e.* (and unlike secure status: 3.19) the Act does not apply to licences.

4.16 Separate dwelling. The tenancy must be of a dwelling-house let as a separate dwelling. Premises which are let with no element of shared living accommodation (3.25) will be a "dwelling" for these purposes, provided that the tenant occupies them as his home. It does not matter if they do not include any kitchen facilities, although the premises probably have to be big enough to sleep in, *i.e.* for a bed: *Uratemp Ventures Ltd v Collins*, 2001.

4.17 Sharing living accommodation. If living accommodation (3.25) is shared with someone other than the tenant's own landlord, however, this will not prevent the tenancy qualifying as assured, even although, strictly, there is no letting as a separate dwelling (3.17). This is, as with Rent Act protected tenancy (5.71), provided by statute (1988, s.3).

4.18   If the tenant shares, or may have to share, living accommodation with his landlord, however, there is no letting as a separate
dwelling and no saving statutory provision.

4.19   This proposition should not be confused with the position
of a resident landlord, with his own separate home elsewhere in
the same building, and which subject to its own express exclusion
(4.43). The proposition applies, rather, where the landlord and the
tenant share living accommodation, *i.e.* neither of them has his
own separate dwelling. In that case, there is no letting as a separate
dwelling, no *prima facie* assured tenancy, and the resident landlord
exclusion never comes into play and need not be relied on.

4.20   There may be no letting as a separate dwelling even if the
landlord does not actually live in the premises, but—whether or
not he has actually ever exercised the right or whether or not he
has a current intention to do so—sharing with his tenant was in
contemplation at the time of the letting, the right to do so was
reserved, and there is at the lowest a real prospect of the landlord
doing so at some future date (*Gray v Brown*, 1992).

4.21   Qualification conditions. Not all residential lettings are
included. There are two qualifying conditions which must also be
fulfilled. They are (s.1(1)):

> (a) That the tenant is an individual rather than a company or
>   other corporation, or if a joint tenancy that all the joint
>   tenants are individuals; and,

> (b) That the tenant, or if a joint tenancy at least one of them,
>   occupies the dwelling as an "only or principal home"
>   (3.32).

4.22   Exclusions. There is a small number of exclusions from
protection which: (a) are rare enough in practice; and (b) are of
sufficient particularity that they do not merit discussion: licensed
premises and lettings of agricultural and/or substantial land.

4.23   The remaining factors which take a tenancy out of assured
protection are as follows.

> (a) **Prior tenancy**. Tenancies preceding commencement (1988,
>   Sch.1, para.1).

> (b) **High rateable value or rent**. The rateable value or high
>   rent of the premises (1988, Sch.1, para.2).

(c) **No or low rent.** Whether any or how much rent is paid (1988, Sch.1, para.3).

(d) **Business lettings.** Whether it is a business letting (1988, Sch.1, para.4).

(e) **Student lettings.** Whether it is a student letting (1988, Sch.1, para.8).

(f) **Holiday lettings.** Whether it is a holiday letting (1988, Sch.1, para.9).

(g) **Resident landlord.** Whether there is a resident landlord (1988, Sch.1, para.10).

(h) **Exempt landlords.** Whether the landlord is exempt from assured protection (1988, Sch.1, paras 11, 12).

(i) **Asylum-seeker accommodation.** Accommodation provided for asylum-seekers (1988, Sch.1, para.12A).

(j) **Other classes of protection.** A tenancy which remains a Rent Act protected, housing association, or Housing Act secure tenancy (1988, Sch.1, para.14).

4.24 Prior tenancy. A tenancy entered into before (or under a contract which pre-dates) the commencement of the Housing Act 1988 will be either Housing Act secure or Rent Act protected (3.17, 5.08).

4.25 High rateable value or rent. Some premises have such a high rateable value or rent that they are considered to be beyond the need for protection.

4.26 It is the part of the premises which the tenant occupies which must be valued, not the whole house in which the tenancy is situated. A block of flats will often, as a whole, have too high a rateable value for 1988 Housing Act purposes, but each individual flat will not.

4.27 A tenancy will not be a Housing Act assured tenancy if the premises have a rateable value in excess of £1,500 (Greater London) or £750 (elsewhere) (1988, Sch.1, para.2A). Where a tenancy has been granted after April 1, 1990 and is for a property which had no rateable value on March 31, 1990 it will be excluded if the rent is greater than £25,000 a year (1988, Sch.1, para.2).

4.28 No or low rent. The 1988 Act is not designed to apply to those who purchase long leases and pay only a small, annual ground rent (1988, Sch.1, para.3). These have been considered as owner-occupiers and were dealt with in Chapter 2.

4.29 This exclusion applies where the annual ground rent is less than two-thirds of the rateable value of the premises (1988, Sch.1, para.3B) or in the case of a tenancy which has been granted after April 1, 1990 and is for a property which had no rateable value on March 31, 1990, where the rent is £1000 or less a year in Greater London or £250 or less elsewhere (1988, Sch.1, para.3A).

4.30 Specifically disregarded in ascertaining the rent is any part of the rent which is expressed to be payable in respect of rates, services, management, repairs maintenance or insurance, unless, even although so expressed, the rent could not have been regarded as so payable (1988, Sch.1, para.2(2)).

4.31 Tenancies at no rent are also excluded (1988, Sch.1, para.3).

4.32 Rent in money. It has been held that rent must mean payment of rent in money if the tenancy is to be brought within protection, *i.e.* not payment in goods, or services (*Hornsby v Maynard*, 1925).

4.33 There is, however, some authority for the proposition that if goods or services represent a quantified, or agreed amount which would otherwise be payable by way of rent, the Act may apply (*Barnes v Barratt*, 1970).

4.34 Where there is a true service tenancy (1.148) and an amount of rent between a landlord/employer and his tenant/employee has been agreed but is merely deducted at source, this will be considered sufficient payment of rent for the purposes of protection (*Montague v Browning*, 1954).

4.35 Business lettings. Tenancies which are subject to the business protection of the Landlord and Tenant Act 1954, and are therefore outside of residential protection (under this Act, as under the Housing Act 1985—see 3.39—and the Rent Act 1977—see 5.14) have been described above (3.39(n)).

4.36 Student lettings. A tenancy will not be an assured tenancy if the landlord under the tenancy is a specified educational institution and the tenant is following or intends to follow a course of study at that or another specified educational institution (1988, Sch.1, para.8).

4.37 Holiday lettings. If the purpose of the tenancy is use as a holiday home, then the tenancy will not be assured (1988, Sch.1, para.9).

4.38 This is an exemption which had been widely used as a device to defeat the Rent Acts (see also 1.73, 5.17, 5.84). The mere fact that someone has been compelled to sign an agreement alleging falsely that the tenancy was for a holiday purpose does not make it so as a matter of law. The principles relating to sham will apply to determine whether the agreement was a mere device to exclude protection, although occupiers should be aware that once they have signed such an agreement, the courts will consider that the burden of proof is upon them to displace the inference that the tenancy is not protected: see *Buchmann v May*, 1976. It may, however, be enough to show that there is a "false label," which is a slightly less pejorative term and was applied in *R. v Rent Officer for LB of Camden Ex p. Plant*, 1981, in which the landlord was found to have known, either before the first or the second of two consecutive "holiday" lettings, that the occupiers were students. What is a holiday is a question of fact and common sense.

4.39 Other classes of protection. Those cases where a letting will be Housing Act 1985 secure notwithstanding that the letting follows the commencement of Pt I of the 1988 Act have already been described (3.15) and those which remain Rent Act protected are described at 5.08. They are therefore not assured (1988, Sch.1, para.13).

4.40 Exempt landlords. Those landlords whose tenants are not assured are (1988, Sch.1, para.12):

- Local authorities (including district and county councils, county borough councils, London Borough Councils, the Common Council of the City of London and the Council of the Isles of Scilly);
- The Commission for the New Towns;
- An urban development corporation;
- A new town development corporation;
- A waste disposal authority;
- A residuary body (under the Local Government Act 1985, which took over the residual affairs of an abolished council, *i.e.* the Greater London Council and the metropolitan counties);

- A fully mutual association housing association (*i.e.* where the rules restrict membership to people who are tenants or prospective tenants of the association, and preclude the grant or assignment of tenancies to persons other than members); and

- A Housing Action Trust (3.252).

4.41　In addition, tenants of the Crown or a government department are not assured unless the tenancy is under the management of the Crown Estate Commissioners (1988, Sch.1, para.11).

4.42　Asylum-seeker accommodation. A tenancy granted to someone being accommodated under the National Asylum Support Service, set up under the Immigration and Asylum Act 1999, Pt VI, is not assured (1988, Sch.1, para.12A).

4.43　Resident landlords. The exclusion of the tenants of resident landlords was developed under the Rent Acts (5.44–5.60) and operates similarly under Housing Act 1988 (1988, Sch.1, para.10).

4.44　The exclusion applies to premises let which are part of a building and, unless the dwelling itself forms part only of a flat, that building is not a purpose-built block of flats (4.47). At the time of the grant of the tenancy, the landlord must have occupied as his only or principal home (3.32, 4.21) another dwelling forming part of the same building (or, where the dwelling forms part only of a flat, another part of the same flat).

4.45　For the landlord to take advantage of this exclusion, he must establish that, since the commencement of the tenancy, he has at all times used the other part of the building or flat which he occupies as an only or principal home.

4.46　The two sets of homes must be within the same building. This will not cover, *e.g.* a terrace of houses, but may include a house which has had an extension added, even if there is no interconnection between the house and extension (*Griffiths v English*, 1981; *Lewis-Graham v Conacher*, 1991).

4.47　The term "purpose-built block of flats" means exactly what it says. A house converted into flats, no matter how long ago, or however separately the living units are now constructed (*Barnes v Gorsuch*, 1982), will not be a purpose-built block (*Bardrick v Haycock*, 1976; *Griffiths*), even if there are separate entrances.

4.48 If the building is a purpose-built block, however, then it avails the landlord not at all that he lives in one and the tenant lives in another flat.

4.49 A corporate landlord, *e.g.* a landlord which is a company, a trust, a partnership, cannot qualify as a resident landlord for these purposes, because it cannot occupy as a home. It is, however, expressly provided that occupation by one of two or more joint owners/landlords is enough to keep the tenant from being a Housing Act assured tenant. There are also provisions to exclude security when "the landlord" is a trustee, and it is the beneficiary who is resident.

4.50 There are two circumstances when residence is treated as continuing, even though it is not:

(a) **Sale.** If the landlord sells the house, residence will be treated as continuing for a further 28 days. If, during that time, the new owner serves notice that he intends to move into the premises for use as a home, then he has a total of six months in which to do so, during which period residence by the landlord will likewise be treated as continuing. If, by the end of the six months, the new owner has not taken up residence, the tenant will become an assured tenant and will so remain, even when the owner moves in, for there will not have been continual residence (or deemed residence) since the start of the tenancy. During the deemed period, the landlord cannot evict otherwise than as if the tenant was assured, *i.e.* if there are grounds.

(b) **Death.** On the death of a resident landlord, the executors effectively have two years, during which the fact that there is no resident landlord will be disregarded. During this period, however, the landlord's executors may freely evict as if there was still a resident landlord.

The two periods (two years under this paragraph, six months under the last) may be added together (*Williams v Mate*, 1982).

2. 1980 ACT ASSURED TENANCIES

4.51 The term "assured tenancy" was first used in Housing Act 1980 and reflected a policy of encouraging the private sector to build housing for rent, with a system of protection modelled on the "new tenancy" mechanism applicable to business lettings under Pt II, Landlord and Tenant Act 1954. The policy was not successful and, subject only to minor qualification and those lettings at the time being kept alive under the adapted 1954 Act, all 1980 assured tenancies were converted into Housing Act 1988 assured tenancies from the commencement of Pt I of the 1988 Act (January 15, 1989) (1988, ss.1, 37).

3. AGRICULTURAL AND FORESTRY WORKERS

4.52 Under the Housing Act 1988, Pt I, Chap. III, agricultural and forestry tied workers, whose occupation commenced on or after January 15, 1989, enjoy a measure of protection, notwithstanding that they may well have licences rather than tenancies.

4.53 It is not possible in this book to consider these provisions in any detail, but the following points of distinction should be noted:

(a) Chapter III applies not only to service tenants but also to service occupiers (1988, s.24), *i.e.* licensees;

(b) The fact that such occupiers will not usually be paying rent does not take them out of protection (1988, s.24(2));

(c) It is usually necessary to show that the employee has been an agricultural worker (though not necessarily with the same employer) for 91 out of the 104 weeks preceding the date when it is claimed that the Act applies (1988, Sch.3).

4.54 The structure allows a landlord to make application to the local authority to provide rehousing "in the interests of efficient agriculture" for both assured agricultural occupiers and those protected by the Rent (Agriculture) Act 1976 (5.15) (1976, Pt IV).

4.55 Agricultural workers not within these provisions may get some temporary security for up to a year, under the Protection from Eviction Act 1977, by way of time granted by the court before a possession order takes effect.

4. ASSURED OR ASSURED SHORTHOLD

4.56 Tenancies created on or since February 28, 1997. As noted above (4.06) lettings granted on or since February 28, 1997 are automatically assured shortholds, unless (1988, s.19A and Sch.2A) certain conditions are fulfilled.

4.57 Those conditions are:

(a) Notice is served by the prospective landlord on the prospective tenant before the tenancy is entered into that it is not to be an assured shorthold; or

(b) Notice is served by the landlord on the tenant after the tenancy has been entered into that it is no longer to be an assured shorthold; or

(c) The tenancy agreement itself contains a provision that it is not to be an assured shorthold; or

(d) The tenancy falls within the transitional provisions considered below, governing new tenancies for existing tenants (4.23); or

(e) The tenancy was a secure tenancy (Chapter 3) which is transferred to a registered social landlord and, accordingly, became an assured tenancy; or

(f) It is an assured tenancy arising on the termination of a long lease (2.17); or

(g) The grant is to a person who (or, if joint tenants, one of whom), immediately beforehand, was an existing assured tenant (or one of a number of assured joint tenants), by someone who (or, if joint landlords, one of whom) is the existing landlord (or one of a number of joint landlords), even if in different premises. (Note: the purpose here is to protect such tenants against deprivation of rights, and provision is accordingly made to allow voluntary removal of protection by means of a notice served on the landlord by the tenant, which must be served before the tenancy begins, and has to be in the prescribed form (in order to warn the tenant of what rights he may be giving up); or

(h) A periodic assured tenancy comes into being following a fixed-term assured tenancy (4.74); or

(i) Certain assured agricultural occupancies (4.52).

4.58 Tenancies created prior to February 28, 1997. It may remain relevant to determine whether a tenancy created prior to February 28, 1997, was at that time fully assured or assured shorthold, as that can affect:

(a) Whether or not the tenant if still in occupation is fully assured or assured shorthold, and

(b) The validity of any new agreement entered into, *i.e.* provisions to protect a fully assured tenant against being tricked into signing an assured shorthold tenancy (4.57(g)) will not operate if the tenant was already assured shorthold.

4.59 Where a tenancy was granted prior to February 28, 1997, and otherwise fulfilled all the requirements for an assured tenancy, it was fully assured unless the landlord had served notice on the tenant that it was to be an assured shorthold tenancy.

4.60 In addition to service of notice, the tenancy had to be for a fixed term of not less than six months (containing no power for the landlord to determine the tenancy within that period, other than by way of forfeiture).

4.61 When the initial shorthold tenancy came or comes to an end, a periodic tenancy came or comes into being, of the same or substantially the same premises, which was or is also an assured shorthold tenancy unless the landlord served or serves notice stating that it is no longer to be considered a shorthold tenancy (1988, s.20(4)).

4.62 In each case, "the landlord" in the case of joint landlords, means at least one of them.

4.63 To prevent a landlord persuading a Housing Act assured tenant to enter into a new arrangement which is shorthold, a tenancy will not be an assured shorthold if, immediately beforehand, the person to whom it is granted (or if joint tenants, one of them) was a fully assured tenant of the same landlord (even if in different premises) (1988, s.20(3)).

5. TEMPORARY ACCOMMODATION FOR THE HOMELESS

4.64 When seeking to house homeless families under the interim housing duties imposed on them by Housing Act 1996, Pt VII, (Chapter 10), local authorities may seek to use accommodation provided by other landlords, whether RSL or wholly private.

4.65 In order to ensure that the homeless do not obtain any security when they are being housed under any of the temporary, interim housing duties, 1996, s.209 provides that a tenancy granted in pursuance of arrangements with authorities in the discharge of one of the interim duties under Pt VII (s.188, accommodation pending enquiries; s.190, accommodation for intentionally homeless; s.200, accommodation pending or following a local connection referral; s.204, accommodation pending appeal to county court— see further Chapter 10) is not assured at all for a period of 12 months (from notification of decision, or decision on review or appeal), unless the tenant is notified by the landlord that the tenancy is to be either assured or assured shorthold.

Security of Tenure

4.66 A number of matters have to be considered under this heading:

(a) Succession;

(b) Loss of assured status;

(c) Continuation and termination; and,

(d) Grounds for possession.

1. SUCCESSION

4.67 **Single succession.** There is a limited right of "statutory succession" to an assured tenancy, similar to (but not as extensive as) that available to Housing Act secure tenants under the Housing Act 1985 (3.40–3.53) and to Rent Act protected and statutory tenants under the Rent Act 1977 (5.33–5.38).

4.68 On the death of an assured tenant, his spouse can succeed, provided that immediately before his death, she was occupying the dwelling-house as her only or principal home (4.21): 1988, s.17(1)(a). For these purposes, "spouse" is not limited to persons legally married, but includes persons who have been living together as husband and wife (see 3.49).

4.69 **Limits on succession.** There can be no statutory succession if the deceased was himself already a successor, whether by reason of this (or another: 5.34) statutory succession provision or because of inheritance (1988, s.17(2)). If the tenancy was a joint tenancy (1.193), and the deceased became the tenant on the death of his joint tenant, there can be no statutory succession (1988, s.17(2)). Statutory succession only applies to a sole tenancy (1988, s.17(1));

on the death of one joint tenant, the other or others become the sole tenant or remaining joint tenants, by right of survivorship.

4.70 Devolution by will or on intestacy. Where there is no statutory succession, a tenancy can pass under a will or on intestacy, and if the inheritor occupies as an only or principal home, the tenancy will still be assured, but as there is to be a mandatory ground for possession available against the successor (provided the proceedings are brought within time limits—4.101) it is a succession potentially of little value.

2. LOSS OF ASSURED STATUS

4.71 There is a number of circumstances in which a tenancy may cease to be assured.

(a) **Want of residence.** The assured tenancy ceases to be assured for want of continued use as an only or principal home, in which case the landlord can terminate the tenancy in the usual way (1.108–1.141).

(b) **Exclusions.** The exclusions from security do not necessarily apply once and for all, see, *e.g.*, resident landlord, low rent. A tenancy may therefore move in to, or out of, assured status.

(c) **New landlord.** The premises are bought by one of the public landlords described above whose tenants are not assured (4.40). The tenancy will usually then become a secure tenancy: see Chapter 3.

(d) **Ground for possession.** The landlord establishes to a court, which will be the county court, that one of the stated sets of circumstances exists, as a result of which he is or may be entitled to an order of the court for possession.

3. CONTINUATION AND TERMINATION

4.72 Continuation by contract. Security of tenure under the Housing Act 1988 operates closer to the Housing Act 1985 than the Rent Act 1977, in so far as a periodic contractual tenancy cannot be brought to an end by the landlord other than by court order (1988, s.5), so that there is no division between a contractual and a "statutory" tenancy as in the case of a Rent Act protected tenancy (5.25). (Note: the periodic tenancy can, however, still be brought to an end by the tenant in the normal way, *i.e.* by notice to quit or surrender (1.108–1.125)). The court order will only be available on specified "grounds" (next heading).

4.73   Fixed-terms. In the case of a fixed-term assured tenancy which contains a forfeiture clause (1.127), the tenancy cannot be brought to an end by the landlord by the exercise of that power. Nor can the tenant apply for relief from forfeiture (1.131–1.141): *Artesian Residential Developments Ltd v Beck*, 1999.

4.74   Instead of forfeiture, the landlord has to obtain an order of the court to determine the tenancy as if it was a periodic tenancy. If the fixed-term ends in any other way, *e.g.* because its time expires, then—unless the tenant voluntarily leaves—there will automatically come into being a "statutory periodic tenancy," which will continue until determined by a court, on specified grounds, in the same way as a tenancy that had been periodic all along.

4.75   There will be no statutory periodic tenancy, however, if the landlord and the tenant agree a new tenancy to start on the determination of the old, whether that is a new fixed term or a new period tenancy.

4.76   Notice of seeking possession. As under the Housing Act 1985 (3.65), in place of notice to quit, the landlord has to serve a notice of seeking possession, specifying the ground he intends to rely on, before he can seek an order for possession (1988, s.8).

4.77   Contents of notice. The notice must be in the form prescribed, and must inform the tenant that the landlord intends to bring proceedings on the grounds specified, and that the proceedings will begin no earlier than a date specified in the notice, but no later than 12 months from service of the notice. The discussion of contents of notices, relative to secure tenants, is equally applicable to assured tenants (3.76).

4.78   Domestic violence and service. There are added requirements where the domestic violence ground (Ground 14A), is relied on (1988, s.8A), analogous to those applicable to secure tenants (3.72).

4.79   Just and Equitable. The court can, however, dispense with such a notice if it considers it just and equitable (3.66) to do so (other than when possession is sought on Ground 8: 4.104).

4.80 Commencement of Proceedings. Proceedings cannot commence before the later of the following:

    (a) Two weeks, or,

    (b) If possession is sought on Grounds 1, 2, 5–7, 9 or 16, two months; or,

    (c) If a periodic tenancy, the earliest date when a notice to quit could have expired; or,

    (d) If reliance is placed on Ground 14, the date of service of the notice.

4.81 A notice of seeking possession can, however, be served during a fixed-term tenancy, to take effect in relation to the following statutory periodic tenancy.

4.82 Grounds. Unless the court dispenses with the notice, or the court gives permission to alter or add to the grounds, possession can only be ordered on a ground specified in the notice.

✳ 4. GROUNDS FOR POSSESSION

4.83 Discretionary and mandatory grounds. As under both the 1985 and the 1977 Acts, grounds for possession (1988, s.7 and Sch.2) are either discretionary or mandatory. The mandatory grounds are set out in Sch.2, Pt I; the discretionary grounds are set out in Sch.2, Pt II.

4.84 The discretionary grounds for possession are those where the landlord has to prove that it is reasonable to make the order: the law on this subject, and the burden of proof, are the same as under the Housing Act 1985 (3.85–3.94).

4.85 Powers of court. In the case of discretionary grounds, the court's powers to suspend or vary an order are the same as under the 1985 and 1977 Act (3.147; 1988, s.9), but the court's powers are otherwise as limited as under those two Acts where no security attaches or where a mandatory ground is available (1980, s.89: 3.145).

4.86 Rent Arrears. There are three rent arrears grounds. One is mandatory (ground 8, 4.104), while the other two are discretionary (grounds 10 and 11, 4.117 and 4.119). Possession may be sought on both the mandatory and discretionary grounds in the same proceedings. If on the face of the order it has not been made on the mandatory Ground 8, however, the court will retain its added powers (4.85) to suspend the order or a warrant for possession: *Capital Prime Plus plc v Wills*, 1998. When making an order under Ground 8 the court should therefore ensure that this is made clear on its face: *Diab v Countryside Rentals 1 plc*, 2001.

(i) *Mandatory grounds*

4.87 There are eight mandatory grounds for possession, *i.e.* those which if proved, leave the court no alternative but to make an order for possession, to take effect within two to six weeks (depending on hardship, 3.145), regardless of whether or not it is reasonable to make the order.

4.88 **Absentee owner-occupiers**. Ground 1 concerns absentee owner-occupiers, although it may be noted that for these purposes the landlord could himself be the tenant of another, while still qualifying as an "owner-occupier" in relation to his sub-tenant.

4.89 The Ground is available to a landlord who has (or, if joint landlords, one of whom has) formerly occupied the property as his only or principal home (4.21). It is also available to a landlord who requires (or, in the case of joint landlords, one of whom requires) to occupy the property as his or his spouse's only or principal home, although this is not an available alternative if the would-be occupier bought the premises (for money or money's worth) with the tenant already in occupation.

4.90 This Ground is only available to a landlord who has served notice no later than the beginning of the tenancy, warning the tenant that the Ground might be used against him.

4.91 If the landlord fails to do so, however, the court may waive this requirement, if it thinks it just and equitable to do so, *e.g.* if the tenant had oral notice, although such other factors as mutual hardship, time in occupation, are also relevant (*White v Jones*, 1993). Persistent late payment of rent may also be relevant (*Boyle v Verrall*, 1996).

4.92 **Mortgaged property**. Ground 2 is available when the property is subject to a mortgage granted before the beginning of the tenancy, and the mortgagee has become entitled to exercise the power of sale under the mortgage (Chapter 2) and requires possession in order to sell with vacant possession.

4.93   Again, there has to have been notice no later than the beginning of the tenancy that this Ground might apply, unless the court uses its power to waive notice on the basis that it is just and equitable to do so.

4.94   Out-of-season holiday letting. An out-of-season fixed-term letting for not more than eight months, of premises occupied within the previous 12 months for a holiday (4.37), is subject to a mandatory ground for possession, provided notice was given no later than the beginning of the tenancy that the Ground would apply (Ground 3). There is no power for the court to waive the notice requirement.

4.95   Off-season student letting. An off-season fixed-term letting for not more than one year, of premises occupied within the previous 12 months as a student letting (4.36), is likewise subject to a mandatory ground for possession, provided notice was given no later than the beginning of the tenancy that the Ground would apply (Ground 4). There is no power for the court to waive the notice requirement.

4.96   Ministers of religion. Ground 5 is a special ground, applicable to property occupied or formerly occupied by ministers of religion.

4.97   Demolition. Possession can be obtained under Ground 6 by a landlord who intends to demolish or reconstruct the whole or a substantial part of the premises, or carry out substantial works on them, if the following conditions are fulfilled:

(a)   The work cannot reasonably be carried out with the tenant in occupation either because the tenant will not agree to a variation in terms such as would allow sufficient access and facilities to permit the work to be carried out, or no such variation is practicable in the light of the intended works; or

(b)   The tenant will not agree to accept an assured tenancy of part only of the property, such as would permit the landlord to carry out the works, or no such "part-property" arrangement would be practicable.

4.98 The Ground is similar to that available under the Housing Act 1985; in particular, a landlord's plans have to be clear and certain before the Ground is available (3.128).

4.99 This Ground is also available in the case of a registered housing association or charitable housing trust (3.30) where the person intending to do the works is not the landlord under the tenancy but a superior landlord.

4.100 This Ground is not available, however, to a landlord who has bought the property for money or money's worth with the tenant in occupation, or when the assured tenant has become an assured tenant by succession under the Rent Act 1977 (5.34).

4.101 **Inherited tenancy.** Ground 7 is available in the case of a periodic tenancy (including a statutory periodic tenancy: 4.74), but not a fixed term tenancy.

4.102 This Ground applies when the tenancy has devolved not on statutory succession (4.67) but under the will of the tenant, or on the tenant's intestacy, and proceedings for possession are commenced no later than one year after the death of the former tenant (or, if the court so permits, one year after the court considers that the landlord—or in the case of joint landlords, one of them— became aware of the death of the former tenant).

4.103 It is expressly provided that if the landlord continues to accept rent from the successor, this will not amount to the creation of a new tenancy (1.54), unless there is a variation in the amount of rent, the terms of the tenancy, its periods or the property itself.

4.104 **Two months' rent arrears.** Ground 8 concerns rent arrears (*cf.* 3.95, 5.145). This mandatory Ground is available if both at the date of service of the notice of seeking possession (4.76) and at the date of hearing of the action, there are at least 8 weeks' or two months' rent arrears.

4.105 There are also two discretionary Grounds concerning rent arrears (4.117, 4.119). If no notice has been served pursuant to s.48 of the Landlord and Tenant Act 1987 (1.107), rent will not yet be due and, therefore, cannot be in arrears (*Marath v MacGillivray*, 1996). Nor will there be arrears if there is a valid set-off for disrepair (or other breach) (11.104), but there will be arrears (at the date of NSP) even if there is a counter-claim for disrepair (or other breach), although (arguably) not at (the end of) the date of hearing, *i.e.* if a (sufficient) award is made on the counter-claim.

(ii) *Discretionary grounds*

4.106 The discretionary grounds for possession are those in relation to which the court enjoys extensive powers, and in which the landlord must prove that it is reasonable to make the order, in addition to showing that the details of each ground are applicable (4.84). There are 10 of them.

4.107 Suitable alternative accommodation. Ground 9 applies when suitable alternative accommodation is available or will be available for the tenant when the order takes effect.

4.108 Suitable alternative accommodation is defined in Pt III of Sch.2 to the 1988 Act. A certificate from the local authority that the tenant will be rehoused by them is conclusive that suitable alternative accommodation will be available (although not necessarily that it is reasonable to make the order).

4.109 In the alternative, a landlord can himself provide another private tenancy or obtain one for the tenant from another landlord. In this case, the Schedule regulates such details as suitability for the needs and means of the tenant and his family as regards extent and character; or its similarity to the existing accommodation; or its proximity to work (*Yewbright Properties Ltd v Stone*, 1980).

4.110 The character of the new premises can be a determining factor. In *Redspring v Francis*, 1973, it was held that premises on a busy road, next door to a fish and chip shop, were not suitable for a tenant who had hitherto been living in a quiet residential street. The extent of the facilities and amenities in an area, including shops, open space, transport, etc., will also influence a decision.

4.111 The new tenancy must either be assured, excluding tenancies in respect of which notices under Grounds 1–5 have been given, and excluding an assured shorthold (see Chapter 6), or else must afford security equivalent to that enjoyed by an assured tenant.

4.112 Alternative accommodation will never be suitable if it will result in overcrowding, even if the tenant's present premises are overcrowded.

4.113 Suitable alternative accommodation may consist of part only of a tenant's present premises, for example, if one room is sublet or disused (*Mykolyshyn v Noah*, 1970). If the part of the premises which the landlord is seeking to recover is used at all, for example, as a study or workroom or a spare room for visiting family, it is extremely unlikely that the court would allow this ground for possession to be used effectively in order to reduce the size of the tenancy (*MacDonnell v Daly*, 1969).

4.114 The landlord must still establish that it is reasonable to make the order. A court will frequently refuse, even where the alternative premises are apparently suitable, because of, *e.g.* the age of the tenant.

4.115 An order may well be made subject to undertakings from the landlord to do specific works to the new premises, or else to pay for various removal or other expenses.

4.116 If such undertakings are not fulfilled, the tenant can apply to the court to set aside or discharge the order, or else sue for the amount owing.

4.117 Arrears of rent. Ground 10 is the first of the further grounds dealing with rent arrears, and applies when rent is in arrears both at the date when the proceedings for possession are commenced, and at the date of service of the notice of seeking possession (4.76), unless such notice is waived by the court (4.79).

4.118 It may be distinguished from the mandatory Ground 8 in that:

(a) There may be no arrears at the date of hearing; and

(b) There is no minimum amount.

4.119 Ground 11 is available where, regardless of whether there are current rent arrears, and regardless of whether there were arrears at date of service of notice of seeking possession, issue of proceedings or date of hearing, the tenant has persistently delayed paying rent. Whether or not there are arrears may be affected by the question of set-off or counter-claim for disrepair (or other breach) (3.96).

4.120 Remaining discretionary grounds. The next series of grounds is familiar:

(a) Ground 12—broken obligation of tenancy (3.98, 5.146);

(b) Ground 13—deterioration of dwelling-house or common parts owing to acts of waste by, or the neglect or default of, the tenant or someone else residing in the property (whom no steps have been taken to try to remove) (3.110, 5.151);

(c) Ground 14 concerns nuisance, annoyance and convictions, as extended by the Housing Act 1996 (3.101);

(d) Ground 14A is the domestic violence ground (3.109);

(e) Ground 15 concerns condition of furniture, with the same qualification in the case of default by someone residing in the premises other than the tenant (3.110, 5.151);

(f) Ground 16 concerns service tenancies (1.148–1.158): it is available when the property was let to the tenant in consequence of his employment, and he has ceased to be in that employment;

(g) Ground 17 concerns tenancies induced by a false statement (3.112).

(iii) *Related issues*

4.121 Forfeiture. In the case of a fixed-term tenancy which contains a forfeiture clause (4.73), the court can only make an order for possession on the discretionary grounds in Sch.2, Pt II, other than Grounds 9 or 16, or Grounds 2 or 8 of the mandatory grounds in Sch.2, Pt I (1988, s.7), and then only if the forfeiture clause itself permits the lease to be ended on that ground.

4.122 The landlord does not need to bring a parallel claim for forfeiture, nor do the provisions for relief from forfeiture (1.131) apply: *Artesian Residential Developments Ltd v Beck*, 1999.

4.123 Misrepresentation. Where possession is ordered on any Ground, and it can later be shown that the order was obtained by misrepresentation or concealment of a material fact, the landlord can be ordered to compensate the tenant (1988, s.12).

4.124 Anti-social behaviour. Registered social landlords are in some circumstances able to secure the attachment of a power of arrest to an order sought in relation to anti-social conduct (1996, Pt V): this has been described above (3.180).

Rent and other terms

1. STARTING RENTS

4.125 Periodic tenancy. The starting-point of such rent control as is applicable to assured tenancies is that what has been agreed is payable; there is no concept analogous to "registered rents" under the Rent Act 1977 (Chapter 5), by which an existing registration might override the rent agreed at the commencement of the tenancy.

4.126 Fixed-term tenancy. In the case of a fixed-term assured tenancy, there is no means for varying the rent, other than as the agreement itself provided, until such time as the agreement becomes a statutory periodic tenancy (4.74).

4.127 Statutory periodic tenancy. Under a statutory periodic tenancy, the terms are *prima facie* the same as under the fixed-term, and its periods are the same as those for which rent was paid under the fixed-term (1988, s.5).

4.128 Within one year of the termination of the fixed-term, however, either the landlord or the tenant may serve notice on the other, in prescribed form, proposing different terms and, if considered appropriate, a variation of rent to reflect the variation of terms (1988, s.6).

4.129 Once such a notice has been served, the landlord or the tenant on whom it has been served has three months within which to refer it to a rent assessment committee (5.204; *N.B.* not the rent officer; rent officers have no role in relation to rent-fixing for assured tenancies) (1988, s.6).

4.130 If the notice is not so referred, then the proposed terms, and rent, become the terms (and rent) of the statutory periodic tenancy (1988, s.6(3)).

4.131 If there is a reference, the rent assessment committee has to consider the proposed terms, and determine whether they, or some other term (dealing only with the same subject-matter as the terms proposed) might reasonably be expected to be found in an assured periodic tenancy of such a property, presuming:

(a) That the tenancy began on the coming to the end of the former, fixed-term; and

(b) That the tenancy was granted by a willing landlord on the terms (other than those now under review) that apply to that tenancy (1988, s.6(4)).

4.132 The committee has to disregard the fact that there is a sitting tenant (1988, s.6(6))

4.133 Even if the notice proposing the new terms did not include a proposal for the variation of rent to reflect them, the committee is entitled to adjust the rent to take account of the adjustment of the terms (1988, s.6(5)).

4.134 Unless the landlord and tenant agree otherwise, the committee decides when the new terms and rent apply from, save that in the case of the rent, it cannot specify a date which is earlier than any proposed in the original notice (1988, s.6(7)).

4.135 The committee is not bound to continue with the process, if the landlord and the tenant give notice in writing that they do not wish it to do so; nor need it continue if the tenancy ends before it reaches its determination (1988, s.6(8)).

2. VARIATION OF RENTS

4.136 In the case of a periodic assured tenancy, or in the case of a statutory periodic tenancy to which the foregoing provisions (4.127–4.134) do not apply, *e.g.* because no variation of terms is proposed or because the one-year time-limit from the expiry of the previous fixed-term has passed, a variation of rent procedure applies, although it can only be initiated by a landlord seeking an increase (1988, s.13).

4.137 This procedure is not available, however, if the periodic tenancy (not being a statutory periodic tenancy following a fixed-term) itself contained its own provisions for determining increases, *e.g.* a procedure by which the landlord can increase it, an index-linked formula, or reference to arbitration (1988, s.13(1)).

4.138 Statutory process for increase of rent. To obtain an increase by the statutory process—when applicable (periodic tenancy without its own provisions, or statutory periodic following fixed-term)—the landlord must serve notice on the tenant, in the prescribed form, proposing a new rent to take effect at the beginning of a period of the tenancy. The period must itself commence no earlier than:

(a) The minimum period (4.139) after service of the notice; and

(b) Other than in the case of a statutory period tenancy, the first anniversary of the date on which the tenancy began; and

(c) If there has been a previous increase under the statutory process, the first anniversary of the date on which that increase took effect (1988, s.13(2)).

(Note: because the effect of this formulation has commonly been to have to push back rent increases to 53 weeks, where 52 weeks would be sooner than the first anniversary limitation, it is anticipated that these provisions will be amended in the near future).

4.139 The "minimum period" is six months in the case of a yearly tenancy, one month in the case of a tenancy the periods of which are less than a month, *e.g.* weekly or four-weekly, or in any other case (*e.g.* quarterly tenancy, six monthly tenancy) one period of the tenancy (1988, s.13(3)).

4.140 Effect of notice. The new rent will take effect unless before the beginning of the (minimum) period specified, the tenant refers the notice to a rent assessment committee, by application in the prescribed form, or else the landlord and the tenant agree a different rent (1988, s.13(4)).

4.141 Decision. If the rent is referred to a rent assessment committee, the committee has to decide:

- What rent the property concerned might reasonably be expected to obtain on the open market;
- By a willing landlord letting an assured tenancy of the same periods;
- Beginning at the period specified in the notice;
- The terms (other than rent) of which are the same, and
- In respect of which the same notices under Sch.2, Grounds 1–5 (mandatory grounds for possession, 4.88–4.96) have been served (1988, s.14(1)).

4.142 Disregards. The committee must disregard the fact that there is a sitting tenant.

4.143   The committee must also disregard:

- Any increase attributable to a "relevant improvement" by a person who—at the time it was carried out—was the tenant (not necessarily the current tenant), and

- Any reduction in value attributable to the tenant's failure to comply with the terms of his tenancy (the tenant's failure only applies to the current tenant and not any predecessor: *N & D (London) Ltd v Gadson*, 1991) (1988, s.14(2)).

4.144   An improvement is not to be disregarded, *i.e.* is not "relevant", if it was an improvement which the tenant was required to do under a term of the tenancy or any other "obligation" to the landlord (unless the obligation arose as a condition of consent given by the landlord on a request by the tenant to execute works) (1988, s.14(2)).

4.145   A "relevant improvement" is otherwise one carried out during the current tenancy, or carried out no more than 21 years before the date of service of the notice proposing the rent increase, during which 21 years the property has always been subject to an assured tenancy on the termination of which the tenant (or if joint tenants, one of them) did not quit (1988, s.14(3)).

4.146   These are the only improvements to be disregarded: the tenant will have to pay for others, by way of increased rent.

4.147   **Powers of committee.** When determining rent, the rent assessment committee is not concerned with any service charge within the Landlord and Tenant Act 1985 (2.75) (1988, s.14(4)), as this can be referred to a leasehold valuation tribunal under that Act, and must determine a rent which exclusive of rates (1988, s.13(5)).

4.148   If there are both a notice seeking an increase in rent and a notice proposing a variation of terms (4.127–4.135) before the committee at the same time, and the notice proposing a variation of terms specifies a date no later than the proposed rent increase, the committee is entitled to hear the applications together, and when it does so is bound to decide the variation of terms before it decides the new rent (1988, s.14(6)).

4.149   Unless the landlord and the tenant otherwise agree, the new rent takes effect from the date specified in the notice of increase unless it appears to the committee that this would cause undue hardship, in which case the committee may determine a later date (but no later than their decision): 1988, s.14(7).

4.150 The committee is not bound to continue with the process if the landlord and the tenant give notice in writing that they do not wish it to do so; nor need it continue if the tenancy ends before it reaches its determination (1988, s.14(8)).

3. OTHER TERMS

4.151 Access. It is an implied term of all assured tenancies that the tenant should afford to the landlord access to the property and all reasonable facilities for executing repairs which the landlord is entitled to execute (1988, s.16; 11.34).

4.152 Assignment and subletting. With two exceptions, all assured periodic tenancies are subject to a prohibition on assignment of the tenancy, in whole or part, and on subletting under the tenancy in whole or part, without the consent of the landlord (1988, s.15(1)).

4.153 In the case of this implied prohibition, there is no qualification that the landlord's consent cannot unreasonably be withheld (1988, s.15(2); 1.175).

4.154 The first exception is if the tenancy agreement itself contains a prohibition, whether absolute or qualified (1.175, 1.224), in which case it is the agreement which determines what rights there are, not the Act. The second is if a premium is paid on the grant or renewal of the tenancy (1988, s.15(3)). "Premium" has the same meaning as under the Rent Act 1977 (1988, s.15(4); 5.216–5.224).

Further Financial Protection and Assistance

4.155 Right to acquire. The assured tenants of registered social landlords have the right to acquire their dwelling if it was provided with "public money", *i.e.* it was funded in whole or in part by social housing grant (paid by the Housing Corporation) or was transferred to the registered social landlord from a landlord whose tenants are secure (3.28) (Housing Act 1996, s.16).

4.156 Operation. The right to acquire essentially mirrors the right to buy (3.183–3.195), save that the Secretary may adapt or modify the provisions (see Housing Act 1996, s.17 and SI 1997/619).

4.157 Miscellaneous provisions. To avoid other forms of exploitation of tenants, or ways of extracting more money from them than permitted, there are other forms of financial protection which may be applicable. In addition, housing benefits are as available for assured tenants as for secure tenants (see 3.265). (Unlike under the Rent Acts, there is no prohibition on premiums and deposits under the Housing Act 1988: *cf.* 5.216–5.227).

4.158 We shall therefore consider:

(i) Accommodation agency charges; and,
(ii) Resale of utilities, *i.e.* gas and electricity.

4.159 Accommodation agency charges. Under the Accommodation Agencies Act 1953, it is a criminal offence either to demand or to accept any payment either for registering or undertaking to register the name and requirements of a person seeking a tenancy of premises.

4.160 It is also an offence under the same Act to demand or accept a payment simply for supplying or undertaking to supply addresses or other particulars of premises to let.

4.161 In *Saunders v Soper*, 1975, it was held that the purpose of the latter provision was to prohibit payments made simply for supplying addresses and particulars of property to let and that it did not prohibit payment for actually finding somewhere for the prospective tenant to live.

4.162 It follows that an illegal payment has been made, and is therefore recoverable by the tenant, if the payment is made simply for the provision of addresses. It is also illegal if made for the provision of addresses even though expressed to be returnable if the tenant does not accept a tenancy through the services of the agency. The payment is not illegal, however, if made after a tenancy has been found and accepted.

4.163 As well as constituting offences, such payments can be recovered as civil debts within six years of the payment being made (Limitation Act 1980).

4.164 Resale of utilities. The public electricity suppliers are entitled to publish a tariff, which may differ from area to area, indicating the maximum amounts which may be charged for the resale of electricity. This will usually be a figure that permits the landlord a small profit per unit, to cover, among other things, the cost of renting the electricity meter which monitors the occupier's use.

4.165 The public gas suppliers are under a duty to fix such maximum prices.

4.166 In either case, the amounts overcharged are recoverable by the occupier as a civil debt.

CHAPTER FIVE

Rent Act Protected Tenancies

Introduction

5.01 In this Chapter, we shall examine the Rent Act 1977 ("1977") protected tenancy, the rights of the protected tenant to security of tenure and regulation of rent, and some further financial protection.

5.02 No new Rent Act protected tenancies. Subject to a limited number of exceptions, it has not been possible to create any new Rent Act protected tenancies since the commencement of Pt I, Housing Act 1988 ("1988"), January 15, 1989.

5.03 It follows that in this Chapter what is discussed either actually is, or is derived from, a letting arrangement that is some years old. It remains necesary to consider the Rent Acts, however, for a number of reasons.

- Tenancies can last not mere years, nor even mere decades, but generations. Although they will overwhelmingly have "settled down" as Rent Act protected tenancies (rather than, *e.g.* licences or holiday lettings or one of the other, sometime well-known devices for defeating Rent Act protection that have been largely replaced since 1980 by security-free "shorthold" lettings—see 4.04, 6.99), there are still many people who occupy under them.

- Much residential security and rent law—perhaps most of it—was developed under the Rents Act. (They were the governing form of residential security from 1915 until 1988). Often, it is only a subordinate part of a Rent Act decision which is still relevant; nonetheless, it cannot be fully comprehended without the context. (Thus, the proposition that for a room to be let as a separate dwelling, it had to comprise—in particular—cooking facilities was "received wisdom" even under Housing Act security— 3.17, 4.16—until critically examined in its original Rent Act context in 2001, see *Uratemp Ltd v Collins*).

5.04 This Chapter will accordingly read somewhat differently than earlier and later Chapters. There is less detail about how an original Rent Act protected tenancy comes into being, and other information that is unlikely today to be of much relevance; and, because its purpose is in part to retain the origins of residential security (and rents) law, even what is left is of less obvious practical relevance. Nonetheless, it may safely be asserted that no one involved in private sector housing advice or action will work for long before needing to come to grips with the tenure.

Outline

5.05 General principles

- Subject to exceptions, there have been no new protected Rent Act tenancies since January 15, 1989 (commencement of Pt I, 1988 Act).

- Security under the Rent Acts applies to private landlords, not social landlords.

- Landlords have used a number of mechanisms to try and avoid security under the Rent Acts, in particular licences, but also holiday lettings and company lettings, although they are of decreasing importance with the passage of time.

- In deciding whether an agreement such as a licence evades Rent Act protection it is necessary to look at its substance and reality, not its form.

- There are two types of full-security tenancy under the Rent Act: protected tenancies:
  - Those where the contract for the tenancy has not terminated; and,
  - Statutory tenancies, which arise on termination of the contractual protected tenancy.

- A spouse can on the death of a protected or statutory tenancy succeed to a statutory tenancy, provided there has been no previous succession.

- If there has been a previous succession, a spouse may succeed to an assured tenancy under the Housing Act 1988 ("1988").

- It there is no spouse entitled to succeed, a member of the family can succeed to an assured tenancy under the Housing Act 1988.

5.06   Rent Act Protected Tenants

- A tenant to whom a dwelling house was let as a separate dwelling prior to January 15, 1989, will be a protected tenant unless one of a number of exclusions applies.

- A protected tenant cannot be evicted unless the contractual tenancy is first brought to an end.

- Once the contractual tenancy is brought to an end a statutory tenancy will arise, provided the tenant occupies the dwelling as his residence.

- A court may only order possession of a protected or statutory tenancy on one of the grounds set out in the 1977 Act.

- Some grounds require the court to be satisfied that it is reasonable to grant possession, which are known as the discretionary grounds, while others are mandatory.

- A protected shorthold tenant is a particular type of protected tenancy, granted under Housing Act 1980. This was a precursor to the 1988 assured shorthold tenancy (4.04). Because, subject only to technical requirements, this meant that the tenant could be easily evicted after an initial two-year period, this conferred only limited security and it is therefore considered in Chapter 6.

5.07   Protection of rents and other financial protection and assistance

- Rent Act protected tenants may apply for a fair rent to be registered.

- A fair rent is a market rent adjusted for scarcity and the statutory disregards.

- A fair rent is initially set by a rent officer.

- In assessing the fair rent, the officer must ignore any scarcity of accommodation in the area and the personal circumstances of the tenant but must take into account the age, character, locality and state of repair of the dwelling.

- Once a fair rent has been registered, it applies to any subsequent Rent Act protected tenancy of the same premises.

- Applications can be made by either the landlord or the tenant to review a fair rent every two years.

- Appeals against the rent registered can be made to the Rent Assessment Committee.

- It is illegal to charge a premium on the grant, continuance or renewal of a Rent Act Protected tenancy.

General Principles

1.   EXCEPTIONS AND EVASIONS

5.08   Exceptions. Notwithstanding the general rule that there can be no new protected tenancies after commencement of Pt I, 1988 Act (5.02), there can be a new Rent Act protected tenancy created on or after January 15, 1989, if either:

(a) **Pre-Act contract.** It was entered into pursuant to a contract for its grant which preceded that date; or

(b) **New tenancy to former tenancy.** It is the grant of a new tenancy (not necessarily of the same premises) to a person who was a former protected or statutory (5.24) tenant of the same landlord, or one of a number of joint (1.193– 1.207) protected or statutory tenants (not including a shorthold tenant (6.99)); or

(c) **Suitable alternative accommodation.** It is the grant of a tenancy resulting from an order for possession on the ground of suitable alternative accommodation (5.170), the premises in question are those which the court has found suitable, and the court directs that the new tenancy should be a protected tenancy because it considers that an assured tenancy (Chapter 4) would not afford sufficient security of tenure; or

(d) **New town corporation to private ownership.** It falls within a small class of tenancy formerly held by a new town development corporation, and passed into the private sector prior to March 31, 1996: 1988, s.34.

5.09   New tenancies normally Housing Act assured. Tenancies granted on or after the commencement of Pt I of the 1988 Act are, subject to its own schedule of exclusions, likely to be assured tenancies, and are considered in Chapter 4.

5.10   Tenants only. Only tenants can enjoy full Rent Act protection, not trespassers or licensees (see, *e.g. Marcroft Wagons v Smith*, 1951), nor, except as described in Chapter 2, owner-occupiers.

5.11   Landlord and Tenant Act 1987, Pt I. Rent Act protected tenants are included as "qualifying" tenants for the purposes of Pt I of the Landlord and Tenant Act 1987, *i.e.* the "right of first refusal" (2.33–2.45).

5.12   Private tenants. In the main, tenants whose landlords are not public bodies, such as local authorities, nor quasi-public bodies, such as housing trusts and registered social landlords, will be Rent Act protected tenants provided that their landlords do not live in the same building as themselves.

5.13   This short description can, however, be misleading, as some who would appear to qualify will not be Rent Act protected tenants, and others who would appear to be excluded may, for one reason or another, in fact enjoy full Rent Act protection.

5.14   Business lettings. As with Housing Act secure tenancies, business tenancies are excluded from protection (1977, s.24): see 3.39(n).

5.15   Agricultural and forestry workers. Under the Rent (Agriculture) Act 1976 ("1976"), protection largely similar to that to be described in this Chapter is available to agricultural and forestry tied workers whose rights of occupation precede the commencement of Pt I of the 1988 Act (January 15, 1989), *i.e.* those living in accommodation belonging to their employers (1.42–1.59).

5.16   It is not possible in this book to consider the 1976 Act in any detail, but the same points made in relation to assured agricultural occupancies are relevant here (4.52).

5.17   Rent Acts and evasion. Landlords commonly sought to avoid the effects of Rent Act protection by granting forms of letting which were not within the ambit of the 1977 Act.

5.18   The most common form of evasion was the licence agreement: we have already considered one form of licence, the non-exclusive occupation agreement (1.209–1.215). We have also considered how the law approaches the task of interpreting an agreement as licence or tenancy (1.69–1.73).

5.19 Substance and reality. In relation to the Rent Acts:

> "It has been said before, and it must be said again, that in the consideration of questions arising under the Rent Acts, the court must look at the substance and reality of a transaction, not its form . . ." (Viscount Simonds, *Elmdene Estates v White*, 1960).

5.20 In an earlier case, *Samrose Properties v Gibbard*, 1958, Lord Evershed M.R., said that a court must always ask itself:

> ". . . Whether the transaction, viewed as a whole and according to the substance of it, is in truth one which . . . is on that side of the line which frees the premises from the impact of the Acts, or whether, so regarded, the transaction is one which is of the mischief which the Acts were designed to avoid."

5.21 More recently, it has been said that:

> "the manufacture of a five pronged implement for manual digging results in a fork even if the manufacturer, unfamiliar with the English language, insists that he intended to make and has made a spade . . . The court should . . . be astute to detect and frustrate sham devices and artificial transactions whose only object is to disguise the grant of a tenancy and to evade the Rent Acts." (*Street v Mountford*, 1986. In *AG Securities v Vaughan, Antoniades v Villiers*, 1988, Lord Templeman said that the word "pretence" should be substituted for sham devices and artificial transactions).

5.22 In this Chapter, two further pretences, to which the same general principles are applicable, are considered in their most appropriate contexts: holiday lettings (5.84) and company lets (5.108).

5.23 The over-riding principle should look always be borne in mind: look at what the parties factually intended to be the arrangement (by which is meant what the law understands the parties to have intended), not how they have described it.

2. STATUTORY TENANCIES

5.24 **Protected and statutory tenancy.** The term Rent Act protected tenant technically refers to a tenant within Rent Act protection who is still a contractual tenant (1977, s.1), *i.e.* one whose contract of tenancy has not come to an end in one of the ways described (1.108–1.141).

5.25 This reflects the somewhat different approach to security under the Rent Acts than under the Housing Act 1985 ("1985", 3.61) and the Housing Act 1988 (4.72), where termination of the tenancy contract can only be effected by the courts. After the termination of a contractual Rent Act protected tenancy under the 1977 Act, security of tenure operates by providing a right to remain or "status of irremovability" which is known as a statutory tenancy (1977, s.2) and which the tenant can enjoy so long as he continues to occupy the property as "a" residence (not necessarily "only or principal" or "only or main").

5.26 If there were joint contractual tenants, each will acquire the personal right of statutory tenancy (*Daejan Properties Ltd v Mahoney*, 1995), and if only one remains, he will be able to sustain it alone (*Lloyd v Sadler*, 1978).

5.27 **Terms of statutory tenancy.** A statutory tenancy continues on exactly the same terms as the prior contractual tenancy save where such terms would be inconsistent with the idea of statutory tenancy (1977, s.3), for example a requirement to yield up vacant possession on termination of the contractual tenancy, or a right to assign or sublet the whole of the premises (*Keeves v Dean*, 1924; *Atyeo v Fardoe*, 1978), and save as regards rent which, obviously, may be increased as the years pass (5.213).

5.28 **Expiry of contractual tenancy.** The distinction between a contractual tenancy and a statutory tenancy may not be without importance as regards both security of tenure and rent regulation. This is especially so if the contractual tenancy is a fixed-term tenancy.

5.29 Before any court proceedings to evict the tenant can be brought on one or other of the grounds described below, the contractual tenancy must have been brought to an end (1.108–1.141). Even if a tenant is in arrears of rent, then it will be necessary for the landlord to forfeit a fixed-term agreement, or serve valid notice to quit. Unless he does so, then no matter how great the tenant's default, the proceedings will be defective and no order will be made. (Note: the tenancy must have expired by the date proceedings are commenced, not just by the date of hearing).

5.30 Fixed term and rent. The tenant may be able to derive an advantage as regards rent from a lengthy fixed-term tenancy. Even if the registered rent increases, the landlord will still be limited by the contractual rent, until such time as he can bring the contractual tenancy to an end: in the case of a fixed term they may not be for some time. (Note: for this reason, many fixed-term agreements came to say that the contractual rent would be a particular sum or the registered rent, if that is higher. Such a clause is valid).

5.31 Periodic tenancy and rent. In the case of a periodic tenancy, however, a notice of increase of rent can double as a notice to quit so as to bring the tenancy to an end and allow a higher rent than originally agreed to be charged. To operate dually in this way, a notice of increase must be in the proper form (*Aristocrat Property Investments v Harounoff*, 1982) and specify a date for the increase to take effect no earlier than a notice to quit could have taken effect (1.111–1.114). It will then have the effect of converting the contractual tenancy into a statutory tenancy (1977, s.49).

5.32 Termination of statutory tenancy. Once the contractual tenancy has been brought to an end, howsoever this is done, there is no need for any further notice to be served to bring the subsequent statutory tenancy to an end before bringing proceedings, even if there is a gap of several years between termination and commencement of proceedings. No new contractual tenancy comes into being unless there is evidence that such was intended, *e.g.* because the landlord and the tenant agreed to vary some term of the tenancy other than rent and it is sufficiently substantial to warrant description as a new tenancy (1.54). The tenant simply occupies as a statutory tenant until such time as a court orders possession to be given up to the landlord.

3. SUCCESSION

5.33 Statutory tenancy by succession. Normally, a tenant will be first a contractual tenant and subsequently a statutory tenant.

This may not be the case, however, when a protected tenant dies and his widow succeeds to the tenancy (1977, s.2). In such circumstances, the successor becomes a statutory tenant at once, and the terms are the same, save as already mentioned, as those of the contractual tenancy of the person to whom the new tenant has succeeded.

5.34 Rent Act succession to Housing Act assured tenancy. Succession to a tenancy where the tenant died on or after the commencement of Pt I of the 1988 Act (January 15, 1989) is subject to the following rules.

(a) **Priority to spouse.** If the tenant who died was married, his spouse will have priority in the succession, provided she was living in the dwelling-house at the time of his death, but for this purpose the terms marriage and spouse includes a couple living together as husband and wife (1977, Sch.1, para.2, as amended by 1988, s.37 and Sch.4).

(b) **Member of family.** If there is no spouse to succeed, then any member of the family who was residing in the dwelling-house at the time of the tenant's death and for two years beforehand is entitled to succeed to the tenancy, but the tenancy will be a Housing Act assured tenancy (Chapter 4), not a Rent Act protected or statutory tenancy (1977, Sch.1, para.3, as amended).

(c) **Death of spouse successor.** On the death of a successor spouse, a member of the family (of both the original tenant and the successor) residing in the dwelling-house at the time of the successor's death and for two years beforehand is entitled to a "second succession," but likewise only to a Housing Act assured tenancy (1977, Sch.1, para.6, as amended).

5.35 Deemed residence. There were transitional provisions governing deaths within the first 18 months following the commencement of Pt I of the 1988 Act, under which a member of the family residing with the deceased for six months before the commencement date was treated as having resided for two years. "Residing" means more than staying at an address, even if the quality of the residence is not permanent or indefinite (*Swanbrae Ltd v Elliott*, 1986, *Hildebrand v Moon*, 1989).

5.36 Cohabitation. Prior to amendment by the Housing Act 1988, when persons living together as husband and wife were specifically defined as spouses, it had been held that a cohabitant of long standing could be treated as a member of the family for the purpose of succession: *Dyson Holdings v Fox*, 1976, *Watson v Lucas*, 1980 (even though still legally married to someone else). A lengthy period of cohabitation may not be needed if there is additional supporting evidence of the nature of the relationship (*Chios Investment (Property) Co v Lopez*, 1987), but in *Helby v Rafferty*, 1979, a man failed in his claim to succeed to his cohabitant's tenancy—they had been together only five years, lived relatively independent lives, and she retained her own name.

5.37 A couple of the same sex cannot be considered "husband and wife" (*Harrogate BC v Simpson*, 1984; *Fitzpatrick v Sterling HA*, 1999).

5.38 Member of the family. While a same sex couple cannot be considered husband and wife, they may be considered members of the same family: *Fitzpatrick*. Member of the family is not otherwise statutorily defined and may be given a wide meaning. It is not used in any technical sense, but in a popular sense (*Longdon v Horton*, 1951; *Brock v Wollams*, 1949). The hallmarks of family membership are essentially that there should be a degree of mutual interdependence, of the sharing of lives, of caring and love, of commitment and support. In respect of legal relationships these are presumed; in other relationships, these are capable, if proved, of creating membership of the tenant's family (*Fitzpatrick*).

Rent Act Protected Tenants

5.39 Two principal issues must be addressed:

1. Who qualifies as a Rent Act protected tenant; and,

2. Security of tenure.

1. WHO QUALIFIES AS A RENT ACT PRO-TECTED TENANT

5.40 Let as a separate dwelling. The Rent Act assumes that all tenants to whom property was let as a separate dwelling before the commencement of Pt I of the 1988 Act (January 15, 1989) are Rent Act protected tenants unless there is some factor which takes them out of protection (1977, s.1).

5.41 The phrase "as a separate dwelling" has been considered in relation both to secure tenancies (3.17) and assured tenancies

(4.16). Because of the provisions including sharers (5.71), it is of much less significance under the 1977 Act.

5.42   Exclusions. The exclusions from protection cover a range of matters.

(i) **Resident landlord.** In respect of tenancies commencing on or after August 14, 1974, whether the landlord lives in the same building or not (Rent Act 1977, s.12).

(ii) **Old furnished lettings and resident landlord.** In respect of tenancies commencing before August 14, 1974, whether the tenancy was considered to be a furnished tenancy in law before that date, and whether the landlord has lived in the same building or not since August 14, 1974 (1977, Sch.24).

(iii) **Sharing living accommodation with landlord.** Regardless of when the tenancy commenced, whether the tenant shares living accommodation with the landlord or not (1977, s.21);

(iv) **Attendances.** Whether the tenant is provided with attendances (1977, s.7).

(v) **Board.** Whether the tenant is provided with board (1977, s.7);

(vi) **Low rent.** Whether the rent is what the law knows as a "low rent" (1977, s.5).

(vii) **Student lettings.** Whether it is a student letting (1977, s.8).

(viii) **No rent.** Whether any rent is paid (1977, s.5).

(ix) **Holiday lettings.** Whether it is a holiday letting (1977, s.9).

(x) **Identity of landlord.** The identity of the landlord (1977, ss.13–16).

(xi) **High rateable value.** The rateable value of the premises (1977, s.4).

(xii) **Agricultural land.** Whether the property qualifies as an agricultural holding (1977, s.10).

(xiii) **Other land.** Whether the letting is with other land (exceeding two acres) (1977, ss.6, 26).

(xiv) **Shared ownership leases.** Whether the letting qualifies as a shared ownership lease, as defined (1977, s.5A).

(xv) **Licensed premises**. Whether the premises qualify as licensed premises (1977, s.11).

5.43 The last four of these do not require further consideration.

(i) *Tenancies commencing on or after August 14, 1974*

5.44 Resident landlord. When the Rent Act 1974 came into operation on August 14, 1974, it brought with it two major changes. One was that it extended full Rent Act protection to the tenants of furnished accommodation who had hitherto been excluded (but enjoyed restricted security: 6.64).

5.45 The other change was to substitute a new class of tenancy subject to the lesser jurisdiction of the Rent Tribunal: those were tenants with resident landlords, as defined. The definition applies where the landlord and the tenant occupy different parts of the same building (not being a purpose-built block of flats), or else (even if a purpose-built block of flats), that they occupy different parts of the same flat. These conditions are defined in the same way as under the Housing Act 1988 (4.47).

5.46 Continuous residence. For a landlord to take advantage of this exception, he must establish that (subject to the provisions governing change of landlord described below), he has at all times since the commencement of the tenancy used the other part of the building which he occupies as a residence (1977, s.12).

5.47 Use as a residence. Legal residence is discussed in greater detail below (5.96–5.112), as the same test applies to the question whether a statutory tenant has sufficient residence to maintain his right to the statutory tenancy (1977, Sch.2).

5.48 Briefly, residence means that premises are being used as a home, even if not the only home. A person may for short periods cease to use premises as a residence and still be treated as sustaining legal residence, provided both that he fully intends to return to live in the premises, and that he has left some physical sign of occupation in the premises, *e.g.* furniture, belongings, family.

5.49 The law accepts that a person may have more than one residence at a time, but a purely token residence will not suffice: a landlord cannot simply keep one room in a house, or in several houses, in order to keep his tenants out of protection.

5.50   The question that must be asked is not whether at all times the landlord has been in residence, or has resided in the part kept for himself, but whether the premises have been a legal residence of the landlord throughout the period in question, *i.e.* since the start of the tenancy.

5.51   When both landlord and tenant moved house together, over a period of about a week, the fact that the landlord happened not to move in until after the tenant did not disqualify him from claiming residence, as he had both the intention to move in, of which there were already signs (*O'Sullivan v Barnett*, 1994). This accords with the usual test of statutory residence (5.96–5.112).

5.52   It is likely that residence by one of two or more joint owners/landlords would be considered to be enough to keep the tenant out of protection (*cf.* 4.49).

5.53   Corporate landlords. Because of this requirement for residence, however, a corporate landlord, *i.e.* a landlord which is a company, a trust, a partnership, etc. cannot "reside" at all because such a landlord has no natural life (*Hiller v United Dairies (London)*, 1934).

5.54   Change of resident landlord. If a landlord sells the house, residence will nonetheless be treated as continuing for a further 28 days. If, during that time, the new owner serves notice that he intends to move into the premises for use as a home, then he has a total of six months in which to do so, during which period residence by the landlord will likewise be treated as continuing (1977, Sch.2).

5.55   If, by the end of the six months, the new owner has not taken up residence, the tenant will become a Rent Act protected tenant and will so remain, even when the owner moves in, for there will not have been continual residence since the start of the tenancy.

5.56   Termination of contractual tenancy during period of disregard. If the contractual tenancy comes to an end within this period, on the one hand no statutory tenancy will arise but on the other, the landlord cannot during this period evict other than as if the tenant was a statutory tenant (1977, Sch.2). In these circumstances, even if he has not moved in, provided he gets a court order (Chapter 8) the (new) landlord can at the end of the period simply evict (*Landau v Sloane*, 1981).

5.57 Death of resident landlord. The position is somewhat different on the death of a resident landlord. In such circumstances, the executors effectively have two years in which the fact that there is no resident landlord will be disregarded (1977, Sch.2). The two periods (two years under this paragraph, six months above) may be added together (*Williams v Mate*, 1982). During this period, the landlord's executors may freely evict (5.56).

5.58 Former tenancy in same building. In certain circumstances, a tenant who would appear to have been excluded from protection because of a resident landlord, may in fact be protected.

5.59 A landlord with good knowledge of the law might have been able to take protection away from a tenant, by moving into a house in which there is an existing protected tenant and offering him a new tenancy of the same or another part of the building, so as to claim that since the start of that tenancy, he has been resident.

5.60 The Rent Act 1977, s.12 provides that a tenant who was formerly a Rent Act protected tenant under a previous tenancy of the same or another part of the building remained a Rent Act protected tenant. This, however, is only so where the presence of the resident landlord would be the only reason for exclusion from protection, not where he is excluded for other reasons. (Likewise, it will not apply if he was not a protected tenancy under a previous tenancy, *i.e.* if he was excluded for some other reason—in particular, because the letting was furnished: 5.61).

(ii) *Tenancies commencing before August 14, 1974*

5.61 Old furnished lettings and resident landlords. The policy of the legislature is to allow people with protection to keep it (see also 5.60). It follows that questions can still arise as to whether or not the tenant was protected before the Rent Act 1974 came into force (*Mann v Cornella*, 1980). If not, then the question is whether there has been a resident landlord since that date, in the same way as already described, with the substitution of August 14, 1974 for the commencement of the tenancy (5.44–5.60).

5.62 Furnished lettings. Deciding whether or not premises were protected prior to August 14, 1974 is not easy business. The class exempted from protection was that of furnished tenancies.

5.63 The law did not, however, treat any amount of furniture, however small, as taking a tenant out of protection. The landlord had to provide enough furniture that the value to the tenant of the furniture formed a substantial proportion of the whole rent paid under the tenancy. (Note: it is the value to the tenant which has to be calculated, in calculating which regard may be had to the social conditions prevailing at the time, *i.e.* the fact that the tenant lost the valuable asset of a protected tenancy, while the landlord gained the ability to evict his tenant with little or no difficulty, so that even a lot of furniture could have little actual value to the tenant: *Woodward v Docherty*, 1974).

5.64 Valuation involves a valuation of the furniture, with a proportion (usually 20 per cent) representing a fair return to the landlord. This sum must then be compared to the rent, ascertained as at the commencement of the tenancy. Courts will normally view anything over 20 per cent as substantial, anything between 15 per cent and 20 per cent as probably substantial, anything between 15 per cent and 10 per cent as possibly substantial, and anything below 10 per cent as insubstantial (see *Nelson Developments Ltd v Toboada*, 1992).

5.65 Furniture or landlord's residence. If the tenancy—approached thus—was furnished, then it was not protected and, as noted (5.61), the test is whether the resident landlord test has been fulfilled since August 14, 1974. If not, then it was protected, then the tenant remains protected, even though there has been a resident landlord in the building since August 14, 1974.

5.66 Neither insubstantial furniture nor want of residence will be relevant, however, if the tenant is excluded from protection by any of the conditions specified below (of which the next is of particular relevance).

(iii) *Sharing living accommodation with landlord*

5.67 Sharing living accommodation with landlord. If the tenant shares what the law recognises as living accommodation (3.17) with his landlord, then regardless of when the tenancy commenced, it will not be a protected tenancy (*Neale v Del Soto*, 1945).

5.68 This is so even if no furniture at all was provided under the tenancy, and even if the degree of residence by the landlord leaves in some doubt whether he qualifies as a resident landlord in the normal way. What is comprised in sharing is considered in relation to assured tenancies (4.19).

5.69 The mere empty retention of a right to share living accommodation, designed to defeat protection, would probably not succeed because it would essentially be a sham reservation (5.17).

5.70 Continuing relevance. This issue is extremely unlikely to arise in connection with a tenancy commencing after August 14, 1974, because it could only apply to a situation in which, on the one hand, the landlord used the premises, but, on the other, he did not establish sufficient residence to qualify as a resident landlord. It may, however, be relevant to an argument over whether or not the tenant was Rent Act protected at the beginning of the tenancy if the landlord took up residence shortly before August 14, 1974 and is trying to establish that the tenancy was not Rent Act protected at that date.

5.71 As with assured tenancy (4.17), the fact that a tenant is sharing living accommodation with other tenants only, does not affect protection at all (1977, s.22).

(iv) *Attendances*

5.72 Attendances. A tenancy will be a protected tenancy unless the tenant is, under the terms of the tenancy, provided with attendances, and the value to the tenant of the attendance forms a substantial proportion of the whole rent (1977, s.7). The substantiality test is the same as that applicable to of furniture and the same principles will apply, although attendances may be somewhat harder to value (5.63–5.64).

5.73 Personal services. Attendance means personal service performed in the premises in question, for the tenant, for example room cleaning, changing the sheets, doing the tenant's laundry, etc. (*Palser v Grinling*, 1948; *Nelson Developments Ltd v Taboada*, 1992).

5.74 Attendances do not include the provision of gas or electricity, or hot water, nor does it include cleaning of the common parts of a house in multiple occupation, *e.g.* hallways, stairs, bathroom, lavatory, etc. (*King v Millen*, 1922).

5.75 The provision of a resident housekeeper does not mean that of definition the tenant is provided with attendances, although it is likely. The full amount of the wages of the resident housekeeper should not be attributed to the tenants, as a whole, even apportioned between them, for the presence of a resident housekeeper is considered to be of value also to the landlord.

5.76 Window-cleaning is another service which is considered to be partly of value to the landlord and partly an attendance upon the tenant (*Engvall v Ideal Flats*, 1945).

Note

5.77 Within jurisdiction of rent tribunal. All tenants whose tenancies precede the commencement of Pt I of the 1988 Act (January 15, 1989) and who are excluded from protection for one of the reasons described above will be subject to the jurisdiction of the Rent Tribunal: Chapter 6.

(v) *Board*

5.78 Board. A tenant who, under the terms of his tenancy, is provided with any amount of board cannot be a Rent Act protected tenant.

5.79 Board means more than a mere morning cup of tea (*Wilkes v Goodwin*, 1923), but no more than a continental breakfast has been upheld as the provision of board for this purpose, provided that at least some services are involved in preparing it and it includes the provision of crockery and cutlery with which to eat it (*Otter v Norman*, 1988).

(vi) *Low rent*

5.80 Low rent. As under the Housing Act 1988, the 1977 Act is not designed to protect those who purchase long leases and pay only a small, annual ground rent (1977, s.5). A low rent is defined in the same way as under the 1988 Act (4.29).

(vii) *Student lettings*

5.81 Student lettings. A tenancy will not be protected if the landlord under the tenancy is a specified educational institution and the tenant is following or intends to follow a course of study at that or another specified educational institution (1977, s.8).

Note

5.82 Possible jurisdiction of rent tribunal. Tenants whose tenancies precede the commencement of Pt I of the 1988 Act (January 15, 1989) and who are excluded from protection for any one of the last three reasons described above may come within the jurisdiction of the Rent Tribunal: see Chapter 6.

(viii)   *No rent*

5.83   No rent. If no rent is paid under the terms of the tenancy, the tenancy cannot be protected (1977, s.5). The same issues as to the meaning of rent apply here, as under the 1988 Act (4.30).

(ix)   *Holiday lettings*

5.84   Holiday lettings. If the purpose of the tenancy was used as a holiday home, then the tenancy will not be protected (1977, s.9).

5.85   This is an exemption which has been widely used as a device to defeat the Rent Acts (see also 1.70, 4.38), and is considered in relation to the same exemption which arises under the 1988 Act (4.37).

(x)   *Identity of landlord*

5.86   Identity of landlord. The tenants of the following landlords will not be Rent Act protected:

> Local authorities,
>
> New Town corporations,
>
> Registered social landlords,
>
> Housing trusts,
>
> The Housing Corporation (1977, ss.14–15).

5.87   Most of these tenants will, however, if pre-Housing Act 1988, be secure tenants: see Chapter 3.

5.88   Tenants of the Crown and a government department will not be protected unless the property is under the management of the Crown Estate Commissioners (1977, s.13).

5.89   Tenants of a housing management co-operative (a body formed to manage or lease land belonging to, *e.g.* a local authority or housing association) will also not be protected (1977, s.16).

5.90   Other kinds of housing co-operative are usually registered social landlords and therefore exempt (1977, s.15).

(xi) *High rateable value*

5.91 High rateable value or rent. This exemption operates in the same way as under the 1988 Act (4.25). Under the 1977 Act this exception is presumed to be so unlikely to apply that it is assumed not to apply unless the landlord shows the contrary (1977, s.4(6)).

Note

5.92 No rent tribunal jurisdiction. None of the tenancies excluded from protection by any of the last three reasons referred to above will fall within the jurisdiction of the Rent Tribunal. They are, therefore, considered in Chapter 7.

2. SECURITY OF TENURE

5.93 Contractual Security. It has been noted (5.29) that no tenant can be evicted, whether lawfully in fact or by court proceedings, so long as the tenancy has not been brought to an end. In the case of a protected tenant, this means the contractual tenancy (5.24).

5.94 The contractual tenancy may have come to an end by expiry of a fixed-term, by notice to quit that complies with the conditions described, by forfeiture or by notice of increase (5.31). It is unlikely to have come to an end by surrender (1.122) if the tenant is still living in the premises.

5.95 Statutory tenancy. Once the contractual tenancy has come to an end, the tenant has an absolute right to continue living in the premises indefinitely and as a statutory tenant on, by and large, the same terms as under the contractual tenancy (1977, s.3) until:

(i)   The statutory tenancy itself terminates for want of continued residence; or

(ii) The premises become overcrowded in law, or are subject to a closing or demolition order because of their condition; or

(iii) The landlord establishes to a court that one of the stated sets of circumstances exists, as a result of which he is entitled to an order for possession; or

(iv) The premises are bought by one of the public or quasi-public landlords described above (5.86) and the tenant is removed from protection. (Note: the tenancy will usually then become a secure tenancy or in the case of registered social landlords, an assured tenancy: see Chapters 3 and 4).

(i)   *Statutory residence*

5.96   Statutory residence. The purpose of the Rent Act is to protect homes (*Skinner v Geary*, 1931). Once the contractual tenancy has come to an end, a statutory tenancy will only come into and remain in being so long as the tenant is in statutory residence.

5.97   This requires exactly the same degree of residence as a landlord must sustain in order to qualify as a resident landlord (5.47–5.53).

5.98   This applies only during a period of statutory tenancy. During the contractual tenancy there is no obligation at all upon a tenant to do so much as set foot in the premises, although one who fails to do so may have a hard time later proving his residence during the statutory period.

5.99   Regular and personal use. Statutory residence, for these purposes as for the purposes of resident landlords, must be continuous although, again, this does not mean that the tenant must constantly be living in the premises, although he must still be able to claim that the premises are in his use as a home, even if not as an only home. Use as a home means "a substantial degree of regular personal occupation by the tenant of an essentially personal nature" (*Herbert v Byrne*, 1964).

5.100   If a tenant is absent from premises for a longish period of time, for example (and at least) a few months, there may, on the face of it, be a claim that he has abandoned use of the premises as a home (*Brown v Brash*, 1948), and if sufficiently prolonged may put the tenant to having to prove continued residence (*Roland House Gardens v Cravitz*, 1974).

5.101   The tenant may nonetheless still be using the premises as a home, even if he is also using somewhere else in the same way. The question is whether the tenant is keeping on the premises in question "as a mere convenience" (*Beck v Sholz*, 1953) or whether in fact he is using both places as homes, even if he only visits one or other of them infrequently (*Langford Property Co v Tureman*, 1949).

5.102 Intention to return. Regardless of whether a person is laying claim to two homes or not, a person who absents himself from premises for a longish period of time can still claim to be a statutory tenant of them so long as he intends to return at some time in the future to use the premises as a home, and leaves in the premises some visible signs of that intention (*Brown v Brash*, 1948). There must be both: intention to return, and some indication of it.

5.103 A tenant who claims that he intends to return subject to a condition, *e.g.* works by the landlord, which he has no reasonable expectation of being fulfilled, will not be considered a statutory tenant (*Robert Thackray's Estate Ltd v Kaye*, 1988).

5.104 Indication of intention could be belongings or furniture, or even leaving a friend in occupation to, as it were, "keep the place warm." But simply leaving a friend in occupation without any intention to return to live there himself, will not be sufficient to allow them to maintain the claim to be a statutory tenant of the premises.

5.105 Residence and spouses. As an exception to the need to show intention to return, a tenant can be treated as still in occupation if he leaves his spouse living in the premises (*Wabe v Taylor*, 1952). This is, however, so only as long as the marriage lasts and will therefore cease to apply on decree absolute (*Metropolitan Properties Co v Cronan*, 1982; *Lewis v Lewis*, 1985).

5.106 A non-tenant abandoned spouse should therefore take steps to have the tenancy transferred into his name before divorce proceedings are concluded: see Chapter 9.

5.107 There is no continued residence without intention to return if the only sign of occupation is by a former cohabitant (*Colin Smith Music Ltd v Ridge*, 1974).

5.108 Residence and companies. As with residence by a landlord, neither a company nor any other "artificial" body can lay claim to residence (*Reidy v Walker*, 1933).

5.109 This requirement that the occupant should not be a corporate body has given rise to yet a further (1.209, 5.17), evasive device, which will only be defeated on the usual principles applicable to sham (5.17).

5.110 In this exercise, a landlord lets not to the tenant, but to a limited company, as whose licensee the tenant occupies (*Firstcross*

Ltd v East West Ltd, 1980; *Tetragon Ltd v Shidash Construction Co Ltd*, 1981; *Hilton v Plustitle Ltd*, 1988). In such a case, the court will probably only allow a statutory tenancy to arise if it believes that the company—to the landlord's knowledge—took as agent or nominee for the tenant, and even then this is not certain. The question to be asked in such a case is whether the company letting is genuine (*Kaye v Massbetter*, 1990).

5.111 Residence by another. In general, the courts will not permit abuse of the requirements of individual statutory residence by the Rent Act protected tenant by permitting the landlord to put the tenancy in one person's name but for the real use of another (*Cove v Flick*, 1954; *Dando v Hitchcock*, 1954), although it will only interfere to let the "true tenant" become the statutory tenant if the arrangement was a device (*Feather Supplies v Ingham*, 1971).

5.112 Thus, one person cannot suddenly step forward and say that he is the true tenant, and the named tenant no more than his agent, without this having been known to the landlord (*Hanstown Properties Ltd v Green*, 1977).

5.113 Effect of bankruptcy. As only the person who was the former Rent Act protected (*i.e.* contractual) tenant can become the statutory tenant, if the tenant goes bankrupt while it is still contractual, the contract of tenancy may vest in his trustee in bankruptcy. When then determined, the bankrupt cannot become the statutory tenant because immediately before determination he was not the tenant (*i.e.* the trustee was) (*Smalley v Quarrier*, 1975).

5.114 If, however, the contractual tenancy was determined before bankruptcy, it does not vest in the trustee because it is not a true tenancy but only a "status of irremovability" (*Jessamine Investments Co v Schwartz*, 1977). Accordingly, the bankrupt can remain in possession as a statutory tenant (*Sutton v Dorf*, 1932).

5.115 At one time, contractual tenancies invariably vested in the trustee. The position today is that Rent Act protected tenancies will not do so unless the trustee elects to adopt the tenancy (1988, s.117), and the bankrupt tenant will be permitted to retain the tenancy in his own name. This averts the worst effects of this rule while retaining the trustee's right to vest the contractual tenancy in himself, *e.g.* if the rent is too high.

5.116 Nor does this provision apply where the tenancy is one in respect of which a premium may lawfully be charged (5.216), *i.e.* because it has a value which the trustee can realise.

5.117 Cessation of residence. Once the statutory residence ceases, the statutory tenancy comes automatically to an end. However, the possibilities of a mistake being made, especially whether the property has been abandoned or it is merely a question of the tenant being absent for a while, especially by a landlord who may be eager to reclaim the premises, are so high that most landlords will commence proceedings for a court order for possession before seeking to take over the premises, and they are well advised to do so.

(ii) *Overcrowding and closing orders*

5.118 Housing conditions. Even if statutory residence is sustained, and even if the contractual tenancy has not been brought to an end, the Rent Act will not apply to premises which are subject to a closing (12.43) or demolition (12.49) order because they are unfit (12.17–12.22) or to premises which are being occupied by so many people that they are statutorily overcrowded (14.09–14.13).

5.119 Even where these exceptions apply, however, the landlord must still terminate the contractual tenancy before recovering possession (1.108–1.141: *Aslan v Murphy*, 1989).

(iii) *Grounds for possession*

5.120 Orders for possession. The most usual way for a person who does not voluntarily give up possession of premises subject to a Rent Act protected tenancy to leave the premises is because a court order for possession is made against him.

5.121 As under the Housing Act 1985 (3.81) and the Housing Act 1988 (4.83), the court may order possession only where the landlord makes out either a mandatory ground for possession (1977, s.98 and Sch.15, Pt II) or a discretionary ground for possession (1977, s.98 and Sch.15, Pt I), *i.e.* one where in addition to the provisions of the ground, the landlord must also provide that it is reasonable to make the order sought. Reasonableness has been considered in Chapter 3 (3.83–3.94).

5.122 Powers of court. In the case of discretionary grounds, the court's powers to suspend or vary an order are the same as under the 1985 and 1988 Acts (3.147; 1977, s.100); likewise, the court's powers are as limited as under those two Acts where no security attaches or a mandatory ground is available (1980, s.89: 3.145).

These powers may not only be exercised for the benefit of the tenant, but also for his spouse or ex-spouse (Chapter 9).

5.123 Mandatory grounds. There are 10 mandatory grounds for possession, *i.e.* those which, if proved, leave the court no alternative but to make an order for possession, to take effect within two to six weeks (depending on hardship, 3.145), regardless of whether or not it is reasonable to make the order.

5.124 Under the Rent Act 1977 the grounds for possession are known as "Cases" (*cf.* Chapters 3 and 4, as "Grounds" under the Housing Acts 1985 and 1988). The mandatory grounds are Cases 11–20. Cases 15–18 are special grounds, applicable to property occupied or formerly occupied by ministers of religion, or people employed in agriculture, and it is not neccesary to consider them any further here. Case 19 is shorthold (6.99–6.128). Cases 11, 12 and 20 may be considered as one group, Cases 13 and 14 as another.

5.125 Owner-occupiers. Case 11 is available to absentee owner-occupiers, *i.e.* someone who, before the letting, had occupied the premises as a residence, although it may be noted that for these purposes the landlord may himself be a tenant, yet still qualify as an "owner-occupier" in relation to his sub-tenant (*cf.* 4.88).

5.126 This Case is only available to a landlord who has served notice at the commencement of the tenancy, warning the tenant that the Case might be used against him, although the court has power, if it thinks it just and equitable to do so, to waive this requirement (see further 3.66, 4.91 and 5.131).

5.127 The Case is only available if the landlord has not let the property out since he last occupied the premises as a residence, other than on terms that include service of one such notice at commencement, although again this requirement may be waived by the court.

5.128 The requirement of former residence can be fulfilled by previous intermittent residence, or something less than permanent residence (*Naish v Curzon*, 1984). Such residence does not have to be as a home (*cf.* 5.99; *Mistry v Isidore*, 1990).

5.129 Retirement homes. Case 12 is available to a landlord who has bought property and intends to retire to it once he ceases regular employment.

5.130   Again, notice must have been served at the commencement of the tenancy warning the tenant that the Case might be used, and again the property must not have been let out to another since the landlord bought it, without the service of such a warning notice, although—again—in each case the court has power to waive the requirements, if just and equitable to do so.

5.131   The court should not exercise this power unless the tenant knew at the outset that he had only limited security, *i.e.* it should only be used where the failure was largely technical (*Bradshaw v Baldwin-Wiseman*, 1985; see also *White v Jones*, 1993). The fact that the occupiers signed licence agreements, which the landlord later conceded amounted to the grant of a tenancy, is not sufficient on its own to make it just and equitable to dispense with notice (*Ibie v Trubshaw*, 1990).

5.132   Member of armed forces. Case 20 is available to a landlord who, both at date of purchase and of letting, is a member of the armed forces: the same requirements of notice, both to tenant and to anyone else to whom the property has been let other than the present tenant, are imposed, though may be waived by the court, again in limited circumstances.

5.133   Applicability of additional criteria. Assuming that a landlord falls within one of these three Cases, he must go on to prove certain additional facts.

5.134   There are seven such additional facts, but they are not all equally available. Under Case 11, the landlord must be able to show the second, fourth, fifth, sixth or seventh; under Case 12, the landlord must be able to show the third, fourth, fifth, sixth or seventh; under Case 20, the landlord must be able to show the first, fourth, fifth, sixth or seventh.

5.135   The additional criteria. The additional factual qualifications are as follows.

(1) The property is required as a residence for the owner.

(2) The property is required as a residence for either the owner or for any member of his family who lived with him when last he occupied the property as a residence.

(3) The owner has retired from regular employment and requires the property as a residence.

(4) The owner has died, and the dwelling is required as a residence for a member of his family who was living with him at the time of his death.

(5) The owner has died, and the dwelling is required by his successor in title, either to live in, or to sell with vacant possession.

(6) The property is subject to a mortgage granted before the tenancy was granted, and the mortgagee requires vacant possession in order to sell the property under the power of sale, *i.e.* for default (by the landlord).

(7) The dwelling is not reasonably suitable to the needs of the owner, having regard to his place of work, and he wants to sell it with vacant possession and use the proceeds of sale to buy somewhere more suitable for himself (1977, Sch.15, Pt V, added by 1980, Sch.7).

5.136 Requirement for residence. Where the landlord is in fact two people, *i.e.* joint owners, the necessary qualifications can be fulfilled by just one of them (*Tilling v Whiteman*, 1980), so that, *e.g.* both do not need to show they want to come and live in the house.

5.137 In each case, the landlord need only show that he requires the property, rather than "reasonably requires" the property. "Requires" means no more than bona fide wants and genuinely intends to occupy as a residence either at once or at any rate within a reasonable time, but so wanted and intended whether reasonably or unreasonably, even from the landlord's point of view (*Kennealy v Dunne*, 1977).

5.138 Once his wish to return to the property has been established, it does not matter if the landlord can be shown to want to sell it as and when he can (*Lipton v Whitworth*, 1993).

5.139 Out of season holiday lettings. Case 13 applies where the letting is for a fixed term of not more than eight months; the tenant must have been given notice at the commencement of the letting that the Case could be used against him; and, within the 12 months preceding the commencement of the letting, the property was occupied under a holiday letting (5.84).

5.140 This Case dealt, in effect, with "out-of-season" holiday lettings. In view of the time requirement, although in theory someone could have remained in occupation as a statutory tenant since, it is extremely unlikely that it will be applicable to any current tenants and it has in practice expired.

5.141 Off-season student lettings. Case 14, concerned property normally used for student lettings (5.81). The letting in question had to be for a fixed term of not more than 12 months; the tenant had to have been given notice at the commencement of the letting that the Case may be used against him; and, within the 12 months preceding the commencement of the letting, the property was occupied under a student letting.

5.142 Again, for time reasons this Case has for all practical purposes expired.

5.143 Discretionary grounds. The discretionary grounds for possession are those in relation to which the court enjoys extensive powers (3.147), and in which the landlord must prove that it is reasonable to make the order, in addition to showing that the details of each Case are applicable (3.83).

5.144 Most of these grounds imply some degree of fault on the part of the tenant, although not all, and many have been reproduced in the Housing Act 1985 or the 1988 Act and have already been described.

5.145 Rent arrears and breach of term of tenancy. Case 1 is available where either the tenant is in arrears with his rent, or the tenant has broken a term of the tenancy (see 3.95–3.100, 4.120, *cf.* 4.117, 4.119).

5.146 Breach of a condition attached to a grant of consent to improve can constitute a breach of a term of the tenancy for these purposes (1980, s.83).

5.147 A clause limiting use to that of the tenant's residence will automatically and impliedly extend to allow residence by his partner (whether or not actually married) and family, in the absence of a clear prohibition to the contrary (*Blanway Investments Ltd v Lynch*, 1993).

5.148 Nuisance, annoyance, illegal or immoral user. Conviction for immoral, or illegal, user is also a ground for possession, as is nuisance and annoyance to adjoining occupiers (Case 2) (3.101, 4.120).

5.149 The nuisance or annoyance must be to an adjoining occupier but this does not mean that the occupier's property is necessarily physically contiguous: it means the same as "neighbour" (*Cobstone Investments Ltd v Maxim*, 1985).

5.150 This ground is narrower than the—recently (1996) extended—corresponding grounds in the Housing Acts 1985 (3.101) and 1988 (4.120).

5.151 Deterioration of premises or furniture. Cases 3 and 4 concern deterioration of the premises, or of any furniture provided by the landlord, attributable to the acts, neglect or default of the tenant, or someone living with him (3.110). (Note: unlike the 1985 and 1988 Acts these Cases do not cover deterioration of common parts or furniture situated in common parts).

5.152 Tenant's notice to quit. Case 5 is peculiar to the Rent Act and is available when the tenant has given notice to quit the premises, in consequence of which the landlord has contracted to sell or let the property, or has taken any other steps as a result of which he would be seriously prejudiced if the tenant were to remain.

5.153 For the Case to apply, the notice to quit must be wholly valid (1.111) (*De Vries v Smallridge*, 1927), which is relatively uncommon.

5.154 Assignment or sub-letting. Case 6 is available when the tenant, without the consent of the landlord, has assigned (1.223) or sub-let (1.163–1.184) the whole of the premises, whether the subletting is in one go, or bit by bit.

5.155 Commonly, although not inevitably, the tenant will in any event lose his statutory tenancy if he does this, for want of residence (5.96–5.104).

5.156 The Case is available even if there was no prohibition in the tenancy agreement on sub-letting (*Regional Properties Co v Frankenschwerth*, 1951). Consent may, however, be express or implied, and may be before or even after the assignment or subletting, at any time before hearing (*Hyde v Pimley*, 1952), so that cases on waiver of illegal sub-letting (1.181) may be prayed in aid by way of analogy.

5.157 Overcharging sub-tenant. If the rent for the sub-tenancy has been registered (5.190–5.212), or if the Rent Tribunal has fixed a rent for the sub-tenancy (6.78–6.80), it is a ground for possession against the tenant that he has overcharged the sub-tenant, *i.e.* charged more than either class of rent (Case 10).

5.158 Required for employee. Case 8 is available only in relation to a service tenant (1.148–1.158). The letting must have been in consequence of the employment, the tenant must have been in the landlord's employment, and the property must now be reasonably required (*cf.* 5.137) by the landlord for the occupation of someone else in his full-time employment, or someone with whom a contract of employment has been agreed, conditional upon the provision of accommodation (*cf.* 1985 Act, Ground 12, 3.132 and 1988 Act Ground 16, 4.120).

5.159 In one case, the landlord was one person, but the employer was a partnership, of which the landlord was but one member: it was held that the case did not apply (*Grimond v Duncan*, 1949).

5.160 Required by landlord. Case 9 is applicable where the property is reasonably required (*cf.* 5.137), by the landlord for occupation as a residence by himself, any of his children over the age of 18, his parents, or his spouse's parents.

5.161 This Case is not available if the landlord became the landlord by purchasing the property with the tenant already in occupation (*Newton v Biggs*, 1953). Purchase does not carry any technical meaning but covers what a reasonable person would consider a purchase (*Ammadio v Dalton*, 1991). It does not include a transfer "in consideration of mutual love and affection" (*Mansukhani v Sharkey*, 1992).

5.162 A landlord cannot use this Case if his true intention is to gain vacant possession in order to sell, no matter how reasonably he wishes to do so. He must want the property for living in it (himself or for one of the other permitted occupiers) for some reasonable period, definite or indefinite (*Rowe v Truelove*, 1976).

5.163 Under this Case (*cf.* 5.136), if the landlord is comprised of two or more joint owners, they must all wish to live there before it can apply (*Macintyre v Hardcastle*, 1948). It is not necessary, however, for any son or daughter for whom the property is required to be the child of both joint owners; it is sufficient if they are the child of any one of them (*Potsos v Theodotou*, 1991).

5.164 Greater hardship. This Case is often referred to as "greater hardship" because the 1977 Act provides a particular defence to a claim under it, that—having regard to all the circumstances of the case including the availability of other accommodation to either landlord or tenant—greater hardship would be caused by granting than by refusing the order (1977, Sch.15, Pt III).

5.165 The court must consider hardship long-term, so that if a tenant who is to be rehoused by a local authority (Chapter 10) will suffer some short-term inconvenience, it is unlikely to amount to "greater hardship" (*Manaton v Edwards*, 1985).

5.166 Burden of defence. The burden of proving the defence lies on the tenant (*Sims v Wilson*, 1946), and he must at the lowest produce evidence of attempts to find other accommodation in order to discharge it (*Alexander v Mohamadzadeh*, 1985).

5.167 Where there are joint tenants, hardship to all of them must be taken into account.

5.168 The extent to which either landlord or tenant may be eligible for rehousing under Pt VII of the Housing Act 1996 (see Chapter 10), may well be decisive under this Case.

5.169 Misrepresentation. If an order for possession is made under either Case 8 (5.158), or Case 9 (5.160), and it is later made to appear to the court that the landlord obtained the order by misrepresenting circumstances to the court or by concealing some material fact, the court has power to order the landlord to pay damages to the tenant (1977, s.102). This can be a difficult claim: a mere change of mind is not the same as a misrepresentation and will not be enough.

5.170 Suitable alternative accommodation. The final "ground for possession," in relation to which reasonableness must still, and additionally, be shown, does not appear in the schedule of discretionary grounds (1977, Sch.15). It is that the landlord can provide or obtain suitable alternative accommodation for the tenant (1977, s.98).

5.171 The meaning of this phrase is, however, defined in Sch.15, Pt IV, and is in similar terms to the 1988 Act (4.108). The ground is subject to reasonableness, although this could include the need for works which cannot be carried out, *e.g.* for want of funds on the part of the landlord (*Trustees of Hungerford Charity v Beazeley*, 1993).

5.172 If the court seems likely to make an order on this ground, it will be in the tenant's interests to seek a ruling that the tenancy of the new premises should be Rent Act protected, rather than a Housing Act assured (Chapter 4) tenancy (5.08).

Protection of rents

5.173 Need for protection of rents. All Rent Act protected tenants, whether statutory or contractual, are entitled to protection of their rents. Indeed, statutory tenancy itself would be valueless if landlords could simply increase rents beyond what tenants can afford to pay, and protection of rents would be valueless if landlords could serve retaliatory notices to quit.

5.174 In this section we shall consider:

  (i) What the fair rent is;

  (ii) How it applies to a tenancy; and,

  (iii) The rent limit for regulated tenancies.

1. THE FAIR RENT

5.175 Rent officers. A fair rent is one that a rent officer— employed by the Rent Officer Service established by the Secretary of State—considers fair for the premises and tenancy in question. An appeal from the rent officer lies to a Rent Assessment Committee ("RAC"), which applies the same principles as the rent officer.

5.176 Statutory considerations. The Rent Act contains guidelines as to what should be considered a fair rent (1977, s.70).

5.177 The rent officer is obliged to take into account all the circumstances (other than personal circumstances) and in particular the age, character, and locality of the residential accommodation, its state of repair, if any furniture is provided for use under the tenancy, the quantity, quality and condition of the furniture, and any premium, or sum in the nature of a premium, which has been or may be lawfully required or received on the grant, renewal, continuance or assignment of the tenancy (5.218) (1977, s.70(1)). He must also assume that there is no scarcity of dwellings in the locality (1977, s.70(2)).

5.178 The rent officer must disregard disrepair or defects attributable to a failure by the tenant or his predecessor in title to comply with any terms of the tenancy, any improvements carried out, otherwise than under the terms of the tenancy, by the tenant or his predecessor in title, and—if furniture is provided—either any improvement to it or deterioration in its condition due to ill-treatment, attributable to the tenant or his predecessor in title (or, in the case of deterioration, attributable to ill-treatment by anyone living with the tenant) (1977, s.70(3).

5.179 Adjusted Market Rent. Following the Housing Act 1988, there was, for the first time since the introduction of fair rents in 1965, the growth of a body of market rents (4.125). This impacted on Rent Act fair rents, which had hitherto functioned by comparison with other fair rents registered by rent officers (rather than with market demand). Indeed, "comparables" (as they were known) had been held to be the best evidence of a fair rent (*Mason v Skilling*, 1974).

5.180 Building on this new market, a number of judicial decisions in the following decade required more emphasis to be placed on the market, albeit adjusted to accommodate the statutory criteria, in place of an earlier focus on the existing body of comparable fair rents.

5.181 Following these decisions, it may be said that a fair rent had become the market rent for a property adjusted for scarcity (5.185) and having regard to (or disregarding) the matters specified in the statute: *Curtis v London RAC*, 1999, *Spath Holme v Greater Manchester & Lancashire RAC*, 1995. The expression is "fair" rent, which is not (necessarily) the same as a "reasonable" rent (*BTE Ltd v Merseyside & Cheshire RAC*, 1991; *Spath Holme*). Comparables remain an alternative approach, only where there continues to be no, or an inadequate, market on the basis of which to proceed.

5.182 Maximum Increases. The new approach led to substantial increases in rent and, in turn, to the Rent Acts (Maximum Fair Rent) Order 1999, made under the Landlord and Tenant Act 1985, s.31. This set a maximum increase on all fair rents registered since February 1, 1999 fixing them by reference to a formula using the retail price index.

5.183 A challenge to the legality of the order was rejected by the House of Lords in *R. v Secretary of State for the Environment Ex p. Spath Holme Ltd*, 2000.

5.184 Current Position. Accordingly, the current position is that the determination of the fair rent involves consideration of the market rent, followed by adjustment for the statutory considerations, followed by limitation (if needed) by the RPI-based formula. If there is no market on the basis of which to determine the rent, then comparison with other registered rents would remain a correct approach, but the RPI-based formula would still be applicable.

5.185 Statutory Criteria. A failure to comply with the statutory criteria would mean that the registration exercise was invalid. The matters to be taken into account or disregarded are as follows:

(i) **Personal circumstances.** The most common example of a personal circumstance is the tenant who is in straitened circumstances, or the landlord who claims that he cannot afford to keep the property in repair. Another example might be that of an elderly person who finds it more inconvenient to live at the top of a flight of stairs than would a hypothetical, average tenant; or a tenant with children who feels the lack of a garden.

The presence or otherwise of a garden, or the fact that a flat is at the top of, perhaps, a long flight of stairs, will, however, affect the value of the premises themselves in any event, just not more so because of the particular characteristics or circumstances of the present tenant.

The extent of a tenant's security of tenure (*e.g.* notice under mandatory ground (5.125–5.132) or housing association landlord—to whose tenants these provisions in some circumstances also apply—(3.237–3.241, 7.70), is a personal circumstance if the approach being taken to assessment is by means of valuing the property (*Palmer v Peabody Trust*, 1975; *Spath Holme v Greater Manchester & Lancashire RAC*, 1995), although it is not if a comparables approach to valuation (5.181) is adopted (*Spath Home*).

(ii) **General conditions in locality.** Although it is not permissible to take into account the tenant's financial circumstances, it is possible for a rent officer to consider the general level of wages throughout a particular locality (*Guppy's (Bridport) Ltd v Carpenter*, 1973).

It is up to the rent officer to determine just what he will consider the locality for the purposes of the determination (*Palmer v Peabody Trust*, 1975). This could benefit a tenant of whatever income, living in a working class district but, equally, could act to the detriment of a poor tenant living in an area that is, or that has become, predominantly middle class.

(iii) **Age, character and locality.** Whether or not premises are on a noisy street is obviously relevant. Consideration of locality means more than just what part of town premises are in, but also whether they are near other amenities, such as parks and recreational facilities, public transport and good shopping centres. In other words, all the factors that would normally be considered as affecting the value of living in particular premises or that would tend to push rents up or down (*Metropolitan Property Holdings v Finegold*, 1975).

State of repair is very important indeed; if premises are in such a bad condition that they are not even habitable, or perhaps only in part habitable, then there is nothing to stop a rent officer determining a purely nominal rent for the premises as a whole, or attributing a purely nominal amount to the uninhabitable part (*McGee v London RAPC*, 1969) although, even technically unfit for human habitation (12.18–12.22) he is not obliged to do so (*Williams v Khan*, 1981).

(iv) **Disregard of tenant's improvements.** The rent officer must disregard, in addition to personal circumstances, any improvements done by the tenant (other than improvements which he is obliged to do under the terms of the tenancy), and any damage or disrepair attributable to the tenant's default.

(v) **Scarcity value.** The major element which the rent officer must disregard, that forms the cornerstone of the fair rent system, is "scarcity value."

It is scarcity, more than anything else, which pushes up the price of property and rents. In order to avoid scarcity value, the rent officer is obliged to adopt the assumption that there are not substantially more people seeking any particular sort of accommodation in the locality than there is such accommodation available (1977, s.70(2)).

The locality for these purposes is very much larger than that relevant for ascertaining the general market rent in the locality under s.70(1) (5.185(iii)): *Queensway Association v Chiltern, Thames and Eastern RAC*, 1998.

5.186   Rent register. The rent officer service is obliged to maintain a rent register, which is open for public inspection. This contains details of all rent registrations in force.

5.187 Normally these are rents which will have been registered by a rent officer since 1965, when the fair rent system was introduced (Rent Act 1965). There is one exception to this. Prior to August 14, 1974, furnished tenancies were subject to the Rent Tribunal (5.45) and rents may have been registered in respect of them with the Rent Tribunal (see Chapter 6). When the Rent Act 1974 came into force, such rent registrations were deemed to be fair rents and were included in the register (1977, Sch.24).

5.188   Comparables. The rent register contains the documentary part of the experience which the rent officer will apply to any particular application. In the past, the practice of rent officers was to look at the register to see if there were any previous registrations for properties of similar size, in similar areas, and with any other similarities. These were what has been referred to above (5.179) as "comparables," formerly considered the best evidence of a fair rent (*Mason v Skilling*, 1974).

5.189   Market rent comparables. As already stated, the starting point for setting a fair rent today is the market rent: *Curtis v London RAC*, 1998. Accordingly, where there are good market rent comparisons available (from assured and assured shorthold tenancies) these should be used in preference to comparables from the register: *Curtis; Spath Holme Ltd v Greater Manchester and Lancashire R.A.C*, 1995; *Northumberland & Durham Property Trust v London RAC*, 1998. (Note: comparables from the register remain as appropriate approach, however, when there is no such market).

2.   APPLICATION OF FAIR RENTS

5.190 A fair rent comes to apply to a tenancy in one of two ways. Either there is a rent already registered, or there is an application for a registration after the tenancy starts.

Existing Registered Rent

5.191   Maximum rent. If there has been a registration before the tenancy starts, then the amount registered will be the maximum rent under a new protected tenancy, even if the tenancy agreement is for a higher figure (1977, s.44), until such time as there is a new registration (5.195). (If, however, the tenancy agreement is for a lower sum, that will—contractually—prevail).

5.192 This is so even where the nature of the letting has changed, *e.g.* from unfurnished to furnished, unless the change is to the structure of the premises such that it can no longer be called the same dwelling-house (*Rakhit v Carty*, 1990). The rent only applies, however, to exactly the same premises, *i.e.* not premises which have been enlarged by the addition of a room, nor even premises reduced in size by allowing them to let one less room (*Gluchowska v Tottenham BC*, 1954).

5.193 Cancellation of Registration. In order to end the registration, application may in some circumstances be made to cancel it:

(i) At least two years after the last registration, at a time when the premises are unlet, by the person who would be the landlord if it were let; or

(ii) Pursuant to a rent agreement taking effect at least two years after the last registration, by the landlord and tenant jointly under a fixed term tenancy on which there is at least one year to run, who agree on a higher rent which is approved by the rent officer (1977, s.73).

5.194 Recovery of Excess. If a tenant has been paying more than the registered rent, then the excess is recoverable for up to two years after it was paid, either by deducting it from future rent owing, or by a normal civil action (1977, s.57).

5.195 New registration. Either landlord, or tenant, or both jointly (1977, s.68) can apply for registration of a rent.

5.196 There cannot normally be an application for a new registration until two years has elapsed since the last even if there is a new tenancy or, indeed, even if there is a new landlord (1977, s.67). Thus, two parties can find themselves bound by a registration secured by two completely different parties.

5.197 Early application. There are three exceptions to the two-year bar.

(i) **Joint Application.** Where a landlord and a tenant apply jointly for a new rent to be registered, this may be done in less than two years.

(ii) **Landlord's Application.** A landlord may apply on his own, one year and nine months after the last registration, but the new rent cannot come into force until two years have elapsed.

(iii) **Change of circumstances.** There can also be an application before the expiry of two years, by either party, if there have been such substantial changes in the terms of the tenancy, the condition of the premises or furniture, that, in all the circumstances, the rent last registered is no longer fair.

A change in the condition of the premises can be as a result of repairs carried out by the landlord, even where the landlord was obliged to carry them out under the terms of the tenancy agreement (11.22) or because of a repairs notice (12.28): *R. v West Sussex Registration Area Ex p. Haysport Properties Ltd*, 2001.

On such an application, the rent officer does not merely consider the changed circumstances and reduce or increase accordingly, but considers the whole rent anew (*London Housing and Commercial Properties v Cowan*, 1976).

This provision is therefore only likely to be of use to a landlord who has, for example, installed some facility such as a hot water system, since the last registration. A tenant who applies because of some deterioration may well find that the amount by which the rent ought to be decreased on account of the deterioration is not as great as the amount by which the rent has increased in respect of the rent of the tenancy, because of inflation.

On the other hand, on a landlord's application for a higher rent because of an improvement, a tenant should not hesitate to point out any deterioration or other new circumstances *e.g.* reduced local amenities), which might prevent too great an increase.

5.198 Procedure. The party making the application completes the appropriate forms, which are available from the rent office and from most aid or advice agencies. The applicant is obliged to state what is the fair rent that he wishes to have registered. The forms will be sent to the other side, for example, the landlord on a tenant's application, who will have an opportunity to comment and to put the case from his point of view.

5.199 If there are joint tenants or, indeed, joint landlords, then all must sign the application form or one must sign as agent for the others (*Turley v Panton*, 1975; *R. v Rent Officer for Camden LBC Ex p. Felix*, 1988).

5.200 Inspection and consultation. Although the rent officer is not obliged to do so, he will normally visit the premises. He will at that time hold a consultation, or else he may hold a consultation at a different time, and at his office.

5.201 He would not normally volunteer to hold a consultation if the rent has previously been registered and there is no change other than the passage of time, but he must do so if either party asks him to.

5.202 The consultation is informal and it is not usual for parties to be represented, nor is legal aid available, although legal advice may be obtained beforehand. A lawyer may be of help if a question of jurisdiction arises, for example whether the tenancy is protected or not, or whether the time is correct for an application. A surveyor may be of more help if the only question is as to the amount of rent.

5.203 Some rent officers give their decision at the hearing, others do so later. In either case, the decision will be in writing.

5.204 Rent Assessment Committee. If either party is dissatisfied with the rent registration, he may appeal to the Rent Assessment Committee (1977, Sch.11). The Rent Assessment Committee is a tribunal, not a court, and legal aid is not available for proceedings before it, although legal advice may be obtained beforehand. Again, representation by a surveyor may be helpful.

5.205 This body has no power to decide an appeal on a point of law, *e.g.* as to jurisdiction (*London Housing and Commercial Properties v Cowan*, 1976). Such a challenge can only be taken to the Administrative Court or to the county court (1977, s.141).

5.206 Hearing *de novo*. When the Rent Assessment Committee hears an appeal, it does not start with the decision of the rent officer and decide whether he is right or wrong; rather, it starts all over again for itself.

5.207 It, too, will normally go to inspect the premises in question and will usually hold a consultation which will be slightly more formal than that before the rent officer and will always be at its office, not at the premises.

5.208 Appeal from Rent Assessment Committee. There is no appeal from a Rent Assessment Committee decision, unless it can be shown to have acted wrongly in law, whether by the wrongful inclusion or exclusion of some consideration or otherwise. This would be made to the High Court. If asked to do so, the Rent Assessment Committee is bound to give its decision, and the reasons for it, in writing (Tribunals and Inquiries Act 1992).

5.209 Relevant date. The date when the registration is finally made, either by rent officer or Rent Assessment Committee, is known as the relevant date (1977, s.67(5)), and it affects the date when a new application can be made. The rent applies to the tenancy from the relevant date (1977, s.72).

5.210 Effecting an increase. The landlord cannot claim an increase unless it is either still within the contractual rent (1977, s.44) or else he has brought the contractual tenancy to an end, either by notice to quit or, in the case of a fixed term tenancy, by expiry of time (1.121). He can also use a notice of increase (5.31) to claim the new rent, specifying a date no earlier than the date when the contractual tenancy could have been brought to an end: this has the effect of terminating a periodic tenancy (1977, ss.45, 49).

Initial Applications

5.211 If there was no rent registration in force when the tenancy began, either party can apply at any time after the start of a tenancy although it will usually only be the tenant who will wish to do so in practice.

5.212 The procedure is the same as when there was an existing registration (5.198–5.210). Most usually, however, the application leads to a decrease, for which reason the notice of increase procedure will not be needed.

3. THE RENT LIMIT

5.213 Maximum rent. The rent limit is the term used to describe the maximum amount which a landlord can claim from the tenant. There is a number of different circumstances that must be considered.

   (i) **Contractual period**. During the contractual period of the tenancy, the rent limit is either the registered rent or the contractual rent, whichever is the lower (1977, s.44).

If there is no registered rent, then the limit is the contractual rent. Any increases up to the amount of the contractual limit can be imposed without notice of increase, but in order to exceed the contractual limit, the tenancy must be determined.

Where there is no registered rent, the parties may agree to an increase, by means of a rent agreement (1977, s.51). Such an agreement will, however, only be valid if it is in writing, and if at the head of the document there appears a statement in writing or print, no less conspicuous than that used elsewhere in the agreement, that the tenant is not obliged to enter into the agreement and that his security of tenure will not be affected if he refuses (1977, s.51(4)).

The statement must also advise the tenant of his right to apply to the rent officer at any time, then or even immediately after it has been signed, for registration of a fair rent.

An agreement which does not comply with these terms is invalid (1977, s.54) and the excess can be reclaimed by the tenant for up to one year after it was paid, as an ordinary civil debt or by deduction from the rent (1977, s.57).

(ii) **Statutory period—pre-registration.** By the time the contractual tenancy comes to an end, there may still be no registered rent.

In this case, the landlord is confined by the former contractual rent limit until such time as he applies for registration of a fair rent (1977, s.45).

If the result of an application is an increase, then the landlord must first serve a notice of increase (1977, ss.45, 49).

The landlord can, however, increase the rent without applying for registration on account of increases in rates (1977, s.46), or the costs of providing services or furniture (1977, s.47). The tenant may be able to challenge the amount claimed in the county court (1977, s.49).

(iii) **Statutory period—post-registration.** Once a rent has been registered for the premises, then this becomes the rent limit and cannot be increased except by a new application and, where applicable, notice of increase (1977, s.45).

It is, however, possible to pass on increases in the cost of providing services without a new application, provided that the rent officer has agreed that the service element should be entered on the register variable and has endorsed the landlord's proposed terms means of calculating any future variations.

Further Financial Protection and Assistance

5.214   Rent in advance. Whether contractual or statutory and whether or not a rent is registered in respect of the premises, it is illegal for a landlord to demand rent further in advance than the beginning of the period for which it is paid, *i.e.* the first day of a week for which a weekly rent is paid, or the first day of a month for which a monthly rent is paid (1977, s.26). If the tenancy is yearly, then the landlord cannot charge the year's rent earlier than half-way through the year for which it is due.

5.215   A tenant can recover any money improperly demanded too far in advance, for up to two years after it was paid. This probably does not mean that the landlord is not entitled to the actual rent at the time when it would be lawful to ask for it; so this would probably only be of any use to a tenant who has been charged a considerable amount in advance, or by way of defence to an action for arrears, or part of them, based on rent improperly charged in advance, *i.e.* because it is, in law, not yet due and therefore not in arrears.

5.216   Premiums and deposits. It is illegal to charge a tenant a premium on the grant, continuance or renewal of a Rent Act protected tenancy (1977, s.119). A tenant who has paid one such premium can sue for its return (1977, s.125). Such a claim must be made within six years of the payment in the same way as for the recovery of a normal civil debt (Limitation Act 1980).

5.217   It is also a criminal offence to require or to receive a premium. Such conduct should be reported to the Tenancy Relations Officer: see Chapter 8. There are two main exceptions where premiums may lawfully be charged (see also 1977, Sch.18 for other limited exceptions).

5.218   The first applies to tenancies where the landlord has no power to determine the tenancy at any time within 20 years, beginning on the date when it was granted and the terms of the tenancy do not inhibit both the assignment and the underletting of the whole of the premises comprised in the tenancy (1977, s.127(2)). Such tenancies are wholly exempt from the illegal premium rules.

5.219 The second exception applies where a tenancy has ceased to fall outside the low rent exception (5.80) because of increases. Where:

(a) The tenancy was granted before July 16, 1980;

(b) A premium was lawfully required and paid on the grant of the tenancy;

(c) The tenancy was when it was granted, a tenancy at a low rent (5.80); and

(d) The terms of the tenancy do not inhibit both the assignment and the underletting of the whole of the premises comprising the tenancy,

the rules relating to premiums do not apply, and are deemed never to have applied (1977, s.127(3A), (3B)).

5.220 Premiums on change of tenant. A premium might be charged by a landlord, or by his agent, or by an outgoing tenant. An outgoing tenant might charge for an assignment, or else for arranging to surrender his own tenancy to the landlord, who contemporaneously consents to grant a new tenancy to the incoming tenant. In such a case, it may well be that there is no profit to the landlord. In all of these cases, however, the premium is an illegal payment (1977, s.120; *Farrell v Alexander*, 1976).

5.221 Premiums paid to or by another. It is a premium whether a person demands that the money is paid to himself, or to someone else, perhaps, for example, in discharge of a debt that the person demanding the premium owes to the other (*Elmdene Estates Ltd v White*, 1960). Another example would be that of the outgoing tenant who agrees to assign the tenancy or arrange for a new tenancy to be granted to the incoming tenant, if the incoming tenant will pay arrears of rent that he owes.

5.222 Premiums in cash or kind. The most obvious form that a premium will take is cash. But an illegal premium might also be demanded or paid other than in cash, for otherwise this protection too could be circumvented without difficulty, *e.g.* by demanding payments in kind, such as goods, or else by demanding excessive prices for fixtures, fittings or furniture.

5.223 Premiums for fittings and furniture. It is lawful to make it a condition of the grant of a tenancy, whether by assignment or from the landlord, that an incoming tenant purchase fittings, or even furniture (1977, s.123). Items such as fitted carpets may well be valueless to an outgoing tenant in his new home and it is considered only fair that he should be able to insist, before the assignment or an arrangement for surrender and new grant, that the incoming tenant, as it were, takes them off his hands.

5.224   Only a fair price for fittings and furniture can be demanded and the excess constitutes an illegal premium (1977, s.123). Anyone seeking to make an incoming tenant pay for furniture is obliged to provide an inventory of it and of the price sought for each item; failure to do so is a criminal offence (1977, s.124).

5.225   Premiums for fixtures, alterations and outgoings. The position is slightly different where "fixtures" are concerned. These are items such as fitted cupboards or double glazing which effectively become a part of the premises and are valueless when removed. No tenant is allowed to remove fixtures in any event; as they attach to the premises, they become, eventually, the property of the landlord.

5.226   An outgoing tenant is permitted to charge an incoming tenant the amount it cost him to install fixtures (1977, s.120). An outgoing tenant is also permitted to charge what it cost him to do any structural alterations to the premises, any amounts paid by way of outgoings on the premises, *e.g.* telephone rental, which are attributable to a period after he leaves, and any amount paid by the outgoing tenant to a former tenant which was payment for fixtures or alterations (1977, s.120).

5.227   Deposits. Landlords frequently require an incoming occupier to pay a deposit, either for furniture, for rent arrears or, for example, damage. Such a deposit will not, however, be illegal if:

(a) It is reasonable in relation to the purpose for which it is claimed; and

(b) It does not exceed one-sixth of the annual rent (1977, s.128, as amended by 1980, s.79). By inference, a larger deposit will be likely to be considered a premium.

5.228   Miscellaneous provisions. Housing benefits are available for protected tenants as for assured and secure (3.265). The provisions governing the resale of utilities (4.162) are the same for protected tenants as for assured. (The provisions governing accommodation agency charges—4.157—are now inapplicable, as the circumstances in which a new protected tenancy can arise—5.09—will not involve such charges).

CHAPTER SIX

Limited Security

Introduction

6.01 Limitations on security. Whenever Parliament has conferred security of tenure on a body of tenants, it has—of definition—also created a body of tenants without that security. In turn, that has given rise to the question of what—if any—security should be enjoyed by those outside full security. Those who are between full security and no security may be considered to enjoy limited security, and are the subject matter of this Chapter.

6.02 Examples of limited security—historic cases. Some of these—both current and past—have already been identified (Chapter 5):

- Furnished tenants, tenants provided with attendance and board, are examples of tenants excluded from full Rent Act protection from its introduction (1915), although it was not until 1946 that they were given limited security;

- When, in 1974, furnished tenants were brought into full Rent Act security, the tenants of resident landlords were moved out and into limited security;

- In 1980, a new exception was created—the protected shorthold tenant—and given only a limited form of security.

6.03 Examples of limited security—current cases. In 1989, when the Housing Act 1988 brought in the assured tenant to replace Rent Act protection, it, too, excluded the tenants of resident landlords (but left them without any security at all—see Chapter 7), and carried with it the assured shorthold, again with limited security. In addition, it reduced the extent of protection available to the tenants of resident landlords still governed by the Rent Acts. The Housing Act 1996, for the first time, created a general exclusion to secure tenancy, the introductory tenancy.

6.04 The assured shorthold tenancy has gone on to become the most prevalent form of tenancy in the private rented sector, and is also used occasionally by registered social landlords. The use of the introductory tenancy has slowly grown amongst local authorities (although probably less than 50 per cent of authorities have adopted such schemes). It is these two types of limited security that we first address in this Chapter. We then return to that now very small group who have limited security under the Rent Act.

Outline

6.05 January 15, 1989 (and post) assured shortholds. The Housing Act 1988 created the assured shorthold tenant (4.56—4.63).

- Such tenancies have been capable of creation since January 15, 1989.

- When originally introduced, such tenancies had to be for a fixed term of at least six months and the tenant had to be given notice that the tenancy was to be an assured shorthold.

- Since February 28, 1997, all new tenancies which otherwise qualify as assured are automatically assured shorthold unless either:

  - The landlord indicates through notice or the tenancy agreement that the tenancy is to be fully assured, or
  - In a number of specified circumstances, it follows an existing tenancy.

- Assured shorthold tenants can be evicted by notice served by the landlord after, either, the fixed term of a tenancy has elapsed or if a periodic tenancy, at least six months has elapsed since the grant of the tenancy

- There is provision for reference of rents to a Rent Assessment Committee, additional to that enjoyed by an ordinary Housing Act assured tenant.

6.06 Introductory tenancies

- The Housing Act 1996 introduced (Pt V, Chapter I) the "introductory tenancy regime," an optional scheme for local authorities and Housing Action Trusts (only), to permit them to "try out" tenants for, in effect, a probationary period, before allowing them to become fully secure.

- Such tenants can be evicted by the landlord without the need to prove a ground for possession.

- A decision to evict may, however, be challenged by judicial review.

- Introductory tenants have some but not all of the additional rights granted to secure tenants.

6.07 Pre-January 15, 1989 restricted contracts

- The first class of occupiers with limited security are those who came within the jurisdiction of the Rent Tribunal, a body the duties of which have subsequently been transferred to the Rent Assessment Committee.

- The RAC has power, where certain types of letting have been granted, to register a reasonable rent for the letting, and in some cases (now very rare), to defer for up to six months at a time, a notice bringing the letting to an end.

- These occupiers have what are known as "restricted contracts," which can be either tenancies or licences.

- No new restricted contracts could be granted after the commencement of Pt I of the Housing Act 1988 ("1988"; January 15, 1989), unless in pursuance of a contract made before that date (1988, s.36).

6.08 Pre-January 15, 1989 protected shortholds

- The "protected shorthold tenant," is a Rent Act protected tenant (see Chapter 5) on whom was served a notice before the commencement of his tenancy that he would be subject to the recovery of possession under the mandatory "protected shorthold" ground introduced by the Housing Act 1980.

- Although ostensibly otherwise a Rent Act protected tenancy (Chapter 5), it is so easy for a landlord to get possession that it is idle to consider the tenant as enjoying Rent Act security of tenure.

- Because (subject to exceptions that are not relevant here—see 5.09, no new Rent Act protected tenancies could be granted on or after the commencement of Pt I, 1988 Act (January 15, 1989), it follows that no new protected shorthold tenancies could be granted after that date.

Assured Shorthold Tenancies

6.09 Pre- and post-1996. To qualify as an assured shorthold tenancy before the commencement of the relevant provisions of the Housing Act 1996 ("1996"), required the service of a notice; since those provisions came into force, the opposite is true—with certain exceptions, all lettings which would have been fully assured are assured shortholds, unless a notice is served to the contrary. The conditions for the creation of an assured shorthold, pre- and post-1996 Act commencement, and the corresponding exceptions (to each), are described in Chapter 4, above.

6.10 Assured and assured shorthold. The assured shorthold tenant is in every other respect a fully assured tenant (Chapter 4). It follows that the provisions governing—*e.g.* grounds for possession, or references of rent—are as applicable to an assured shorthold, save so far as adapted. It is, in substance, only the adaptations which fall to be described in this Chapter.

 ## 1. SECURITY

6.11 Mandatory ground for possession. The assured shorthold tenancy works by the addition of a mandatory (4.87) ground for possession, so that the landlord still enjoys all the usual grounds (Chapter 4). A challenge to the mandatory quality of the right to possession, based on art.8 of the European Convention on Human Rights (right to respect for the home) was rejected in *Poplar HARCA v Donoghue*, 2001. The decision of Parliament to restrict the jurisdiction of the court when ordering possession was a policy decision to which the courts had to defer.

6.12 Pre-1996 Act. In the case of a pre-1996 assured shorthold, the landlord could only claim possession during the initial fixed term in the same way and in the same circumstances as under a fully assured tenancy (4.83), *i.e.* if there were grounds for terminating the letting early, but, once it is over, a court is obliged to make an order for possession provided the requisite notice of seeking possession has been served.

6.13   There are two kinds of notice. One notice is served before the initial fixed term comes to an end, or on its last day; such a notice merely has to be in writing, and for a minimum of two months. If no notice is served during the fixed term, however, the landlord's notice must fulfil additional criteria: it must still be in writing and of at least two months, but:

   (a)   It must end on the last day of a period of the tenancy;

   (b)   That date must be no earlier than the tenancy could otherwise have been brought to an end by notice to quit (1.111–1.114); and

   (c)   The notice must state that possession is required under these provisions (1988, s.21).

 6.14   Post-1996 Act. Following the 1996 Act changes, an assured shorthold need not be for a fixed term, but may be. If fixed term, it can only be brought to an end in the same way and in the same circumstances as under a fully assured tenancy (4.83). Whether fixed term or periodic, however, no order on the shorthold ground may be made so as to take effect any earlier than six months after the shorthold was granted (or, if one shorthold of the same or substantially the same premises with the same landlord and tenant has followed another, after the original shorthold was granted) (1988, s.21(5)).

2.   POSSESSION PROCEEDINGS

6.15   Accelerated procedure. Pt 55 of the Civil Procedure Rules 1998 provides an accelerated possession procedure enabling landlords to recover premises let under an assured shorthold tenancy without a hearing. The procedure cannot be used if the landlord is making any other claim in the proceedings (*e.g.* for arrears of rent).

6.16   If the tenant wishes to dispute the claim for possession, he must complete the form of reply within 14 days of service of the application. On consideration of the application and the reply (if any), the judge may order possession without a hearing. If the judge is not satisfied that the claim was served or that the claimant landlord is entitled to possession, he may fix a day for a hearing and give case management direction.

6.17 A hearing day must be fixed if the documents filed by the claimant might arguably disclose a defect in his claim, or where, on its face, the defendant's reply raises an issue which, if true, would constitute an arguable defence to the claim for possession: *Manel v Memon*, 2001.

3. RENT

6.18 Additional protection. Assured shorthold tenants are subject to the normal provisions governing rents which are applicable to Housing Act assured tenants generally, with the following qualification, that the tenant may refer the rent to the Rent Assessment Committee (1988, s.22) even though the landlord is not seeking an increase (4.140).

6.19 In the case of a pre-1996 Act assured shorthold, this power is only available once, and it is not available if the initial fixed-term tenancy has already expired, *i.e.* if the tenancy has become periodic. After that, only a request for an increase can trigger the reference.

6.20 In the case of a post-1996 Act assured shorthold, the power is only available during the first six months from the commencement of the original (6.14) tenancy, and otherwise it is likewise reliant on a request for an increase from the landlord.

6.21 Comparison with other rents. A determination to fix a rent under this additional power arises only if the rent under the tenancy is significantly higher than rents under other assured tenancies (whether or not shorthold). But merely because the rent is referred does not mean that the Rent Assessment Committee are bound to make a determination: they can only make a determination if satisfied that there are sufficient other assured tenancies with which to make a comparison (and that the rent payable is significantly higher than other Housing Act assured tenancies). If they refuse to make a determination, the tenant may accordingly reapply in the future, if it seems that other rents are now available with which to make a comparison, or much lower.

6.22 Procedure. Rent for this purpose excludes any service charges or rates (4.147). A reference may be withdrawn by written agreement between the landlord and the tenant (4.150).

6.23 If the Rent Assessment Committee does proceed to a determination, they will decide from when it is to take effect, although that cannot be earlier than the date of the application to them. Any excess rent over the determination is irrecoverable from the tenant (1988, s.22(4)(b)).

6.24 Once the Committee has determined a rent, the landlord cannot serve a notice seeking an increase (4.138) for a year after the determination takes effect (1988, s.22(4)(c)).

6.25 The Secretary of State has power to disapply this additional means of referring a rent to the Rent Assessment Committee (1988, s.23).

4.   WRITTEN STATEMENT OF TERMS

6.26   Post-1996 Act. If a post-1996 Act assured shorthold tenant asks him in writing to do so, the landlord must provide him with a written statement of any term of the tenancy which is not (already) evidenced in writing and which governs:

(a) The date on which the tenancy began (or if a statutory periodic tenancy—4.72, or an assured shorthold by succession, *i.e.* succession to a Rent Act protected shorthold—6.111, the date on which it came into being),

(b) The rent and dates for payment,

(c) Any rent review clause, and

(d) The length of a fixed-term shorthold (1988, s.20A(1),(2)).

6.27 Once the landlord has complied with such a request, he need not comply again unless the term has subsequently been varied (1988, s.20A(3)). The statement is not, however, to be treated as conclusive evidence of the terms (1988, s.20A(5)).

6.28   Non-compliance. Non-compliance with a request within 28 days of its receipt is liable on summary conviction to a fine (1988, s.20A(4)).

Introductory Tenants

1.   INTRODUCTORY TENANCY REGIME

6.29   Optional Regime. The introductory tenancy regime is optional: it has no effect at all unless a local housing authority, or a

Housing Action Trust, decide to operate it (1996, s.124(1)). If at any time the landlord decides to cease operating the regime (without prejudice to its reintroduction: 1996, s.124(5)), an introductory tenancy ceases to be such and becomes secure (1996, s.125(5)(c)).

6.30 Who may be an introductory tenant. Only a periodic tenant can be introductory; only someone who would otherwise be a secure tenant can be introductory, so that someone who would be excluded from full security (3.32–3.39) will likewise be excluded from being an introductory tenant (s.124(2)); indeed, if during the life of the tenancy, the tenant (or, if joint tenants, all of them) ceased to occupy as an only or principal home—which would cause the loss of security—so also would it cause the loss of status as an introductory tenant (6.37).

6.31 Introductory tenancy has no application to fixed-term tenancies.

6.32 Exclusions. If, immediately before the tenancy is granted, the tenant (or, if joint tenants, one or more of them) was a secure tenant of any premises (of any landlord, whether or not the same) (1996, s.124(2)(a)), or a fully assured tenant of a registered social landlord (but not a mere assured shorthold tenant), again of any premises (1996, s.124(2)(b)), the tenancy cannot be introductory.

6.33 The regime also does not apply to those whose tenancies are granted pursuant to a contract entered into before the decision was made to adopt the regime (1996, s.124(3)).

6.34 Licensees. As with secure tenancy (3.19), the introductory tenancy regime is applicable to licences, other than those granted as a temporary expedient to people who entered the property, or other land, as a trespasser (1996, s.126).

6.35 Period of introductory tenancy. The intention is that introductory tenants will become secure tenants unless the tenancy (or licence) is determined while the regime still applies to the tenant—"the trial period" (1996, s.125(1)).

6.36 The trial period lasts one year starting with the date when the tenancy was entered into or, if later, the date on which the tenant was first entitled to take possession under it (1996, s.125(2)). Where there are two (or more) introductory tenancies in immediate succession, or where the tenant formerly held an assured shorthold from a registered social landlord—in neither case necessarily of the same premises—the earlier period (or periods) counts (or count) towards the trial period (1996, s.125(3)). (Where there are joint tenants, one or more of whom has an earlier period to be taken into account, the earliest starting-date is to be applied: 1996, s.125(4)).

6.37 Cessation of introductory tenancy. Unless terminated, or the introductory tenancy regime is abandoned, the tenancy becomes secure at the end of the trial period, unless before that time something has happened that means that the tenancy would not otherwise be secure, *e.g.* cessation of occupation as an only or principal home, or someone other than a local authority or Housing Action Trust becomes the landlord, or the introductory tenancy ceases because of succession (1996, s.125(5)).

6.38 Once a tenancy ceases to be introductory, it cannot become introductory again (1996, s.125(6)).

6.39 A person will not become secure, however, if proceedings for possession have been commenced, and are not finally resolved (1996, s.125(7)).

6.40 Succession. The succession provisions are similar to those applicable to secure tenancies (3.40–3.53), and the succession will be to an introductory tenancy (1996, ss.131–133).

6.41 If there is no one entitled to succeed under the statutory provisions (1996, s.133(3)), then once the tenancy has vested pursuant to the provisions applicable to the devolution of property on death, it will cease to be introductory.

6.42 This is not so, however, if it is vested by an order of a court using powers under one of a number of family statutes, governing both partners and children, in which case the tenancy may remain introductory, notwithstanding the absence of a qualifying successor, *e.g.* if it is vested by the court in a child who had not been residing with the tenant, or a former spouse (likewise not residing with the deceased tenant). In the interregnum, it will therefore remain introductory.

2. POSSESSION PROCEEDINGS

6.43 Terminating the tenancy. Like the secure tenancy (3.64), an introductory tenancy can only be brought to an end by obtaining an order of the court, in which case the tenancy comes to an end on the date when the tenant must give up possession pursuant to the order (1996, s.127).

6.44 The court cannot make an order for possession unless there has first been served a notice of proceedings (NOP), which states that the court is to be asked to make an order, sets out the reasons for the decision to apply for it, and specifies a date after which the proceedings may be begun, being a date no earlier than when the tenancy could be brought to an end by a notice to quit (1.111) given on the same date as the NOP (1996, s.128(1)–(4)).

6.45 The proceedings cannot be begun before that date (1996, s.128(5)). The notice must inform the tenant:

(a) Of the right to seek an internal review of the decision, and the time within which the review may be sought (1996, s.128(6)), and

(b) That if the tenant needs help or advice about the notice, and what to do about it, that he should take it immediately to a Citizens Advice Bureau, housing aid centre, law centre or solicitor (1.119) (1996, s.128(7).

6.46 Reasons. While there are no "grounds for possession" (3.81–3.140), the landlord has to give its "reasons" for the decision to seek an order (1996, s.128(3)). This means that the reasons must be "good" reasons, in the sense that all public authorities (which includes both local authorities and Housing Action Trusts) must reach decisions which accord with the principles of public law (10.73–10.80), in the sense that they cannot be absurd, irrational or whimsical, or reached in bad faith, nor can they disregard relevant considerations or take into account irrelevant matters.

6.47 Powers must also be used for the purposes for which they have been conferred. Much, therefore, may turn on how the courts view the purpose of the introductory regime. On a narrow approach, they may consider that it is purely related to issues of conduct (for the provisions appear in 1996, Pt V, which is headed "Conduct of Tenants"); in that case, the reasons will likewise have to relate to conduct. On a broader approach, the courts may consider that—although this Pt of the Act is from where the powers derive—there is no reason why authorities should not use their regimes in order, *e.g.* to give themselves some flexibility in relation to the use of their stock. In that case, wider questions of policy may be admissible, to which tenant-conduct may be irrelevant. Reasons will, however and in either event, have to be intelligible (10.91).

6.48 Review. The tenant is entitled to apply for an internal review of the decision to seek an order, but the application must be made within 14 days of the date on which the NOP is served (1996, s.129(1)).

6.49 The landlord is bound to carry out a review which has been properly asked for (1996, s.129(2)).

6.50 The Secretary of State has power to decide the procedure to be followed on a review (s.129(3,(4)). The current regulations (the Introductory Tenants (Review) Regulations 1987 (SI 1997/72)), require that any review is carried out by a person who was not involved in the decision to apply for possession and, if made by an officer, that the officer is senior to the officer who made the original decision.

6.51 There are also detailed provisions about the right to make representations, depending on whether or not a hearing is held. If there is a hearing the tenant has a right to attend with the assistance of representation. The tenant also has the right to call witnesses and may put questions to any person who gives evidence.

6.52 Notification. The landlord has to notify the tenant of the outcome of the review and, if it is to uphold the decision to evict, of its reasons (1996, s.129(5)). The review must be completed, and the tenant notified of the outcome, before the date when proceedings for possession may be begun (6.45) (1996, s.129(6)).

6.53 Challenge. If the review upholds the decision to evict, the tenant may challenge that decision by an application to the High Court for judicial review: *Manchester CC v Cochrane*, 1999. (See paras 10.173 to 10.180, below for a discussion of the basis on which the High Court could quash the decision of the landlord.)

6.54 The county court may adjourn possession proceedings to allow the challenge to be made. In order for the county court to make an informed decision as to whether to allow an adjournment, the landlord should provide an affidavit spelling out how the procedure operated in the individual case, dealing with the degree of independence of the tribunal from persons who took the original decision, the way the hearing was conducted and the reason for taking the decision to continue the proceedings: *R. v Bracknell Forest BC Ex p. McLellan*, 2001.

6.55 ECHR Compliance. The review by the authority of its own decision does not provide an impartial and independent tribunal to determine a tenant's civil rights in accordance with art.6 of the European Convention on Human Rights. The availability of a challenge through judicial review (6.53), however, is sufficient to ensure compatibility with Art.6: *McLellan*.

6.56 Proceedings and status as introductory tenant. Proceedings might not be completed before either an introductory tenancy would otherwise become secure because of the expiry of the trial period (6.36) or circumstances arise such that the tenancy ceases to be secure, so that the tenancy would also cease to be an introductory tenant (6.37) (1996, s.130(1)).

6.57 In either case, the tenancy remains an introductory tenancy until the proceedings are finally determined by a court, withdrawn or abandoned (including on appeal), and the date arrives when the tenant has to give up possession pursuant to the court order (6.43) (1996, s.130(2),(5)).

6.58 If no order is made, the normal rules will continue to apply to determine whether the tenancy is still introductory. If the tenancy would have ceased to be introductory because of a change of landlord, or the introductory tenancy regime is abandoned, or on succession (6.37, 6.40), then the tenancy will cease to be introductory notwithstanding the proceedings, but the landlord may continue with the proceedings as if it was still introductory (1996, s.130(3)). If no order is then made, the tenant may become secure, or assured (but not introductory), and will indeed in substance have been declared to have been secure or assured pending the outcome.

3. OTHER RIGHTS

6.59 Assignment. An introductory tenancy is incapable of assignment (1996, s.134(1)), unless it is in pursuance of a court order made under one of a number of family statutes, governing both partners and children, or else it it to a person who would be qualified to succeed to the introductory tenancy (6.40) (1996, s.134(2)).

6.60   If the introductory tenancy has ceased to be introductory for want of occupation as an only or principal home, the same provisions apply (1996, s.134(3)).

6.61   Rights to repair. The Secretary of State has power to apply the "right to repair" (3.222) to introductory tenants and has amended the regulations to do so.

6.62   Consultation and information. There are similar provisions governing introductory tenancies to those governing secure tenancies in respect of:

    (a) Consultation on housing management (3.228), and

    (b) The publication and provision of information about the terms of tenancies (3.232) (1996, ss.136, 137).

6.63   Right to buy. Introductory tenants do not have the right to buy. Where proceedings have been brought on the ground of change of landlord, abandonment of introductory regime or succession (6.56), and the tenant ceases to be an introductory tenant pending their outcome, that tenancy may prove to have been secure (6.58). Pending the outcome, however, a tenant claiming to have become secure cannot exercise the right to buy (3.183) (1996, s.130(4)), although in the event of a successful defence, the intervening time will count towards qualification and discount (3.184).

Restricted Contracts

6.64   Tenants with resident landlords. The largest class of occupiers with restricted contracts are tenants who have resident landlords (5.44–5.60). In addition, those who are provided with sufficient attendances to take them out of full Rent Act protection (5.72–5.76) or board, provided it is not substantial (5.63), have restricted contracts. Hostel-dwellers will frequently have restricted contracts, as will those in long-stay hotels. The class does not normally cover lettings from landlords who are in some way publicly accountable (*e.g.* local authorities) nor family/friendly arrangements, nor those where no long-stay is involved.

1. DEFINITION

6.65 Categorising restricted contracts. There are two ways in which restricted contracts are defined: by general definition and by specific definition. Some lettings, however, are specifically excluded from the jurisdiction.

6.66 General definition. Restricted contracts are generally defined in Rent Act 1977, s.19. Restricted contracts are those "contracts . . . whereby one person grants to another person, in consideration of a rent which includes payment for the use of furniture or for services, the right to occupy a dwelling as a residence."

6.67 In every case, it is the relationship between the occupier and the person who granted the right of occupation which is relevant: an occupier might be the restricted occupier of a protected tenant, or of a secure tenant, or of an owner-occupier or, indeed, even of a wholly unprotected tenant.

6.68 Tenancy and licence. The use of the term "contracts" has been interpreted to include both tenancies and licences: *Luganda v Service Hotels Ltd*, 1969. The arrangement must, however, be contractual, *i.e.* it has to be intended to be binding on the parties.

6.69 Services. "Services" includes attendances (5.72–5.76) and also the provision of heating or lighting, the supply of hot water and any other privilege or facility connected with the occupancy of a dwelling, other than a privilege or facility necessary for the purposes of access to the premises let, the supply of cold water or sanitary accommodation (1977, s.85). Furniture means any amount of furniture.

6.70 Exclusive occupation. The key element of a restricted contract is that of exclusive occupation. A hostel-dweller who is given a room to share with another will not have exclusive occupation, unless the occupiers approached the hostel together and took the room jointly.

6.71 Any tenant will of definition have exclusive occupation (1.98).

6.72 A hostel dweller with his own room will usually have exclusive occupation sufficient to amount to a restricted contract (*R. v South Middlesex Rent Tribunal Ex p. Beswick*, 1976).

6.73 In every case, it will be a question of fact whether or not an occupier has exclusive occupation. It will not be missing just because, for example, a landlord retains a key to the room, or because one of the landlord's employees comes in to clean.

6.74 There will still be enough exclusive occupation for these purposes if, in addition to the exclusive use of at least one room, there is shared use of other rooms (1977, s.19), even if those shared rooms constitute "living accommodation" (3.23).

6.75 Specific definition. Even if a tenant does not qualify under the general definition, above, the tenants of resident landlords who are excluded from full Rent Act protection for that reason, have restricted contracts, even if no furniture or services are provided (1977, s.20).

6.76 Those who are excluded from full protection because they share living accommodation with their landlords (5.67–5.69) are also included regardless of the provision of furniture or services (1977, s.21).

6.77 Specific exclusion. There are certain conditions which exclude an occupier from the definition of restricted contract, whether or not he qualifies under the general definition, or by specific inclusion (1977, s.19).

> (a) **Rateable values.** The rateable value of the (occupier's part of the) premises exceeds £1,500 (Greater London) or £750 (elsewhere). This is so unlikely to be the case that it may be assumed not to apply unless the landlord shows the contrary.

> (b) **Regulated tenancy.** The letting creates a regulated tenancy (5.24). This provision is inserted to ensure that there is no overlap between full Rent Act protection and Rent Tribunal restriction (*Baldock v Murray*, 1980).

> (c) **Public landlords.** The landlord under the letting is the Crown, a government department or a local authority. if Crown property is under the management of the Crown Estate Commissioners, however, it is not so excluded.

> (d) **Quasi-public landlords.** The landlord under the tenancy is a registered housing association, housing trust, the Housing Corporation, or a housing co-operative. Note that this

only excludes the tenants of such landlords, and does not prevent their licensees from using the powers of the Rent Tribunal, if they otherwise qualify.

(e) **Board.** Under the terms of the letting, the occupier is provided with board and the value to the occupier of the board forms a substantial proportion of the whole rent paid. This is a similar application of the test applicable to whether or not premises were let furnished in law before August 14, 1974, and whether or not sufficient attendances are provided to keep a tenancy out of protection (5.72–5.76). Board may be hard to value and is almost certainly worth more than the mere cost of the food. What constitutes board has already been considered (5.79). If any board is provided, a tenancy cannot be Rent Act protected but if the value of the board forms an insubstantial proportion of the rent, then it will be restricted. Otherwise, it will be wholly outside of both protection and restriction.

(f) **Holiday lettings.** If the letting is for the purposes of a holiday (4.38) the Rent Tribunal will not have jurisdiction over it.

2. RENT RESTRICTION

6.78 Reasonable rents. In respect of all restricted contracts, the Rent Tribunal can fix a reasonable rent (1977, s.78), which is to say, a rent which it considers reasonable in all the circumstances. There are no guidelines analogous to those to which the rent officer must pay heed, but, under different legislation, it has been said that it would not be reasonable to make a tenant pay for general shortages in the availability of accommodation, *i.e.* scarcity value: *John Kay Ltd v Kay*, 1952.

6.79 Rent jurisdiction. In comparison with the systems of rent regulation considered in Chapter 5, Rent Tribunal powers over rents are easy to describe. An application may be made in respect of any letting within its jurisdiction, so long as the letting lasts, and the Tribunal can reduce, confirm or increase the existing rent.

6.80 It can do this in respect of a periodic letting, or a fixed-term letting, and irrespective of any contractually agreed rent. The Rent Tribunal rent, if one exists in respect of the letting, forms the only rent limit which binds the landlord (1977, s.81), other, of course, than the actual terms of the agreement, *e.g.* for a fixed-term at a specified rent. The likelihood of such an application now being made is so rare that we do not consider the procedure any further.

3. SECURITY PROVISIONS

6.81 Lettings pre- and post-November 28, 1980. The security provisions governing restricted contracts are completely different in relation to contracts starting before November 28, 1980 (the date when the relevant parts of the Housing Act 1980 came into force), and in relation to contracts starting on or after that date.

6.82 Pre-1980 Act security. Even if rent is not really a problem, security of tenure is obtained by application to the Rent Tribunal for consideration of the rent, plus security. The Tribunal has no powers at all unless the application is made also for a rent registration.

6.83 An occupier can only apply for security of tenure (together with the rent to be considered) if a notice bringing the right of occupation to an end has been given and has not yet expired. This means that a fixed-term agreement cannot be referred to the Tribunal for security of tenure. It can, however, before the time runs out, be referred for consideration of rent.

6.84 Suspension and deferral of notice to quit. The existence of a pre-1980 restricted contract is now so unlikely that we only set out the provisions here in outline.

6.85 Where the landlord has served a valid notice to quit, and the rent has been referred to the tribunal, the notice is automatically suspended (1977, s.104).

6.86 If a notice has been served before application, then the Tribunal will not only decide what rent is payable under the letting, but also when the notice should take effect (1977, s.104).

6.87 The Rent Tribunal can defer the notice for up to six months at a time. Before the six months run out, there is nothing to stop an occupier applying for more time. The Tribunal may order no security at all, or a period shorter than six months. Deferral is automatic once the rent has been registered (1977, s.103).

6.88 The landlord is entitled to apply during the period of deferral for a reduction in security, which will be granted if there has been misconduct, *e.g.* non-compliance with the contract, by the tenant (1977, s.106).

6.89 Post-1980 Act security. The position relating to these contracts is very different. Rent Tribunal jurisdiction over security was entirely abolished (1977, s.102A).

6.90 In its place, the county court has a more limited power, to allow suspension of an order for possession, to a maximum of three months from the date of its order (1977, s.106A).

6.91 If the court grants less than three months initially, it can on a later application grant further suspension, to a maximum of three months from the date of the original order. These powers may be exercised not only for the benefit of the tenant or licensee, but also for the benefit of his spouse or ex-spouse (1977, s.106A(5), (6)).

6.92 The court's power may be exercised on terms or conditions, which must include terms as to payment of rent and of any arrears, unless the court considers that to do this would cause exceptional hardship or would otherwise be unreasonable.

6.93 The power is not limited to a former periodic restricted contract (6.83).

6.94 Although the obligation to take legal proceedings before evicting most licensees is less clear cut than former tenants (see Chapter 8), court proceedings must always be taken before evicting a former restricted licensee whose licence is a post-1980 Act contract (Protection from Eviction Act 1977, s.3(2A), added by 1980, s.69). If it were not for this amendment then the court's powers replacing the former security jurisdiction of the Rent Tribunal might well not have availed restricted licensees at all.

4. FURTHER PROVISIONS

6.95 Premiums and deposits. The prohibitions against premiums and excessive deposits described above (5.216–5.227), only applied to restricted contracts if there was an effective rent registration with the Rent Tribunal, *i.e.* one which applies to the letting in question (1977, s.122). If there was not, then there were no prohibitions on premiums. But if a rent registered with the Tribunal did apply to the letting, then all the remarks made under this heading in Chapter 5 will apply in the same way.

6.96   Change of terms. If the rent under a restricted contract is varied after the commencement of Pt I of the 1988 Act (January 15, 1989), then a new contract is deemed to come into existence at the time of the variation and the contract will cease to be a restricted contract.

6.97   The only exceptions to this are if the variation is one resulting from an application to the Rent Tribunal, or if the variation is by agreement, but only in order to alter the rent to match one that is registered by the Rent Tribunal (1988, s.36).

6.98   If other terms of the contract are varied, then it is a question of fact in each case whether it is a sufficiently substantial variation to amount to a new contract (which will not be a restricted contract if after January 15, 1989), or only a minor variation which leaves the old contract in existence.

Protected Shorthold Tenancies

6.99   The protected shorthold tenancy was introduced by the Housing Act 1980, and abolished by the 1988 Act (when it was replaced by the assured shorthold).

1. NOTICE

6.100   Valid prior notice. A valid notice must have been given by the landlord to the tenant before the tenancy was granted that the tenancy was to be a shorthold tenancy (1980, s.52(1)(b); 6.103(c)). The notice must be in the prescribed form of notice. A notice given after the tenancy has begun will not suffice.

6.101   On proceedings for possession under the shorthold ground, a court can, however, waive the requirement for notice if it considers that it is just and equitable to do so (1980, s.55(2)). This would be an extremely severe decision: in effect, the court would be retrospectively deeming the tenancy to have been a shorthold; the court should only use this power when the omission to serve notice was known to the tenant, perhaps known to be an oversight or accident of which the tenant now seeks to take advantage in a way that the court considers unmeritorious, or the notice was in very slightly the wrong form.

6.102   In *RJ Dunnell Property Investments Ltd v Thorpe*, 1991, where the tenancy agreement had stated that the letting was a protected shorthold but no notice had in fact been served, a decision to dispense with notice was upheld by the Court of Appeal. It should not be used, however, to take away from a tenant full security where the tenant had reason to believe that was what he enjoyed.

2. CONDITIONS

6.103 The protected shorthold tenancy (Housing Act 1980—"1980"—s.51), is a tenancy which is in all other respects a fully Rent Act protected tenancy (5.39–5.92), granted after November 28, 1980 (when the provisions were brought into force), which fulfilled the following conditions.

(a) **Fixed-term.** The tenancy had to be fixed-term as distinct from periodic (1.97), granted for a minimum of one year, and a maximum of five (1980, s.52(1)).

A tenancy granted on one date, but expressed to have commenced on an earlier date, would only be likely to be considered to fulfil the minimum/maximum time-limits if they were fulfilled from the date when the tenancy was actually granted, rather than from any such earlier date (*Roberts v Church Commissioners for England*, 1971; *Brikom Investments Ltd v Seaford*, 1981).

(b) **No break clause.** There had to be no provision in the agreement for bringing the tenancy to an end by the landlord, other than by way of forfeiture (1.126–1.141) for non-payment of rent or breach of some other term of the tenancy (1980, s.52(1)(a)).

Thus, a "break-clause" allowing the landlord to give notice in the middle of, or any other time during, the term would defeat the shorthold.

A clause which allowed a landlord to forfeit if the tenant went bankrupt was construed as creating an obligation on the part of the tenant not to go bankrupt, with the effect that the tenancy was still shorthold (*Paterson v Aggio*, 1987).

(c) **Prior notice.** Before the tenancy was granted, the landlord had given the tenant a valid shorthold notice (1980, s.52(1)(b)).

(d) **Registered rent.** In some cases, either there must have been a registered rent (5.190–5.212) at the commencement of the tenancy, or the landlord must have secured a certificate of fair rent (now no longer available), by the time the tenancy was granted (1980, s.52(1)(c)). This, too, is considered further below (6.112–6.114).

(e) **Previous Rent Act protected or statutory tenant.** The tenancy was not granted to a person who, immediately before the grant, was a Rent Act protected or statutory (5.24) tenant of the same premises (1980, s.52(2)).

This is designed to prevent landlords persuading existing tenants to sign shorthold agreements. However, it only protects the tenant if the new tenancy was of exactly the same premises as the pre-existing tenancy (*cf.* 5.60). Thus, another flat in the same building would not keep the tenant out of shorthold, nor even a new agreement in respect of, *e.g.* the same premises less or plus one room (*Gluchowska v Tottenham BC*, 1954).

6.104 Notice by tenant. Although the landlord could not reserve the right to give notice during the life of the shorthold (6.103(b)), the shorthold tenant is absolutely entitled to give notice, even if the written agreement prohibits him from doing so (1980, s.53(1)).

6.105 Furthermore, any clause purporting to penalise the tenant for giving notice under the provision, *e.g.* imposing additional rent, is wholly void and of no effect (1980, s.53(2)).

6.106 The notice may be given at any time during the fixed term: if the fixed term was for more than two years, the notice must be of three months; if for two years or less, it need only be of one month; in either event, it must be in writing (1980, s.53(1)).

6.107 Continuation of protected shortholds. A protected shorthold tenancy is only technically a shorthold during the initial fixed-term tenancy (1980, s.52(5)). This is only technical, because the power of the landlord to recover possession under the shorthold ground continues indefinitely (6.119; *Gent v De La Mare*, 1987) and references to "shorthold tenants" include those whose shorthold has ended, but who remain vulnerable to the shorthold ground. The shorthold tenant is also subject to the usual grounds for possession (5.120–5.172).

6.108 Limited assignability. A protected shorthold tenancy cannot be assigned (1.223), other than by order of the court under

Matrimonial Causes Act 1973, ss.23A or 24 (9.06), at any time during the shorthold (6.107), or afterwards, *i.e.* so long as the tenant remains subject to the possibility (6.107) of use of the shorthold ground (1980, s.54(2)).

6.109 It is unclear whether the Family Law Act 1996 (9.40–9.43) could be used to order a transfer of tenancy between spouses or cohabitants, though this seems likely on balance as there is no express prohibition against it.

6.110 Subletting. While there is no restriction on subletting, a sub-tenant to whom some part of the premises, or even the whole of the premises, has been let at any time while the tenant is still subject to the possibility (6.107) of use of the shorthold ground cannot avail himself of Rent Act 1977, s.137 (1.163; 1980, s.54(1)), and so will only become the landlord's tenant directly if the circumstances would put him in that position at common law, *i.e.* if the tenant surrenders (1.186).

6.111 Succession. If there is a succession to a Rent Act protected tenancy (5.33) which is a protected shorthold, the succession takes effect as an assured shorthold (above) (1988, s.39(7)).

3. RENT

6.112 Need for registered rent. Under the Act, there must, at the time the tenancy was granted, either already have been a registered rent, or a certificate of fair rent, in relation to the premises (1980, s.52(2)(c); 6.103(d)). Registration of fair rents has already been considered (5.190–5.212).

6.113 The certificate of fair rent was repealed with the introduction of the Housing Act 1988. The certificate of fair rent was usually used by a landlord intending to let out premises on a fully Rent Act protected tenancy, after the execution of works, and who wanted to know what was likely to be his return on the property. The same procedure used to be available to a landlord intending to let out on shorthold, even though no works were to be carried out by him beforehand.

6.114 If the landlord let out the premises when there was only a certificate of fair rent:

(a) Prior to full registration, no more rent should have been charged than stated in the certificate; and

(b) The landlord had to apply for full registration within 28 days of the beginning of the tenancy (1980, s.52(1)(c)).

6.115 Waiver of need for registered rent. The Secretary of State reserved powers under the Act to waive the requirement for a registered rent or a certificate of fair rent (1980, s.52(4)). He used this power in 1981 to waive the requirement outside London (SI 1981/1578) and from 1987 throughout the whole of the country (SI 1987/265).

6.116 In any event, the court may still order possession on the shorthold ground (6.119–6.128) even when there has been a failure to comply with the registered rent requirement, if it is just and equitable to do so (1980, s.55(2)).

6.117 Again (*cf.* 6.101), this power is only likely to be used when there has been a technical defect, or an application pursued a matter of days late. It is highly unlikely to be used if a very high rent has been charged, but where the failure was an honest mistake, and the rent set was fully acceptable to both parties, it may be (*RJ Dunnell Property Investments Ltd v Thorpe*, 1991).

6.118 Where a rent was already the subject of a certificate or registered, the tenant could still apply for registration himself (5.211–5.212), and if the rent officer registers a rent lower than that stated in a certificate, it is the lower rent that will be payable from registration (5.213).

4. THE SHORTHOLD GROUND

6.119 Mandatory ground for possession. The shorthold ground remains available for use as long as the original shorthold tenant remains the tenant of the premises (1980, s.54(3)).

6.120 The ground itself is to be found, by way of amendment, in Rent Act 1977, Sch.15, Case 19, as an added mandatory ground for possession, although it was originally contained in 1980, s.55(1).

6.121 The landlord must show not only that the preliminary conditions were fulfilled (6.103), save in so far as he hopes to rely on the court's discretion (6.101, 6.116), but also that since the technical end of the shorthold tenancy, *i.e.* the termination of the original fixed-period (6.107), there has been no further grant of a tenancy of the premises to anyone other than the original shorthold tenancy. In addition, he must comply with the "warning" notice provisions (*Ridehalgh v Horsefield*, 1992).

6.122 Warning notices. The purpose of the warning notice provisions is to ensure that the tenant is not constantly subject to the likelihood of proceedings. Accordingly, before applying for possession under Case 19, the landlord must serve the appropriate notice. These notice provisions do not, however, need to be fulfilled once the tenancy has become statutory (5.24) if grounds for possession (5.120–5.172) other than the mandatory ground (6.119) are used instead.

6.123 The landlord can only commence proceedings within three months after the expiry of the notice (1977, Sch.15, Case 19(b)).

6.124 The notice must be in writing and must state that proceedings may be brought under Case 19 after it expires. The notice must give a minimum of three months: but it can be for an unlimited length, *i.e.* before it expires. It may be served during the last three months of the fixed term, or else during the same three months of any succeeding year, and no earlier than three months after the expiry of the last notice.

6.125 Warning provisions exemplified. These provisions are difficult to untangle. They are best approached by way of illustration. A fixed term was granted on April 1, 1988 to expire on March 31, 1990. A warning notice may be served at any time between the beginning of January and the end of March during 1990 or any subsequent year in which the ground remains available to the landlord. It must give the tenant at least three months: if served on January 1, therefore, proceedings could commence on April 1: if not served until March 1, however, they could not commence before June 1. If the landlord gave longer than three months, the proceedings could not be commenced before the time allowed expires.

6.126 Commencement of proceedings. Once the notice expires, the landlord must bring his proceedings within three months, or else the notice lapses. He cannot serve a further notice during this three months. Thus, if the notice was for three months, and was served on January 1, proceedings must be commenced between April 1, and June 30, and during that time no further notice can be served. Accordingly, July 1 would be the earliest date when a new notice could be served, but as the notice can only be served during the January-March "season," he cannot serve a further notice until January 1 next. If, however, he gives nine months, from January 1, he can commence his proceedings at any time between October 1, and December 30. If he fails to do so, he can serve a new notice immediately after December 30, as: (a) he will be back in the notice season; and (b) three months will have passed since the notice lapsed.

6.127 Eviction season. It follows that while it is true that a tenant cannot be subject at any given moment to proceedings for possession under Case 19, the landlord has a generous discretion to select his eviction (as opposed to notice) season, and may in practice, by careful choice of the length of notice, keep the tenant in the position where proceedings are always looming, or to be anticipated.

6.128 These notice provisions do not, however, dispense with the normal requirement to bring the tenancy to an end at common law, by notice to quit (1.108–1.120), or forfeiture (1.126–1.130).

5. FURTHER PROVISIONS

6.129 Premiums and deposits. The premium and deposit provisions applicable to Rent Act protected tenants are also applicable to protected shorthold tenancies in the same way.

Further Protection and Assistance

6.130 Miscellaneous provisions

   (i) Accommodation Agency Charges;

   (ii) Resale of Utilities; and

   (iii) Housing Benefit.

6.131 These are all applicable to assured shorthold tenants, those with restricted contracts and protected shorthold tenants, as they are to Housing Act assured or fully Rent Act protected tenants (4.159–4.166). Only the latter is likely to be relevant to Housing Act introductory tenants (3.265).

CHAPTER SEVEN

Occupation without Security

Introduction

7.01 Residual classes of occupation. This Chapter examines the remaining classes of occupation, being those without any security at all. There are five such classes.

1. Trespassers.

2. Unrestricted licensees.

3. Non-secure public tenants.

4. Non-secure/assured quasi-public tenants and

5. Unrestricted tenants.

Outline

7.02 Trespassers

- There is a special, speedy eviction procedure available against trespassers.

- Interim possession orders may also be obtained, breach of which creates a criminal offence.

- It is an offence to use violence to evict a trespasser.

- Trespassers may themselves commit offences in some circumstances, particularly if required to leave by a displaced residential occupier or a protected intended occupier and they fail to do so.

7.03   Unrestricted licensees

- Most licensees do not enjoy any security of tenure.

- Unless it is an "excluded licence," a periodic license must be brought to an end by the service of a notice complying with the Protection from Eviction Act 1977.

- A court order is generally required to evict a licensee.

- The special procedures for eviction may be used against former unrestricted licensees.

7.04   Non-secure public tenants

- Some tenants of public landlords may fall outside security of tenure all together.

- Before eviction, any tenancy must be properly terminated and, save in the case of an "excluded tenant," a minimum of four weeks notice to quit given to a periodic tenant.

- A court order is generally required to evict a non-secure tenant.

- A decision to evict a non-secure tenant by a local authority can be challenged by judicial review.

- There are special provisions relating to notices of increase of rent for non-secure, local authority tenants.

7.05   Non-secure/assured quasi public tenants

- Before eviction, any tenancy must be properly terminated and, unless "excluded", a minimum of four weeks notice to quit given to periodic tenants.

- A court order is generally required to evict such tenants.

7.06   Unrestricted tenants

- These are tenants of private sector landlords who are not protected by the Rent Act 1977 or the Housing Act 1988.

- Before eviction, any tenancy must be properly terminated, and, unless "excluded", a minimum of four weeks notice to quit given to periodic tenants.

- A court order is generally required to evict an unrestricted tenant.

Trespassers

1. EVICTION

7.07 Least security. Unless they have been in occupation for long enough to claim a right by adverse possession (1.35), trespassers have no rights of occupation and, because they pay no rent, are subject to no rent control. They have the least security of all. Court proceedings can be taken against them at any time, without any warning, and special, speedy procedures can, and in all probability will, be used: CPR 55 and Sch.1, Ord.24 (county court) and Ord.113 (High Court).

7.08 Proceedings for possession. These procedures do not even require the landlord to identify the occupiers. A landlord can issue proceedings against a named person on his own, or against persons unknown, or against both a named person and persons unknown. A claim is issued, stating the landlord's interest in the property, that the property in question has been occupied without his consent and, if the claim is also against persons unknown, that the landlord does not know the names of some or all of the people on the property.

7.09 Orders for possession. The summons is served by personal service save in the case of persons unknown, where it can be by fixing the summons to the door of the premises. Once it has been served, there need only be a delay of five days, in the case of residential premises (two otherwise), before a court hearing.

7.10 If the court finds that the occupiers are, indeed, trespassers, then it is obliged to make an immediate order for possession (*McPhail v Persons Unknown*, 1973) not even subject to the normal 14-day delay to which, for example, a final order against a secure, or indeed any other tenant, will normally be subject (3.145).

7.11 Eviction. Landlords will still normally need to effect eviction by using court bailiffs, which may provide some slight delay of, perhaps, a week or 10 days.

7.12 When bailiffs attend on an eviction, they must turn out of the premises all those people found there, whether or not they were parties to the proceedings, or even if they moved into the premises between the date of the court order and the actual eviction, unless an occupier can claim to have some separate right of occupation, *e.g.* a tenant who is on the premises (*R v Wandsworth County Court Ex p. Wandsworth London BC*, 1975).

7.13 Negotiated suspension. Although the court is obliged to make the immediate order, it is possible that the landlord will consent to a suspension of, for example, two or four weeks. They may agree to this before the actual hearing. If there is any prospect of a dispute, representatives of the landlord are likely to be amenable to granting such a delay by agreement, to avoid the need for the hearing. Even if there is no prospect of dispute, more responsible landlords, such as public and quasi-public landlords, will usually be willing to agree to some time.

7.14 Damages. Although the court can order costs against an occupier during the course of proceedings brought under one of these speedy procedures, there is no provision for awarding any monetary compensation by way of damages to the landlord. If a landlord wants to seek such damages, he must use normal possession proceedings and claim damages for use and occupation.

7.15 Interim possession. The interim possession order provides an even quicker remedy, allowing for a hearing only three days from the application to court. An application for an interim possession order may only be made against persons who have entered the premises without the applicant's consent (CPR Sch.2, CCR, Ord.24, Pt II).

7.16 An application for such an order must be made on the prescribed form and the applicant must give specific undertakings, in particular as to damages and putting the defendant back into possession if it turns out the interim possession order was wrongly granted. The court hearing date may be set at any time after three days from the making of the application. For the hearing to go ahead, there must be evidence that the order has been served on the defendant.

7.17 Order and breach. An interim possession order requires the defendant to vacate the premises within 24 hours. The order must also fix a return date (for a full hearing) not less than 7 days after the date on which the interim order was made, and the order expires on this return date.

7.18 Eviction takes place through the police, rather than the court bailiffs. Failure to leave is a criminal offence, as is returning within 12 months to the premises to which the order applies or knowingly or recklessly giving false information in order to obtain or resist such an order: Criminal Justice and Public Order Act 1994, ss.76, 75.

2. CRIMINAL OFFENCES

7.19 Criminal offences. The only protection that a trespasser has against eviction is such as is provided by the Criminal Law Act 1977, which created certain offences in connection with squatting, and repealed the earlier Forcible Entry Acts. The Act also, however, created offences which a trespasser may commit in connection with squatting.

7.20 Anyone who commits a criminal offence under the Criminal Law Act 1977 ("CLA 1977") in the course of evicting a trespasser who is using premises as a residence is likely also to commit an offence under the Protection from Eviction Act 1977 ("PEA 1977"): see Chapter 8.

7.21 The offence which serves to protect trespassers is that of:

(i) Violent eviction.

The offences a trespasser must be careful not to commit are those of:

(ii) Trespass with an offensive weapon;

(iii) Trespass on diplomatic or consular premises;

(iv) Resisting or obstructing an officer of a court in the course of an eviction;

(v) Refusing to leave premises when requested.

(i) *Violent Eviction*

7.22 Violent entry. Any person, whether or not the landlord, who uses or threatens violence against either people or property in order to gain entry into premises, commits an offence if, but only if, the person seeking entry knows that there is someone present on the premises at the time of the attempted entry, and that that person is opposed to the entry (CLA 1977, s.6).

7.23 The offence is not committed if the person seeking entry has lawful authority to do so, *i.e.* a court bailiff. It does not constitute lawful authority that the person trying to get in has some greater interest, *e.g.* licence, tenancy or ownership of the property.

7.24 Displaced residential occupier. There is an important exception to this offence. The offence is not committed by a person otherwise offending against its provisions if he or someone on whose behalf he is acting is a "displaced residential occupier" of the premises.

7.25 A displaced residential occupier is any person, other than another trespasser, who was using the premises or part of them as a residence immediately before the trespasser entered (CLA 1977, s.12). This exception is designed to permit the owner-occupier, or tenant, who goes away on holiday and finds on his return that the premises have been "squatted," to evict the trespassers without any need to take court proceedings and without fear of committing an offence. In practice, such incidents of squatting in people's homes have been very rare, as it is no part of the ethos of the squatter to make another homeless.

7.26 A displaced residential occupier must also take great care when using this privilege for he may still commit any of the ordinary, criminal offences of assault, actual or grievous bodily harm, etc.

7.27 Protected intending occupier. A second exception is made for "protected intending occupiers". There are three categories of protected intending occupier.

(i) A person is a protected intending occupier if he either has a freehold or a leasehold interest in the property, and requires the premises for his own occupation (CLA 1977, s.12A). The leasehold interest must have not less than two years to run at the relevant time.

(ii) A private tenant (whose tenancy may be less than two years) or a licensee with a licence granted by a freeholder or leaseholder (whose lease has more than two years to run) may be a protected intending occupier if he requires the accommodation for his own occupation.

(iii) A person is also a protected intending occupier if he has been given permission to occupy the premises as a residence by any of the public or quasi-public landlords described below (7.55, 7.69).

7.28 In each case, the protected intended occupier must produce a statement which proves his status as a protected intending occupier. In the first and second cases, the statement has to specify the interest which the would-be occupier has, must state the requirement for use of the premises as a residence for himself, and must have been signed either in the presence of a justice of the peace or commissioner of oaths who has also signed the statement as a witness. In the third case, the statement must specify that the would-be occupier has been authorised to occupy the premises and that the landlord is one of the bodies referred to.

(ii) *Trespass with an Offensive weapon*

7.29 Offensive weapon. It is a criminal offence for a person on the premises as a trespasser, having entered as such, to have with him any weapon of offence, *i.e.* anything which has been made or adapted for causing injury to another (CLA 1977, s.8). This, too, raises the spectre of "violent squatting" which has been virtually unknown in the recent history of the squatting movement.

7.30 Because such a weapon can either be made or adapted for causing violence, a person can, in theory, be charged with causing violence on the basis of possession of virtually any common household implement, *e.g.* a kitchen knife or screwdriver. But for a person to have committed this offence, he must not only be a trespasser, but must have entered as such. This refers to the common law rule that a former licensee and, strictly, even a former tenant, remaining on premises after the end of the licence or tenancy, becomes a trespasser (1.74). Such people are not trespassers for the purposes of this provision.

(iii) *Trespass on Diplomatic or Consular Premises*

7.31 Diplomatic premises. This provision was designed to deal with "political squatting" (*Kamara v DPP*, 1974) and makes it an offence for a trespasser to enter diplomatic or consular buildings, unless he can show that he does not believe them to be diplomatic or consular premises (CLA 1977, s.9).

(iv) *Resisting or Obstructing an Officer of the court in the course of an Eviction*

7.32 Resisting official eviction. It is an offence to resist or intentionally obstruct any person who is an officer of a court executing a possession order issued by a county court or the High Court (CLA 1977, s.10). This offence is only committed by someone in premises in circumstances that are also defined in the Act.

7.33 Briefly, the Act is intended to catch anyone resisting or intentionally obstructing an officer who is executing a possession order made under one of the speedy procedures referred to above, Ords 24 and 113. It is so worded, however, that it applies to resistance or intentional obstruction of an officer executing any order which could have been brought under those procedures but which have in fact been brought under normal proceedings, for example because the owner wishes to claim damages for use and occupation.

7.34 The Orders can be used against any trespasser, which includes a former licensee and has been held to include illegal sub-tenants (*Moore Properties (Ilford) Ltd v McKeon*, 1976; 1.174–1.184). The orders do not catch illegal tenants of mortgagors (*London Goldhawk Building Society v Eminer*, 1977; 1.221–1.222).

(vi)   *Refusing to Leave Premises when Requested*

7.35 Refusal to leave. This was the major new offence introduced by the Act (CLA 1977, s.7). It makes it an offence for any trespasser, who enters as a trespasser, to fail to leave premises if asked to do so by a displaced residential occupier or by a person who is, within the terms of the Act, a protected intending occupier.

7.36 Displaced residential occupier and protected intending occupier have been described above (7.24, 7.27). In either case, the displaced residential occupier or the protected intending occupier must have been kept out of occupation by reason of the trespass and, obviously, there can be no offence of failing to leave when requested until a request has been made. The request does not need itself to be in writing but protected intending occupiers have to produce the required statement (7.27).

7.37 Defences. It is clear that a protected intending occupier could be a licensee, *e.g.* for short-life use, of one of the public or quasi-public landlords; as it is necessary for a protected intending occupier to specify that the premises are to be used as a residence, it can only be used in connection with premises fit for use, *i.e.* not in connection with premises yet to be renewed or redeveloped.

7.38 It is a defence for the trespasser to prove that he did not believe that the person asking him to leave was either a displaced residential occupier or a protected intending occupier, or that the premises in question are or form part of premises used mainly for a non-residential purpose and that he was only on that part. It is also a defence to prove that a protected intending occupier did not produce the required statement (7.27).

Unrestricted Licensees

7.39 Resort to common law. Most licensees do not enjoy any statutory protection at all and must therefore rely upon their common law rights of occupation. The exceptions are: a licensee within public sector security (3.19); a licensee whose licence pre-dates the commencement of the Housing Act 1988 ("1988"), and who has a restricted contract (6.68), and certain licensees who are service occupiers (1.159) who may either fall within the Housing Act 1988 (4.52) or the Rent (Agriculture) Act 1976 (5.15).

7.40 Service tenants and occupiers who work in agriculture but who are not protected by either the 1988 or 1976 Acts may also enjoy a degree more protection against eviction than others, as the county court enjoys power to suspend the operation of a possession order against them for up to six months in certain circumstances (PEA 1977, s.4, as amended by the 1988 Act).

7.41 Notice requirement. At common law, no licensee can be evicted until the licence has been brought to an end (1.79–1.84). A bare licence (1.76) can be brought to an end by reasonable notice, and a contractual licence by either reasonable notice or the contractually agreed period (and form), whichever is the longer (1.81).

7.42 A fixed-term contractual licensee requires no notice and the licence terminates on the expiry of the term (1.79). An example of such an arrangement might be a letting for short-life use which is for a specific period only.

7.43 If notice has to be given to determine a licence, then, since the commencement of Pt I of the 1988 Act (January 15, 1989), such notice has to be in writing, of a minimum of four weeks, and contain such information as may be prescribed (PEA 1977, s.5(1A), added by 1988, s.32; 1.119), even if the licence began before the commencement of the 1988 Act. This is not so, however, if the licence is an "excluded licence" (s.5(1B)): excluded licences (and tenancies) are described in Chapter 8 (8.19), below.

7.44 Licensees and rent protection. Only those contractual licensees whose licences pre-date the commencement of Pt I of the 1988 Act (January 15, 1989) and fall within Rent Tribunal jurisdiction (Chapter 6) enjoy any protection over the levels of rent they have to pay.

7.45 Strictly, a licensee's rent cannot be increased without terminating the existing licence in the normal way and offering a new one. Most licensees, however, will consent to a mutual variation of the rent terms unless they are actually prepared to leave because, lacking any legislative protection, they are in no bargaining position.

7.46 Status of former licensee. Once the licence has terminated, the former licensee is in strict law a trespasser. Indeed, both the former bare licensee and the former contractual licensee are in exactly the same position as a trespasser (7.08–7.14), save that they are not liable to be convicted for certain of the offences described (7.30).

7.47 Court proceedings have to be taken to evict a former licensee, however, unless the licence is an "excluded licence" (PEA 1977, s.3(2B), (2C), added by 1988, s.30), even if the licence was granted before the commencement of the 1988 Act.

7.48 This will not apply to hotel accommodation, as it is not occupied "as a residence" and therefore does not have the protection of the Act: *Mohamed v Manek*, 1995.

7.49 It is also necessary to take legal proceedings to evict a former service occupier, who enjoys a special privilege of remaining in occupation until a court order is made, provided that he enjoyed exclusive occupation of the premises which he held with his job (PEA 1977, ss.3 and 8).

7.50 Use of speedy procedures. Proceedings may be brought against any former licensee under the speedy procedures provided by CPR Pt 55 and Sch.1, Ords 24 and 113.

7.51 These proceedings should not, however, be used where there is a triable issue (*Cooper v Varzdari*, 1986), *e.g.* that the licence is a sham arrangement concealing a tenancy (*Crancour Ltd v Da Silvaesa*, 1986) or that the occupier is a tenant holding over (*Henderson v Law*, 1984).

7.52 Any licence must have been determined before the issue of these proceedings (*GLC v Jenkins*, 1975), though where normal possession proceedings are used, the landlord need only show determination of the licence by the date of the hearing.

7.53 In all cases, it is in any event practicable and advisable for the landlord to take court proceedings to evict a former licensee, because there is a risk that if he does not do so, he will commit a criminal offence, for example under CLA 1977, or of common law assault, etc. If a landlord commits a criminal offence in evicting a former licensee, then he will also commit an offence under PEA 1977 (Chapter 8).

7.54 Offences. Former licensees are not subject to proceedings for being on premises with an offensive weapon (7.29), nor are they required by law to leave when asked to go by a displaced residential occupier or a protected intending occupier (7.35–7.38). They can, however, commit the offence of resisting or intentionally obstructing an officer of the court in the execution of an order of the court for possession, because they are liable to CPR Pt 55, and Sch.1, Ords 24 and 113, even if those proceedings are not actually used against them, for example, because the landlord was claiming damages for use and occupation during or continuing after the licence and therefore chose to use normal possession proceedings (7.14), or because the proceedings are inappropriate on account of a dispute (7.51).

Non-Secure Public Tenants

7.55 Public landlords. Those who are described as public tenants are the tenants of the Crown, a government department, or a local authority.

7.56 Where the tenancy began before the commencement of 1988, Pt I (January 15, 1989), a tenant of the Crown, in property under the management of the Crown Estates Commissioners, is Rent Act protected (5.88); later lettings, however, are within Housing Act assured protection (Chapter 4).

7.57 Most tenants of local authorities are now secure tenants (3.17–3.38), and some may be introductory tenants (6.29–6.42).

7.58   In this section, we are concerned with tenants who are not secure or introductory (or protected or assured).

7.59   All former tenants are entitled to remain in occupation until such time as a court order is obtained against them (PEA 1977, s.3), save for those who qualify as "excluded tenants" (for the definition of which, see 8.19); it would be illegal eviction to regain possession in any other way: see Chapter 8.

7.60   **Eviction.** It is, of course, illegal to evict a tenant before the expiry of the tenancy. The rules relating to determination or expiry of a tenancy have been described above (1.108–1.141). Notices to quit must normally be in writing, contain prescribed information and be of a minimum period of four weeks, and are also subject to the other common law rules described: if the tenancy commenced on or after January 15, 1989, when Pt I of the 1988 Act came into force, however, the requirement for a minimum period and for writing, and for prescribed information, has been waived for "excluded tenants" (as to the definition of which, see 8.19), so that only compliance with common law is required.

7.61   **No rent protection.** There is no rent control for the public tenant. In order to increase the rent, the landlord must normally bring the tenancy to an end in the usual way and, of course, in the case of a fixed-term tenancy, he will not be able to do that simply in order to raise the rent.

7.62   A fixed-term tenant could consent to an increase during the period, but it is fairly likely to be unenforceable should he subsequently change his mind, because, in effect, the landlord will have given nothing in exchange for the unplanned increase.

7.63   A periodic tenant could likewise consent to an increase without compelling the landlord to serve notice to quit and offer a new tenancy, but this might be enforceable because of the ease with which the landlord could otherwise bring the tenancy to an end, *i.e.* there could be said to be some consideration from the landlord, by way of failure to serve notice to quit. For this reason, many public periodic tenants would be inclined to consent to an increase.

7.64   **Local authority notices of increase.** Local authorities are under an obligation to keep rents in their areas under review. They have a discretion to charge such rents as they consider reasonable.

These matters have been considered in Chapter 3 (3.234). They apply as much to their tenants without any security as to those with.

7.65 Local authority tenancies are almost invariably periodic. Local authorities have a particular privilege, now to be found in the Housing Act 1985, s.25, to raise rents without serving a notice to quit. They may, instead, serve a notice of increase.

7.66 A notice of increase cannot take effect earlier than the authority could otherwise have brought the tenancy to an end by notice to quit, *i.e.* not less than four weeks, and the notice must warn the tenant of his right to leave rather than pay the increase. In addition, the notice must tell the tenant what he must do in order to bring the tenancy to an end if he chooses to leave, and by what date the tenant must serve his own notice to quit to the local authority, if he—as he rarely will in practice be able to do (especially if he may wish to apply as homeless: see Chapter 10)— chooses this course of action.

7.67 Reasonable use of powers. As regards security, although we are considering tenants without security of tenure as such, local authorities are obliged by common law to act within their powers. Powers are so defined at law as to preclude authorities acting in an unreasonable fashion, and to require authorities to act reasonably.

7.68 Where eviction is concerned, this means that a local authority could not serve a notice to quit, say, whimsically. Before making a decision to evict, the authority must take into account all proper and relevant considerations, and must exclude from consideration anything which it would be improper to take into account. For example, a corrupt decision will always be outside their powers, as will a decision borne of malice. These principles are sometimes called the principles of administrative law (see further 10.173–10.180). As the authority will be determining the right to occupy the tenant's "home," Art.8 of the ECHR is considered also to be applicable, so that a decision to evict must be proportionate (see 3.94).

Non-Secure/Assured Quasi-Public Tenants

7.69 Quasi-public landlords. Non-secure and non-assured quasi-public tenants are the tenants of registered housing associations, housing trusts, or registered social landlords as they are now termed (Housing Act 1996, Pt I), or of the Housing Corporation, and housing co-operatives who for one reason or another do not qualify as Housing Act secure (3.17–3.38) or Housing Act assured (4.13–4.21) tenants.

7.70   Rents. Very little remains to be said of this class that cannot be achieved by cross-reference. If Housing Act secure, *i.e.* if preceding the commencement of 1988, Pt I (January 15, 1989), their rents are governed by the fair rent system, subject to minor variations (3.237–3.242). Landlords may increase rents without having to serve a notice to quit (Rent Act 1977, s.93). Otherwise, tenants are subject to no rent control.

7.71   Eviction. Such tenants cannot be evicted without the tenancy being determined (1.108–1.141). The same principles of notice and requirements for a court order under the Protection from Eviction Act 1977 apply as to non-secure public tenants (7.59 and 7.60).

7.72   It has been held that housing associations are not normally subject, as are local authorities (7.67), to the principles of administrative law (*Peabody Housing Association v Green*, 1978). In view of developments generated by the Human Rights Act 1998, however, this may no longer be absolutely true, where, *e.g.* a housing association has been created to take over the stock of a local authority (*Donoghue v Poplar HARCA*, 2001); in such circumstances, they are also likely to be considered subject to that Act, and—as such—to the same considerations as local authorities (above, para.7.68).

Unrestricted Tenants

7.73   Minimal rights. This class will include the pre-Housing Act 1988 tenant who is provided with substantial board and the tenant occupying premises of very high rateable value. Unrestricted tenants enjoy the protection of their contracts against both eviction and rent increase but are in a weak bargaining position when it comes to increases, as the landlord can easily terminate the tenancy, *e.g.* if it is a periodic tenancy. Unless an "excluded tenancy" (as to the definition of which, see 8.19, below), the notice to quit must be in writing, contain the prescribed information, and be of a minimum of four weeks, and must otherwise comply with the common law (1.111–1.116). Unrestricted tenants benefit from no system of rent protection.

Further Financial Protection and Assistance

7.74 Miscellaneous provisions. As trespassers do not pay for their occupation of premises, there is no financial protection available to them. All of the other classes described in this chapter are subject to protection in respect of:

(a) Accommodation Agency Charges (4.159–4.163);

(b) Resale of Utilities (4.164); and

(c) Housing Benefit (3.265).

7.75 There are no restrictions on the charging of premiums which apply to these classes of occupation.

CHAPTER EIGHT

Harassment and Illegal Eviction

Introduction

8.01   In Chapters 1, 4, 5 and 7, we considered some of the ways used by landlords who seek to evade the effects of protective legislation. Some landlords, however, still resort to force or other crude tactics in order to get rid of their occupiers when they want to do so, without taking proceedings in court. To counter this, there are criminal offences of harassment and illegal eviction, now to be found in the Protection from Eviction Act 1977 .

8.02   In practice, however, individual occupiers may be able to get much more help from the civil courts than the criminal law. Thus, there are only limited circumstances in which the magistrates' courts can make an order for compensation, and they will rarely order damages for suffering or inconvenience. Similarly, the magistrates' court has no power to make an order compelling a landlord to readmit an evicted occupier, either immediately—which is when it will be most needed—or at all. Strictly, it cannot even order a landlord to cease harassing an occupier, although it can bind a landlord over to keep the peace, or could discharge a landlord without punishment, conditional on no further offences being committed.

8.03   The position is different in the civil courts (primarily the county courts), where remedies are pursued between the parties. These courts have power to order a landlord to readmit an evicted occupier, and they can exercise this power so quickly that an occupier may be able to get back in the same day as the eviction, or, at least, the same day as he has sought advice. They can also make orders restraining further harassment or eviction. At the end of a case, civil courts can make permanent orders which remain in force indefinitely and breach of which would be contempt of court.

They can also order the landlord to pay the occupier damages for actual loss suffered, for distress, shock, suffering, and for the wrong that has been done him.

8.04 The phenomenon of harassment is, however, by no means limited to those suffering at the hands of their landlords. In recent years there has been an increasing concern with harassment and anti-social behaviour committed by neighbours and others, which may severely disrupt people's lives. This has been met by legislation (the Housing Act 1996) which has strengthened the powers of social landlords to evict those guilty of anti-social behaviour (see 3.101 and 4.120, above) and which also provides for local authorities to obtain injunctions (3.163).

8.05 Another response has been less specifically related to housing law, but nonetheless provides important remedies which we will consider here. First the Protection from Harassment Act 1997 ("1997") created both criminal offences of harassment and the right to seek an injunction to prevent it. Secondly, the Crime and Disorder Act 1998 ("1998") permits local authorities and the police to obtain anti-social behaviour orders against perpetrators of anti-social behaviour.

Outline

8.06 Criminal proceedings

- The Protection from Eviction Act 1977 creates offences of unlawful eviction and harassment.

- They are committed against "residential occupiers", *i.e.* someone occupying premises as a residence, whether under a contract or by virtue of any enactment or rule of law.

- Some of the offences may be committed by anyone; others only by landlords.

- Cases are generally heard in the magistrates' court.

- Local authorities have powers to prosecute these cases.

8.07 Civil Proceedings

- Two civil remedies are available: injunctions and damages.

- Injunctions may be sought in interim proceedings, sometimes without giving notice to the defendant.

- Damages may be general, aggravated or exemplary.

- A cause of action is necessary if civil action is to be taken; the most common cause is breach of the landlord's covenant to afford the tenant quiet enjoyment of the premises; others include trespass and nuisance.

- The Housing Act 1988, ss.27 and 28 provide a separate cause of action, with damages based on the financial benefit to the landlord of obtaining vacant possession.

8.08 Protection from Harassment Act 1997

- The Protection from Harassment Act 1997 creates four offences in connection with harassment.

- In addition, the magistrates' court may impose a restraining order on someone convicted of an offence under the Act.

- Injunctions under the Act may be sought by the individual victim.

8.09 Anti-social behaviour orders (ASBOs)

- Either the police or a local authority may apply for an ASBO in the magistrates' court.

- The court may make such an order where a person (aged 10 or over) has acted in a manner that causes, or is likely to cause, harassment, alarm or distress to one or more persons not within his own household, if the order is necessary to protect persons in the area from further such behaviour.

- The order may prohibit a person from doing anything described in the order.

- Breach of an ASBO is a criminal offence.

Criminal Proceedings

8.10 Principal definitions. The definitions of the criminal offences of illegal eviction and harassment are contained in the Protection from Eviction Act 1977 ("PEA 1977"), s.1, as amended by the Housing Act 1988:

> "(2) If any person unlawfully deprives the residential occupier of any premises of his occupation of the premises or any part

thereof, or attempts to do so, he shall be guilty of an offence unless he proves that he believed, and had reasonable cause to believe, that the residential occupier had ceased to reside in the premises.

(3) If any person with intent to cause the residential occupier of any premises—

(a) to give up occupation of the premises or any part thereof; or

(b) to refrain from exercising any right or pursuing any remedy in respect of the premises or part thereof;

does acts likely to interfere with the peace or comfort of the residential occupier or members of his household, or persistently withdraws or withholds services reasonably required for the occupation of the premises as a residence, he shall be guilty of an offence.

(3A) The landlord of a residential occupier or an agent of the landlord shall be guilty of an offence if—

(a) he does acts likely to interfere with the peace or comfort of the residential occupier or members of his household, or

(b) subject to subsection (3B) below, he persistently withdraws or withholds services reasonably required for the occupation of the premises in question as a residence,

and (in either case) he knows, or has reasonable cause to believe, that that conduct is likely to cause the residential occupier to give up the occupation of the whole or part of the premises or to refrain from exercising any right or pursuing any remedy in respect of the whole or part of the premises.

(3B) A person shall not be guilty of an offence under subsection (3A) if he proves that he had reasonable grounds for doing the acts or withdrawing or withholding the services in question."

1. RESIDENTIAL OCCUPIER

8.11 Application of Act. The Act applies to "residential occupiers." The term is also defined in s.1 of the Act:

"(1) In this section 'residential occupier,' in relation to any premises, means a person occupying the premises as a residence, whether under a contract or by virtue of any enactment or rule of law giving him the right to remain in occupation or restricting the right of any other person to recover possession of the premises."

8.12 Occupation as a residence. Occupation as a residence is a question of fact and common sense, not law. It is not necessary to show, for example, that the occupier had sufficient residence to sustain a claim to statutory tenancy (5.96–5.112). Obviously, someone who merely visits a friend is not residing in premises, not even if he stays overnight or, perhaps for a few nights. The same is no doubt true of a short-term hotel guest. But once a person begins to use premises to live in, in any normal sense of the expression, then the premises are being occupied as a residence.

8.13 A person can have two residences, *e.g.* a student who lives away from home during the term-time will normally be considered resident both at home and at college. A person does not stop residing in premises just because, for example, he goes away for a holiday, or for some other reason is temporarily absent. The residence will continue during such breaks as if the occupier was actually present.

8.14 Residential occupation by status. All tenants (including long leaseholders) and licensees (including service tenants and occupiers) whose tenancies and licences have not been brought to an end are residential occupiers because they are occupying under contract. It does not matter if the person harassing or evicting is not a party to the contract: what is in question is whether or not the occupier is a residential occupier.

8.15 Secure, assured and introductory tenants occupy both under contract and by virtue of statute (Chapters 3, 4), as do secure and introductory licensees.

8.16 Rent Act protected tenants whose contractual tenancies have been brought to an end and who occupy as statutory tenants (see Chapter 5) do so "by virtue of an enactment," and remain so protected until evicted by the bailiff (*Haniff v Robinson*, 1992).

8.17 Unless the tenancy was entered into on or after the commencement date of Pt I of the 1988 Act (January 15, 1989) and qualifies as an "excluded tenancy", all other former tenants (together with those lawfully living with them, even if the former tenant has himself departed) are residential occupiers because there is an enactment (PEA 1977, s.3) "restricting the right of any other person to recover possession of the premises."

8.18 Excluded Tenancy. If the tenancy was entered into on or after January 15, 1989, however, s.3 is disapplied, *i.e.* the former tenant will not be within s.3 and, the tenancy having ended, there will be no restriction on the right of the landlord to recover possession. It follows that neither eviction without court order, nor harassment, are illegal as against such a former excluded tenant.

8.19 The following are excluded tenancies:

(a) The tenant shares any accommodation (other than storage space, passages, corridors or other means of access, *i.e.* a bathroom or lavatory is accommodation for this purpose, *cf.* above, 3.25) with the landlord, who was himself in occupation of another part of the premises as an only or principal home (3.32) both before the tenancy was granted and at the time it comes to an end.

(b) The tenant shares any accommodation (other than storage space, passages, corridors or other means of access, so that again a bathroom or lavatory is included) with a member of the family of the landlord, who was in occupation of another part of the premises as an only or principal home (3.32) both before the tenancy was granted and at the time it comes to an end, and immediately before the tenancy was granted and at the time it comes to an end, the landlord occupies as his only or principal home (3.32) premises in the same building (not being a purpose-built block of flats: 4.47).

(c) The tenancy was granted as a temporary expedient to someone who originally entered premises as a trespasser, *i.e.* a former squatter who is granted a tenancy for a period of time (*cf.* para.3.21).

(d) The tenancy was a holiday letting (4.37) or was granted other than for money or money's worth, *i.e.* was not a commercial arrangement.

(e) The tenancy was granted in order to provide accommodation under Pt VI of the Immigration and Asylum Act 1999;

(f) The tenancy is in part of a hostel provided by one of a specified number of public bodies, including local authorities, development corporations, Housing Action Trusts, and a housing trust which is a charity or a registered social landlord.

8.20　Former licensees. S.3 also protects former licensees who have occupied under restricted contracts commencing on or after November 28, 1980 (see Chapter 6), former service occupiers who were granted some exclusive occupation of their accommodation under the employment arrangement (PEA 1977, s.8), and all other former licensees other than those with "excluded licences".

8.21　This has the same meaning as "excluded tenancy", in each case including anyone lawfully living with such a licensee at the end of the occupancy.

8.22　Spouses and cohabitees. In addition, there are enactments restricting the right of another person to recover possession of premises which serve to protect deserted spouses and, in some cases, even trespassers. The Family Law Act 1996 (Chapter 9) prohibits an owner or tenant-spouse/cohabitee from evicting a non-owner or non-tenant-spouse/cohabitee from the matrimonial home without an order of a court. Such an order will normally be made during the course of domestic proceedings and this subject is considered in the next Chapter. Because, however, there is an enactment which restricts the right of some other person to recover possession, meaning the owner/tenant-spouse/cohabitee, the deserted partner qualifies as a residential occupier for the purposes of the Protection from Eviction Act, even if it is not the other partner who is attempting to recover possession.

8.23　Trespassers. The criminal offence of violent entry for the purposes of eviction of a trespasser has been described in Chapter 7. In so far as a trespasser is protected from eviction by that provision, so also will he be protected from eviction under this Act.

8.24　Advisability of proceedings. The definition of residential occupier is, therefore, very wide indeed. It is possible to evict certain occupiers, *e.g.* trespassers, and some former licensees and tenants, without taking court proceedings, so long as the Criminal Law Act 1977 is not broken, so long as no other criminal offence is committed, so long as the licence or tenancy is already at an end (*R v Blankley*, 1979), and so on. This list of reservations should deter any landlord from seeking to recover possession without taking court proceedings, for the risk of committing an offence when doing so will otherwise be very high. It is for this reason that landlords are invariably advised—and well-advised—by lawyers to take court proceedings before evicting an occupier.

2. ACTS OF HARASSMENT

8.25 Intention and knowledge. The difference between s.1(3) and s.1(3A) is that the former creates an offence when the landlord does the specified acts with the intention of causing the occupier to quit or to refrain from exercising a right, while the latter creates an offence when the landlord does those acts knowing or having reasonable cause to believe that the consequence is likely to be to cause the occupier to quit or refrain from exercising a right.

8.26 The most common intention is that of wanting the occupier to give up possession of the premises or part of them, *e.g.* one room, and that is also the most common consequence. Harassment also occurs with the other objective in mind, *e.g.* to try and deter an occupier from applying to the rent officer or Rent Assessment Committee, or to deter him from complaining to an environmental health officer (see Chapter 13), about the condition of the property.

8.27 Services, peace and comfort. The criminal action can also be committed in different ways: by persistently withholding or withdrawing services, such as gas and electricity, reasonably required for the occupation of the premises as a residence; or, by doing an act (*R. v Polycarpou*, 1983) or acts, which are likely to interfere with the peace or comfort of the residential occupier or members of his household.

8.28 "Persistently" means more than just once or twice. Withholding or withdrawal of services can be justified under s.1(3B) if the landlord proves there were reasonable grounds for it, *e.g.* that services were dangerous to use. Mere non-payment of rent or other charges by the occupier is not sufficient justification, for the landlord has other remedies for this, *i.e.* to seek an order for possession.

8.29 Other conduct. The breadth of the definition allows the law to catch odd actions which may not be obvious acts of harassment, such as hanging around a sensitive and perhaps elderly occupier, or coming into the premises so frequently that the occupier ceases to feel secure in his home.

8.30 The act in question does not need also to be a civil wrong, so that a criminal offence may be committed by an act with the appropriate intention, even if it does not conflict with an occupier's other rights, *e.g.* refusing to supply a spare key when the occupier has lost his (*R. v Yuthiwattana*, 1984), or deliberately disconnecting the door bell and preventing use of a particular bathroom and lavatory (*R. v Burke*, 1990).

3. ACTS OF EVICTION

8.31 Definition. There are three points to note in connection with the definition of eviction:

(a) Eviction can be from the whole or part of the premises in question;

(b) An offence is committed either by a successful eviction or by an attempted eviction; and

(c) The defence which is available to an accused requires him to show that he believed and had reasonable cause to believe that the residential occupier had ceased to reside in the premises.

8.32 The requirement of reasonable cause means that a subjective but unreasonable belief will not be a defence.

8.33 Eviction or harassment. Eviction means more than intending to lock the occupier out for only a short time, *e.g.* overnight; such an action is more likely to be one of harassment (*R. v Yuthiwattana*, 1984).

8.34 Homelessness and eviction. An occupier who is illegally evicted will be homeless, and will qualify for assistance under Pt VII, Housing Act 1996 (see Chapter 10), although how much will depend on priority need (10.29–10.44).

4. THE ACCUSED

8.35 Under s.1(2) and 1(3), anyone can be charged with either illegal eviction or harassment, not only a landlord or his friends or agents. It may, however, be difficult to establish the necessary intention for harassment unless the act is done by someone with connections to the landlord. On the face of it, no one else is likely to have the incentive to try and make the occupier get out.

8.36 Where s.1(3A) is alleged, the perpetrator must be or be acting on behalf of the landlord. In addition, the acts must have been committed with the knowledge—actual or deemed—that it will cause the occupier to quit or to refrain from exercising a right or remedy.

8.37 For this purpose, however, the definition of "landlord" is extended (PEA 1977, s.1(3C)) to include anyone who would have a right to occupation of the premises but for the occupier's protection, or a superior landlord from whom the immediate landlord derives his right.

8.38 A prospective future occupier could qualify in this way (*Jones v Miah*, 1992). If the harassment or eviction is performed on behalf of a limited company, then a director or any officer of the company will also be guilty of an offence if he consented to or connived at the harassment, or it happened because of his negligence (PEA 1977, s.1(6)).

5. CRIMINAL PROCEEDINGS

8.39 Magistrates' court. Criminal proceedings are initiated in the magistrates' court. The landlord may elect trial in the Crown Court, but most cases are tried in the magistrates' court.

8.40 Local authorities have power to prosecute offences under the Act (PEA 1977, s.6), and almost all prosecutions are brought by them, usually through a tenancy relations officers employed to deal with private sector disputes.

8.41 Role of police. The police are not liable for a failure to prevent an offence being committed under PEA 1977, even where the tenant has requested them to attend (and prevent) an unlawful eviction. It has been held that they cannot be expected to inform themselves about landlord and tenant law before attending such a call: *Cowan v Chief Constable of Avon & Somerset Constabulary*, 2001.

8.42 Role of tenancy relations officer. In the event of any act of harassment or eviction, the tenancy relations officer ("TRO") should be contacted without delay. If it is urgent, he will normally call straight round to the premises and try to sort the problem out face to face with the landlord and the occupier. Some TROs have radio-linked cars. In addition or, if the matter is not urgent, in the alternative, he may write to the landlord, warning him of the possible offences and penalties, and inviting comment.

8.43 The TRO does not usually make prosecution the goal of his job. The officers tend to work by way of conciliation, reinforced by the possibility of prosecution, although the degree of emphasis will vary between officers and/or authorities.

8.44 A TRO cannot normally decide on his own initiative to prosecute: the prosecution will be handled by the local authority's legal service (internal or external).

8.45 Private prosecution. If the TRO will not prosecute, then it is still open to the individual occupier who has been harassed or illegally evicted to do so. Legal aid will not be available for a prosecution, although publicly funded legal advice can be sought beforehand. Unsurprisingly, not many occupiers are prepared to shoulder the responsibility of a private prosecution unassisted, and run the risk of having to pay the landlord's costs if he is acquitted.

8.46 Penalties. The court can impose a fine or up to six months' imprisonment, or both. If the landlord elects trial in the Crown Court, then he could be fined up to an unlimited amount, or sent to prison for up to two years, or both.

8.47 Compensation. Either sort of court has power to award compensation for "personal injury, loss or damage resulting from [an] offence" (Powers of Criminal Courts (Sentencing) Act 2000, s.130). The power is only used in relation to ascertainable loss, such as damaged property, time off work through injury, cost of overnight accommodation or eating out, etc. It is not used for shock, distress, inconvenience or discomfort. Nor, in the case of illegal eviction, will the power be used for loss of the home itself as this does not have an easily identified value. Awards are limited to £5,000 (s.131). Any documentary evidence of loss sustained by the occupier, such as bills, should be brought to court.

Civil Proceedings

8.48 County courts. Civil proceedings are brought in either the county court, usually for the area in which the incident happens, or in the High Court. Most cases of harassment and illegal eviction will be brought in the county courts, as a case which includes a claim for damages may not be started in the High Court unless the value of the claim is more than £15,000 (CPR Pt 7 PD 7A 2.1). If the claim includes a claim for damages for personal injury, the claim may not be started in the High Court unless the value of the claim is more than £50,000 (CPR Pt 7 PD 7A 2.2).

8.49 Remedies. The county court has the jurisdiction to make any order which the High Court can, *e.g.* an injunction (County Courts Act 1984, s.38).

8.50 The civil remedies which may be awarded by either sort of court are:

   (i) Injunctions; and

   (ii) Damages.

1. INJUNCTIONS

8.51 Injunctions. An injunction is an order of the court. It will always identify the person, or persons, who is or are to be bound by it. Failure to comply with the terms of an injunction is a contempt of court. Contempt can be punished by either a fine or imprisonment. It is uncommon for civil courts to send a landlord who is in breach of an injunction to prison, unless he persists in his refusal to obey it.

8.52 Final injunctions. Injunctions are either final or interim. A final injunction is awarded at the end of a trial when the factual disputes between the parties have been resolved.

8.53 Interim injunctions. The trial may not, however, take place for some months after the commencement of proceedings and the prospect of a final injunction is of little assistance to the victim of an ongoing campaign of harassment or other anti-social behaviour or someone locked out of his home who is sleeping rough or staying with friends.

8.54 In such circumstances, the victim may apply for an interim injunction, which may be granted at any time from the commencement of proceedings in order to maintain the *status quo* pending the trial. In extremely urgent cases, an injunction may even be awarded on an undertaking to go through the formal process of issuing proceedings within a specified time afterwards.

8.55 Without notice orders. Likewise, a matter can be so urgent that it cannot even be left for the few days necessary to give the other side an opportunity to attend court. In cases of such urgency, the court will grant a "without notice" interim order, *i.e.* one that is based upon the unchallenged evidence of the occupier only.

8.56 The matter must be serious, for example, eviction or disconnection of utilities, before a court will make an order on a without notice hearing.

8.57   No delay. The courts will only use their powers to make a without notice order if there has been little or no delay before they are asked to do so. A without notice order should always be sought immediately.

8.58   On notice hearing. If an order is granted without notice, it will usually be for only a few days or a week, until a further hearing—on notice—at which the court can hear the other side of the case and decide whether or not the order should be continued until a full trial of the matter.

8.59   An on notice hearing may also be suitable if a matter is not serious enough to merit a without notice order, but the matter cannot be left until the full trial.

8.60   Balance of convenience. When a judge is deciding whether or not to grant an interim injunction, he does not decide the full merits of the case. He only decides what order should be made, pending the full trial, on a balance of convenience (*American Cyanamid Co Ltd v Ethicon*, 1975).

8.61   Unless the premises have already been reoccupied by someone else, or by the landlord himself, the balance of convenience in a case of illegal eviction will almost always be in the occupier's favour, although it may be subject to an undertaking by the occupier to pay rent pending the trial. The balance of convenience will also almost invariably be with the occupier where harassment is in issue.

8.62   Strength of claim. Although the issue is one of balance of convenience, the strength of a case may still affect the decision of the court. If the occupier's case is a strong one, on the face of it, then even if the landlord has relet the premises, or is himself in occupation, the court will be reluctant to allow the landlord to benefit from what appears to be both the commission of a criminal offence and a very serious breach of the civil law, by allowing him to remain in occupation until trial.

2.   DAMAGES

8.63   Types of damages. Damages are not awarded until the end of the case. There are several different sorts of damages:

    (i)   A person claims special damages for specific sums of money, *e.g.* damage to furniture, cost of eating out or overnight accommodation, lost property, etc. These are the same sorts of damages which may be awarded in the magistrates' courts as compensation.

(ii) General damages are unquantified sums which are claimed in respect of, for example, suffering, shock, distress, physical injury, inconvenience, the lost right of occupation itself or any other harm to which a specific value cannot be attached, *e.g.* additional electricity costs because gas is cut off.

(iii) Aggravated damages are awarded to compensate for injury to proper feelings of dignity and pride, and for aggravation generally (*Ramdath v Daley*, 1993), *e.g.* where the manner of that which is being sued for was especially mean, unpleasant, brutal, etc.

(iv) Exemplary damages are awarded where it would appear that the landlord has, for example, evicted a tenant, calculating to himself that any profit made, for example from sale of the property with vacant possession, will be more than any damages awarded against him. In other words, that he can make a profit, even out of doing something wrong.

8.64 Exemplary damages. In *Cassell & Co Ltd v Broome*, 1972, the House of Lords considered when exemplary damages might be awarded. Lord Hailsham L.C., said:

"How, it may be asked, about the late Mr. Rachman, who is alleged to have used hired bullies to intimidate statutory tenants by violence or threats of violence into giving up vacant possession of their residences and so placing a valuable asset in the hands of the landlord? My answer must be that if this is not a cynical calculation of profit and cold-blooded disregard of a plaintiff's rights, I do not know what is . . ."

8.65 In the case of *Drane v Evangelou*, 1977, Lawton L.J. said that to deprive a tenant of a roof over his head was one of the worst torts (wrongs) that could be committed. It brought the law into disrespect. He also expressed his surprise that the landlord had not been prosecuted under what is now s.1 of the PEA 1977. Lord Denning M.R. applied the words of an earlier case:

"Exemplary damages can properly be awarded whenever it is necessary to teach a wrongdoer that tort does not pay."

8.66 Exemplary damages cannot, however, be claimed where there is only a claim based on breach of contract (see further below).

3.   CAUSE OF ACTION

8.67   Need for cause of action. Neither the county court nor the High Court can make any order at all, however, until an action has been commenced (or an undertaking to commence it has been accepted, see above, 8.54). Legal aid will generally be available for a civil action based on harassment or illegal eviction

8.68 In order to commence an action in a civil court, it is necessary to show that the plaintiff has a "cause of action". A court does not have power to make an order because, for example, someone does not like the colour of his neighbour's hair, or because someone jumps in front of someone else in a bus queue, or because another person calls someone a silly idiot. On the other hand, there will be a cause of action if a neighbour plays music so loudly or at anti-social hours that he disturbs someone else's enjoyment of his own home, or if the queue-jumper used so much force that he assaulted someone, or if what was said was of a defamatory character.

8.69   Causes of action classified. All of the causes of action referred to at the end of the last paragraph are "torts," or civil wrongs. A tort is an action which the law recognises that it is wrongful for one person, who is the person complained about, to do to the person complaining. There are several torts which may be used in connection with harassment and illegal eviction.

8.70 In addition, there is always a cause of action when one party breaks a contract with another, whether completely or in a material particular. Breach of contract will also often be appropriate to cases of harassment and illegal eviction.

(i)   *Breach Of Contract*

8.71   Tenancies and licences. Both tenancy and licence are contracts. A licensee may sue for breach of contract or breach of a term of the contract (*Smith v Nottinghamshire CC*, 1981). A term of a contract may actually be stated, or it may be implied, although only where it is a term which is necessary for the contract to be effective. In the case of a residential licence, this will usually mean such terms as are necessary for the property to be capable of use as a residence, although standards may vary depending on the type of licence, *e.g.* a hostel licence normally implies a "full" or "high" standard of occupancy, but a licence to share property scheduled for demolition or refurbishment, *i.e.* what is called short-life use, would probably be at the opposite end of the spectrum.

8.72 Quiet enjoyment. In addition, into every tenancy (but not a licence) there is implied, unless it is actually spelled out in the agreement, a promise by the landlord that the tenant will have the "quiet enjoyment" of the premises so long as the tenancy lasts.

8.73 In *Kenny v Preen*, 1962, it was said that the promise was broken by an act which was an invasion of the right of the tenant to remain in possession undisturbed. Clearly, this includes an actual or threatened eviction, and almost every act of harassment. In *McCall v Abelesz*, 1975, disconnection of utilities was described as both a breach of implied term, and as an interference with quiet enjoyment. Any conduct by a landlord which interferes with the tenant's freedom of action in exercising his rights as tenant will be an interference with the covenant for quiet enjoyment.

8.74 Excessive noise. Excessive noise made by the landlord is capable of amounting to breach of the covenant: *Southwark LBC v Tanner*, 2001. In *Tanner*, however, the disturbance arose from tenants being able to hear their neighbours due to poor sound insulation. There was no breach of the covenant for quiet enjoyment because the landlord had not caused the noise (other than by letting the flats, as it was obvious and intended that it would).

8.75 Derogation from grant. In addition, some actions by a landlord in common parts, or in neighbouring property under his control, could amount to derogation from his grant of the tenancy to the tenant (see further, 11.35). This is also an action in contract.

(ii) *Housing Act 1988, ss.27 and 28*

8.76 Breach of Housing Act 1988, s.27. In *McCall v Abelesz*, 1975 it was held that, even though a landlord had committed an act or offence of illegal eviction or harassment, the occupier did not necessarily have a civil remedy, *i.e.* a right to sue.

8.77 Accordingly, s.27, 1988 Act, affords an express right to sue where either illegal eviction within the PEA 1977, s.1(2) has taken place, or such harassment within s.1(3), (3A) (8.10) has been committed (after June 9, 1988), that it leads to the occupier's departure. This right is conferred on all residential occupiers, as defined (8.11–8.24), and carries an express right to damages.

8.78 The action can be brought against the landlord (but not someone acting as his agent—*Sampson v Wilson*, 1995), or anyone else who, but for the occupier's right to occupy, would be entitled to occupy, or any superior landlord from whom that person derives his right (8.37).

8.79 The action is an action in tort (8.69) and is additional to any other rights, save that damages for loss of occupation are not to be awarded twice over. A landlord can defend the action by showing that he believed, and had reasonable cause to believe, that the residential occupier had already quit, or—in the case of a departure based on withholding of services—that there were reasonable grounds for withholding services.

8.80 Damages may be reduced if either the court considers that the occupier's conduct provoked the eviction or harassment, or (where eviction is concerned) that the landlord has offered to reinstate the occupier, before the proceedings under the 1988 Act were begun, and the offer was unreasonably refused. (There can be unreasonable refusal even if the occupier had found somewhere else before the offer). The offer of reinstatement must be genuine, and merely handing the tenant a key to a lock which does not work, and inviting her to resume occupation of a room which has been totally wrecked, will not suffice (*Tagro v Cafane*, 1991).

8.81 Amount of damages. There are detailed provisions (1988, s.28) governing the amount of damages for breach of this "statutory tort", designed to deprive the landlord of the financial benefit of vacant possession. No damages at all are payable if before the action is commenced, or at any time before it is finally over, the occupier is actually reinstated.

8.82 Where the evicting landlord holds only an intermediate interest, that is the interest which must be valued for the purpose of preventing him securing a profit (*Jones & Lee v Miah*, 1992). The nature of the interest of the tenant, and the fact of other occupiers should be taken into account, so that where the tenancy which has been lost is an assured shorthold in a house still occupied by other tenants, the award is likely to be quite low (*Melville v Bruton*, 1996).

iii. *Other Torts*

8.83 Trespass to land. If there is a tenancy, the tenant has possession of the premises to the exclusion of all others including the landlord. A landlord can, therefore, trespass on the premises of his own tenant.

8.84 There is some legal authority for the proposition that the sort of exclusive occupation which most licensees have is enough possession for the purposes of trespass. This is because it is possession in fact, rather than legally defined possession, which matters.

8.85 A person is a trespasser whenever he enters the land or premises of another without permission. It is also a trespass to place anything on someone else's property without permission. In one case it was held to be a trespass to drive a nail into someone else's wall, which, by analogy, would apply to a landlord who nails up a door or blocks up a lock. A person is also a trespasser if he has permission to be on someone's premises for one purpose but uses it for another. For example, a landlord calling around to collect the rent or inspect for repairs will become a trespasser if he uses the occasion to abuse, threaten or harass the occupier.

8.86 A person given permission to enter must leave once he is asked to do so and, once a reasonable time has been given for the exit, becomes a trespasser. Reasonable time here, as with residential licence (1.83), is reasonable in all the circumstances and, where a person is just visiting, will be a matter of however long it would normally take to get to the door.

8.87 Trespass is a tort and anyone who trespasses can be sued for it. A landlord is liable for the torts of his agents, if they were committed with his approval or on his behalf. An evicted or harassed occupier can sue the landlord and, if the landlord got someone else to do the job for him, that person as well.

8.88 Assault. Harassment and eviction will often be accompanied by assaults. An assault is not necessarily a directly physical act. It may be no more than some gesture which suggests that the person to whom it is made is about to be attacked physically. Threatening words on their own are not an assault, and it is difficult to prove unless there has been some sort of physical attack, although this might be with a weapon, piece of furniture or merely by shoving an occupier around. An assault is a tort and the remarks in the last paragraph will, therefore, apply in the same way to assault.

8.89 Nuisance. Like trespass, this is a cause of action which can be used by someone in possession of land, which certainly includes a tenant and may include a licensee. It includes a "tolerated trespasser" (1.42): *Pemberton v Southwark LBC*, 2001. It is, however, only the person with the interest in the land who can sue, not other family members: *Hunter v Canary Wharf*, 1997.

8.90 A nuisance is anything which interferes with the reasonable use and enjoyment of property, *e.g.* noise, smells, even hanging about outside someone's home. Most acts of harassment will constitute a nuisance, although this may not be so if the act is negative, *e.g.* a withdrawal of services. Nuisance is also a tort.

8.91 Trespass to goods. Any direct interference with another person's belongings is a trespass to goods. If belongings are actually removed, this may also be conversion. Conversion is the act of dealing with someone else's property in any manner that is inconsistent with the right of the other person to possession of it. Trespass to goods and conversion are torts.

Protection from Harassment Act 1997

8.92 Criminal offences. The 1997 Act generally prohibits harassment, breach of which is actionable in both the civil and criminal courts. It creates four criminal offences:

  (i) Harassment;

  (ii) Putting another person in fear of violence;

  (iii) Breach of a restraining order; and,

  (iv) Breach of an injunction.

8.93 The Act gives a criminal court the power to make a restraining order, which has similar effect to an injunction.

8.94 Harassment. The PHA 1997, s.1(1) prohibits a person from:

  ". . . pursuing a course of conduct:

(a) which amounts to harassment of another; and
(b) which he or she knows or ought to know amounts to harassment of the other."

8.95 It is an offence to pursue a course of conduct in breach of the prohibition against harassment (1997, s.2).

8.96 There is no exhaustive definition of harassment for this purpose. It includes, but is not limited to, alarming or causing distress to a person (1997, s.7(2)). It is a matter for the court to determine on the facts of the particular case whether the conduct complained about "amounts to harassment", in the everyday sense of the word. The prosecution must also prove that the defendant was aware that the conduct amounted to harassment or, if not, that he "ought to have known".

8.97 Conduct is not defined, but includes speech. To amount to a "course of conduct" there must be conduct on more than one occasion (1997, s.7(4)).

8.98 Putting another person in fear of violence. S.4(1) makes it an offence to pursue a course of conduct (8.97) which:

". . . causes another to fear, on at least two occasions, that violence will be used against him. . . if he knows or ought to know that his course of conduct will cause the other so to fear on each occasion."

8.99 Restraining orders. The court may impose a "restraining order" on a defendant to protect the victim (or any other specified person) from further conduct which may amount to harassment or causing a fear of violence (1997, s.5).

8.100 The power is available where a court is sentencing or otherwise dealing with a defendant convicted of an offence under s.2 (8.95) or 4 (8.98). The order must describe the prohibited conduct and the order may be for a specified period or until a further order is made.

8.101 Breach of a restraining order. It is an offence for a person to do anything prohibited under a restraining order, without reasonable excuse (1997, s.5(7)).

8.102 Breach of an injunction. Where proceedings are taken under the 1997 Act in a civil court, it may grant an injunction to prevent further harassment. If it does so, then it is a criminal offence for the defendant, without reasonable excuse, to do anything which he is prohibited from doing by the injunction (1997, s.5(6)). This offence cannot be pursued, however, if the defendant has already been punished for contempt of court for breach of the injunction.

8.103 Obtaining an injunction. PHA 1997, s.3 specifically provides a civil claim for actual or apprehended harassment, as defined in 1997, s.1 (8.94) allowing the victim to seek an injunction and damages.

8.104 Damages. It is expressly provided that damages may be awarded for any anxiety caused by the harassment as well as any financial loss (1997, s.3(1)).

Anti-social behaviour orders

8.105 Acting in an anti-social manner. An anti-social behaviour order ("ASBO") may be sought against a person aged 10 or over who has acted in an anti-social manner, *i.e.* in a manner "that causes or is likely to cause harassment, alarm or distress to one or more persons not of the same household as himself," if the order is necessary to protect persons in the local government area from further such behaviour by the individual (Crime and Disorder Act 1998, s.1(1)).

8.106 Use of the phrase "likely to cause" enables someone other than the victim of the behaviour to give evidence, particularly professional witnesses who can provide evidence to a court where victims feel unable to come forward for fear of reprisals or intimidation.

8.107 Who can apply for an ASBO. An application for an ASBO can only be made by a relevant authority, which is either:

(a) The council for the local government area (which, in two-tier areas, is the district, not county, council) in which the anti-social behaviour is alleged to have occurred; or

(b) Any chief police officer, any part of whose area lies within the local government area in question.

8.108 Consultation and application. An authority wishing to apply for an ASBO must first consult every other authority which could apply for an ASBO in that area, *i.e.* the police must consult the local authority and vice versa. Application for an ASBO is made by complaint to the magistrates' court in whose area the alleged behaviour took place.

8.109 Civil proceedings. Proceedings for an application for an ASBO—as opposed to its enforcement for breach—are civil, not criminal (*R. v The Crown Court at Manchester Ex p. McCann*, 2002). Accordingly, the civil rules of evidence apply (so that hearsay evidence is admissible) but the case needs to be proved to the criminal standard.

8.110 Criteria for making an ASBO. The court may make an ASBO if (1998, s.1(1) and (4)):

(a) The person has acted in an anti-social manner to one or more persons not of the same household as himself; and

(b) The order is necessary to protect persons in the local government area in which that behaviour was caused or was likely to be caused from further such behaviour by the individual.

8.111 In deciding whether these conditions are satisfied, the court must disregard any act which the defendant shows was reasonable in the circumstances. What is reasonable is for the court to decide on the facts of the individual case.

8.112 Terms of ASBO. The ASBO may prohibit a person from doing anything described in the order. Accordingly, the terms must be negative in character, *i.e.* they must prohibit the person from doing something. The 1998 Act does not constrain the court as to the terms other than requiring that the prohibition(s) must be necessary to protect the public from further anti-social acts by the person subject to the ASBO in the local government area and in any adjoining local government area specified in the application for the order. The court must specify a period for the duration of the ASBO, subject to a minimum of two years.

8.113 Breach of ASBO. An ASBO is breached if, without reasonable excuse, the person subject to it does anything which he is prohibited from doing by it (1998, s.1(10)). Whether an excuse is reasonable is to be determined objectively. It is for the defendant to establish both the excuse and that it is reasonable. The standard of proof is the balance of probabilities. The existence of a reasonable excuse is a question of fact for the court to decide.

8.114 Criminal offence. Breach of an ASBO is a criminal offence, triable in the magistrates' court or the Crown Court. The maximum penalty that can be imposed on an adult by a magistrates' court is six months imprisonment and/or a fine not exceeding level 5 on the standard scale (currently £5,000) and, in a Crown Court, five years' imprisonment or a fine or both.

8.115 Appeal. A person against whom an ASBO is made may appeal to the Crown Court, which is empowered to make such orders as are necessary to give effect to its decision on the appeal (1998, s.4(1)).

8.116 Proposals for reform. At the time of writing, the Police Reform Act includes a number of significant changes to ASBOs, which are yet to be brought into force, in particular:

- Enabling registered social landlords to apply for ASBOs;

- Introducing interim ASBOs to enable a court to order an immediate stop to behaviour;

- Extending the geographical area over which an ASBO can be made, *i.e.* extending beyond one local government area;

- Enabling county courts to grant ASBOs in, for example, possession proceedings involving persistent anti-social behaviour;

- Enabling criminal courts to make ASBOs whenever a person has been convicted of an offence involving anti-social behaviour.

CHAPTER NINE

Break-up of Relationship

Introduction

9.01 **Housing law and relationship breakdown.** In this Chapter, we shall consider in outline only (see Introduction on p.v) some of the law as it relates to housing in the event of the break-up of a relationship. This is in one sense an artificial study, because decisions cannot and will not be taken on the basis of housing law, or law itself, alone. There will be many other considerations to bring to bear, including that of the desirability of exercising particular rights and (always) the best interests of any children of the relationship. The law affecting domestic breakdown is substantial, and a study in its own right: the purpose of this Chapter is merely to indicate some of the possibilities which it raises.

Outline

9.02 **Relevant Provisions.** There is a number of relevant provisions which are considered briefly in this Chapter:

- The Matrimonial Causes Act 1973 which contains broad powers to divide up matrimonial property on divorce, separation or nullity proceedings;

- Matrimonial homes rights under the Family Law Act 1996 which gives rights to spouses to occupy the home during the currency of a marriage;

- Occupation rights under the Family Law Act 1996 which gives the court power to regulate who may occupy the home in the case of spouses, ex-spouses and co-habitees; the extent of the powers depend on whether the applicant has a legal right to occupy the home or not;

- Non-Molestation orders under the Family Law Act 1996, which provide protection against violence and other molestation;

- Transfering tenancies under the Family Law Act 1996, giving the court power to transfer tenancies between spouses, former spouses and cohabitees;

- The Matrimonial and Family Proceedings Act 1984, which deals with divorce or legal separation in another country;

- The Children Act 1989 which regulates the residence of children on relationship breakdown.

9.03 Further considerations

- Matrimonial and family proceedings have to be brought in a properly accredited court.

- When women are fleeing violence they may apply as homeless and it is important to consider the provisions of the Housing Act 1996, Pt VII.

- When rehousing, landlords must comply with the Sex Discrimination Act 1975.

9.04 Cumulative provisions. None of these Acts or laws is mutually exclusive: it will be common for provisions contained in more than one Act to apply in the same case. In addition, the courts have a fairly broad discretion to make such orders as are considered appropriate at any stage in proceedings: interim orders are commonplace. It is also necessary to consider the common law position, and the rights of any spouse or cohabitee under trust law, set out at 1.23–1.29, above).

Relevant provisions

1. MATRIMONIAL CAUSES ACT 1973

9.05 Division of property. It is this Act which contains the broad powers which a court has to divide up matrimonial property when a marriage is in the course of breaking up or has broken up. These powers are only exercisable between married partners. They can be exercised during the course of divorce, separation or nullity proceedings.

9.06 The court has power to apportion property between the parties and, if necessary, to order that property, including a home, be transferred from the name of one party to that of another or be sold (Matrimonial Causes Act 1973—"MCA 1973"—ss.23A, 24,

24A as amended by the Family Law Act 1996). S.23A deals with the position on divorce or separation, while s.24 makes provision for nullity. As the latter is a relatively rare event we shall throughout the remainder of this Chapter refer to s.23A.

9.07 Former position. At one time, a wife who did not work and who had not contributed financially to the value of the property was not entitled as of right to any share in the property when the marriage broke up. She had to rely on common law provisions, if there was any direct financial contribution (1.27). She might, of course, have been entitled to maintenance, and there may have been a settlement which took the form of a transfer of ownership of the matrimonial home. Alternatively, property might be transferred into her name, but for the benefit of children of the marriage, in which case she would become the trustee of it herself, but only the trustee, which could have serious implications when children reached the age of majority.

9.08 Relevant considerations. Over the years, however, the courts came to recognise that the contribution of the non-earning spouse could not be measured purely in terms of direct financial contribution. A husband's earning power is enhanced by the provision of domestic services by the wife who remains at home, including but not exclusively those involved in care of the children. Similarly, the courts came to recognise that a woman should not live with and be dependent upon her husband for a period of time and suddenly be discarded by him without any further provision for her accommodation or support.

9.09 Use of section 23A. Accordingly, s.23A may be used to divide up matrimonial property, including the matrimonial home, in proportions which do not necessarily reflect the limited financial or quasi-financial considerations to which the common law will be limited.

9.10 These rights are mainly of interest only to owner-occupiers, even though a court can order the transfer of a tenancy under these provisions (*Hale v Hale*, 1975; *Newlon Housing Trust v Alsulaimen*, 1998) regardless of whether the tenancy is protected or not. But it seems likely that this will only be possible if there is no provision in the tenancy agreement prohibiting assignment. The powers could not be used in connection with a licence, however, as a licence does not constitute "property" which a court can transfer.

9.11 Section 24A. While s.23A permits adjustment of property rights, *e.g.* transfer between the parties, s.24A permits the court to order sale of the home, so that the proceeds may be divided between the parties.

9.12 Criteria for making an order. When deciding whether or not to make an order for adjustment or sale, MCA 1973, s.25 sets out a number of matters to which the court must have regard. These include the income, earning capacity and other financial resources each party has or is likely to have in the forseeable future, the financial needs, obligations and responsibilities each party is taking on, the age of the parties and duration of the marriage, any physical or mental disability, and the conduct of the parties (whatever its nature) but only if it is such that in the opinion of the court it would be inequitable to disregard it.

9.13 Dealing with the home. S.37(2) prevents one spouse trying to dispose of or otherwise deal with the assets once the other spouse has commenced proceedings. S.37(2)(b) relates to "dispositions" of property and it has been held that the service of a notice to quit by one joint tenant (1.199, above) is not a disposition for the purposes of MCA 1973: *Newlon Housing Trust v Alsulaimen*, 1998. It has been suggested, however, without being decided, that s.37(2)(a), which provides a broader power to prevent "dealing" with the property and/or the inherent powers of the court may be used to prohibit the service of a notice by a spouse (*Bater v Greenwich LBC*, 1999).

2. MATRIMONIAL HOMES RIGHTS UNDER THE FAMILY LAW ACT 1996

9.14 Matrimonial homes rights. The Family Law Act 1996 ("FLA 1996") introduces the concept of matrimonial homes rights. The rights arise where one spouse has the right to occupy a dwelling-house by virtue of ownership of the property, tenancy or a contractual licence and the other does not.

9.15 In those circumstances, the spouse who does not have legal rights over the property is given the right not to be excluded by the other from occupation of the matrimonial home without an order of the court (FLA 1996, s.30(1), (2)).

9.16 Such an order will normally be made in the course of matrimonial proceedings dealing with a number of considerations, but it could be made on application under this Act alone. The court also has power to make an order permitting a spouse who has been wrongfully evicted or excluded from the matrimonial home to re-enter. The court can make the order in respect of part only of the premises, *e.g.* excluding a husband from the residential part of the premises but allowing him to carry on his business in another part.

9.17   Effect of terminating tenancy. These rights under s.30 do not prevent a tenant from otherwise validly terminating his tenancy. Thus, if the spouse who is the tenant validly surrenders that tenancy (*Sanctuary Housing Association v Campbell*, 1999) or serves a notice to quit (*Harrow LBC v Johnstone*, 1997), there are no rights which can be protected under this provision.

9.18   Acceptance of payments. Where the spouse with matrimonial homes rights (9.14) takes over mortgage or rent payments under these provisions, the landlord or mortgage company is obliged to accept them as though they were made by the owner-occupier, tenant or licensee (FLA 1996, s.30(3)).

9.19   Registrable right of occupation. A spouse who has matrimonial homes rights (9.14) over an owner-occupied home is entitled to register these rights as a charge on the dwelling (FLA 1996, s.31). The effect of this is that, if the house is sold, the purchaser buys it subject to her right of occupation and is deemed to have known that she was and can remain in occupation. This is to prevent, for example, a husband selling the home over the head of a wife, before a court has an opportunity to make any order for transfer.

3.   OCCUPATION RIGHTS UNDER THE FAMILY LAW ACT 1996

9.20   Spouses, cohabitees and associated persons. While basic matrimonial homes rights have been dealt with above, the FLA 1996 also makes provision for occupation rights to be enforced where the parties are already divorced or where they are merely cohabiting, and indeed even if they they are only "associated persons".

9.21   Associated person. A person is associated with another if:

(a)   They are or have been married to each other;

(b)   They are cohabitants or former cohabitants (see 9.22);

(c) They live or have lived in the same household, otherwise than merely by reason of one of them being the other's employee, tenant, lodger or boarder (this would include, *e.g.* carers);

(d) They are relatives;

(e) They have agreed to marry one another;

(f) If they are both parents of, or have or had parental responsibility for, the same child;

(g) They are both parties to other family proceedings (FLA 1996, s.62).

9.22 For these purposes, cohabitants are a man and a woman (*N.B.* not a same sex couple) who, although not married to each other, are living together as husband and wife (FLA 1996, s.62(1)).

9.23 Termination by tenant. FLA distinguishes between those applicants with legal rights of occupation and those with no such rights. The same point made above (9.18) in relation to matrimonial homes rights not preventing a tenant from validly terminating the tenancy, also apply to occupation rights.

9.24 Applicants with legal rights. Where an applicant has a legal right to occupy the home (as an owner, tenant or contractual licensee), or is entitled to occupy under matrimonial homes rights (9.14), he may apply for an occupation order in relation to a dwelling-house which was or is his home or was intended to be his home (*e.g.* where a home has been bought for renovation but not moved into) against an ex-spouse, current or former cohabitee or an other associated person (above, 9.21).

9.25 The court has power to make one of the following orders (FLA, s.33):

(a) Enforcing the applicant's entitlement to remain in occupation;

(b) Requiring the associated person to permit the applicant to enter and remain in the home;

(c) Regulating the occupation by either or both parties;

(d) Limiting the legal right to occupy of the associated person;

(e) Requiring the associated person to leave the home; and

(f) Excluding the associated person from a defined area around the home.

9.26   Criteria. In deciding whether to make an order under s.33 the court must have regard to all the circumstances including:

(a) The housing needs and housing resources of each of the parties and of any relevant child;

(b) The financial resources of the parties;

(c) The likely effect of any decision on the health safety or well-being of the parties or any relevant child; and

(d) The conduct of the parties towards each other.

9.27   Former spouses. Where the former spouse is in occupation of the home she may apply for an order for a specified period excluding her ex-husband from the home or giving her the right not to be evicted or excluded from the home. Where she is not in occupation she may be given the right to enter and occupy. In either case, any of the orders set out at 9.25(c)–(f) may also be granted.

9.28   The criteria to be applied in making an order where the applicant is a former spouse are as set out in 9.26 above, with the addition of:

(a) The length of time since the parties ceased to live together;

(b) The length of time since the marriage was dissolved or annulled;

(c) The existence of any pending proceedings which will adjust the legal rights in the home (*e.g.* under the MCA 1973, para.9.04).

9.29   In the unlikely event of neither former spouses having any legal rights to occupy the matrimonial home (*e.g.* where a mortgage company has obtained a possession order but is allowing a period of grace), a short-term order excluding one former spouse and allowing the other into possession may be made under FLA 1996, s.37.

9.30   Cohabitants. Where one cohabitant has legal rights to occupy the home, and the other does not, the party with no rights may apply to the court for any of the orders set out at 9.25(c)–(f) (FLA 1996, s.36). Former cohabitants may also apply.

9.31 The criteria to be used in deciding whether to make an order are the same as those set out at 9.26, above, together with the following:

(a) The nature of the parties' relationship (including the fact that they have not made a commitment to marriage (FLA 1996, s.41);

(b) The length of time during which they have lived together as husband and wife;

(c) Whether there are or have been any children who are children of both parties or for whom both parties have or have had parental responsibility;

(d) The length of time which has elapsed since the parties ceased to live together;

(e) Any pending legal proceedings in relation to the home (*e.g.* under the Children Act 1989, 9.46).

9.32 As with former spouses, where neither has any legal occupation rights (9.29), short-term orders may be made (FLA 1996, s.38).

9.33 Additional orders. When making an occupation order against a spouse, former spouse or cohabitant, (other than in cases where neither party has any legal occupation rights), the court may also require one party to repair and maintain the home and pay the rent or mortgage, or other outgoings.

9.34 The court may also order the party who is given occupation to make payments to the other party, where that person would otherwise be legally entitled to occupy the home. Orders may also be made in relation to furniture (FLA 1996, s.40).

4. NON-MOLESTATION ORDERS UNDER THE FAMILY LAW ACT 1996

9.35 Earlier provisions. Statutory powers to protect against molestation were originally introduced in the 1970s. Two Acts— the Domestic Violence and Matrimonial Proceedings Act 1976 and the Domestic Proceedings and Magistrates Courts Act 1978—

created two separate jurisdictions, the former in the county court and the latter in the magistrates' court. One of the purposes of the Family Law Act 1996 was to unify this jurisdiction. The FLA also significantly widens the availability of molestation orders through the concept of "associated persons", who may apply for such an order.

9.36 Content of orders. A non-molestation order is one which prohibits a respondent from molesting another person with whom he is associated (9.21) and/or from molesting a relevant child (FLA 1996, s.42(1)).

9.37 Applications. An application for a molestation order may be made by a person associated with the respondent or in the course of other family proceedings (FLA 1996, s.42(2)). An order can be made without notice where the court considers it just and convenient to do so (FLA, 1996, s.45).

9.38 Molestation. Molestation is not defined by the Act, nor was it in earlier legislation. It is wider than violence, and can include pestering and harassment. In *Horner v Horner*, 1982, it was held that handing the plaintiff menacing letters and intercepting her on her way to work amounted to molestation. In *Johnson v Walton*, 1990, sending partially nude photographs of the plaintiff to a national newspaper, to cause her harm, was also molestation.

9.39 Power of arrest. The court has an additional power, to "back" the injunction for arrest. This means that a police officer can arrest without warrant any person whom he suspects is in breach of an order under the Act. The person must be brought back before the judge within 24 hours. This power can, however, only be used where there has been actual violence or the threat of violence (FLA 1996, s.47).

5. TRANSFER OF TENANCY UNDER THE FAMILY LAW ACT 1996

9.40 Transfer of tenancy. The court has power to order the transfer of tenancies under the FLA 1996, s.53 and Sch.7, between spouses, former spouses, cohabitants and former cohabitants (9.22).

9.41 The tenancy must have been the matrimonial home, or—in the case of cohabitants—one in which they lived together as husband and wife. The tenancies which may be transferred are protected or statutory tenancies under the Rent Act 1977, statutory tenancies under the Rent (Agriculture) Act 1976, secure tenancies under the Housing Act 1985, assured and assured agricultural occupancies within the Housing Act 1988 and introductory tenancies within the Housing Act 1996.

9.42 Criteria. In deciding whether to make a transfer, the court must consider the circumstances in which the tenancy was granted, and the criteria set out at 9.26(a)–(c) above. Where cohabitants are involved the courts must also consider those at 9.31(a)–(d).

9.43 Statutory tenancies. Although transfer may take place after divorce or the cohabitation, the law is unclear as to whether a transfer order can effectively be made after decree absolute if the tenancy is statutory and the tenant-spouse is no longer in occupation. From the one case which has touched upon this point (*Lewis v Lewis*, 1985), it would seem that it cannot. For this reason it is essential to seek the order before decree absolute. The same powers apply to Housing Act secure and Housing Act assured tenancies, but there are similar difficulties if a divorce is already final or the cohabitant tenant has moved out, since it will cease to be secure/assured if the tenant is not occupying it as his only or principal home (3.32, 4.21).

6. MATRIMONIAL AND FAMILY PROCEEDINGS ACT 1984

9.44 Relationship to foreign orders. This Act is intended to deal with divorce or legal separation in another country but which is entitled to be recognised as valid in this, where one of the parties is domiciled or has been habitually resident in this, or either or both of the parties had at the date of application under the Act an interest in a dwelling-house in this country which has at some time during the marriage been a matrimonial home (ss.12, 15).

9.45 The Act permits applications for financial relief, of various kinds, including (1984, s.17) a property adjustment order under ss.23A and 24 of the 1973 Act (9.06), sale under s.24A of that Act, and (1984, s.22) transfer of tenancy under the 1996 Act (9.40).

7. CHILDREN ACT 1989

9.46 Orders. Under the Children Act 1989 there is a number of specific orders—"contact order"—"prohibited steps order"—

"residence order"—"specific issue order"—which may be sought in proceedings under any of the above Acts, or under the inherent jurisdiction of the High Court in relation to children, some of which orders (*e.g.* "an order settling the arrangements to be made as to the person with whom a child is to live," *i.e.* a residence order) will concern housing.

9.47 If such an order is sought during proceedings under these Acts, the general principles of the Children Act 1989, s.11, will be applied, and ancillary powers will be available (*e.g.* a family assistance order under s.16). In general terms, the Act does not substantively alter the description in the foregoing paragraphs of this Chapter, nor is it possible here to describe its terms in any detail.

Further Considerations

1. WHICH COURT?

9.48 Accredited courts. All matrimonial proceedings have to be brought in a properly accredited court. The High Court has power to conduct matrimonial proceedings which means that, in London, the Family Division of the High Court will hear the case, and—in other cities where the High Court sits—the case will be brought in the Divorce Registry.

9.49 Some county courts, however, also have power to hear matrimonial disputes, provided that they have been listed as a divorce county court. Under the Family Law Act, the court is defined as "the High Court, a county court or a magistrates' court" (FLA s.57(1)). For cases involving transfer of tenancies (9.40), the court excludes the magistrates' court.

9.50 The Lord Chancellor has power to specify by order the level of court at which proceedings may or must be commenced.

2. REHOUSING

9.51 Homelessness. A woman who leaves the domestic home because of violence or the fear of violence is considered to be homeless for the purposes of Pt VII of the Housing Act 1996.

9.52 In deciding whether it was reasonable for her to continue to occupy the home for the purposes of deciding homelessness or intentional homelessness, authorities may not take into account the fact that she could have taken proceedings under the provisions considered in this Chapter, unless they are in fact proceedings which have commenced or which are going to commence (*Bond v Leicester CC*, 2001; 10.22).

9.53   Discrimination. A woman who is not rehoused by the local authority may have difficulties finding anywhere else to live. She should bear in mind the provisions of the Sex Discrimination Act 1975 which make it unlawful for those concerned in the management, sale or rental of property to treat a woman any the less favourably than they would treat a man, for example, by refusing to grant a mortgage to a woman, or adding some term such as a demand for a guarantor for rent or mortgage payments.

9.54   Exemptions. This Act does not apply to resident landlords or buildings so small that they are either subdivided into no more than three separate units of accommodation or can only accommodate a maximum of six people within them. A housing association set up to cater for the needs of one sex only, *e.g.* single mothers, female ex-prisoners, male ex-mental patients, etc. is also exempt from the Act.

9.55   Court. Unlawful discrimination can be the subject of a normal county court action.

CHAPTER TEN

Homelessness and Allocations

Introduction

10.01 Homelessness. Since 1977, local authorities have been under a duty to secure that accommodation is made available for many of those who are homeless: the provisions, first contained in the Housing (Homeless Persons) Act 1977, were later consolidated into Pt III of the Housing Act 1985 ("1985"). Major changes were made by Pt VII of the Housing Act 1996 ("1996") and further amendments by the Homelessness Act 2002.

10.02 Allocations. In large part because of the extent to which housing the homeless was affecting the allocation of housing stock, Pt VI of the 1996 Act also introduced a new regime governing the allocation of housing, which was also amended by the Homelessness Act 2002. Because of this link between the two Parts, they are both considered in this Chapter.

Outline

10.03 Homelessness duties

- Pt VII places an obligation on local housing authorities to secure that suitable accommodation is made available for a person who is homeless, in priority need of accommodation, who did not become homeless intentionally, but subject to the requirements of Pt VI as to allocation of their own accommodation.

- The obligation is subject to local connection provisions which permit one authority, in some circumstances, to pass the responsibility for complying with the legislation to another authority (ss.193(2) and 198(1)).

- The obligation is the peak housing duty under Pt VII, but permanent housing will only be available once the applicant is allocated accommodation under Pt VI.

- Persons from abroad are excluded from assistance, including asylum-seekers who made their claim on or after April 3, 2000. Earlier asylum-seekers are in any event excluded if they have some accommodation, however, temporary.

- There are also obligations in respect of those who are not yet homeless, those who do not have a priority need, those who have a priority need but become homeless intentionally, and those who may be the responsibility of another authority while the position is resolved.

10.04   Additional homeless duties

- Authorities have duties to make enquiries, to notify applicants of their decisions and the reasons for them, and to protect the property of the homeless.

- Where there is no duty under Pt VII, duties to accommodate or assist may arise under other legislation such as the Children Act 1989 and the National Assistance Act 1948.

- There are ancillary provisions governing obtaining accommodation by deception, and funding voluntary agencies.

- There are provisions for an internal review of decisions and appeal to the county court on a point of law.

- The Homelessness Act 2002 introduced a new strategic duty requiring authorities to formulate a homelessness strategy.

10.05   Allocation duties

- Local authorities no longer need to maintain a housing register governing the allocation of housing, whether their own or by way of nomination to another landlord's stock, but they must maintain a scheme to ensure that housing is preferentially (although not exclusively) allocated to those statutorily defined as being most in need of it.

- The scheme must include a statement of the authority's policy on offering applicants a choice of housing accommodation or an opportunity to express their preferences as to the housing to be allocated.

- Certain persons from abroad are excluded from allocation, as are those whom an authority decide to treat as ineligible on the ground of anti-social behaviour, although there are provisions enabling the latter class to reapply if the applicant considers that he should no longer be excluded on this ground.

10.06 Additional allocation duties

- Authorities have to make advice and information about allocations freely available in their areas.

- The allocation scheme has to be framed so as to afford applicants the information that will allow them to assess how applications are likely to be treated and whether accommodation is likely to be made available under it and, if so, when it is likely to become available.

- Applicants have to be notified of decisions and there is provision for internal review, although not for appeal to the county court (on a point of law or otherwise).

- Before adopting a scheme, or making major changes to it, authorities must consult with registered social landlords with whom they have nomination arrangements.

- There are ancillary provisions governing false statements.

Homelessness

10.07 Key Concepts. The approach adopted here is to deal first of all with the key concepts contained in Pt VII before matching them to the duties which Pt VII imposes, considering separately and under their own headings the ancillary provisions and review and appeal.

10.08 Definitions. The key definitions are:

- Authorities;
- Eligibility for assistance;
- Homelessness;
- Priority need;
- Intentional homelessness; and
- Local connection.

10.09 Duties. The duties which have to be considered are:

- Preliminary duties;
- Principal duties; and
- Local connection provisions.

10.10 Other matters. The other matters which must be considered are:

- Duties under other Acts;
- Protection of property;
- Homelessness strategies
- Advice, information and voluntary organisations;
- Code of Guidance;
- Review and appeal;
- Criminal offences;
- Co-operation between authorities.

1. AUTHORITIES

10.11 Three classes. Pt VII refers (1996, s.217) to three classes of authority—local housing authorities, relevant authorities and social services authorities.

10.12 Local Housing Authority. "Local housing authority" means a district council except in London, where it means the London borough council or the Common Council of the City of London, or in Wales where it means the county or county borough council (1985 s.1, as amended). Unitary authorities under Local Government Act 1992 will have the functions conferred on them by order, which mean that they, too, are housing authorities.

10.13 Contracting Out. Some of the functions of the local housing authority may, however, be contracted out: see the Local Authorities (Contracting out of Allocation of Housing and Homelessness Functions) Order 1996 (SI 1996/3205).

10.14 Relevant authorities. "Relevant authority" means, in England and Wales, a local housing authority and a social services authority (1996, s.217).

10.15 Social services authority. "Social services authority" means a non-metropolitan county council, a metropolitan district council, a London borough council or the Common Council of the City of London, and in Wales a county or county borough council (1996, s.217 and Local Authority Social Services Act 1970 s.1, as amended). The same point may be made (see 10.12) about unitary authorities.

2. INELIGIBILITY FOR ASSISTANCE

10.16 Two categories. There are two categories of person who are simply ineligible for assistance (although they may still be able to benefit from the general 'advice and information' duty—s179; 10.158):

(a) "Persons from abroad" are altogether ineligible for assistance; these are persons who are subject to immigration control under the Asylum and Immigration Act 1996, unless requalified by regulations (s.185(1) and (2)).

No person who is excluded from entitlement to housing benefit by the Immigration and Asylum Act 1999, s.115 may be reincluded by such regulations (s.185(2A)). In addition, the Secretary of State may by regulation add categories of people who are to be treated as persons from abroad for these purposes (s.185(3), see the Homelessness (England) Regulations 2000 (SI 2000/701), reg 3, applied to Wales by the Homelessness (Wales) Regulations 2000 (SI 2000/1079)). Note too that, when determining whether another person is homeless or threatened with homelessness, or has a priority need for accommodation, ineligible persons from abroad are to be disregarded (s.185(4)).

(b) Those asylum-seekers, or dependants of an asylum-seeker, who are not excluded as persons from abroad (including all asylum-seekers who made their claim on or after April 3, 2000) will nonetheless still be ineligible for assistance if they have accommodation in the United Kingdom, however temporary, which is available for their occupation (as to the meaning of which, see further below, 10.28) (s.186(1)).

Provision is made for determining when a person becomes, and ceases to become, an asylum-seeker (or a dependant of an asylum-seeker) for these purposes (s.186(2)–(5)).

10.17 Information. In order to reach a decision on the question of eligibility, a local housing authority may seek such information as they require from the Secretary of State, who is bound to provide it (and—whether or not the original request for information was in writing—to provide it in writing if the authority in writing ask for it so to be provided) (s.187(1) and (2)).

10.18   The Secretary of State is under an additional duty to notify the authority in writing if it subsequently appears to him that any application, decision or other change of circumstance has affected the status of a person about whom he had previously provided information (s.187(3)).

3. HOMELESSNESS

10.19 No rights in accommodation. A person is homeless for the purposes of Pt VII if he has no accommodation in the United Kingdom or elsewhere in the world, and a person is deemed to lack accommodation if there is no accommodation:

(a) Which he is entitled to occupy by virtue of an interest in it (*e.g.* ownership, tenancy); or

(b) Which he is entitled to occupy by virtue of an order of a court, (*e.g.* in the course of domestic proceedings, see Chapter 9); or

(c) Which he has an express or implied licence to occupy (*e.g.* service occupants, members of the family), or

(d) Which he is occupying as a residence by virtue of any enactment or rule of law giving him the right to remain in occupation or restricting the right of any other person to recover possession of it (1996, s.175(1)).

10.20 Available accommodation. Accommodation is only available for an applicant's occupation if it is available for him, together with any other person who normally resides with him as a member of his family, and any other person who might reasonably be expected to reside with him (1996, s.176). Persons from abroad, disqualified for assistance in their own right, will also fall to be disregarded when considering availability (10.16). Accessibility to accommodation (*e.g.* whether the applicant can travel to it) is a relevant factor in determining whether it is available (*Begum (Nipa) v Tower Hamlets LBC*, 1999).

10.21 Accommodation reasonable to continue to occupy. Accommodation is disregarded if it is not accommodation which it would be reasonable to continue to occupy (1996, s.175(3)), *e.g.* if it is in such bad condition that no one could be expected to stay in it. When deciding whether or not it would be reasonable for a person to remain in occupation, an authority to which application has been made can take into account the general housing circumstances prevailing in their area (1996, s.177(2)), *i.e.* whether many others are living in accommodation just as bad. The meaning of the term "reasonable to continue to occupy" is considered below, in relation to intentional homelessness (10.64), as the purpose of this part of the definition is in substance to secure that if an applicant could quit accommodation without being considered homeless intentionally, he ought to be treated as, in effect, already homeless.

10.22 Violence. It is also not reasonable to continue to occupy accommodation if it is probable that to do so will lead to violence (domestic or otherwise) against the applicant, or against someone who normally resides with the applicant as a member of his family, or against anyone else who might reasonably be expected to reside with the applicant (s.177(1)). Violence means violence from another person or threats of violence from another person which are likely to be carried out (s.177(1A)). In deciding whether it is reasonable for an applicant to continue to occupy under s.177(1), the only question the authority may ask is whether it is probable that continued occupation of the accommodation will lead to violence against that person; that is purely a question of fact devoid of value judgments about what an applicant should or should not do, *e.g.* whether he should take out an injunction against the perpetrator: *Bond v Leicester CC*, 2001.

10.23 Domestic Violence. Violence is domestic if it is from a person who is associated with the victim (s.177(1A)).

10.24 Associated Persons. Persons are associated if:

(a) They are or have been married to each other;

(b) They are cohabitants or former cohabitants (meaning a man and a woman who are living together without being married to one another);

(c) They live or have lived in the same household;

(d) They are relatives, meaning:

(i) Parent, step-parent, child, step-child, grandparent or grandchild of a person or of that person's spouse or former spouse; or

(ii) Sibling, aunt or uncle, niece or nephew of a person or that person's spouse or former spouse, whether of full or half-blood, or by affinity;

(e) They have or had formerly agreed to marry;

(f) In relation to a child, each of the persons is a parent of the child, or has or has had parental responsibility (within the meaning of the Children Act 1989) for the child; and

(g) In relation to a child who has been adopted (or subsequently freed from adoption), if one person is a natural parent or natural parent of a natural parent, and the other is the child, or is a person who has become a parent by adoption, or who has applied for an adoption order, or with whom the child was at any time placed for adoption (s.178).

10.25 Additional categories of homelessness. In addition, a person is homeless if he has accommodation which he is entitled to occupy, and which is available for his occupation, and which it is reasonable to continue to occupy, but

(a) He cannot secure entry to it, or

(b) The accommodation consists of a movable structure, vehicle or vessel, designed or adapted for living in, and there is no place where he is entitled or permitted both to place it and to reside in it, *i.e.* houseboat, caravan (1996, s.175(2)).

10.26 Threatened with homelessness. A person is threatened with homelessness if it is likely that he will become homeless within 28 days (1996, s.175(4)).

10.27 Meaning of accommodation. Under the equivalent provisions of the 1985 Act, it was held that the only gloss which can be put on the word "accommodation" is that which the statute imports, *i.e.* availability (10.20) and reasonableness to continue to occupy (10.21). Other than that, it simply means "a place which can fairly be described as accommodation", *per* Lord Hoffman in *R. v Brent LBC Ex p. Awua*, 1996. (Although a person may not be homeless because of the low level of this test, he may still be threatened with homelessness).

10.28 Homelessness and temporary accommodation. Before *Awua*, a number of cases which are still likely to be followed had also considered the meaning of accommodation. Thus, in *R. v Ealing LBC Ex p. Sidhu*, 1982 (not considered in *Awua*), the local authority held that a woman temporarily housed in a women's refuge was not homeless because she had a licence to occupy a room in the hostel: the court rejected this argument. Likewise, the court rejected the argument that a man who usually slept in a night shelter, on a day-to-day basis, but who could be turned away if the shelter was full at the time of his arrival, was not homeless: *R. v Waveney DC Ex p. Bowers*, 1982 (approved in *Awua*).

4. PRIORITY NEED

10.29 Statutory definition. A person has a priority need for accommodation under Pt VII if:

(a) He has dependent children who are residing with him, or who might reasonably be expected to reside with him; or

(b) He, or anyone who resides or might reasonably be expected to reside with him, is vulnerable as a result of old age, mental illness or handicap or physical disability or other special reason; or

(c) She is a pregnant woman, or the applicant resides or might reasonably be expected to reside with a pregnant woman; or

(d) He is homeless or threatened with homelessness as a result of an emergency such as flood, fire or other disaster (1996, s.189).

10.30 Further classes. The Secretary of State may specify further classes of person as having a priority need for accommodation, or may amend or repeal any of the present classes (s189(2)).

10.31 Wales. In Wales, this power has been exercised in the Homeless Persons (Priority Need) (Wales) Order (SI 2001/607) to specify:

(a) All those who are aged 18 or over, and under 21, if at any time while they were a child they were looked after, accommodated or fostered, or they are at particular risk of sexual or financial exploitation;

(b) All 16 and 17 year olds;

(c) Those without dependent children who have been subject to domestic violence, who are at risk of such violence or who would be if they returned home;

(d) Those who formerly served in the regular armed forces and have been homeless since leaving;

(e) Former prisoners who have been homeless since leaving custody, provided they have a local connection (10.67) with the local housing authority.

10.32 England. In England, the following additional classes have been specified in the The Homelessness (Priority Need for Accommodation) (England) Order 2002 (SI 2002/2051):

(a) All 16 and 17 year olds, provided they are not a relevant child (as defined by the Children Act 1989, s.23A) or owed a duty under the Children Act 1989, s.20;

(b) Any person who is aged 18 to 20 who at any time while 16 or 17 was, but is no longer, looked after, accommodated or fostered but not a relevant student (as defined by the Children Act 1989, s.24B(3));

(c) Those aged 21 or over who are vulnerable because they have previously been looked after, accommodated or fostered;

(d) Those who are vulnerable as a result of service in Her Majesty's regular armed forces;

(e) Those who are vulnerable as a result of having served a custodial sentence, having been committed for contempt of court or having been remanded in custody;

(f) Those who are vulnerable because they have had to cease to occupy accommodation because of violence or threats of violence which are likely to be carried out.

10.33 Dependent children. Dependent children are usually treated as those still in full-time education or training, or otherwise up to the age of 16: *R. v Kensington and Chelsea RLBC Ex p. Amarfio*, 1995. Even where a 16 or 17 year old is financially independent, however, it is possible that he is dependent in other ways (*Amarfio*).

10.34 Residence. The issue is solely one of fact: are dependent children residing, or are there dependent children who ought reasonably to be expected to reside, with the applicant? In *R. v Hillingdon LBC Ex p. Islam*, 1981, in the High Court, the authority suggested that priority need only arose if children both are residing, and might reasonably be expected to reside, with the applicant. But, as the court held, Pt III (now Pt VII) says "or."

10.35 Split families. It is not a requirement that the child is wholly dependent on—or wholly and exclusively residing with— the applicant, so in a genuine case of split custody an applicant may be in priority need even though the child is with him only for part of the week: *R. v Lambeth LBC Ex p. Vagliviello*, 1990. In *R. v Port Talbot BC Ex p. McCarthy*, 1990, however, it was held that where a father was granted staying access to his children, under an order of joint custody, but it was the mother who had care and control of the children, the children were not necessarily to be treated as residing with their father. Again where children were residing with their mother, even though they were dependent on their father and a joint residence order had been made under the Children Act 1989, s.8, it did not necessarily follow that the children were reasonably to be expected to reside with both parents (*R. v Oxford CC Ex p. Doyle*, 1997).

10.36 Custody. In *Sidhu* (10.28), the authority argued that until the applicant had what they called a "final" or "full" custody order, in the course of pending divorce proceedings, they need not consider her as in priority need. The court held that custody was irrelevant to priority need, for a custody order can be varied at any time until the child reaches 18, or one parent may have custody, while another has care and control.

10.37 Children in priority need. A dependent child is not entitled to apply under the Act in his own right, and will not qualify as vulnerable (10.38) simply because of youth or any disability. Dependent children are expected to be provided for by those on whom they are dependent: *R. v Oldham LBC Ex p. G*, 1993.

10.38 Vulnerability. Vulnerability means "less able to fend for oneself so that injury or detriment will result where a less vulnerable man will be able to cope without harmful effects" (*R. v Waveney DC Ex p. Bowers*, 1983 and *R. v Camden LBC Ex p. Pereira*, 1998).

10.39 Assessing Vulnerability. In *R. v Kensington & Chelsea RLBC, Hammersmith & Fulham LBC, Westminster CC*, and *Islington LBC Ex p. Kihara*, 1996 the Court of Appeal said that whether someone is vulnerable—for one of the stated reasons (10.29, 10.32)—should preferably be approached as a composite question, rather than in two separate stages, *i.e.* it should not be approached by asking first whether there is vulnerability at all and, secondly and separately, whether that vulnerability (if any) is attributable to any of those factors.

10.40 Mental illness and handicap. A distinction may be drawn between mental illness (*i.e.* psychotic) and "mere" mental handicap, although subnormality will not necessarily amount to vulnerability in every case (*R. v Bath CC Ex p. Sangermano*, 1984). Nor will every case of epilepsy render a person vulnerable (*R. v Reigate and Banstead BC Ex p. Di Domenico*, 1987).

10.41 Medical assessment. The authority must reach their own decision, and not merely "rubber-stamp" a medical opinion, unless it is decisive on the only relevant issues (*R. v Lambeth LBC Ex p. Carroll*, 1987 and *R. v Wandsworth LBC Ex p. Banbury*, 1986).

10.42 Mental capacity. Where vulnerable, an applicant must have the capacity to understand and respond to the offer of accommodation and to undertake its responsibilities. If incapable of doing so, he may not apply at all, notwithstanding his vulnerability (*R. v Tower Hamlets LBC Ex p. Begum*, 1993).

10.43 Other special reason. In *Kihara* (above) the Court of Appeal rejected an argument that "other special reason" was limited to the applicant's mental or physical characteristics. The category is free-standing, unrestricted by any notion of physical or mental weakness other than that which is inherent in the word "vulnerable". The word "special" imports a requirement that the housing difficulties faced by an applicant are of an unusual degree of gravity, enough to differentiate him from other homeless persons and does not include financial impecuniosity by itself: an absence of means does not mark out one case from the generality of cases to a sufficient degree to render it "special".

10.44 Emergency. A person who has been unlawfully evicted from his home is not in priority need due to an emergency. If not actual flood or fire, the emergency must be of a similar nature which—while not needing to be a natural disaster—must encompass some physical damage: *R. v Bristol CC Ex p. Bradic*, 1995 (see also *Noble v South Herefordshire DC*, 1983).

5. INTENTIONAL HOMELESSNESS

10.45 Principal Definition. A person becomes homeless intentionally if he deliberately does anything or fails to do anything in consequence of which he ceases to occupy accommodation which is available for his occupation and which it would have been reasonable for him to continue to occupy (1996, s.191(1)).

10.46 Threatened with homelessness. Becoming threatened with homelessness intentionally is similarly defined (1996, s.196(1)). There is no distinction in principle between the two concepts (*Dyson v Kerrier DC*, 1980). (All future references to intentional homelessness may, accordingly, and save where an express distinction is drawn, be taken to refer also to becoming threatened with homelessness intentionally.)

10.47 Different elements. The principal definition (10.45) of intentional homelessness incorporates a number of elements:

(a) Something must be done deliberately, or there must be a deliberate failure to act;

(b) The act or omission must have a consequence;

(c) The consequence must be that accommodation ceases or will cease to be occupied;

(d) That accommodation must be or have been, 'accommodation available for [the] occupation' of the homeless person (see 10.20, above); and

(e) It must have been reasonable to continue in occupation of that accommodation (see 10.64, below).

10.48 Good faith. An act or omission in good faith, on the part of a person who was unaware of any relevant fact (*e.g.* the availability of financial assistance towards rent, etc. the right to remain in occupation after notice to quit or expiry of tenancy), is not to be treated as deliberate for these purposes (1996 ss.191(2), 196(2)). Good faith in these circumstances can encompass honest blundering and carelessness (*e.g.* in a business deal) and should be contrasted with dishonesty (where there can be no question of good faith): *R. v Hammersmith & Fulham LBC Ex p. Lusi*, 1991.

10.49 Whose conduct. One preliminary question is whose conduct is to be taken into account, when an application is by or on behalf of more than one person? In *R. v North Devon DC Ex p. Lewis*, 1980, a woman lived with a man by whom she had a child, but to whom she was not married. He quit his job and in consequence lost his tied accommodation. When he applied as homeless, he was held to have become homeless intentionally. The woman then applied in her own right. The authority said two things: (a) they did not have to consider her application, because she was governed by the decision on his application; and (b) she had in any event acquiesced in his decision to quit his job, so that she, by association, had done an act of intentionality in her own right. The court rejected the authority's first argument but upheld the second on the facts of the case. It would not, however, have been appropriate for her to be deemed to have acquiesced if she had done all she could to prevent him, but he had gone ahead notwithstanding, *e.g.* a woman who has done all she can to prevent her husband spending the rent money on drink or otherwise.

10.50 Lewis applied. In *R. v West Dorset DC Ex p. Phillips*, 1984, *Lewis* was applied so as to compel an authority to house a woman who turned on her husband during their homelessness interview and attacked him for spending money on drink. In *R. v Mole Valley DC Ex p. Burton*, 1988, the authority failed to consider that a wife had acted in good faith when she had believed her husband's assurances that they would be rehoused if he quit his job and accordingly lost his tied accommodation, for which reason their decision could not be upheld. In *R. v East Northamptonshire DC Ex p. Spruce*, 1988, it was said that a spouse's mere knowledge of, *e.g.* rent or mortgages arrears would not be enough to amount to acquiescence, or he or she might have learned so late that the arrears were too big to do anything about.

10.51 Lewis not applied. In other cases, attempts to apply the *Lewis* principle have failed. In *R. v Nottingham CC Ex p. Cain*, 1995, in particular, the Court of Appeal held that an authority were entitled to infer that the applicant had known of her partner's conduct in withholding the rent, even though there was no direct evidence that she had done so. (The intentionality of parents cannot be circumvented by a child's application, as a dependent child is not in priority need in his own right—*R. v Oldham LBC Ex p. G; R. v Bexley LBC Ex p. B*, 1993–10.37).

10.52 Deliberate act or omission. The definition does not require that the applicant deliberately became homeless so much as that he deliberately did (or failed to do) something as a result of which he became homeless. The word "deliberate" only governs the act or omission: *Devenport v Salford CC*, 1983. The link between the act and the homelessness must be judged objectively: *Robinson v Torbay BC*, 1982.

10.53 In Consequence. The homelessness must be "in consequence of" the deliberate act or omission. This is a question of "cause and effect" (*Dyson v Kerrier DC*, 1980; *Din v Wandsworth LBC*, 1983). The principal issue which has arisen in practice is the attribution of present homelessness to past act or omission. That is to say, there is commonly a past act which has or could have been the subject of a finding of intentionality and the argument then becomes whether or not that act or omission is the cause of the present homelessness.

10.54 Cause and effect. A causal link may continue to subsist following the act of intentionality even though the applicant ceases to be homeless in the interim, *e.g.* because he finds some temporary accommodation from which he is subsequently evicted: *R. v Brent LBC Ex p. Awua*, 1996. The authority has to look back to the original cause of the homelessness and determine whether it was intentional (*Din*). This derives from the distinction between tenses within what is now s.190(1) ("is" homeless, but "became" homeless intentionally; see also s.189(2), "has" a priority need, and s.191 "is homeless ... and has a priority need, and did not become homeless intentionally").

10.55 Prison. Commission of a criminal offence may be considered deliberate conduct and lead to a finding of intentionality, where it can properly be regarded as having caused the homelessness, *e.g.* where subsequent imprisonment leads to repossession of the home, *i.e.* for want of ability to pay rent. The test is whether the loss of accommodation could reasonably have been regarded at the time as a likely consequence of the commission of the offence (*R. v Hounslow LBC Ex p. R*, 1997; *Stewart v Lambeth LBC*, 2002)

10.56 Loss of tied accommodation. It will not always be appropriate to treat someone who has quit or been dismissed from his job and thus lost tied accommodation as intentionally homeless. There must be a sufficient link, or proximity, between the act which caused the loss of job, and the loss of accommodation (*R. v*

Thanet DC Ex p. Reeve, 1981). A direct act, *e.g.* theft from an employer, which could reasonably be foreseen to lead to loss of job and accommodation, may well amount to intentional homelessness; loss of job through, *e.g.* a period of incompetence, should, however, not do so.

10.57 Assessing loss of tied accommodation. The fact that someone appears voluntarily to have quit employment does not necessarily mean that he has become homeless intentionally: he may have been forced into it, so that his resignation was constructively dismissal (*R. v Thurrock BC Ex p. Williams*, 1982).

10.58 Burden in intentionality. If there is any doubt about whether or not someone has done a sufficiently direct act to qualify as intentionally homelessness, it should be resolved in the applicant's favour (*Williams*). In every case, it is for the authority to satisfy themselves that a person became homeless intentionally, not for an applicant to satisfy the authority that he did not do so (*Lewis, Williams*).

10.59 Grounds for possession. Rent arrears, non-payment of mortgage instalments, and nuisance and annoyance causing eviction (3.95–3.108, 4.120, 5.143–5.148), can qualify as acts of intentional homelessness, although in each case there must be sufficient proximity, or foreseeability, between act and loss of home. In each case, too, ignorance of ways of avoiding loss of the home will be a defence.

10.60 Arrears and resources. In *R. v LB Hillingdon Ex p. Tinn*, 1988, which only secondarily concerned this issue, it was said by the court that it could not be reasonable to continue to occupy accommodation if an applicant could not pay the rent or mortgage without depriving himself of the ordinary necessities of life, such as food, clothing, heat and transport. Authorities must therefore consider whether the applicant has adequate resources when deciding whether failure to pay the rent amounts to a deliberate act: *R v Wandsworth LBC Ex p. Hawthorne*, 1994. In *R. v Leeds CC Ex p. Adamiec*, 1991, however, a sale before the commencement of possession proceedings by a building society was upheld as intentional, even though it was likely that in the long run the applicant would not have been able to afford to continue living in the house. See now the specific regulations relating to affordability which authorities must consider: The Homelessness (Suitability of Accommodation) Order 1996 (SI 1996/3204).

10.61 Breaking the chain of causation. Where an applicant has done a deliberate act, which has caused homelessness, the question becomes how the chain of causation may be broken. It will be broken by a period of "settled accommodation" (*Din, Awua*). It may also be broken by other events (*e.g.* separation from husband, reduction in housing benefit payments), provided that the event is unconnected with the temporary nature of the accommodation (*R. v Camden LBC Ex p. Fahia*, 1997, in the Court of Appeal).

10.62 Settled accommodation. There is no judicial or other definition of settled accommodation, but accommodation which is indefinite at its outset should qualify, although an intention that it should be indefinite will not always be sufficient where the accommodation is of a precarious nature (*R. v Merton LBC Ex p. Ruffle*, 1988). An assured shorthold may be settled (*R. v Rochester-upon-Medway CC Ex p. Williams*, 1994).

10.63 Available accommodation. Accommodation is only available for a person's accommodation if it is available for himself and for anyone with whom he might reasonably be expected to reside (1996, s.176).

10.64 Reasonable to continue to occupy. When considering whether or not it was reasonable for the applicant to remain in occupation of his former accommodation, the authority are entitled to have regard to the general circumstances prevailing in relation to housing in their own area (1996, s.177(2)), *i.e.* they may consider others who are putting up with bad housing conditions. This permits authorities to claim that applicants should have remained in what objectively may be considered appalling conditions. It means in practice that people can rarely safely quit their current accommodation on account of its physical condition without a real likelihood of a finding of intentionality.

10.65 Range of questions. In *R. v Hammersmith and Fulham LBC Ex p. Duro Rama*, 1983, it was said that "reasonable to continue to occupy" involves a range of questions, not confined to the condition of the housing formerly occupied, and in *R. v Tower Hamlets LBC Ex p. Monaf*, 1988, that it calls for a "balancing exercise" between the reasons for leaving accommodation and coming to the area where application has been made, and housing conditions in that area. In *R. v B Hillingdon LBC Ex p. H*, 1988, political and racial harassment was considered relevant to the question of reasonable to continue to occupy. When applicable, the specific provisions relating to violence will make it not reasonable to continue to occupy accommodation (10.22).

10.66 Collusive arrangements. There is one "added" definition of intentional homelessness. A person becomes homeless intentionally or threatened with homelessness intentionally if he enters into an arrangement under which he is required to cease to occupy accommodation which it would have been reasonable for him to continue to occupy, the purpose of which arrangement is to enable him to qualify for assistance under Pt VII, and there is no other, or independent, good reason for the actual or threatened homelessness (1996 ss.191(3), 196(3)).

6.   LOCAL CONNECTION

10.67 Statutory definition. A person has a local connection with an area:

(a) Because he is, or in the past was, normally resident in it and that residence was of choice; or

(b) Because he was employed in it; or

(c) Because of family associations; or

(d) For any special circumstance (1996, s.199(1)).

10.68 Residence of choice. Residence is not "of choice" if:

(i) It is in consequence of service in the armed forces; or

(ii) It is in consequence of detention under an Act of Parliament (*e.g.* imprisonment, compulsory in-patient) (1996, s.199(3), (4)).

10.69 Employment. Employment does not count if it is employment in the armed forces (1996, s.199(2)).

10.70 Temporary accommodation. An applicant housed in temporary accommodation by an authority (under *e.g.* s.188, 10.93, below) will still be normally resident in that accommodation (*Mohamed v Hammersmith & Fulham LBC*, 2001).

10.71 Relation between local connection and grounds. The overriding term is "local connection," which must be attributable to one of the specified "grounds"; merely demonstrating that there is, *e.g.* employment, or family connection, without a finding sufficient to amount to a "local connection" will not be enough (*Re Betts*, 1983).

10.72 Timing of decision. Whether an applicant has a local connection or not is established as at the date of the decision, not at the date of the application (*Mohamed v Hammersmith & Fulham LBC*, 2001). Furthermore, where the applicant seeks an internal review of the decision (see 10.161, below), it is the facts at the date of the decision which must be considered (*Mohamed*).

10.73 Conditions. The local connection provisions allow one housing authority to shift the burden of making accommodation available to another housing authority. The provisions apply when the authority are satisfied that the applicant is homeless (N.B., not merely threatened with homelessness), in priority need, and not homeless intentionally, and either:

(a) The applicant was—within the previous five years—placed in accommodation in their area by another authority, in pursuance of Pt VII functions (1996, s.198(4) the Homelessness Regulations 1996 (SI 1996/2754) reg.6; see also 10.114 for the notification requirements imposed on the other authority at the time of the placement); or

(b) The authority consider that all of the following conditions applies:

(i) Neither the applicant nor anyone who might reasonably be expected to reside with him has a local connection with their area, and

(ii) The applicant or a person who might reasonably be expected to reside with him does have a local connection with the area of another housing authority, and

(iii) Neither the applicant nor any person who might reasonably be expected to reside with him will run the risk of domestic violence in the area of the other authority (1996, s.198(1),(2)).

10.74 Further condition. In addition, a local connection referral may not be made where the applicant or any person who might reasonably be expected to reside with him has suffered non-domestic violence in the area of the other authority and it is probable that the return to that area of the victim will lead to further violence of a similar kind against him (s.198(2A)).

10.75 Violence and domestic violence. These are defined in the same terms as when determining whether or not it is reasonable to remain in occupation (s.198(3); 10.22–10.23).

10.76 Passing responsibility. The housing duty passes to the other authority if the conditions are satisfied (1996, s.200(4)). The other authority's obligation is to house under 1996, s.193 (10.107).

10.77 Keeping responsibility. The housing duty under s.193 remains with the notifying authority if the conditions are not satisfied (1996, s.200(3))

10.78 No local connection. If an applicant has no local connection with anywhere in England, Scotland or Wales, the local connection provisions do not apply, and the burden of housing will remain with the authority to which application is made, as in *R. v Hillingdon LBC Ex p. Streeting*, 1980, a case concerning a refugee from Ethiopia.

10.79 Interim accommodation and notification. Pending resolution of the question which authority will have final responsibility, the authority to which the application is made will provide temporary accommodation (1996, s.200(1)). Once the question has been decided, it is they who must notify the applicant of the decision and of the reasons for it, as well as of his right to request a review (and the time within which it must be requested, 10.162) (1996, s.200(2)). Notification is effected in the same way as under 1996, s.184(6) (1996, s.200(6), 10.91). The temporary housing duty ceases when the notification is given, even if a review is requested, although the authority still have a discretion to continue to provide it pending review (1996, s.200(5)).

10.80 Arbitration. These provisions are clearly a breeding ground for differences of opinion between authorities. Pt VII provides elaborate machinery for the determination of disputes between them either by agreement or, if necessary, by reference to an independent arbitrator (1996, s.198(5)). An arbitration decision can none the less be the subject of internal review, and thence appeal to the county court (10.160 *et seq.*) (1996, s.198(5), s.202(1)(d), (e)).

10.81 "Merry-go-round". Decisions of the authority to which the application has been made on the issues of homelessness, priority need and intentionality are binding on an authority to whom they subsequently refer the application. This remains true even if the applicant had formerly applied to one authority, been found homeless intentionally, and moved on to apply to another authority: the second authority can still reach a decision, different from that of the first authority, that the applicant did not become homeless intentionally, and then invoke the local connection provisions to refer the applicant back (*R. v Slough BC Ex p. Ealing LBC*, 1980). This produces what has been described as a "merry-go-round," for the first authority will be bound by the decision of the second, notwithstanding that it contradicts their own, earlier decision. The proposition illustrates how views may differ as to whether or not someone has become homeless intentionally. There is nothing to stop an applicant applying to authority after authority in the hope of a favourable decision.

10.82 Enquiries by second authority. In one of these cases, where there has been no intervening change of circumstances, the authority to which the later application has been made must treat the application carefully and must give the authority which had made the earlier decision and to which the applicant will be returned an opportunity of discussing the case and, above all, of discussing any discrepancies in the explanations offered for the homelessness by the applicant (*R. v Tower Hamlets LBC Ex p. Camden LBC*, 1988) Before deciding to refer, the second authority must take into account the general housing circumstances in the area to which they are referring the application (*R. v Newham LBC Ex p. Tower Hamlets LBC*, 1990).

10.83 No change of mind. An authority who find that an applicant is unintentionally homeless and who then refer the applicant to another authority cannot change their mind on intentionality simply because the referral is unsuccessful and the applicant comes back to them (*R. v Beverley DC Ex p. McPhee*, 1978).

10.84 Local authority agreement. As a first stage, authorities will try to reach agreement as to who should house the applicant, (1996, s.198(5)). In default of agreement, disputes are to be resolved in accordance with arrangements made by the Secretary of State by order. The current arrangements are to be found in the Homelessness (Decision on Referrals) Order 1998 (SI 1998/1578) and the agreement reached between the relevant association of local authorities (the Local Authority Agreement). The terms of this document do not bind anyone, not even an authority who are party to it: it is a voluntary guideline, for administrative purposes only, and if an authority choose to depart from it in a particular case, they are free to do so; indeed, it will be irrelevant to any court or arbitration proceedings which may arise under the 1998 Order (*R. v Mr Referee McCall Ex p. Eastbourne BC*, 1981).

7. PRELIMINARY DUTIES

10.85 Applications. The preliminary duties described below arise where a person applies to a housing authority for accommodation, or for assistance in obtaining it, and the authority have reason to believe that he may be homeless or threatened with homelessness (1996, s.184(1)). There is no provision for any particular form of application, or even that the application should be in writing (*R. v Chiltern DC Ex p. Roberts*, 1990).

10.86 Illegal immigrants. While certain immigrants are precluded from assistance (10.16), illegal immigrants are precluded from applying altogether (*Tower Hamlets LBC v Secretary of State for the Environment*, 1993).

10.87 Mental capacity. As noted above (10.42), the applicant must have sufficient capacity to understand and respond to the offer of accommodation, and to undertake its responsibilities: *R. v Bexley LBC Ex p. B, R. v Oldham MBC Ex p. G, R. v Tower Hamlets LBC Ex p. Begum*, 1993.

10.88 Three preliminary duties. The three main preliminary duties are to make enquiries, to notify the applicant of the decision and, in the case of an eligible homeless person in priority need, to accommodate pending the outcome of enquiries and notification. These duties are immediate: the authority cannot avoid them by keeping their offices shut for prolonged periods; in the major cities, they may be expected to maintain a 24–hour service, *i.e.* an emergency, out-of-hours service as well as a normal office service (*R. v Camden LBC Ex p. Gillan*, 1988). Nor can an authority postpone a decision in the hope of a change of circumstances that will reduce their duty (*R. v Ealing LBC Ex p. Sidhu*, 1982).

10.89 Enquiries. Where the authority have reason to believe there is actual or threatened homelessness, then they must make enquiries:

> (a) Such as are necessary to satisfy them whether the applicant is eligible for assistance (10.16); and,

(b) If so, whether any, and what, duties are owed to him under Pt VII (1996, s.184(1)).

10.90 Local connection enquiries. The authority may also make further enquiries as to whether there is a local connection with the district of another authority (1996, s.184(2)).

10.91 Notification. It follows that if the authority are not satisfied as to homelessness, they need not proceed to make any further enquiries. If they do make enquiries, then the authority must, on their completion, notify the applicant of their decision and "so far as any issue is decided against [the applicant's] interests" inform him of the reasons for the decision (1996, s.184(3)). If the decision is to notify another authority under the local connection provisions (10.73), the applicant must also be notified of this decision and its reasons (1996, s.184)). Notification must also inform the applicant of the right to request a review (within 21 days) (1996, s.184(5); 10.160).

10.92 In writing. A notification must be in writing; if the applicant does not receive the notification, he will be treated as having done so if the notice is made available at the authority's office for a reasonable period, for collection by him or on his behalf (1996, s.184(6)). The burden is on the applicant who does not receive the decision to go to the authority's office and ask for it.

10.93 Accommodation pending enquiries. Enquiries may take some time. If the authority have reason to believe that the applicant may be homeless and eligible for assistance, and in priority need, then—pending their decision—they are obliged to secure that accommodation is made available (1996, s.188(1)). This is so whether or not the applicant may have a local connection with another authority (1996, s.188(2)).

10.94 Accommodation for whom. The accommodation must be made available for the applicant and for any other family member who normally resides with, or anyone else who might reasonably be expected to reside with, him (1996, ss.176, 188(1)).

10.95 Cessation of interim accommodation duty. The duty ceases on notification of decision, even if the applicant requests a review, but the authority have a discretion to continue to house pending the review (1996, s.188(2),(3)).

8. LESS THAN THE FULL HOUSING DUTY

10.96 Types of duties. Duties towards the homeless depend on the findings of the authority as to priority need and intentionality.

10.97   Priority need but homeless intentionally. If the authority are satisfied that an applicant is homeless, and in priority need of accommodation, but they are also satisfied that he became homeless intentionally, they have two duties:

(a)   To secure that temporary accommodation is made available for such period as they consider will give him a reasonable opportunity to secure his own accommodation (s.190(2)(a)); and

(b)   To assess the applicant's housing needs and provide him (or secure that he is provided) with advice and assistance (s.190(2)(b), (4)).

10.98   Advice and assistance. The advice and assistance must include information about the likely availability in the authority's area of types of accommodation appropriate to the applicant's housing needs, including as to the location and sources of such types of accommodation (s.190(5), added by Homelessness Act 2002, Sch.1, para.10).

10.99   Local authority accommodation. If the authority provide their own accommodation, it will not be secure unless and until the authority notify the applicant otherwise (1985 Act Sch.1 para.4, substituted by 1996 Act Sch.17 para.3), which they may not do otherwise than in accordance with the allocation provisions considered below.

10.100   Private accommodation. If the authority secure accommodation through a landlord whose tenants are not secure, then this temporary accommodation will likewise not be within any statutory protection at all, albeit only for a year from when the authority first gave notification of their decision (above, 10.91), or—if there is a review (or an appeal)—from its final determination, and again unless the tenant is previously notified by the landlord that it is to be regarded either as an assured shorthold or a fully assured tenancy (s.209(2)).

10.101   Priority need but threatened with homelessness intentionally. If the authority are satisfied that the applicant is threatened with homelessness intentionally, eligible for assistance and in priority need, then the advice and appropriate assistance duty (above, 10.97(b)) arises (s.195(5)(b), (6), (7)), on the basis that once the homelessness itself occurs, an application will entitle the applicant to a period of temporary accommodation (10.97(a)).

10.102 No priority need. If the authority are satisfied that the applicant is homeless—whether intentionally (s.190(3)) or unintentionally (s.192)—or threatened with homelessness (intentionally or not) (s.195(5) (a)), and eligible for assistance, but they are also satisfied that he is not in priority need, they owe an identical advice and appropriate assistance obligation (10.97(b)) to the applicant.

10.103 Additional powers. In addition, if the authority are satisfied that the applicant is unintentionally homeless but not in priority need, they still have a power to secure that accommodation is made available for occupation by the applicant (s.192(3), as added by the Homelessness Act 2002, s.5), even if no duty. Likewise, an applicant not in priority need who is unintentionally threatened with homelessness may benefit from reasonable steps taken by the authority to secure that accommodation does not cease to be available for his occupation (s.195(6)).

10.104 Priority need and unintentionally threatened with homelessness. If the authority decide that the applicant is threatened with homelessness and eligible for assistance, and has a priority need, but did not become threatened with homelessness intentionally, their duty is to take reasonable steps to secure that accommodation does not cease to be available for his occupation (s.195(1) and (2)), *i.e.* either to help him remain in his current accommodation (s.195(2)), or else to have other accommodation waiting for him once homelessness occurs.

10.105 No limits on obtaining possession. This duty cannot be used to prevent the authority themselves obtaining vacant possession of any accommodation (s.195(3)), *i.e.* the fact that the authority have this duty cannot be raised as a defence in any action by the authority against one of their own tenants. If the authority provide their own accommodation when the homelessness itself occurs, then s.193 applies in the same way as it applies to those who apply when already homeless (10.107 *et seq.*) (s.195(4)).

10.106 Other Acts. Other statutory provisions may be available to afford housing, when there is no duty, or no full duty, under the 1996 Act—see below 10.119 *et seq.*

9. FULL HOUSING DUTY

10.107 Full duties. If the authority are satisfied that the applicant is homeless, eligible for assistance, in priority need and not intentionally homeless, then their duty is (subject to the possibility of referral to another authority, 10.67 *et seq.*) to secure that accommodation is made available for his occupation (and, therefore, for any other family member who normally resides with, or anyone else who might reasonably be expected to reside with, the applicant: 10.20) (s.193(2)).

10.108 Provision of allocation policy statement. In addition, the authority must give the applicant a copy of the statement included in their allocation policy (10.205) on offering choice to people allocated housing accommodation under Pt VI (s.193(3A)).

10.109 Securing accommodation. The duty to secure that accommodation is made available for the applicant's occupation can be discharged by:

   (a) Making available suitable accommodation held by the authority under the Housing Act 1985 Pt II, or under any other powers; or

   (b) Securing that the applicant obtains suitable accommodation from some other person; or

   (c) Giving the applicant such advice and assistance as will secure that he obtains suitable accommodation from some other person (s.206(1)).

10.110 Suitability. Suitability is governed by 1996, s.210, which states that, when determining whether accommodation is suitable, the authority must have regard to Pts IX, X and XI of the Housing Act 1985 (slum clearance, overcrowding and houses in multiple occupation—see Chapters 12 and 14).

10.111 Personal Circumstances. In determining suitability, the authority must also take into account the particular circumstances of the applicant and his family, *e.g.* medical evidence (*R. v Brent LBC Ex p. Omar*, 1991). Accommodation must be adequate as regards size for the family's needs as well as appropriate having regard to such other factors as nature of area and employment prospects (*R. v Wyre BC Ex p. Parr*, 1982).

10.112 Affordability. Regulations have been made to govern consideration by authorities of affordability: the Homelessness (Suitability of Accommodation) Order 1996 (SI 1996/3204). The Order requires the authority to take into account:

  (i) The financial resources available to the applicant,

  (ii) The costs of accommodation,

  (iii) Payments being made under a court order to a spouse or former spouse,

  (iv) Any payments made to support children whether under a court order or under the Child Support Act 1991, and

  (v) The applicant's other reasonable living expenses.

10.113 Accommodation in own area. So far as reasonably practicable, authorities are bound to secure accommodation within their own area (s.208(1)).

10.114 Out-of-area accommodation. If the authority nonetheless place an applicant in another area, they must give notice to the local housing authority with responsibility for that area, stating:

  (a) The name of the applicant,

  (b) The number and description of other members of his family normally residing with him, or of anyone else who might reasonably be expected to reside with him,

  (c) The address,

  (d) The date on which the accommodation was made available to the applicant, and

  (e) What Pt VII function the authority were discharging when securing the accommodation for him (s.208(2) and (3)).

  (f) The notice must be given in writing within two weeks from when the accommodation was made available (s.208(4)).

10.115 Security. Where an authority provide their own accommodation in discharge of the full duty, it cannot be a secure tenancy, but continues to be provided under Pt VII, hence the expression "Pt VII" accommodation, in contrast to accommodation allocated under Pt VI (10.191), which—if owned by the authority—is normally held by them under Pt II, Housing Act 1985 (see 3.09).

10.116 Charges. Authorities have a general power to make reasonable charges for the provision of their own accommodation under Pt II of the 1985 Act (s.24). Pt VII entitles them to make charges to a homeless person for accommodation which they provide, or for or towards accommodation which they arrange for some other person to provide, under Pt VII (s.206(2)). This applies to both accommodation under s.193 and accommodation provided under any of the temporary duties (10.93, 10.97).

10.117   Continuation of duty. The duty continues to be owed to an applicant until it is brought to an end by any of the circumstances set out in s.193 (s.193(3)).

10.118   Cessation of duty. The duty comes to end in any of the following circumstances:

(a) If the applicant refuses an offer under Pt VII, which the authority are satisfied is suitable for him (10.110), and the authority have informed the applicant that if he does not accept the offer, they will regard themselves as having discharged the duty (s.193(5)).

(b) If the applicant ceases to be eligible for assistance (s.193(6)(a)) (10.16).

(c) If the applicant becomes homeless intentionally (10.45) from the Pt VII accommodation (s.193(6)(b)).

(d) If the applicant accepts an allocation under Pt VI (s.193(6)(c)).

(e) If the applicant accepts an offer of an assured tenancy (other than an assured shorthold tenancy) from a private landlord, *i.e.* one whose tenants are not secure (s.193(6)(cc)).

(f) If the applicant voluntarily ceases to occupy the Pt VII accommodation as his only or principal home (s.193(6)(d); see 3.32).

(g) If the applicant, having been informed of the possible consequences of refusal, and of his right to request a review of the suitability of accommodation refused, refuses a written final offer of a Pt VI allocation, and the authority are satisfied that the accommodation was suitable for him (10.110), and that it was reasonable for him to accept it (s.193(7), (7A), (7F)).

For this purpose, an applicant may reasonably be considered to accept an offer even though he is under a contractual or other obligation in respect of his existing accommodation, if (but only if) he can bring that other obligation to an end before he is obliged to take up the offer (s.193(8)).

(h) If the applicant accepts a qualifying offer of an assured shorthold tenancy from a private landlord (s.193(7B)).
An offer is only a qualifying offer if:

   (i) It is made with the approval of the authority, in pursuance of arrangements made by the authority with the landlord with a view to bringing the duty towards the applicant to an end;

   (ii) The offer is of a fixed term tenancy; and,

   (iii) It is accompanied by a statement in writing which states the term of the tenancy being offered and explains in ordinary language that there is no obligation on the applicant to accept it but that if it is accepted the authority will cease to be under a duty to the applicant (s.193(7D).
   Acceptance of a qualifying offer is only effective if the applicant acknowledges in writing that he has understood the authority's statement (s.193(7E)).
   An authority may not make a qualifying offer unless they are satisfied that the accommodation is suitable for the applicant and that it is reasonable for him to accept the offer (s.193(7F)).
   For this purpose, an applicant may be reasonably be considered to accept an offer even though he is under a contractual or other obligation in respect of his existing accommodation, if (but only if) he can bring that other obligation to an end before he is obliged to take up the offer (s.193(8)).

10. OTHER ACTS

10.119 Social service legislation. As well as discharging their duty under Pt VII itself, authorities may also choose to discharge their duties towards the homeless under other statutory provisions, such as through housing in an old person's home accommodation under the National Assistance Act 1948, Pt III, or else, in the case of a minor, by using powers under the Children Act 1989, Pt III. A duty may arise under Pt III of the Children Act even though no duty—or, in practice, no full housing duty—exists under Pt VII.

10.120 Social service authorities. Duties under these Acts are imposed on social service authorities (10.15).

10.121 Pt III, Children Act 1989. The 1989 has two relevant sections which must be considered: ss. 17 and 20.

10.122 Section 17. S.17 provides:

"(1) It shall be the general duty of every local authority . . .

> (a) to safeguard and promote the welfare of children within their area who are in need; and
>
> (b) so far as is consistent with that duty, to promote the upbringing of such children by their families by providing a range and level of services appropriate to those children's needs . . ."

10.123 Social service power. Although this section does not positively require authorities to provide accommodation, it does comprise a further—"safety net"—power permitting authorities to assist a family, including with the provision of accommodation (*R (W) v Lambeth LBC*, 2002, following *AG Ex rel. Tilley v Wandsworth LBC*, 1981, and *R. v Tower Hamlets LBC Ex p. Monaf*, 1988.)

10.124 Section 20. S.20 of the Children Act 1989 provides:

"(1) Every local authority shall provide accommodation for any child in need within their area who appears to them to require accommodation as a result of—. . .

> (c) . . . the person who has been caring for him being prevented (whether or not permanently, and for whatever reason) from providing him with suitable accommodation or care . . .

(3) Every local authority shall provide accommodation for any child in need within their area who has reached the age of sixteen and whose welfare the authority consider is likely to be seriously prejudiced if they do not provide him with accommodation . . . "

10.125 Social Service Duty. The effect of the section is to impose a duty on social services authorities to house children in the circumstances set out in subs.(1) and to house young people in the circumstances set out in subs.(3). The duty is exclusive to the child and does not confer a duty (or even a power) on the authority to accommodate a child's family: *R (G) v Barnet LBC*, 2001.

10.126 Co-operation. Where not themselves also the housing authority, as they will be in unitary authorities and London borough councils, these authorities may request assistance in discharging their duties under the 1989 Act (1989, s.27(1)). An authority whose help is requested "shall comply with the request if it is compatible with their own statutory or other duties and obligations and does not unduly prejudice the discharge of any of their functions" (1989, s.27(2)).

10.127 Pt VII v Pt III. In *Smith v Northavon DC* (1994), the housing authority found the applicant to be intentionally homeless and sought to evict him from his temporary accommodation. The applicant applied to the social services authority for assistance. The social services authority considered that the applicant's children would be in need when the eviction took place and therefore requested the housing authority to provide accommodation. The housing authority declined. The House of Lords refused to quash their decision. The request of the social services authority did not give the applicant any priority over other homeless persons or waiting-list applicants for housing. In the event of the housing authority being unable to provide assistance, the social services authority remained under a responsibility to protect the applicant's children.

10.128 Referrals to social services. The Homelessness Act 2002 makes specific provision for applicants with children who are not owed a full Pt VII duty to be referred to social services. Where a local authority have reason to believe that an applicant with whom children reside or normally reside may be ineligible for assistance (10.16), may be homeless or may have become so intentionally (10.45), or may be threatened with homelessness intentionally (10.46), they must make arrangements for ensuring that the applicant is invited to consent to the referral of his case to the social services authority (or department in the case of a unitary authority) and, if consent is given, must make the social services authority/department aware of the facts of the case and the subsequent decision in relation to it (s.213A(1), (2)). (The decision is subsequent because the duty arises when the housing authority form the view that the applicant may be disqualified from full assistance for one or other relevant reason, even though they have not yet reached a final decision).

10.129 Social service response. Following a referral, the social services authority/department may request the housing authority to provide them/it with advice and assistance in the exercise of their functions under Pt III of the Children Act 1989, and the housing authority must provide them with such advice and assistance as is reasonable in all the circumstances (s.213A (5), (6)).

10.130 National Assistance Act 1948. The National Assistance Act 1948, s.21(1) (as amended) provides that:

> ". . . a local authority may with the approval of the Secretary of State, and to such extent as he may direct shall, make arrangements for providing—
>
> (a) residential accommodation for persons aged eighteen or over who by reason of age, illness, disability or any other circumstances are in need of care and attention which is not otherwise available to them."

10.131 Assessment of need. Once an applicant has sought assistance from a local authority under s.21, the authority must assess his needs: see National Health Service and Community Care Act 1990, s.47.

10.132 Immigrants and asylum-seekers. S.21(1A) of the 1948 Act (as added by the Immigration and Asylum Act 1999) provides:

> "A person to whom s.115 of the Immigration and Asylum Act 1999 (exclusion from benefits) applies may not be provided with residential accommodation under subsection (1)(a) if his need for care and attention has arisen solely—
>
> (a) because he is destitute; or
> (b) because of the physical effects or anticipated physical effects of his being destitute."

10.133 The effect of this provision is to exclude those who are subject to immigration control (unless reincluded by regulations—10.17) from making an application under s.21 of the 1948 Act, where their need for care and attention arises solely from destitution. Their needs are, instead, intended to be met under the Asylum and Immigration Act 1999, through the National Asylum Support Service. Local authorities have no power to provide any accommodation for non-asylum-seeking immigrants who are merely destitute and who do not have children.

10.134 In the case of asylum-seekers whose need for care and attention does not arise because of destitution, however, but because, *e.g.* of disability, responsibility for meeting their care needs remains with the local authority (*R. (Westminster CC) v Secretary of State for the Home Department*, 2001).

10.135 Provision of accommodation. Once the local authority have assessed an applicant's needs as satisfying the criteria in s.21, they must provide accommodation on a continuing basis so long as the need of the applicant remains as originally assessed (*R. v Kensington & Chelsea RLBC Ex p. Kujtim*, 1999). Residential accommodation may include "ordinary" housing accommodation (*Khana v Southwark LBC*, 2001). A duty to supply such accommodation will arise where a person needs care and attention, including housing accommodation, that is not otherwise available. The need for care and attention remains, however, a precondition of such a duty.

10.136 Discharge of duty. The duty under s.21 is not, however, absolute and may be brought to an end by an applicant's unreasonable behaviour (*Kujtim*, above) or by the unreasonable refusal of an offer of accommodation (*Khana*, above).

10.137 Local Government Act 2000. A final safety net may also be available under the Local Government Act 2002, s.2, which provides that:

> "Every local authority are to have power to do anything which they consider is likely to achieve any one or more of the following objects— (a) the promotion or improvement of the economic well-being of their area, (b) the promotion or improvement of the social well-being of their area, and (c) the promotion or improvement of the environmental well-being of their area."

10.138 Safety net. In *R. (J) v Enfield LBC*, 2002, which was decided prior to the decision in *W*, above (10.123), it was held that in order to ensure that there was no breach of an applicant's right to respect for family right under the ECHR Art.8, s.2 could be used in order to provide financial assistance and, if no other power was available, that the authority would have to use it in order to assist. Given the decision in *W*, the need for reliance on s.2 seems unlikely.

11. PROTECTION OF PROPERTY

10.139 Duty to protect property. If an authority are or have been under a (temporary or permanent) duty under 1996, s.188

(10.93), ss.190, 193, 195 (10.97–10.118), or s.200 (10.79), they may also be under a duty to take reasonable steps to prevent the loss of an applicant's property, or to prevent or mitigate damage to it (1996, s.211(2)). The applicant's personal property, for these purposes, includes that of any person reasonably to be expected to reside with him (1996, s.211(5)).

10.140　When the duty arises. This duty arises if the authority have reason to believe:

   (a) That there is a danger of loss of or damage to property because of the applicant's inability to protect or deal with it, and

   (b) That no other suitable arrangements have been or are being made (1996, s.211(1)).

10.141　Power to protect property. If the authority have not been under one of the identified duties (10.139), but have reason to believe there is such a danger, they nonetheless have power to protect property (1996, s.211(3)).

10.142　Terms and charges. The authority may, however, refuse to take action under these provisions other than on such conditions as they consider appropriate, including for reasonable charges, and the disposal of property (1996, s.211(4)).

10.143　Relocation of property. If the applicant asks the authority to move the property to a nominated location, the authority may (if they consider that the request is reasonable) discharge their responsibilities under these provisions by doing so, and treat their responsibilities as being at an end (1996, s.212(2)).

10.144　Powers of entry. In connection with these provisions, the authority have power, at all reasonable times, to enter any premises which are or were the usual or last usual place of residence of the applicant, and to deal with his property in any way that is reasonably necessary, including by way of storage (1996, s.212(1)).

10.145　Termination. Duties and powers end when the authority consider that there is no longer any danger of loss or damage, by reason of the applicant's inability to protect or deal with his personal property, although if the authority have provided storage, they have a discretion to continue to do so (1996, s.212(3)).

10.146 Notification. Where the authority's responsibilities end, they must notify the applicant, and of the reasons for it (1996, s.212(4)). Notification may be given by delivery, or by leaving it or sending it to the applicant's last known address (1996, s.212(5)).

12. HOMELESSNESS STRATEGIES

10.147 Duty to review and publish strategy. The Homelessness Act 2002 ("2002") imposed a new duty on local housing authorities to carry out a homelessness review (10.149) in their area and formulate and publish a homelessness strategy (10.151) based on the results of that review (2002, s.1(1)). The first strategy must be published within twelve months of s.1 coming into force, and thereafter a new one must be published at least every five years (2002, s.1(3), (4)).

10.148 Authorities. Where they are a different authority, the social services authority (10.15) for the area of the authority must give assistance in the review and in the formulation of the strategy (2002, s.1(2)). The strategy must be taken into account by both the local housing authority and the social services authority in the exercise of their functions (2002, s.1(5), (6)).

10.149 Review. For these purposes a homelessness review means a review of:

    (a) The level, and likely future levels of homelessness in the authority's area;

    (b) The activities which are carried out in the area to:

        (i) Prevent homelessness in the authority's area;

        (ii) Secure that accommodation is or will be available for people in the area who are or may become homeless; and,

        (iii) Provide support for people in the area who are or may become homeless or who have been homeless and need support to prevent it happening again; and,

    (c) The resources available to the authority, the social services authority, other public authorities, voluntary organisations and other persons for such activities (2002, s.2(1), (2)).

10.150 Information about review. On completion of the review, the authority must arrange for the results to be available for inspection at their principal office, at all reasonable hours, without charge, and provide (on payment of a reasonable charge, if required) a copy of the results (2002, s.2(3)).

10.151   Strategy. A homelessness strategy means one formulated for:

(a) Preventing homelessness in the authority's area;

(b) Securing that sufficient accommodation is and will be available for people in the area who are or may become homeless; and,

(c) Securing that there is satisfactory provision of support for people in the area who are or who may become homeless or who have become homeless and need support to prevent them becoming homeless again (2002, s.3(1)).

10.152   Content of strategy. The strategy may include specific objectives to be pursued as well as specific action planned to be taken in the course of the exercise of the authority's housing functions and also of the functions of the social services authority for the district (2002, s.3(2)).

10.153   Other action. The strategy may also include specific action which the authority expects to be taken by any other public authority or by any voluntary organisation or other person, who can contribute to the objectives of the strategy, but only with the approval of the body or person concerned (2002, s.3(3), (4)).

10.154   Partnership. The authority must consider how far the objectives of the strategy can be met by joint action between itself, the social service authority or any other body or persons (2002, s.3(5)).

10.155   Review and modification. The strategy must be kept under review and may be modified (2002, s.3(6)). Before adopting or modifying the strategy, the authority must consult such public or local authorities, voluntary organisations or other persons as they consider appropriate (2002, s.3(7), (8)). Any modification must be published.

10.156   Information about strategy. A copy of the strategy must be available at the authority's principal office for inspection at all reasonable hours, free of charge, and provided to members of the public on request, on payment (if required) of a reasonable charge (2002, s.3(8)).

13. ADVICE, INFORMATION AND VOLUNTARY ORGANISATIONS

10.157 Voluntary organisations. Provision is made in Pt VII for giving grants, loans, premises or goods in kind to voluntary organisations concerned with the homeless (1996, ss.180). The assistance may be given on terms and subject to conditions and subject to undertakings as to the use of the assistance (1996, s.181).

10.158 Advice and information. In addition, authorities have an obligation to ensure that advice and assistance about homelessness and its prevention are available to any person in their areas, free of charge (1996, s.179(1)). This duty can be discharged by providing assistance (grant or loan, use of premises, furniture or other goods, or making staff available) through another person (not necessarily a voluntary organisation, although on the same terms and conditions as would apply to a voluntary organisation: 1996, s.181(1)) (1996, s.179(2), (3)).

14. CODE OF GUIDANCE

10.159 The Code. In the exercise of their functions under Pt VII, authorities are bound to have regard to such guidance as may from time to time be given by the Secretary of State (1996, s.182). This is not the same as saying that they are bound to comply with its contents in the same way as they are bound to comply with Pt VII itself (*De Falco v Crawley BC*, 1979). It is, rather, something they are bound to take into account; in practice, if an authority deviate from the provisions of the Code, they may find themselves obliged to explain their reasons for doing so in any challenge.

15. REVIEW AND APPEAL

10.160 Right to internal review. Applicants have a statutory right to request an internal review of any of the following decisions:

   (i) As to eligibility for assistance (10.16);

   (ii) As to the duty (if any) owed (10.96–10.118);

   (iii) To notify another authority (10.91);

(iv) Whether the conditions for referral are met (10.73);

(v) What duty is owed following a local connection referral (10.76); or,

(vi) Any decision as to suitability of accommodation offered in discharge of duty, including a part VI offer (10.110).

10.161 Request for review. The right of review does not, however, entitle the applicant to a review of an earlier review (1996, s.202(2)). This does not prevent an authority from further reconsidering a decision if they are minded to do so (*R. v Westminster CC Ex p. Ellioua*, 1998), although if an applicant wishes still to challenge the decision after a further review, he must do so by way of appeal to the county court on the original decision (*Demetri v Westminster CC*, 2000).

10.162 Time limits for request. A request for a review must be made within 21 days of notification of the decision (10.91), or such longer period as the authority may in writing allow (1996, s.202(3)).

10.163 Review procedure. The Secretary of State has power to regulate the review procedure, including requiring the review to be conducted by a person of "appropriate seniority . . . not involved in the original decision", and the "circumstances in which the applicant is entitled to an oral hearing, and whether and by whom [the applicant] may be represented at such a hearing" (1996, s.203(2)). The Allocation of Housing and Homelessness (Review Procedures) Regulations 1999 (SI 1999/71), require that an officer of the authority conducting a review was not involved in the original decision and is senior to the original decision-maker. In carrying out the review, the reviewer must have regard not only to the information available at the time of the original decision, but also to that obtained thereafter and to matters occurring after the initial decision: *Mohamed v Hammersmith & Fulham LBC*, 2001.

10.164 Time limit for review. The review must generally be carried out within eight weeks, although a longer period is permitted in the case of local connection reviews: see Review Procedure Regulations, reg.9. The parties may agree a longer period.

10.165 Notification. The authority have to notify the applicant of the outcome of the review and, if it is adverse to his interests or confirms a local connection referral, of the reasons for it (1996, s.203(4)). In any event, they must notify the applicant of the right to appeal to the county court on a point of law (1996, s.203(5)). If either of these requirements is not fulfilled, the notification is treated as not having been given (1996, s.203(6)). Otherwise, notification is given in the same way as under 1996, s.184 (1996, s.203(8); 10.91).

10.166 Accommodation pending review. Pending the outcome of the review, the authority may provide accommodation for the applicant (s.188(3)). Any challenge to a decision not to house pending the review must, however, be made by judicial review: *R. v Camden LBC Ex p. Mohammed*, 1997.

10.167 Appeal to the county court. Appeal lies to the county court if the applicant is either dissatisfied with the outcome of the review, or if he has not been notified of the outcome within any time that may be prescribed (1996, s.204(1)). Exercise of the right to a review is therefore an essential precondition of appeal. Appeal lies only on a point of law, whether it arises from the original decision or the decision on review (1996, s.204(1)).

10.168 Time for appeal. The appeal must be brought within 21 days of notification, or of when the applicant ought to have been notified of the outcome (s.204(2)). The court may give permission for appeal out of time where there is good reason for the applicant being unable to bring the appeal within the 21–day limit (s.204(2A)).

10.169 Housing pending appeal. Pending an appeal (and any further appeal), the authority may continue to provide accommodation (1996, s.204(4)). If the authority refuse to do so, the applicant may appeal that decision to the county court (s.204A).

10.170 Powers of court on interim housing appeal. The court may order accommodation to be made available pending the outcome of the appeal (or such earlier time as it may specify), and may confirm or quash the decision of the authority not to provide accommodation (s.204A(4)(a), (b)). In considering whether to confirm or quash the decision, the court must apply the principles applied by the High Court on an application for judicial review (s.204A(4)). If the court quashes the decision, it may order the authority to exercise the power to accommodate pending appeal in the applicant's case for such period as it specifies (s.204A(5)). Such an order may, however, only be made if the court is satisfied that failure to exercise the accommodation power in accordance with its order would substantially prejudice the applicant's ability to pursue his substantive appeal (s.204A(6)(a)).

10.171 Powers of court on appeal against decision. The court may make such order as it thinks fit, confirming, quashing or varying the decision (1996, s.204(3)).

10.172 Basis of appeal. The right of appeal is on a point of law, as distinct from an appeal on the facts. Point of law includes issues of jurisdiction or vires. The distinction between a point of law and a question of fact is not always straightforward, in so far as a conclusion of fact for which there is no, or insufficient, evidence may in itself comprise an error of law. Furthermore, even a straightforward error or mistake of fact may itself serve to vitiate a decision as a matter of law. For practical purposes, the grounds of intervention will be the same, therefore, as have been available on judicial review hitherto (*Begum v Tower Hamlets LBC*, 1999), both under Pt III, 1985 Act, and indeed on issues of allocation, and as will remain available where there is no appeal.

10.173 General principles. The general principles are those of administrative law, which have been largely developed in the course of proceedings for judicial review, and which now comprise both a growth area of legal activity and case-law, and of legal literature. What these principles import is that a straightforward difference of opinion or judgment between an authority and an applicant as to what decision should have been reached will not suffice to justify the intervention of the courts. If Parliament has entrusted a decision to a local authority, it is that authority's view of what is reasonable which must prevail, rather than that of a court (*Associated Provincial Picture Houses Ltd v Wednesbury Corp*, 1948).

10.174 Judgment of the authority. It follows that it is not sufficient merely to know what rights and duties are set out in Pts VI or VII, or of knowing what the Code of Guidance under either 1996, s.168 (10.219), or s.182 (10.159), suggests is appropriate in a particular case. The principal Pt VI duty arises only when "it appears to the authority" that a state of affairs exists: see 1996, s.163. Under Pt VII, duties only arise when the authority have "reason to believe," "consider," or are "satisfied" that a certain state of affairs exists: see 1996, ss.183, 184, 188, 190, 193, 195, 197,

198, 211. An applicant's rights therefore only arise and can only be enforced once the authority's satisfaction, belief or view has been established (*Cocks v Thanet DC*, 1983) and it is, accordingly, essential to distinguish between the actual—undisputed, or indisputable—facts of a particular case, and whether the authority are "satisfied", have "reason to believe", or are "of the opinion" that those facts exist.

10.175 Intervention. At first glance, one might think that this subjective assessment of rights and duties would mean that an authority's decision could never be challenged at all:

> "The section is framed in a 'subjective' form . . . This form of section is quite well-known and at first sight might seem to exclude judicial review . . . "

per Lord Wilberforce, *Secretary of State for Education and Science v Tameside MBC* (1977). It is here, however, that the principles that have evolved come into play.

10.176 *Ultra vires.* What the principles invariably involve is that authorities should always approach their decisions in a lawful manner. If it can be shown that a public body such as a local authority have approached their decision unlawfully, the decision will be void and the courts will not give effect to it. A decision improperly reached is *ultra vires, i.e.* outside the authority's powers, and without effect in law, whether it is because on the face of the statute there was no power to reach a decision or engage in an act at all, or because the statute has been misconstrued, or because the authority have misapplied the statute in another sense, *e.g.* by failing to use the powers to implement the purpose of the statute, or by reaching a decision under the statute by reference to something which is irrelevant—or in ignorance of something which is relevant—to the way the power under the statute is intended to be operated.

10.177 Proper decision-making. At the heart of the case law is the proposition that Parliament intends that bodies such as local authorities should always act properly, in the sense of reasonably and lawfully. That is not to say that they would always arrive at "the" reasonable decision: one person's view of what is reasonable will often quite properly differ from that of another, and again, Parliament has entrusted decision-making under Pts VI and VII to authorities, not to the courts.

10.178 *Puhlhofer*. The House of Lords, in *R. v Hillingdon LBC Ex p. Puhlhofer*, 1986 stressed that in cases where the wording of an obligation is subjectively qualified (in the *Tameside* sense, 10.175), it is the local authority and not the court who Parliament intended to be the judge of fact:

> "I am troubled at the prolific use of judicial review for the purpose of challenging the performance by local authorities of their functions under the Act of 1977. Parliament intended the local authority to be the judge of fact. The Act abounds with the formula when, or if, the housing authority are satisfied as to this, or that, or have reason to believe this, or that. Although the action or inaction of a local authority is clearly susceptible to judicial review where they have mis-construed the Act, or abused their powers or otherwise acted perversely, I think that great restraint should be exercised in giving leave to proceed by judicial review. The plight of the homeless is a desperate one, and the plight of the applicants in the present case commands the deepest sympathy. But it is not, in my opinion, appropriate that the remedy of judicial review, which is a discretionary remedy, should be made use of to monitor the actions of local authorities under the Act save in the exceptional case. The ground upon which the courts will review the exercise of an administrative discretion is abuse of power—*e.g.* bad faith, a mistake in construing the limits of the power, a procedural irregularity, or unreasonable-ness in the *Wednesbury* sense—unreasonableness verging on an absurdity . . . Where the existence or non-existence of a fact is left to the judgment and discretion of a public body and that fact involves a broad spectrum ranging from the obvious to the debatable to the just conceivable, it is the duty of the court to leave the decision of that fact to the public body to whom Parliament has entrusted the decision-making power save in a case where it is obvious that the public body, consciously or unconsciously, are acting perversely."

10.179 **Classification**. The principles of administrative law may be expressed, and classified, in a number of different ways. In *Council of Civil Service Unions v Minister for the Civil Service*, 1985, Lord Diplock re-classified them under three headings: "illegality," "irrationality" and "procedural impropriety."

> "By 'illegality' as a ground of judicial review I mean that the decision-maker must understand correctly the law that regu-lates his decision-making power and must give effect to it.

Whether he has or not is par excellence a justiciable question to be decided, in the event of dispute, by those persons, the judges, by whom the judicial power of the state is exercisable.

By 'irrationality' I mean what can by now be succinctly referred to as '*Wednesbury* unreasonableness' . . . It applies to a decision which is so outrageous in its defiance of logic or of accepted moral standards that no sensible person who had applied his mind to the question to be decided could have arrived at it. Whether a decision falls within this category is a question that judges by their training and experience should be well equipped to answer, or else there would be something badly wrong with our judicial system . . . 'Irrationality' by now can stand upon its own feet as an accepted ground on which a decision may be attacked by judicial review. I have described the third head as 'procedural impropriety' rather than failure to observe basic rules of natural justice or failure to act with procedural fairness towards the person who will be affected by the decision. This is because susceptibility to judicial review under this head covers also failure by an administrative tribunal to observe procedural rules that are expressly laid down in the legislative instrument by which its jurisdiction is conferred, even where such failure does not involve any denial of natural justice . . ."

10.180 Practical classification. In practice, the principles tend to overlap with one another. They may be considered under one or more of the following sub-headings:

(i) A statutory authority must take into account all the relevant factors before making their decision, and must disregard the irrelevant: *Wednesbury*. See also *Bristol DC v Clark*, 1975.

(ii) The decision must be based on the facts; a decision totally at variance with the facts or for which there is no factual basis cannot be sustained:

"If a judgment requires, before it can be made, the existence of some facts, then although the evaluation of those facts is for the Secretary of State alone, the courts must enquire whether those facts exist, and have been taken into account, whether the judgment has been made on a proper self-direction as to those facts, whether the judgment has not been made on other facts which ought not to have been taken into account . . ." (*Tameside*).

(iii) The authority must not act in bad faith or dishonestly: *Wednesbury*.

(iv) The authority must direct themselves properly in law, so that a decision based on a misunderstanding or misapplication of the law will not have been reached properly: *Wednesbury*. This is the point in *Wednesbury* that is restated as "illegality" in *Council of Civil Service Unions* (10.179).

(v) The authority must act so as to promote, and not to defeat, the objects or policy of the Act in question. Powers conferred for public purposes must be used in a way that Parliament can be presumed to have intended (*Padfield v Minister of Agriculture, Fisheries & Food*, 1968).

(vi) The decision must not be one to which no reasonable authority could have come: this is conclusive evidence that the decision is improper (or irrational)—*Wednesbury*.

(vii) The authority must reach their own decision on each individual case; they must not fetter their discretion by approaching a decision with a predetermined policy as to how they will deal with any case falling within a particular class.

The leading case on this is probably still *British Oxygen Co Ltd v Minister of Technology*, 1971. While a public authority can adopt a policy or limiting rule in order to guide the future exercise of their discretion if they think good administration requires it, they must consider its application individually in every case where it is sought to make an exception (*Stringer v Minister of Housing and Local Government*, 1970). *British Oxygen* was adopted and applied by the House of Lords in *Betts* (10.71).

(viii) It is the authority who are entrusted with the decision-making power and must make the decision. The authority cannot avoid their duties by adopting the decision of another body: *Lavender & Sons v Minister of Housing and Local Government*, 1970).

A distinction must be drawn, however, between adoption of the decision of another body and the proper use of resources when reaching a decision. The authority may employ staff (Local Government Act 1972, s.112), and have implied power to employ contractors or agents, and to enter into contracts with them (*Crédit Suisse v Allerdale BC*, 1997. There is now an express power to contract: see s.1,

Local Government (Contracts) Act 1997.) These resources can all be used when reaching a decision. What cannot be abdicated is responsibility for the essential elements of a decision which are to determine what is to be done or what is to happen. See further 10.189 below. See, also, the express power to contract out functions (10.13).

(ix) The authority's decision must be reached properly. Under the Local Government Act 2000, local authorities now function in what may be described as two parts: an executive (of one of three kinds: mayor and cabinet, leader and cabinet or mayor and council executive—see Local Government Act 2000, s.11), and the full authority.

Decisions not conferred on the authority by statute, statutory instrument or (where the power is left to the authority to decide) conferred by the authority on themselves under "local choice" (2000 Act, s.13(3)(b)), must be taken by the executive (2000 Act, s.13(2), (10)). Decisions on allocations and homelessness are—by this route—matters for the executive (2000 Act, s.13 and SI 2000/2853).

Decisions to be taken by the executive may be dealt with in any way that the 2000 Act permits, which includes delegation to an individual member of the executive, or to a committee or sub-committee of the executive, or to an officer (or, in some circumstances, an area committee not of the executive but of the authority themselves) (2000 Act, ss.14–16 and 18). For the first time, therefore, individual decisions can properly be taken by an individual councillor, although this is not only unlikely but, it must be said, undesirable, and it is probable that they will continue to be delegated to officers.

Decisions which the authority are to take themselves cannot, however, be delegated to an individual member, only to a committee, sub-committee or officer of the authority (Local Government Act 1972, s.101).

(x) In all cases, an authority must act fairly, or in accordance with natural justice (*Ridge v Baldwin*, 1964). The extent of this duty will depend upon circumstances, and the nature of the decision. Even if a statute or other instrument contains its own procedural requirements to ensure fairness, including to give reasons for decisions, the courts may—if they consider that the circumstances of an individual case (or, presumably, class of case) call for it—impose yet further requirements to ensure that a matter has been decided fairly and/or give reasons (*Wiseman v Borneman*, 1971). This requirement means that, if relevant to the decision, an applicant must know what is being said against him (*Board of Education v Rice*, 1911).

The requirement of fairness will also mean that an authority must respect any legitimate expectations which an applicant may enjoy. Conventionally, the expression refers to a legitimate procedural expectation, *i.e.* as to how a matter is to be handled, such as an assurance that no decision will be taken, at all on an aspect of a matter, until there has been a further opportunity to comment, or until the authority have managed to contact someone, or that it will only be taken by an officer of a particular level of seniority, or by a panel (member or officer) (*Schmidt v Secretary of State for Home Affairs*, 1969; *R. v Devon CC Ex p. Baker*, 1995), provided always that to do so would not interfere or conflict with the authority's statutory duty (*R. v AG of Hong Kong Ex p. Ng Yuen Shiu*, 1983).

Less frequently it has been held to encompass a legitimate substantive expectation, *i.e.*, of a particular outcome of a decision-making process, as opposed to its procedure, where there has been a clear and unambiguous statement, devoid of qualification, on which it was reasonable to rely (*R. v IRC Ex p. MFK Underwriting*, 1990).

The court has to determine the nature of the legitimate expectation which has been engendered, and whether it would be an abuse of power for the court to frustrate it or whether there is a sufficient overriding interest to justify a departure from what had been promised (*R. v North and East Devon Health Authority Ex p. Coughlan*, 2001).

In *R. v Newham LBC Ex p. Bibi and Al-Nashed*, 2001 the local authority had promised a "permanent" home to homeless applicants. A legitimate expectation had arisen, which was sufficient to justify derogation from the authority's housing allocation scheme, and which required the authority to provide reasons if the expectation was not to be fulfilled.

10.181 Human Rights Act 1998. As public authorities within the meaning of the Human Rights Act 1998, s.6, local housing authorities must act in a way which is compatible with the European Convention on Human Rights (ECHR). Two Articles of the ECHR are particularly relevant in homelessness and allocations cases.

10.182 Article 6. First, Art.6 provides that in the determination of his civil rights, everyone is entitled to a fair and public hearing within a reasonable time by an independent and impartial tribunal. This is particularly relevant to review and appeal processes. In *Runa Begum v Tower Hamlets LBC*, 2002, it was held that homelessness rights comprised civil rights. Although an officer of an authority conducting an internal review (10.163) could not be said to provide an independent and impartial tribunal, the county court appeal process (10.167) was nonetheless held to be a sufficient safeguard to ensure compliance with Art.6. The different stages could be considered cumulatively to decide whether Art.6 had been complied with.

10.183 Article 8. By Art.8 of the ECHR: "Everyone has the right to respect for his private and family life, his home and his correspondence". This does not amount, however, to a right to housing to be provided by the state (*X v Federal Republic of Germany*, 1956; *Chapman v UK*, 2001). Given this interpretation of Art.8, it is unlikely that any claim for breach of Art.8 will succeed, where an authority have properly applied the provisions of Pt VII and reached the conclusion that there is no substantive duty to house an applicant, as the provisions of Pt VII are themselves compliant with ECHR (and, indeed, go further than any duties under Art.8).

16. CRIMINAL OFFENCES

10.184 False statements. It is a criminal offence knowingly or recklessly to make a statement which is false in a material particular, or knowingly to withhold information which an authority have reasonably required in connection with the exercise of their functions under Pt VII, with intent to induce an authority to believe that the person making the statement, or any other person, is entitled to accommodation or assistance (or accommodation or assistance of a particular kind) (1996, s.214(1)). The offence is punishable on summary conviction by a fine of up to level five on the standard scale (1996, s.214(4)), *i.e.* £5,000).

10.185 Change of circumstances. An applicant has a duty to notify an authority as soon as possible of any material change of facts material to his case which occurs before he receives the notification of the authority's decision on his application (1996, s.214(2)). The authority are under a corresponding obligation to explain to an applicant, in ordinary language, the nature of this duty, and the effect of the statutory defence to a charge of non-compliance (1996, s.214(2)).

10.186 Defence. The statutory defence to a charge of non-compliance is that no such explanation was given, or that although such an explanation was given there is some other reasonable excuse for non-compliance (1996, s.214(3)).

10.187 Penalty. In the absence of such a defence, it is a criminal offence to fail to comply with the duty to notify of material changes, punishable on summary conviction at up to level five on the standard scale.

17. CO-OPERATION BETWEEN AUTHORITIES

10.188 Requests for assistance. In the discharge of their functions under Pt VII, a local housing authority may request assistance from another local housing authority, a new town corporation, a registered social landlord or a housing action trust, or a Scottish local authority, development corporation, registered housing association or Scottish Homes (1996, s.213(1)(a), (2)). They may also ask a social services authority (in England, Wales or Scotland) to exercise any of their functions on their behalf (1996, s.213(1)(b)). The other authority (or body, etc.) must co-operate with the housing authority, by rendering such assistance as is reasonable in the circumstances (1996, s.213(1)).

10.189 Assistance. Although an authority may request assistance under s.213, they may not delegate their substantive duty to inquire under s.184 except as expressly permitted (under the regulations permitting contracting out—10.13): *R. v West Dorset DC Ex p. Gerrard*, 1994. Even prior to those express provisions, however, in *R. v Hertsmere BC Ex p. Woolgar*, 1995, it was held that so long as the key decision-making function was preserved by the authority, the inquiries themselves could be carried out by another body on their behalf.

10.190 Discretion. Whether or not to seek assistance is a matter for the authority, and the court will be slow to interfere with the exercise of such a discretion (*R. v Wirral MBC Ex p. Bell*, 1994.

Allocation

10.191 Homelessness Act 2002. Allocation of housing by local housing authorities is regulated by the Housing Act 1996, Pt VI.

This was extensively amended by the Homelessness Act 2002. At the time of writing (Summer 2002) these amendments had not yet been brought into force but were expected by December 2002 in England, and a date of January 27, 2003, had been set in Wales by the Homelessness Act 2002 (Commencement) (Wales) Order 2002 (SI 2002/1736). The remainder of this text is accordingly based on Pt VI as amended by the 2002 Act. Readers needing to apply the unamended law are referred to the 6th edition.

1. DEFINITION OF ALLOCATION

10.192 Meaning of allocation. When allocating housing, local housing authorities are obliged to comply with the provisions of Pt VI (1996, s.159(1)). For these purposes, allocation has the following meanings.

(i) Selecting a secure (3.17) or introductory (6.30) tenant for their own accommodation. This includes notifying an existing tenant or licensee that his tenancy is to be secure (1996, s.159(3)), *e.g.* under 1985 Act, Sch.1, paras 2 (employment-related accommodation), 5 (temporary accommodation for people taking up employment), or 10 (student accommodation), each of which has been amended (Sch.16) to substitute a requirement for notice for the previous conditions which related to the expiry of time (3.39).

(ii) Nominating a person to be a secure or introductory tenant of another. Nomination includes formal and informal such arrangements (1996, s.159(4)).

(iii) Nominating (in the same sense: 1996, s.159(4)) a person to be an assured tenant (4.15) of a registered social landlord (3.12) (1996, s.159(2)).

10.193 Excluded allocations. Allocations to existing secure or introductory tenants are excluded, unless the allocation involves a transfer of housing accommodation for that tenant, and the transfer is made on his application (s.159(5)). In effect, therefore, management transfers to which the tenant accedes (or are ordered by the court—see above 3.120 *et seq.*) do not count as allocations to which Pt VI applies.

10.194 Additional exclusions. In addition, there is a number of other cases which are not treated as allocation:

(i) Succession and devolution on death, or assignment to a potential successor (3.40);

(ii) Assignment by way of exchange (3.214);

(iii) Vesting under a number of family or domestic law provisions (Chapter 9); and,

(iv) Other cases as may be prescribed by regulations (1996, s.160).

2. ELIGIBILITY

10.195 Eligibility. Any person may be allocated housing, provided that he is not ineligible under s.160A (s.160A(1), (2). An allocation may not be made to two or more persons jointly if even one of them is ineligible (s.160A(1)(c)).

10.196 Persons from abroad. Persons subject to immigration control under the Asylum and Immigration Act 1996 are ineligible unless reincluded by regulations (s.160A(3)). The Secretary of State may not include in regulations any person who is excluded from entitlement to housing benefit by the Immigration and Asylum Act 1999, s.115 (s.160A(4)). The Secretary of State may prescribe other persons from abroad who are ineligible, either in relation to local housing authorities generally or any particular local housing authority (s.160A(5)). See under the unamended 1996 Act, the Allocation of Housing (England) Regulations 2000 (SI 2000/702, applied to Wales by the Allocation of Housing (Wales) Regulations 2000 (SI 2000/1080) (note new regulations in similar terms are expected to accompany the bringing into force of the Homelessness Act 2002, provisions). These provisions do not affect the eligibility of someone who is already a secure or introductory tenant or an assured tenant of housing accommodation allocated to him by a local housing authority (s.160A(6)).

10.197 Unacceptable behaviour. A local authority may decide that an applicant is to be treated as ineligible, if they are satisfied that:

(a) The applicant or a member of his household has been guilty of unacceptable behaviour serious enough to make him unsuitable to be a tenant of the authority; and,

(b) By reason of the circumstances at the time his application is considered is unsuitable to be a tenant of the authority by reason of that behaviour (s.160A(7)).

10.198 Definition. Unacceptable behaviour is that which would (if the applicant was a secure tenant of the authority) entitle the authority to a possession order under s.84 of the Housing Act 1985 on any of grounds 1–7 of Sch.2 to that Act (see 3.82–3.116), or behaviour by a member of the applicant's household which would (if he were a person residing with a secure tenant of the authority) entitle the authority to such a possession order (s.160A(8)).

10.199 Reapplication. An applicant who is treated as ineligible because of unacceptable behaviour may (if he considers that he should no longer be so treated) make a fresh application (s.160A(11)).

10.200 Notification. If the authority decide that the applicant is ineligible for an allocation, they must notify him of that decision and the grounds for it (s.160A(9)). Notification must be given in writing, and, if not received by the applicant, shall be treated as having been given if made available at the authority's office for a reasonable period for collection by him or on his behalf (s.160A(10)).

10.201 Applications–advice and assistance. Authorities must ensure that there is free advice and information available in their area about the right to make an application for an allocation of housing (s.166(1)(a)). Authorities must also ensure that any necessary assistance in making an application is available free of charge to those who are likely to have difficulty in doing so without assistance (s.166(1)(b)). Authorities must ensure that applicants are aware of their right to request information about the likely availability of accommodation (10.214) (s.166(2)).

10.202 Consideration of applications. Every application for an allocation of housing made in accordance with the procedural requirements of the authority's allocation scheme must be considered by the authority (s.166(3)). The fact that a person is an applicant for an allocation may not, without the applicant's consent, be divulged by the authority to any member of the public (s.166(4)).

3. ALLOCATION SCHEMES

10.203 Allocation schemes. The authority have to maintain an allocation "scheme" governing both priorities and procedures (including all aspects of the allocation procedure, including by whom decisions may be made) (s.167(1)).

10.204 Choice Policy. The allocation scheme must include a statement of the authority's policy on offering people who are to be allocated housing:

(a) A choice of housing accommodation; or

(b) The opportunity to express preference about the housing accommodation to be allocated to them (s.167(1A)).

10.205 Preference. The scheme must be framed to ensure that a reasonable preference is given to the following:

(a) Persons who are homeless (10.19, above);

(b) Persons who are owed a duty by a local housing authority under s.190(2) (10.97), 193(2) (10.107), or 195(2) (10.104) (or under s.65(2) or 68(2) of the Housing Act 1985) or who are occupying accommodation secured by any such authority under s.192(3) (10.103);

(c) Persons occupying insanitary or overcrowded housing or otherwise living in unsatisfactory housing conditions;

(d) Persons who need to move on medical or welfare grounds; and

(e) Persons who need to move to a particular locality in the authority's area, where failure to meet that need would cause hardship to themselves or to others (s.167(2)).

10.206 Reasonable preference. To afford a reasonable preference means that the criteria must be an "important factor in making a decision about the allocation of housing," (*R. v Lambeth LBC Ex p. Ashley*, 1996) and that "positive favour should be shown to applications which satisfy any of the relevant criteria" (*R v Wolverhampton MBC Ex p. Watters*, 1997). "Reasonable preference does, however, imply a power to choose between different applicants on 'reasonable grounds' . . . it is not unreasonable to prefer good tenants to bad tenants" (*R. v Newham LBC Ex p. Miah*, 1995 at 288).

10.207 Quotas. The requirement to give a reasonable preference to the specified groups does not prevent an authority allocating a quota of all vacancies to one particular group (*e.g.* the homeless) (*R. v Islington LBC Ex p. Reilly and Mannix*, 1998; *R. v Westminster LBC Ex p. Al-Khorshan*, 2000). Where a separate quota is kept for a group, that list may not, however, be run in simple date order, but must reflect the different priorities of applicants within the group (*Al-Khorshan*).

10.208 Composite assessments. Any allocation scheme must be able to take into account multiple categories of need so as to reach a composite assessment of the needs of the applicant; the categories of need can be cumulative and are not to be treated separately (*Reilly and Mannix*).

10.209 Additional preference. The scheme may be framed so as to give additional preference to those within these categories who have an urgent housing need (s.167(2)).

10.210 Determining priorities. The scheme may also include provision for determining priorities between those in the reasonable preference categories, taking into account:

(a) The financial resources available to a person to meet housing costs;

(b) Any behaviour of a person (or a member of his household) which affects his suitability to be a tenant;

(c) Any local connection (10.67) which exists between a person and the authority's area (s.167(2A)).

10.211 Unacceptable behaviour. The scheme does not have to provide for any preference to an applicant where the authority are satisfied that:

(a) He, or a member of his household, has been guilty of unacceptable behaviour (10.197) serious enough to make him unsuitable to be a tenant of the authority; and

(b) In the circumstances at the time his case is considered, he deserves by reason of that behaviour not to be treated as a member of one of the groups to whom a reasonable preference is to be given (s.167(2C), (2D)).

10.212 Regulations. The Secretary of State has power to add to, amend or repeal any part of the list of those to whom a reasonable preference is to be accorded (s.167(3)). He also has power to specify factors which are not to be taken into account when allocating housing (s.167(4)).

10.213 Other allocations. Subject to the reasonable preference categories, the scheme may contain provision about the allocation of particular accommodation to a person who makes a specific application for it and to persons of a particular description, whether or not they are within the reasonable preference categories (s.167(2E)).

10.214 Procedure. The scheme must be framed so as to give an applicant the right to request general information that will enable him to assess:

(a) How his application is likely to be treated under the scheme (including whether he is likely to be regarded as in one of the reasonable preference categories); and

(b) Whether accommodation appropriate to his needs is likely to be made available to him and, if so, how long it is likely to be before such accommodation becomes available for allocation to him (s.167(4A)(a)).

10.215 Notification. The scheme must be framed so that an applicant is notified:

(a) In writing of any decision that he is a person being given no preference because of a decision as to behaviour under s.167(2C) (10.197); and

(b) Of the right to request the authority to inform him about the facts of his case which are likely to be, or have been, taken into account in considering whether to allocate housing accommodation to him (s.167(4A)(b), (c)).

10.216 Review. The scheme must include the right for applicants to request a review of a decision as to whether they are to be given no preference under s.167(2C) (10.211), about the facts of their case or that they are considered ineligible under s.160A (10.195) (s.167(4A)(d)).

10.217 Regulations. The Secretary of State may require that the procedures are framed in accordance with such principles as he may prescribe (s.167(5)).

10.218 Changing the scheme. Priorities and procedures are otherwise in the discretion of the authority (s.167(6)). Before adopting or making any major policy change to a scheme, the authority must send a copy of it in draft to every registered social landlord with which they have nomination arrangements, and afford them a reasonable opportunity to comment (s.167(7)).

10.219 Code of Guidance. As under Pt VII (10.159), there is provision for the Secretary of State to issue guidance to which authorities must have regard (s.169).

10.220 Co-operation. When an authority ask a registered social landlord to offer accommodation to people with priority under the authority's allocation scheme, such landlords are bound to cooperate to such extent as is reasonable in the circumstances (s.170).

10.221 Information. An authority must publish a summary of their scheme, and provide a copy of it free of charge to any member of the public who asks for it (s.168(1)). The full scheme must be made available for inspection at the authority's principal office, and a copy must be made available to any member of the public who asks for it, on payment of a reasonable fee (s.168(2)).

10.222 Changes. When the authority make a major policy alteration to their scheme, they have to take such steps as they consider reasonable to bring the effect of the alteration to the attention of those likely to be affected by it (s.168(3)).

4. CRIMINAL OFFENCES

10.223 Criminal offences. It is a criminal offence knowingly or recklessly to make a statement—in connection with the exercise by an authority of their functions under Pt VI—which is false in a material particular, or knowingly to withhold information which an authority have reasonably required in connection with the exercise of their functions under Pt VI (1996, s.171(1)).

10.224 Penalty. The offence is punishable on summary conviction by a fine of up to level five on the standard scale (1996, s.171(2)), *i.e.* £5,000.

CHAPTER ELEVEN

Disrepair

Introduction

11.01 Civil proceedings. In this Chapter, we consider civil proceedings for disrepair, primarily from the viewpoint of the occupier who suffers its effects. Redress by way of complaint to a justice of the peace under s.606 of the Housing Act 1985, that a house (or an area of housing) is unfit for human habitation is considered in Chapter 12 (12.163). Proceedings by way of a summons for statutory nuisance, under s.82 of the Environmental Protection Act 1990, are considered in Chapter 13 (13.23–13.38).

11.02 Repair and Improvement. In practice, there is a considerable overlap between what is or is perceived to be an issue of disrepair, and what calls for what is considered improvement. Although the overlap between the two concepts or activities is considered in this Chapter, improvement powers—and financial assistance for their exercise—are themselves considered in Chapter 12.

11.03 Cumulative remedies. It should be remembered that these other proceedings and possibilities remain available, however, and that they, as well as other remedies considered in the following three Chapters, are additional to those considered in this.

11.04 Contract and tort. In this Chapter, therefore, we are concerned with remedies in contract and tort. Contract will assist when there is a specific agreement, whether express or implied; tort is the body of law governing relations between individuals where there is no contractual relationship, or where the contractual relationship does not itself cover the harm alleged to have been suffered.

Outline

11.05 Contract

- The starting-point is the written agreement governing the occupation in question, if any, but contractual terms may be implied by common law or statute, which may add to or even override written terms.

- Landlords are generally not in breach of any obligation to repair until they have notice of the disrepair.

- The Unfair Contract Terms Act 1977 and EC regulations may impose a requirement that any contractual terms are reasonable.

- Common law implies a number of terms into tenancies: that a furnished tenancy is fit for habitation at the start of the letting; that the landlord will keep any common parts in a reasonable condition; that the tenant will use the premises in a "tenant-like manner".

- The Landlord and Tenant Act 1985, s.8 imposes an obligation on landlords to keep premises fit for human habitation; the obligation only applies, however, to tenancies at a very low rent, and is therefore rarely applicable today.

- The most important statutory obligation is that implied by the Landlord and Tenant Act 1985, s.11, which requires landlords of dwellings let on short leases (*i.e.* fixed terms of less than seven years and periodic tenancies) to keep in repair the structure and exterior of the dwelling, and the water, gas, electrical and heating installations.

- An obligation to repair a dwelling is not an obligation to improve it, although there may be an overlap.

- There are also special provisions aplicable to repairs when a long leaseholder becomes a statutory tenant.

- There is a number of contractual remedies for disrepair.

- Both the landlord and tenant may seek damages for breach of any repairing covenant.

- In certain circumstances, the tenant may "set off" any repairing costs against his rent.

- A court may order specific performance of a repairing covenant or an injunction requiring works to be carried out.

- A receiver or manager of the property may be appointed by the court.

- In cases where the tenant under a long lease is in breach of a repairing covenant, the landlord may seek to forfeit the lease.

11.06 Tort

- A number of torts—arising at common law or by statute— may be committed in cases of disrepair or unacceptable housing conditions.

- Certain relationships will give rise to a legal duty of care, so that a failure to take reasonable care may lead to a claim in negligence. These relationships include: the landlord in relation to the users of common parts of premises; builders in relation to occupiers of a house; developers and other professionals involved in building in relation to future occupiers; and, surveyors in relation to purchasers of a house.

- Failure to comply with the Building Regulations gives rise to an action in tort.

- The Defective Premises Act 1972, s.3 imposes a liability on anyone who carries out construction, repair, maintenance or demolition or any other work in relation to premises in respect of persons who might reasonably be expected to be affected by any resulting defects in the premises.

- S.1 of the 1972 Act imposes a duty of care on anyone doing any work for or in connection with the provision of a dwelling by erection, conversion or enlargement, to ensure that the dwelling when completed is fit for human habitation.

- The Occupiers Liability Act 1975, s.2 imposes a duty on "occupiers" of property to ensure that the premises are reasonably safe for any visitors.

- Liability is imposed on landlords by the Defective Premises Act 1972, s.4 where the landlord is under an obligation to repair. The obligation is to take reasonable care to ensure that any persons who might be affected by a defect are reasonably safe from personal injury or damage to their property.

- In some circumstances, landlords may be liable in nuisance and tenants liable for waste (*i.e.* an act causing deterioration to the premises).

- The main remedies in tort are damages and injunctions.

11.07 Limitation

- There is generally a six-year time limit on bringing claims in contract or tort.

- Where damages for personal injury are being claimed, the limit is three years.

- Where a defect is "latent" and does not become obvious until later, more time may be available.

Contract

11.08 Contractual and statutory provisions. The starting-point will always be what—if anything—is set out in any written agreement that may exist. In the main, it is landlords who draw up letting agreements, and consequently the object of the agreement will be to impose upon the tenant the most extensive obligations that the law permits, while limiting the landlord's own obligations.

11.09 In a number of cases, however, the law will intervene: these circumstances are considered in context, but it should be noted that in short leases, and periodic tenancies, any such attempts by a landlord are likely to contravene the provisions of s.11 of the Landlord and Tenant Act 1985 (11.47–11.79), that other leases, at low rents, may have to comply with the provisions of s.8 of the Landlord and Tenant Act 1985 (11.43–11.46), that relief may be obtainable under the provisions of the Unfair Contract Terms Act 1977 or regulations (11.15–11.21). Further, remedies in tort may be available where there are none in contract.

11.10 Notice of disrepair. There is one principle that is common to almost all of the provisions to be considered under this heading. That is, that a landlord's obligation to repair does not arise until he has had actual notice of conditions such as to put him, if not on actual notice of what is in disrepair, then at least on sufficient notice to cause him to inspect and find out. The only exception to this is the case of an express repairing covenant which does not state that the tenant has to give notice (*Minchburn v Peck*, 1987).

11.11   Cases. The leading cases on the need for notice usefully illustrate its operation. In *O'Brien v Robinson* (1973), works had been executed to a ceiling, several years before it fell down. There had been no further complaint or warning, by tenant or otherwise, to the landlord before it came down and the landlord was, accordingly, held not to be in breach of the obligation to repair. In *Sheldon v West Bromwich Corp.*, 1973, however, a plumber employed by the defendant corporation inspected a water tank. The tank was corroded although it was not yet weeping. Subsequently, it burst. It was held that the condition of the water tank at the time of the inspection, even without the weeping (which would be a sure and final sign of corrosion calling for repair) was sufficient to put the corporation on notice that something needed to be done.

11.12   In *McGreal v Wake*, 1984, a repairs notice was served on the landlord by the local authority. When the landlord did not carry out the works, the local authority carried them out in default (see Chapter 12). For the period from after the landlord had a reasonable opportunity to comply with the notice, until the authority completed the works, the landlord was held to be in breach of his obligation to repair.

11.13   From these and other cases (see also *Dinefwr BC v Jones*, 1987, *Hall v Howard*, 1988) emerge the following propositions.

(a) **Actual Notice.**   Notice need not come from the tenant. It is sufficient that the landlord has actually had notice, *e.g.* by way of a notice under one of the many provisions considered in the next three Chapters.

(b) **On Notice.**   Notice must be sufficient to warn the landlord that there may be a problem. It is not necessary for the tenant actually to identify causes, or to specify defects in such detail to serve as a schedule of (necessary) works.

(c) **Unequivocal Notice.**   Notice must, however, be unequivocal. Where a tenant gave notice of disrepair, saying that he would subsequently provide the landlord with the details, the landlord was entitled to await the further information (*Al-Hassani v Merrigan*, 1987).

11.14   Notice and common parts. The rule that notice has to be given does not apply in relation to any part of the premises still in the landlord's control (*British Telecommunications plc v Sun Life Assurance Society plc*, 1996). In *Passley v Wandsworth LBC*, (1996), the landlord authority were held responsible for burst pipes, even though they had no notice of any defect, because the pipes were located in a roof space above a top floor flat which was a part of the property which was not within the flat but rather was within a part of the property under the landlord's control.

1. UNFAIR CONTRACT TERMS ACT 1977

11.15 Application. Although this Act does not apply to the creation or termination of an interest in land (Unfair Contract Terms Act 1977, s.1 and Sch.1), it may apply to other terms in a tenancy, and applies generally to licences. It follows that it may affect the operation of a repairing obligation imposed on an occupier (which is not already excluded by another statutory provision, *e.g.* Landlord and Tenant Act 1985, s.11). The Act only applies to "consumers" dealing with a person, on his written standard terms of business (Unfair Contract Terms Act 1977, s.3), and so is unlikely to apply, *e.g.* in the case of a resident landlord (4.43–4.50, 5.44–5.60).

11.16 Requirements. Under the provisions of this Act, a landlord may neither limit his own liability for breach of contract, nor claim to be entitled to offer either no service at all or a service substantially different from that which might reasonably be expected of him, save to the extent that is reasonable (Unfair Contract Terms Act 1977, s.3). In this context, no service or a substantially different service than that expected, may be the provisions most relevant to repairing obligation, *i.e.* if the landlord seeks to abdicate responsibility altogether or seeks to limit his responsibility unreasonably.

11.17 Reasonableness. For these purposes, reasonableness means that the term in question is or is not one that is fair and reasonable to include in the contract,

  (a) Having regard to the circumstances actually known to the parties when the contract was made, or which ought to have been so known, and

  (b) Having particular regard to:
    (i) The relative bargaining positions of the parties,
    (ii) Alternative possibilities, (*i.e.* here, alternative accommodation) open to the consumer, and

(iii) Trade or custom (Unfair Contract Terms Act 1977, s.11).

11.18   EC regulations. In addition to the 1977 Act, contracts are also governed by the Unfair Terms in Consumer Contracts Regulations 1999 (SI 1999/2083), which directly implement European Council Directive 93/13 (and which do not exclude the creation or termination of interests in land).

11.19   The regulations import a requirement of good faith into contracts between a "seller or supplier" and a "consumer". The requirement of good faith is almost an identical requirement to that of "reasonableness" under the Unfair Contract Terms Act 1977 (11.17).

11.20   The regulations list a variety of illustrations of unfair terms. In the context of disrepair, the most relevant will be any term "excluding or hindering the consumer's right to take legal action or exercise any other legal remedy," *e.g.* clauses which seek to limit the right of the tenant to set-off against arrears of rent (11.103).

11.21   Detailed guidance on unfair terms in relation to assured and assured shorthold tenancies is now available from the Office of Fair Trading, which offers a number of further examples of possible exclusions and limitations of liability which would be unfair.

2.   CONTRACTUAL TERMS

11.22   In the following paragraphs we shall consider:

(i) Express terms which may be found in tenancy agreements;

(ii) Terms implied by law, which may be additional to those expressed in an agreement, or may provide a basic and minimum statement of liabilities when there is neither written nor verbal agreement between the parties; and,

(iii) Terms implied by statute, which may override what has expressly been agreed or may operate where nothing express has been agreed.

(i) *Express Terms*

11.23   Content. The express terms are exactly that—express and explicit. What they say is—subject to being overridden by statute (including the Unfair Contract Terms Act and Regulations, above, 11.15)—what they mean. While there is a number of common terms, which have given rise over the centuries to a considerable body of law as to their interpretation (most of the relevant aspects of which have fed through to the interpretation of statutorily implied terms and are considered, so far as relevant, in that context), they are essentially idiosyncratic in the sense that the parties may seek to allocate responsibilities between themselves and/or expressly to address specific repairing items in any way they see fit.

11.24 Higher standards. Although most landlords seek to limit their repairing obligations to a minimum, this is not always the case. Some local authorities have expressly agreed to higher standards than those imposed by the Landlord and Tenant Act 1985, s.11 (11.47, below). In *Welsh v Greenwich LBC*, 2001, the authority covenanted to keep the premises in "good condition" which was held to include liability for severe condensation dampness which would not have fallen under a mere covenant to repair (11.66).

11.25 Reasonable steps. Another term concerned a covenant to "take all reasonable steps to keep the estate clean and tidy." It was held that this was not discharged by the mere appointment of outside contractors, however, competent, without also putting in place an adequate system for the landlord to monitor the contractor's performance and effectiveness (*Long v Southwark LBC*, 2002).

(ii) *Terms Implied By Law*

11.26 Fitness for human habitation. There is no general term implied into contracts for the letting of residential accommodation either that a dwelling is fit for human habitation at the start of the tenancy, or that it will be so kept by the landlord during the tenancy (*Hart v Windsor*, 1844). It is, however, implied that a furnished lettings will at the start of the tenancy be fit for human habitation (*Smith v Marrable*, 1843).

11.27 Fitness for these purposes means fitness at common law, not fitness for human habitation as defined for the purposes of the Housing Acts (12.18–12.22). What is meant by fitness, therefore, must be considered as a matter of common law, although statute may on occasion afford a helpful guide to contemporary standards: it is clear that what one generation means by fitness is not the same as another.

11.28 Licences. It would seem that today a similar covenant will normally be implied into a licence of furnished accommodation (*Smith v Nottinghamshire CC*, 1981), although there could be cases where it would not be consistent with the nature of the licence to do so.

11.29 Weekly tenancies. Nor, in the absence of any express agreement as to repair, will the courts necessarily assume that under a weekly or monthly periodic tenancy, the landlord will take responsibility for "major" repairs, even though the courts readily accept that it is unlikely to have been intended that the tenant will do so instead, for want of any sufficient interest in the property to merit substantial expenditure (*Mint v Good*, 1950; *Sleafer v Lambeth London Borough*, 1959).

11.30 Under a weekly, or probably other short, periodic tenancy, the landlord will, however, have a right to do repairs, and correspondingly to enter to view the state of the property, but whether or not it is implied at law that he is obliged so to do will depend on whether anything was written or said, or otherwise on the court's view as to what was intended.

11.31 In *Barrett v Lounova*, 1988, where the tenant was liable for internal repairs but nothing had been agreed or said about structural or external repairs, the court concluded that it must have been intended that the landlord would have liability, in order to make the agreement work effectively, *i.e.* to give it business efficacy, because the tenant could not otherwise comply with his obligations.

11.32 In practice, this issue rarely arises today, because lacunae in responsibility are cured by the provisions of s.11 of the Housing Act 1985, although there remains in existence a number of tenancies which predate its predecessor (Housing Act 1961, s.32), and to which, accordingly, its provisions do not apply, as in *Barrett*.

11.33 Licences. In the case of a licence, it will not only be the case that the landlord will usually be assumed to undertake liability to keep the property in repair (*Smith v Nottinghamshire CC*, 1981), but it may be considered inconsistent with the nature of licence for the licensee to be under any significant repairing obligation (*Addiscombe Garden Estates v Crabbe*, 1958). There could, however, be exceptions if some particular aspect of the licence so suggested.

11.34 Common parts. A clear distinction must be drawn between the premises the subject of the tenancy, and other parts of a house or building which are not included in the letting. These parts, *e.g.* stairs, roof, halls, corridors, foundations and—in some houses—bathrooms and toilets, are kept in the landlord's possession and control, and are consequently his responsibility. He is wholly responsible for their upkeep (*Cockburn v Smith*, 1924). He must keep them reasonably safe (*Dunster v Hollis*, 1918). Where they form the means of access to a house, flat or room, and in the absence of any express agreement to the contrary, he is to keep them in a reasonable condition (*Liverpool CC v Irwin*, 1977; *King v South Northamptonshire DC*, 1991), probably in a condition reasonably approximating that in which they were at the commencement of the letting. (It is thought that this obligation is related to, or derived from, that considered in the next paragraph).

11.35 Non-derogation from grant. Where a tenant occupies property which adjoins that occupied by the landlord (whether actually so occupied or as a matter of law, *e.g.* common parts), it is implied that the landlord will not use his retained property so as to "derogate from the grant" of the tenancy, *i.e.* in such a way as to interfere with the tenant's use of the property for the purpose for which it was let.

11.36 Quiet enjoyment. This covenant has been considered above (8.72). It is not usually considered in relation to disrepair. As, however, a covenant by the landlord that the tenant will be able quietly to enjoy the premises the subject of the tenancy is implied into every letting, it may be a useful catch-all where, *e.g.* repairs take an undue time to complete or are executed with such disregard for the tenant's convenience that it may be said unreasonably and unnecessarily to interfere with his use of the premises. There is no reason why disrepair should not also be considered breach of the covenant for quiet enjoyment (*Gordon v Selico Co*, 1986).

11.37 The covenant can only be used, however, in relation to a complaint about conditions arising after the grant of the tenancy. The tenant takes the premises in the physical conditions which he finds them and subject to the uses contemplated for those premises. Thus, everyday noise from neighbouring flats arising because of a lack of soundproofing does not amount to a breach of the covenant (*Southwark LBC v Mills*, 1999).

11.38 Estoppel and rent registration. In some circumstances, even where one party has no direct or express legal rights against another, the law will stop the other party denying an obligation. This is known as "estoppel".

11.39 One circumstance related to repairs, and which relies heavily upon estoppel, was at one time quite common although is of decreasing contemporary relevance.

11.40 It is noted below (11.49) that the provisions of s.11 of the Landlord and Tenant Act 1985 apply only to tenancies granted after October 24, 1961. Where a tenancy commenced before that date, therefore, there might have been no repairing obligations implied into the tenancy at all (as in *Barrett v Lounova*, 1988, above, 11.31, 11.32). Over time, however, there may have been applications for registration of a fair rent (5.190–5.212) in the course of which it is possible—perhaps even likely—that the rent officer will have assumed, or even been informed, either that s.11 applies or that the landlord is in any event responsible for major and structural repairs, and will have assessed the rent on this basis.

11.41 As the tenant will therefore be paying—and the landlord receiving—a higher rent than if the tenant were responsible for the major repairs, or than if no one had any such responsibility, the landlord will be "estopped" from denying the liability (*Brikom Investments v Seaford*, 1981), although he can subsequently apply for a variation in the registration. The estoppel will not, therefore, guarantee future responsibility. In an appropriate case, estoppel may override even the express terms of an agreement.

11.42 Use in a tenant-like manner. The tenant is under an obligation to use premises in a "tenant-like manner." That is to say, he:

> "must take proper care of the place. He must, if he is going away for the winter, turn off the water and empty the boiler. He must clean the chimneys, when necessary, and also the windows. He must mend the electric light when it fuses. He must unstop the sink when it is blocked by his waste. In short, he must do the little jobs about the place which a reasonable tenant would do. In addition, he must, of course, not damage the house, wilfully or negligently; and he must see that his family and guests do not damage it; if they do, he must repair it. But apart from such things, if the house falls into disrepair through fair wear and tear or lapse of time, or for any reason not caused by him, then the tenant is not liable to repair it." (*Warren v Keen*, 1953, *per* Denning L.J.).

(iii) *Terms Implied By Statute*

Landlord and Tenant Act 1985, s.8

11.43 Fit for human habitation. Contrary to the normal rule (11.26)—that there is no covenant that premises are fit for human habitation at the commencement of a tenancy or that they will so be kept throughout the tenancy—statute implies such a term into tenancies at a very low rent (Landlord and Tenant Act 1985, s.8). For these purposes, fitness bears the same meaning as under the Housing Act 1985 prior to its amendment in 1989, *i.e.* it is unfit if it is defective in respect of one or more of the following: repair, stability, freedom from damp, internal arrangement, natural lighting, ventilation, water supply, drainage and sanitary conveniences, facilities for preparation of food and for the disposal of waste water, and by reason of that is not reasonably suitable for occupation.

11.44 As discussed above (11.10–11.13), there will be no obligation until the landlord has had notice of the disrepair (*Morgan v Liverpool Corp.*, 1927), and the term has no application where the premises cannot be rendered fit for human habitation at a reasonable expense (*Buswell v Goodwin*, 1970; see 12.70). The term will, however, carry over into a statutory tenancy (11.81). The term carries with it a right on the part of the landlord, on not less than 24 hours' notice in writing, to enter to view the state and condition of the premises.

11.45 Rent limits. The covenant is, however, implied only into tenancies at such low rents that the covenant is today rarely encountered in practice. The rent levels are as follows:

(a) Where the contract was made before July 31, 1923, the rent at the beginning of the tenancy must not have been more than £40 per annum in the administrative county of London, nor more than £26 per annum in a borough of an urban district outside London, nor elsewhere more than £16 per annum;

(b) In relation to contracts made on or after that date, but before July 6, 1957, the rent at the commencement of the tenancy must not have been more than £40 per annum in the administrative county of London, nor more than £26 elsewhere; and,

(c) In relation to contracts made on or after that date, the rent at the commencement must not have been more than £80 in what was until April 1, 1965 the administrative county of London and thereafter Greater London, or £52 per annum elsewhere.

11.46   Short and long leases. The covenant is implied into both short lettings and, unless excluded, into longer leases. In relation to a lease for not less than three years, the covenant will not take effect if the lease contains a term that the tenant put the property into a condition reasonably fit for human habitation, and the lease cannot be brought to an end by the landlord or by the tenant, other, perhaps, than by forfeiture (1.126–1.130), within the first three years.

Landlord and Tenant Act 1985, s.11

11.47   Principal repairing covenant. This is the principal repairing covenant now implied into most lettings of residential accommodation. It does not apply if the letting is for a term of seven years or more (Landlord and Tenant Act 1985, s.12), which means seven years from the commencement of occupation, either under the tenancy or under a binding agreement for a tenancy (*Brikom Investments v Seaford*, 1981).

11.48   The Act allows the parties to apply to the county court for an order excluding or modifying the operation of s.11, but in the absence of any such order the Act overrides the express terms of any agreement, and any contract purporting to exclude the provisions of s.11—or to penalise the tenant because the landlord has to comply with them—is void and of no effect.

11.49   Old tenancies. The section applies only to tenancies granted after commencement of the Housing Act 1961, when the provision was introduced (October 24, 1961).

11.50   Periodic tenancy. A periodic tenancy is not for seven years or more, even though it may last or have lasted that long or longer, so that the covenant accordingly applies to it.

11.51   The implied covenant. The term is that:

"In any lease of a dwelling-house, being a lease to which this section applies, there shall be implied a covenant by the lessor —

(a) to keep in repair the structure and exterior of the dwelling-house (including drains, gutters and external pipes); and

(b) to keep in repair and proper working order the installations in the dwelling-house
  (i) for the supply of water, gas and electricity, and for sanitation (including basins, sinks, baths and sanitary conveniences but not, except as aforesaid, fixtures, fittings and appliances for making use of the supply of water, gas or electricity), and
  (ii) for space heating or heating water . . . "

11.52 The covenant carries with it a right on the part of the landlord, on giving not less than 24 hours' notice in writing, to enter to view the state of the premises (Landlord and Tenant Act 1985, s.11(6)).

11.53 The obligation extends to essential means of access to the premises (*Brown v Liverpool Corp*, 1969).

11.54 Part of house or building. The provision applies as much to part of a house or building—even as little as a single room—as to a house (Landlord and Tenant Act 1985, s.16).

11.55 Where only a part of house or building is involved, then the covenant extends to an obligation to keep the structure and exterior of the house or building in repair, and to keep in repair and proper working order an installation (for the same purposes) which serves the part of the house the subject of the tenancy, provided it forms part of a building in which the landlord has an interest or the installation itself is owned by the landlord or is under his control (Landlord and Tenant Act 1985, s.11(1A), added by Housing Act 1988, s.116).

11.56 This will not be so, however, unless the disrepair actually affects the tenant's enjoyment of his property or of the common parts (Landlord and Tenant Act 1985, s.11(1B)).

11.57 These provisions extending s.11 beyond the premises the subject of the tenancy relate only to tenancies granted on or after November 15, 1988 (unless pursuant to a contract for a tenancy which predates November 15, 1988).

11.58 Limits of covenant. The provisions do not, however, go so far as to require the landlord to do works for which the tenant is liable under the duty to use premises in a tenant-like manner

(11.42), nor do they require him to rebuild or reinstate the premises in the case of destruction or damage by fire, tempest, flood or other inevitable accident, nor to keep in repair or maintain such of the tenant's own belongings as he is entitled to remove from the property (Landlord and Tenant Act 1985, s.11(2)).

11.59 It is a defence to an action based on failure to repair a building in which the premises are situated, or installations outside the premises but which service them, that the landlord was unable to obtain sufficient rights to do the works (Landlord and Tenant Act 1985, s.11(3A)), *e.g.* under the Access to Neighbouring Land Act 1992 (11.166).

11.60 There will only be a breach of the covenant if the landlord has had notice of disrepair (11.10–11.13), but the covenant will carry over into any statutory tenancy (11.81).

11.61 Standard of repair. The main problem arising under this provision is that of the standard of repair it imposes. The Act itself provides that regard shall be had to the age, character and prospective life of the property, and the locality in which it is situated (Landlord and Tenant Act 1985, s.11(3)). This may mean that patch repairs are adequate even where a higher standard of repair would be desirable (*Trustees of Hungerford Charity v Beazeley*, 1993).

11.62 It is not a defence to an allegation that installations are not in proper working order to show that they suffer from a design defect (*Liverpool CC v Irwin*, 1976). Indeed, although the covenant requires only that the landlord keep the premises in repair to the extent set out, this is interpreted as meaning that the landlord must also put them in repair, for that which is not in repair at the commencement of the tenancy can hardly be kept in repair (*Saner v Bilton*, 1878).

11.63 Exterior. A dividing wall between two terraced houses will be part of the exterior of each (*Green v Eales*, 1841), and the walls of a flat—whether to the outside or the inside of the building,—and the ceiling and floor, will all be part of the exterior for the purpose of the covenant (*Campden Hill Towers v Gardner*, 1976).

11.64 Windows. Windows are part of the exterior (*Quick v Taff Ely BC*, 1985; *Ball v Plummer*, 1979; *Boswell v Crucible Steel*, 1925; *Irvine v Moran*, 1990). That is not to say that the landlord is liable for a breakage by the tenant, for that would be the tenant's responsibility as part of his duty to use the premises in a tenant-like manner (11.42), but it does mean that breakage by someone else, or because, *e.g.*, the frame broke or warped, would be the liability of the landlord.

11.65 Structure. Structure is perhaps a more difficult concept. A house is a complex whole, and anything which touches upon that complex unit may properly be deemed to be part of the structure (*Pearlman v Keepers and Governors of Harrow School*, 1978). The roof of a block of flats or a house converted into flats may be part of the structure of the top floor flat, but then again it may not, depending on, *e.g.* whether there is a roof space or an attic (*Douglas-Scott v Scorgie*, 1984).

11.66 Disrepair to structure. Disrepair must be to the structure or exterior, not merely resulting from it. Thus, dampness caused by a leak or defective brickwork will mean that the structure or exterior is in disrepair, but where the construction of the structure and exterior results in dampness from ordinary use of the premises (*i.e.* "condensation dampness"), without actual disrepair, this will not class as disrepair within this implied covenant (*Quick v Taff Ely BC*, 1985).

11.67 Thus, in *Stent v Monmouth DC*, 1987, it was held that if a door "merely" fails to keep out water, there will be no disrepair to the structure, although if the water ingress damages the door itself, there will be.

11.68 In *Staves v Leeds CC*, 1990, condensation dampness meant that the physical condition of the plaster required renewal. It was conceded that the plaster was part of the structure and it therefore followed that there was disrepair.

11.69 In *Irvine v Moran*, 1990, however, it was held that internal wall plaster was not part of the structure of a dwelling-house since it was more in the nature of a decorative finish than an essential material element of the house.

11.70 Repair. It is "repair" which the covenant requires. For many years, it was believed that the proper way to define the word repair in a repairing covenant was by distinguishing it from such other terms as "improvement," "renewal" or "replacement," *i.e.* if the works needed to cure the problem amounted to improvement, renewal or replacement, they would not comprise a repair. For this reason, it was commonly believed that an inherent defect could not be cured within a repairing obligation, because that would comprise an improvement.

11.71 The key test was—and to this extent remains—whether the works executed would result in the delivery up of something different in quality to that which was originally let. Thus, for example, it was thought that a repairing obligation could not be used to require a landlord to introduce a damp-proof course (*Pembery v Lamdin*, 1940), or to provide underpinning (*Sotheby v Grundy*, 1947).

11.72 Extent of works. More recently it has been held, however, that these older cases turned on their own facts rather than setting precedents as to what works are or are not within a covenant to repair: *Ravenseft Properties Ltd v Davstone (Holdings) Ltd*, 1978, a case involving the same block of flats as the subject of the action in *Campden Hill Towers v Gardner*, 1976.

11.73 In that case, the block had been constructed without expansion joints to retain a stone cladding once natural movement ("settling") commenced. Accordingly, the stone cladding threatened to fall away. The only proper way to rectify this, however, was by the introduction of the missing expansion joints. It was argued that such works to the structure, involving the introduction of a new method of construction and the curing of a construction defect, could not be within the covenant to repair. Having regard to the sort of works involved (which were not, in comparison to the whole block, that extensive), to the necessity for the joints, and to the cost of the works compared to the value of the block as a whole, it was held that the works could be compelled within the repairing obligation.

11.74 Contemplation of parties. In another case (*Smedley v Chumley and Hawkes*, 1981), a riverside restaurant was built on a pier, or raft. It was a recent construction, and there was inadequate underpinning. The restaurant threatened to sink into the river. The court asked itself what had been in the contemplation of the parties, and was influenced by the fact that these were modern premises, not an old and deteriorating property: it was held that underpinning could be compelled within a covenant to repair.

11.75 Principles in practice. How do these principles work in housing? In *Wainwright v Leeds CC*, 1984, the older authorities prevailed. In *Elmcroft Developments Ltd v Tankersley-Sawyer*, 1984, and most recently in *Quick v Taff Ely BC*, 1985, however, the Court of Appeal upheld the *Ravenseft* approach.

11.76 Accordingly:

(a) Where a modern property is in issue, works can be required within s.11 of the Landlord and Tenant Act 1985, even though they comprise works to cure an inherent or constructional defect and which involve the introduction of a new construction method; and,

(b) Where an older house is in issue, the courts are—having regard both to contemporary values and to the comparatively small cost of such works as damp-proof coursing, and perhaps also influenced by the modern emphasis on retention in use of older housing stock—also now prepared to order whatever works are necessary to keep a house in a reasonable condition, provided they are not so extensive or expensive as to involve virtual reconstruction or such overall improvement as will turn the old house into a new dwelling.

11.77 Thus, in *Murray v Birmingham CC*, 1987, it was held that the covenant could (in principle) extend to the provision of a new roof, although in that case such extensive works were in fact not held necessary.

11.78 Three tests. In *McDougall v Easington DC*, 1989, the Court of Appeal considered whether a major rehabilitation programme requiring over £10,000 worth of works to each property, but only increasing their value from £10,000 to £18,000, amounted to their repair and concluded that the works amounted to an improvement not within the repairing obligation.

11.79 The court identified three tests which could be applied separately or concurrently to decide whether works amounted to a repair within s.11 of the Landlord and Tenant Act 1985:

(a) **Whole or subsidiary structure.** Whether the alterations went to the whole or substantially the whole of the structure or only to a subsidiary part;

(b) **Character.** Whether the effect of the alterations was to produce a building of a wholly different character than that which had been let; and,

(c) **Cost.** The cost of the works in relation to the previous value of the building and their effect on the value and life span of the building.

Other statutory provisions

11.80   Rent Act 1977; Housing Act 1988. Though the Rent Act 1977 and the Housing Act 1988 are not directly concerned with repairs, they contain a number of provisions affecting the subject.

(a) **Continuation of covenants.** Both a Rent Act statutory tenancy (5.25) and a Housing Act assured statutory periodic tenancy (4.74) are on the same terms as the preceding contractual tenancy (1977, s.3(1); 1988, s.5), from which it follows that any express or implied repairing obligations will be continued (*McCarrick v Liverpool Corp.*, 1947).

(b) **Access.** It is an implied term of all Rent Act protected tenancies (whether contractual or statutory, see Chapter 5), and of all Housing Act assured tenancies (Chapter 4), that the tenant will afford the landlord all reasonable facilities for access and the execution of any repairs which the landlord is entitled to carry out (1977, ss.3(2), 148; 1988, s.16).

(c) **Grant-aided works and court order.** Where a landlord wishes to carry out works which qualify for a grant under the Housing Grants, Construction and Regeneration Act 1996 (12.95), and a Rent Act protected tenant will not consent to their execution, the landlord may apply to the court for an order compelling the tenant's consent, which may be subject to terms (*e.g.* tenant's housing during works), and which will be granted or refused bearing in mind such alternative accommodation, the age and health of the tenant, and any disadvantages that might be expected to result to the tenant from such works (1977, s.116). There is no equivalent provision under the Housing Act 1988, although extensive works may constitute a ground for possession (4.97).

11.81   Landlord and Tenant Act 1954. On termination of a long lease, a tenant at a low rent may become a statutory tenant under the Rent Act 1977 (2.11–2.15). Under the long lease, the tenant will usually have been responsible for repairs. It would be inconsistent with the nature of a statutory tenancy for the tenant to retain such an obligation, but on the other hand it might be considered unfair were the landlord suddenly to find himself having to rectify breaches of the tenant's covenant, *i.e.* the tenant's failure to repair during the lease.

11.82 To this end, amongst the provisions governing "conversion" of the long leaseholder to the status of statutory tenant, is to be found provision for the execution of "initial repairs" (Landlord and Tenant Act 1954, s.7). The notice proposing the statutory tenancy (2.13) must itself propose:

(a) What initial repairs are to be carried out; and,

(b) What balance of repairing obligation is to pertain during the statutory tenancy.

11.83 There are no equivalent provisions where the termination of the long tenancy falls to be dealt with under the Local Government and Housing Act 1989, Sch.10 (2.16–2.20).

11.84 Initial repairs. These matters are to be agreed between landlord and tenant at least two months before the statutory tenancy comes into existence, or otherwise application must be made to the county court for a determination (Landlord and Tenant Act 1954, s.7). The purpose of the provision is to ensure that the property is in an acceptable state for the commencement of the statutory tenancy, for which purpose it is assumed that the state will be the same as if the tenant had fulfilled all his contractual obligations.

11.85 The burden of initial repairs will, then, commonly fall on the tenant. Unless the tenant is willing to have them carried out himself, however, the court cannot order him to do so; instead, the landlord is ordered to execute the works, and the tenant to pay for them.

11.86 The works are required to be to a maximum standard of "good repair," or such higher standard of works as the landlord indicates he is willing to attain (Landlord and Tenant Act 1954, s.9). The court may order payment for the initial repairs in instalments, or in a lump sum (Landlord and Tenant Act 1954, s.8).

11.87 Continuing repairs. The court can also determine the balance of obligations to follow the initial repairs, but cannot order the landlord to maintain the premises at a higher standard than at the completion of the initial repairs or, if there are no initial repairs, than the state of the premises at the date of the court's hearing (Landlord and Tenant Act 1954, s.9).

11.88 The court is under no obligation to make any order governing continuing repairing obligations (Landlord and Tenant Act 1954, s.8). It is, however, common to order or agree that the balance will be as under the Landlord and Tenant Act 1985, s.11 (11.47–11.79).

11.89 Leasehold Reform Act 1967. On the extension of a lease under this Act (2.21–2.25), there is a general provision for variation of the repairing terms of the original lease by consent or by court order (Leasehold Reform Act 1967, s.15).

3. CONTRACTUAL REMEDIES

11.90 Either landlord or tenant may wish to obtain a remedy against the other for breach of a repairing obligation. If the tenant breaks his obligations, the landlord may seek possession of the premises, by way of an action for forfeiture and under the Rent Act 1977, the Housing Act 1985 and the Housing Act 1988. He may also seek damages. More commonly, it is the tenant who will be seeking redress against the landlord: here, possession will not be in issue, but the tenant will want an order for works to be executed and may also seek compensation for the period of disrepair.

11.91 The remedies which fall to be considered are therefore:

(a) Damages for breach by landlord;

(b) Damages for breach by tenant;

(c) Set-off and counterclaim by tenant;

(d) Specific performance/injunctions;

(e) Receiving orders;

(f) Forfeiture; and,

(g) Possession.

(i) *Damages for breach by landlord—1. unfitness*

11.92 If furnished premises are not fit for human habitation, the tenant can quit and will not be liable for the rent. Unfortunately, that is rarely an option available for most tenants, especially as this could lead to a finding of intentional homelessness under Pt VII of the Housing Act 1996 (10.45–10.66). It would seem at the least arguable that if premises are not fit at the commencement of the tenancy, the breach by the landlord should today be treated as the breach of any other repairing obligation, *i.e.* that the tenant can remain in occupation, press for repairs to be executed (11.114) and claim damages (11.93).

(ii) Damages for breach by landlord—2. disrepair

11.93 Where a landlord is in breach of a repairing covenant, the tenant is entitled to damages which, so far as money can, will put the tenant in the position in which he would have been but for the breach of covenant (*Pembery v Lamdin*, 1940; *Calabar Properties Ltd v Stitcher*, 1983).

11.94 Special damages. The tenant is entitled to special damages for any losses such as the cost of alternative accommodation while the repairs are carried out, the value of damaged belongings, or the costs of redecoration (*Calabar*).

11.95 General damages. The tenant will also usually be entitled to an award of general damages to reflect any discomfort, inconvenience and ill health suffered. Such an award may include damages for the tenant's mental distress (*Personal Representatives of Chiodi v De Marney*, 1988).

11.96 Prior to the decision in *Wallace v Manchester CC*, 1998, the Court of Appeal had approved a number of approaches to the assessment of general damages:

(a) An award for the diminution in the value of the property to the tenant calculated by reference to a proportion of the rent payable (*McCoy & Co v Clark*, 1982);

(b) Global assessment of the discomfort and inconvenience suffered made without reference to the rent payable (*Personal Representatives of Chiodi v De Marney*, 1988); and,

(c) A combination of an award for diminution in value calculated as a percentage of the rent payable and a separate sum for discomfort and inconvenience (*Sturolson & Co v Mauroux*, 1988).

11.97 In *Wallace*, the Court of Appeal restated the principles for awarding general damages:

(a) For periods when the tenant remains in occupation of the property, the loss requiring compensation is the loss of comfort and convenience which results from the disrepair;

(b) Expert evidence is of no assistance in assessing this figure; the question is the monetary value of the discomfort and inconvenience suffered by the tenant which is a question for the judge;

(c) Compensation for the distress and inconvenience may be ascertained in a number of different ways, including diminution in value assessed as a notional reduction in the rent; some judges may prefer to use that method alone, some may prefer a global award for discomfort and inconvenience, and others may prefer a combination of the two;

(c) The judge is not, however, bound to assess damages separately under heads of both diminution in value and discomfort and inconvenience; they are merely alternative ways of expressing the same concept;

(d) A judge who decides that he will assess the award on a global basis should cross-check his prospective award by reference to the rent payable for the period during which the landlord is in breach of covenant; and,

(e) The source of the money used to pay the rent is irrelevant to the amount of compensation so that it is irrelevant that the rent is paid by housing benefit.

11.98 Where the tenant does not remain in occupation but, being entitled to do so, sells or sublets the property, he is not entitled to damages for discomfort and inconvenience after he has vacated the property. He may, however, be entitled to damages reflecting the reduction in the purchase price, or the reduction in the rent obtained for the subletting (*Calabar*; *Wallace*).

11.99 Reinstatement of premises. Finally, the tenant is entitled to require the premises to be reinstated, including by way of any internal redecoration necessitated by the landlord's works, and in the absence of such reinstatement or redecoration will be entitled to damages for having to do them himself (*McGreal v Wake*, 1984; *Bradley v Chorley BC*, 1985).

(iii) *Damages for breach by tenant*

11.100 Reversionary interest. The principles governing a breach of an obligation to repair on the part of a tenant are different. The amount which the landlord can recover is the amount by which his reversionary interest in the premises, (*i.e.* the interest which he enjoys on account of his future repossession of the premises), has been depreciated (*Smith v Peat*, 1853; *Drummond v S & U Stores*, 1980).

11.101 If the landlord has already repossessed the premises, the damages represent the depreciation in the value of that of which he has recovered possession compared to what he ought to have got back (*Hanson v Newman*, 1934).

11.102 If the tenant is to remain in occupation, *e.g.* as a statutory tenant on account of the Landlord and Tenant Act 1954 (2.11–2.14), then it would seem that unless "initial repairs" (11.84–11.86) serve to eliminate any deterioration in the value of the landlord's reversion, the valuations of repaired and unrepaired property are based on the fact that a sitting tenant is, and will remain, in occupation (*Jeffs v West London Property Corp*, 1954).

(iv) Set-off and counterclaim by tenant

11.103 One of the most common responses by tenants to repairs inactivity by the landlord is to withhold the rent.

11.104 What set-off covers. "Set-off" is the main principle with which we are here concerned. It is now accepted that breach of a repairing covenant is so closely related to the obligation to pay rent that it is appropriate for a tenant to set-off his damages (11.93) against the rent.

11.105 In the earlier stages of its recent development, this privilege extended only to money actually expended by the tenant on arranging for his landlord's obligations to be executed in default and was not technically a set-off, but an ancient common law entitlement achieving the same effect (*Lee-Parker v Izzet*, 1971).

11.106 Initially, it was thought this could only be done when the landlord had been given a warning, an opportunity to review estimates, and the money was to be taken out of future rent. Subsequently, it was held that the same principle could apply in relation to past rent withheld, *i.e.* rent arrears (*Asco Developments Ltd v Lowes*, 1978).

11.107 In the most recent development, it was held that not only could the tenant withhold money so expended, but he could also set-off his general damages, *i.e.* reduction in value of premises/loss of enjoyment, or his special damages, *e.g.* destroyed property (*British Anzani (Felixstowe) v International Marine Management (UK)*, 1978; *Televantos v McCulloch*, 1990).

11.108 Caution. Nonetheless, a tenant should, if possible, withstand the temptation to resort to this way of trying to force the landlord to carry out repairs. It is much better to pay the rent, and then to claim damages, in the course of proceedings, calculated as described above (11.93). Otherwise, there is a risk that the tenant will lose the monetary claim and find himself in arrears.

11.109 It is true that, where there is a discretion, a court is unlikely to find it reasonable to make an order for possession if rent has been withheld because of a dispute over repairs (*Lal v Nakum*, 1982, but *cf. Haringey LBC v Stewart*, 1991), even where in the end result the tenant fails to prove his case: nonetheless, there remains a risk.

11.110 Furthermore, in the case of a Housing Act assured tenant (Chapter 4), if the tenant fails to establish his entitlement to damages, he may even find himself subject to a mandatory ground for possession, *i.e.* with no room for the exercise of discretion by the judge (4.104).

11.111 There are probably only two circumstances in which set-off should be considered:

(a) When there is a clear breach, and the tenant, after giving his landlord ample warning of his intentions, causes the work to be carried out in default; and

(b) When arrears have already accrued by the time an adviser is in a position to assist.

11.112 Even so, in the first circumstance there will continue to be a danger that the tenant will be incorrect as to the his rights (and the landlord's obligations), for which reason if withholding can be avoided it should be. In the second circumstance, it will remain preferable to pay as much off the arrears as possible.

11.113 Unless the amount claimed by way of set-off is clearly substantially less than the amount owing to the landlord in rent, a counterclaim should in any event be added, with which to recoup the excess of damages over rent unpaid.

(v) *Specific performance and injunctions*

11.114   An order for specific performance is an order of the court requiring someone to fulfil a contractual obligation; an injunction is an order to do something, which may or may not arise under contract, (*i.e.* it may also be used in relation to tort, 11.131).

11.115   Although there has been contention in the past as to whether the county court has had power to grant an order for specific performance, there is now no practical difference between the two remedies: either may be sought in the county court (Landlord and Tenant Act 1985, s.17, governing specific performance; County Courts Act 1984, s.38, governing injunctions), unless the remedy sought is attached to a claim for damages which exceeds the level of the county court jurisdiction (which—currently at £50,000–is unlikely).

11.116   A landlord's want of financial ability to comply with an order is no defence to such an order (*Francis v Cowcliffe*, 1976).

11.117   Neither class of order may, however, be made against a tenant (*Hill v Barclay*, 1811; *Regional Properties v City of London Real Property*, 1980).

11.118   Court procedure. Where no injunction is claimed and the value of a claim is less than £5,000, a matter will normally be dealt with in the county court on the small claims track. Where, however, there is a claim for an order requiring the landlord to carry out work, it will not be allocated to the small claims track provided that the cost of the works is estimated to be more than £1,000 or the financial value of the remainder of the claim is more than £1,000 (CPR Pt 26.6(1)(b)).

(vi) *Receiving orders*

11.119   Where a landlord fails to carry out his obligations, the High Court has power (Supreme Court Act 1981, s.37)—where it considers it just and convenient to do so—to appoint a receiver to take over the whole or part of the management of a property, including the receipt of rents and/or the execution of works.

11.120   A court will not, however, appoint a receiver under this power where the landlord is a local authority carrying out their statutory housing duties, *i.e.* to provide and manage housing, because to do so would usurp Parliament's express conferral of those powers on the authority (*Parker v Camden LBC*, 1985).

11.121 Landlord and Tenant Act 1987, Pt II. This power has been codified into Pt II of the Landlord and Tenant Act 1987 and, where Pt II applies, it replaces earlier powers. Pt II applies, however, only to a building where there are two or more flats, where at least 50 per cent of the floor area of the building (excluding its common parts) is occupied for residential purposes, and the landlord is neither a resident landlord (defined in similar terms as under the Housing Act 1988; see 4.43), nor an "exempt landlord," defined to include local authorities and a number of other public bodies (Landlord and Tenant Act 1987, s.21).

11.122 Action under Pt II requires a prior notice fulfilling statutory requirements to be found in s.22 of the Act, followed—if the landlord does not comply with the notice—by application under s.23 for the appointment of a manager. (See now also the general power to seek the appointment of a manager even in cases of no default—2.69).

(vii) *Forfeiture*

11.123 Forfeiture is one of the means of bringing a tenancy to an end (1.126–1.141). There is no right to forfeit a tenancy unless such a right is expressly reserved in the agreement. The right is, however, commonly reserved in most written tenancy agreements, and is commonly drafted in such terms as to apply on breach of a tenant's repairing obligation.

11.124 Waiver. If the obligation in question is to put (not also to keep) the premises in repair, a landlord who has known of a breach by the tenant, but has so conducted himself as to be considered to have waived the breach (*cf.* waiver of illegal sub-letting; 1.181), will also have waived his right to forfeit the tenancy (*Doe d. Morecraft v Meux*, 1825).

11.125 If, however, the obligation in question is also to keep the property in repair, both the obligation and the breach continue so long as the tenant fails to repair and there is, accordingly, no waiver (*Doe d. Hemmings v Durnford*, 1832).

11.126 Remedying the breach. Before seeking to forfeit, the landlord must serve notice specifying his complaint and, if the breach is remediable, requiring remedy and demanding compensation (Law of Property Act 1925, s.146). The landlord must also allow sufficient time for remedy of a repairing breach.

11.127 Leasehold Property (Repairs) Act 1938. In relation to a long lease of which at least three years remain unexpired, the s.146 notice must also advise the tenant of his right to claim by way of counter-notice the protection of the Leasehold Property (Repairs) Act 1938, under the terms of which the landlord cannot proceed with an action for forfeiture based on disrepair other than with the leave of the court.

11.128 The court will not grant leave unless an immediate remedy is needed in order to prevent a substantial reduction in the value of the landlord's interest, or where remedy would now be cheap compared to remedy later, or in order to comply with any statute, or where the tenant is not in occupation and repair is needed for the protection of other occupiers, or where in all the circumstances the court considers it just and equitable to grant leave.

11.129 Relief. Where a landlord seeks to forfeit a tenancy, the tenant can usually apply to the court for relief from forfeiture, which will, however, almost invariably be on conditions, in this case meaning conditions requiring the tenant to rectify the breach, although not if the court considers that the extent of the obligation is unreasonable (Law of Property Act 1925, s.147): a Housing Act assured tenant (Chapter 4), however, cannot apply for relief (4.73).

(viii) *Possession*

11.130 Even if a tenancy is determined by forfeiture, or where—without forfeiture—proceedings against either a Rent Act protected or statutory (Rent Act 1977; see Chapter 5) tenant, or a Housing Act secure (Housing Act 1985; see Chapter 3 above) or Housing Act assured (Housing Act 1988; see Chapter 4) tenant are taken based on breach of the tenant's repairing obligation (3.98, 4.120, 5.145), it will still be necessary to prove that it is reasonable to make an order for possession.

Tort

1. INTRODUCTION

11.131 In this section, we shall briefly consider remedies for disrepair, or other unacceptable housing conditions, which arise independently of contract. They may be available to those with a contract, or those without.

2. CAUSES OF ACTION

11.132 The torts with which we are here concerned are:

(i) Negligence;

(ii) Breach of the Building Regulations;

(iii) Defective premises;

(iv) Occupier's liability;

(v) Nuisance; and,

(vi) Waste, a tort peculiar to the relationship of landlord and tenant.

(i) Negligence

11.133 Duty of care. Action in negligence only arises when there is a legal duty of care. This means:

> "you must take reasonable care to avoid acts or omissions which you can reasonably foresee would be likely to injure your neighbour. Who, then, in law is my neighbour? The answer seems to be: persons who are so closely and directly affected by my act that I ought reasonably to have them in contemplation as being so affected when I am directing my mind to the acts or omissions which are called into question" (*Donoghue v Stevenson*, 1932, *per* Lord Atkin).

11.134 Duty to tenants and visitors. Thus, in addition to the landlord's contractual duty to make sure that common parts are kept reasonably safe (11.34), he also owes a duty of care to tenants or others who may visit premises to ensure that they are safeguarded against damage from any danger of which he knows, or ought to have known (*Cunard v Antifyre Ltd*, 1933).

11.135 Duty of builders. Anyone carrying out work on premises is under a general duty to use reasonable care for the safety of those whom he knows or ought to know might be affected by those works, or who are lawfully in the vicinity of those works (*AC Billings & Son v Riden*, 1958). A builder of a house, whether or not he is also the landlord, owes a duty of care in the construction of the building to potential occupiers of it, but the liability only extends to personal injury and not to economic loss, *i.e.* because, *e.g.* it is worth less than was paid for it (*Murphy v Brentwood DC*, 1990) or cannot be used for the purpose for which it was acquired.

11.136 Developers. Developers (whether or not also the owner) of, *e.g.* housing for sale, owe a duty of care to purchasers (*Sutherland v Maton (CR) & Son*, 1976; *Batty v Metropolitan Property Realisations; Rimmer v Liverpool CC*, 1985; *Targett v Torfaen BC*, 1991).

11.137 Building professionals. Architects, engineers, surveyors, and others involved in the construction of a dwelling owe a similar duty to future occupiers to take reasonable care in the execution of their functions (*Cedar Transport Group v First Wyvern Property Trustees Co*, 1980). In the light of *Murphy*, any such liability will be limited to damages for personal injury and not extend to economic loss (*Preston v Torfaen BC*, 1993).

11.138 Works by the landlord. A landlord may also be responsible in negligence for other works, *e.g.* for the manner of carrying out his repairing obligations (*Sharpe v Manchester MDC*, 1977) or for the quality of works done prior to the commencement of a letting.

11.139 Whether the landlord has complied with his duty of care will normally turn on whether, in selecting a particular design or materials for the repair or maintenance, the landlord has acted "in accordance with a practice accepted as proper by a reasonable body of. . .men skilled in that particular art" (*Adams v Rhymney Valley DC*, 2000). There is no negligence, however, in failing to carry out works before a letting (*Arden v Pullen*, 1842; 11.26).

11.140 Home purchase. A further, and important, illustration of negligence arises in the course of home purchase. Most people buying their own homes will take advice from a surveyor and a solicitor. The surveyor will report on the condition of the house: if he does so negligently, he will be liable for the effects of his default. A solicitor will have a number of legal functions to carry out, including finding out information about the purchaser's title, and whether the local authority have any plans, *e.g.* for clearance (12.76–12.86) which may adversely affect the purchaser's intended occupation. He, too, may be liable in negligence.

11.141   Report to building society. Where a purchaser failed to have his own survey carried out, but instead relied on the fact that a building society was willing to advance the mortgage, knowing that the building society had themselves sought a survey, the surveyor was held liable to the purchaser, even though the purchaser never saw his report to the building society (*Yianni v Evans (Edwin) & Sons*, 1981; see also *Smith v Bush*, 1987; *Harris v Wyre Forest DC*, 1987; *Davies v Idris Parry*, 1988). The surveyor is deemed to know that the consequences of his negligence would not only affect the building society's decision on mortgage, but also the purchaser's decision as to whether or not to buy. In practice today, many building societies (and banks) release such reports to the borrower.

11.142   Local authorities. It should also be remembered that local authorities may commit negligence in the execution of their functions. Alternatively, they may be liable for breach of statutory duty, which is technically a separate tort, for failing properly to carry out their obligations under an Act of Parliament.

11.143   Thus, where an authority were obliged to inspect property in the course of construction to see whether there had been compliance with Building Regulations (see also 11.146), and were alleged to have done so negligently, action was available at the instigation of later occupiers (*Anns v Merton LBC*, 1977).

11.144   Causation and consequence. The fact that there is a defect, however, is not enough to give rise to action: that defect must be caused by an act which a reasonable man would not have done or an omission to do something which a reasonable man would have made sure was done (*Bolton v Stone*, 1951).

11.145   Further, the act or omission must cause the harm (or the likelihood of harm). There must be a line of causation between act or omission and harm, so that the latter is not too remote a consequence of the former. Another way of putting the same proposition is that it must have been reasonably foreseeable (which is not to say reasonably foreseen) that harm of the order which has resulted would result.

(ii)   *Breach Of The Building Regulations*

11.146   Health and Safety at Work Act 1974, s.71. In a large number of cases where housing is constructed, improved or altered, or its use changed, it will be obligatory to comply with the Building Regulations. Anyone who is obliged to comply with the Regulations and who fails to do so will, save where the Regulations themselves otherwise specify, be liable to an action in tort at the instance of a person harmed by his failure (Health and Safety at Work Act 1974, s.71).

(iii) *Defective Premises*

11.147 Defective Premises Act 1972, s.3. Anyone who carries out work of construction, repair, maintenance or demolition, or any other work in relation to premises, owes a duty of care to persons who might reasonably be expected to be affected by resulting defects in the state of the premises (Defective Premises Act 1972, s.3).

11.148 The duty of care persists through any subsequent sale or letting of the premises, and is co-extensive with the duty of care in negligence (11.133). It does not, however, apply to omissions to repair or execute other works which may be needed.

11.149 The duty applies only in relation to works carried out prior to a sale or letting which itself followed the commencement of the Act (January 1, 1974).

11.150 Defective Premises Act 1972, s.1. The same Act imposed a duty of care on anyone doing any work for or in connection with the provision of a dwelling by erection, conversion or enlargement (Defective Premises Act 1972, s.1).

11.151 The duty of care is to see that work is done in a workmanlike manner and with proper materials or—if the person involved is a professional, *e.g.* architect, engineer—that it is done in a professional manner, so as to ensure that the dwelling will be fit for habitation when completed.

11.152 The duty is owed to, among others, purchasers and tenants. The duty is also additional to the duty of care in negligence (11.133) but again applies only to work following the commencement of the Act (January 1, 1974).

11.153 Defective Premises Act 1972, s.4. Further, whenever a landlord is under an obligation to repair (however arising, *i.e.* implied by law (11.26–11.42); implied by statute (11.43–11.79); or express), he owes:

"to all persons who might reasonably be expected to be affected by defects in the state of the premises a duty to take such care as is reasonable in all the circumstances to see that they are reasonably safe from personal injury or from damage to their property . . . ": Defective Premises Act 1972, s.4.

11.154 The duty arises whenever the landlord knows of the defect, or even if he only ought to have known of it, so that it may be an appropriate cause of action if, for want of notice (11.10–11.13), action cannot be taken under a contractual obligation. The duty is owed both to tenants, and to the tenant's visitors. (Although there is no notice requirement, however, damages may be reduced on the basis on contributory negligence by a tenant who has failed to notify the landlord of the defect: *Sykes v Harry*, 2001).

11.155 The duty only arises, however, in relation to "relevant defects." A relevant defect is one arising from or continuing because of an act or omission by the landlord which actually constitutes a breach of his repairing obligation, or which would have constituted a breach of his repairing obligation if he had had notice of it. In substance, this means any defect which is within the obligation to repair, of which the landlord knew, or ought to have known.

11.156 Even if repairing obligations are obscure, however, if the landlord has a right to repair (as distinct from a duty), he is treated for these purposes as if he were under a repairing obligation (Defective Premises Act 1972, s.4(4), and see *McCauley v Bristol CC*, 1991), so that in weekly tenancies (11.29), Rent Act protected and statutory tenancies, and Housing Act assured tenancies (11.80), and those to which the Landlord and Tenant Act 1985, ss.8 (11.44) and 11 (11.52) apply, there will be an obligation for the purposes of this provision, in relation to any class of works which the right of entry is designed to permit the landlord to execute. The Act does not create any obligation wider than the landlord's repairing obligation (*McNerney v Lambeth LBC*, 1988).

(iv) *Occupier's Liability*

11.157 Occupier's Liability Act 1957, s.2. The occupier of premises is the person in possession and control of them. Thus, a tenant is an occupier, but only of the premises the subject of the letting. In a block of flats, the landlord is the occupier of the block, just as in a house let out in bedsitting-rooms or flats the landlord retains possession and control of the house itself.

11.158 An occupier owes a common duty to take such care as is reasonable in all the circumstances of the case to see that "visitors" to premises will be reasonably safe in using the premises for the purposes for which he was allowed in (Occupier's Liability Act 1957, s.2). The term "visitors" will include those on the premises with the express or implied permission of the occupier, *e.g.* a tenant or licensee of some part, or the tenant's or licensee's own visitors. The extent of the duty may vary with circumstances, including factors affecting the class of visitor: *e.g.* the elderly, children. In some circumstances, there is even a duty of care to those not lawfully on the premises, *i.e.* trespassers: see Occupier's Liability Act 1984.

(v) *Nuisance*

11.159 Act or state of affairs. The concept of nuisance has been considered earlier (8.89). It is mentioned here because, like breach of covenant for quiet enjoyment (11.36), a landlord's control of neighbouring property may in appropriate circumstances be such that it interferes with the tenant's reasonable use of the premises let. To constitute a nuisance, there must be some act or state of affairs in one set of premises, which adversely affects use and enjoyment of another. Only someone with a right to occupy the premises suffering the nuisance can sue (*Read v Lyons & Co*, 1946), not a mere visitor.

(vi) *Waste*

11.160 Alteration of nature of premises. Waste is a tort peculiar to the law of landlord and tenant. In some ways, it may be considered the equivalent in tort of action in contract for breach of the tenant's duty to use premises in a tenant-like manner (11.42). An act of waste is an act by the tenant which alters the nature of the premises let.

11.161 Normally, this will be an act of deterioration of the premises, *e.g.* cutting down a tree or knocking down an outhouse, or any other act of damage, including to the premises themselves. Technically, it can also be something which might otherwise be regarded as an improvement, *e.g.* an alteration. There will be no waste, however, if the landlord's consent to the act in question has been secured, and an act of waste will only give rise to a claim for possession (3.110, 4.120, 5.151) if it is also an act of deterioration.

3. REMEDIES IN TORT

11.162 Classes of damages. If one person commits a tort which causes harm to another, that other is to be put in the position he would have enjoyed had the tort not occurred. Thus, damages will be available on this principle, whether the claim is against landlord or tenant, for such harm as has ensued.

11.163 "Special damages" are those which are identifiable, such as loss of earnings, loss of property, including clothing, medical expenses, alternative accommodation, travelling expenses. In addition, there are "general damages," for pain and suffering, personal injury, and nervous shock, although not, as a general rule, for inconvenience or discomfort (*cf.* 11.95).

11.164 Two points to note. Two points on damages are of importance to occupiers of housing. First, there is no reduction in a claim for damages because the claim is against a public body, engaged in a socially useful task, such as the discharge of their housing functions (*Taylor v Liverpool Corp.*, 1939). Secondly, where the claim is in relation to damage to a house, *e.g.* by an owner-occupier suing someone who has negligently advised on the purchase (11.140), damages will be the cost of repairs, assessed as at the date when, having regard to all the circumstances, the repairs could reasonably have been undertaken, rather than when the harm occurred: in this connection, the financial ability or inability of the person suing may be a factor in requiring the deferral (and so the increased cost) of repairs (*Perry v Sidney Phillips & Son*, 1982). In some cases, however, any claim will be limited to damages for personal injury and will not cover any loss of value in the house or cost of repairs (11.135, *Murphy v Brentwood DC*, 1990).

11.165 Injunction. In addition, and in principle, there is no reason why an injunction should not be sought, either to prevent harm arising from a tort, or to rectify it. Although the prospect of damage should not be too remote, it is not necessary to wait until a building is about to collapse, and assistance may be secured by way of injunction as soon as it is clear that if something is not done, the harm feared will indeed occur (*Anns v Merton LBC*, 1977; *Crump v Torfaen BC*, 1982).

11.166 Access to Neighbouring Land Act 1992. Where, in order to preserve the condition of land, works are required to neighbouring land, it is possible to obtain an order for access to that neighbouring land in order to carry out the required works (Access to Neighbouring Land Act 1992).

Limitation

11.167 Six years or three years. As a general rule, actions both in tort or contract must be brought within six years of the date on which the cause of action accrued, *i.e.* when the right to sue arose (Limitation Act 1980, ss.2, 5). If, however, the claim is for personal injuries, it must be brought within three years (Limitation Act 1980, s.11). The three years run from when the person injured knew of the injury, knew that it was serious enough to merit action, knew that it was attributable to the landlord's default, and knew who the landlord was (Limitation Act 1980, s.14). Time does not, however, start to run against a minor until he achieves his majority (18) (Limitation Act, 1980, s.28).

11.168 An obligation to keep property in repair is a continuing breach, not a breach only at its outset, so that time can run from any point until the landlord rectifies the defect.

11.169 Latent damage. More problematic is from when times run if a defect is not obvious, perhaps for many years. In such a case, the limitation period will be the longer of the usual six-year period, accruing from the date when the damage came into existence, or three years from the date when the complainant discovers (or could have discovered) the damage (Limitation Act 1980, s.24A, added by Latent Damage Act 1986). An overriding time-limit (or "long-stop") of 15 years is applied, during which the complainant must bring the action (Limitation Act 1980, s.24B, added by Latent Damage Act 1986). A successor in title, who buys in ignorance of the damage, may also benefit from the extended time-limits (Latent Damage Act 1986, s.3).

CHAPTER TWELVE

Housing Acts—Disrepair and Improvement

Introduction

12.01 Purpose of legislation. One of the principal purposes of the Housing Act 1985 ("1985") is to ensure that buildings used for housing are only so used if they are of acceptable standard. Standards are as defined in the 1985 Act. There are several standards which relate to the condition or repair of housing; the principal standard—that of fitness for human habitation—was substantially revised by the Local Government and Housing Act 1989 ("1989"). Additional procedures were introduced by the Housing Grants, Construction and Regeneration Act 1996 ("1996").

12.02 Improvement. Demolition, closure or clearance were, until 1969, the main means of dealing with unfitness. Since then, however, there has been a shift in emphasis towards improvement. The Housing Act 1974 introduced new provisions for improving inadequate housing:

    (a) By way of improvement grants for individual houses, which can sometimes lead to compulsory improvement notices; and,

    (b) By way of the declaration of improvement areas.

12.03 1989 Act. The 1989 Act reflected a further shift in emphasis: it brought in a new test to decide between repair, demolition or closure; the provisions for compulsory improvement notices were repealed; a new set of grants was introduced; new provisions were made for area improvement.

12.04 Grants. The grants provisions have since been replaced by those in the 1996 Act which, in turn, have now been replaced by the Regulatory Reform (Housing Assistance) (England and Wales) Order 2002 (SI 2002/1860, "the regulatory reform order") which introduces a much less prescriptive scheme with wide-ranging power for authorities to provide assistance for housing renewal.

12.05 Other Provisions. Disrepair and unfitness overlaps with issues of environmental health, dealt with in Chapter 13. In addition, there are special provisions governing overcrowding, and multiple occupation, dealt with in Chapter 14. The provisions considered in this Chapter and in those are cumulative. Nor does action under the provisions to be considered in this Chapter exclude civil proceedings by the occupier (Chapter 11).

Outline

12.06 Preliminary matters

- Local authorities are defined for the purposes of the relevant legislation by the Housing Act 1985, s.1.

- These authorities are under a duty to consider the housing conditions in their area at least once a year.

12.07 Unfitness

- The main thrust of the 1985 Act is to ensure that houses which are unfit for human habitation are either repaired or else closed to domestic use (1985, Pts VI and IX).

- A dwelling-house is unfit if it fails to meet one or more of the requirements specified in 1985, s.604 and by reason of that failure is not reasonably suitable for occupation. There are additional requirements relating to flats.

- Once satisfied that a dwelling-house is unfit the authority must serve a repairs notice, a demolition or closing order, or a deferred action notice;

- The authority must, between these options, choose the most satisfactory course of action in accordance with central government guidance.

- Before taking action, however, the authority must in most cases serve a "minded to"—or warning—notice.

- A repairs notice, under 1985, Pt VI, specifies the works which the authority consider necessary to render the premises fit, and is served on the "person having control" of the property the subject of the action (or, in the case of a house in multiple occupation, the "person managing" it).

- A closing order (1985, Pt IX) prevents the premises being used for human habitation; while a demolition order (1985, Pt IX) requires them to be demolished.

- There are provisions for appealing any notice or order; subject thereto, any breach of the requirements of the notice or order is a criminal offence. Authorities may also carry out works in default in some circumstances.

- A deferred action notice does not require any action by the person served, but notifies him of the state of the property, thus giving him a period in which to take voluntary action to remedy the position.

- Onto the framework designed to deal with unfitness in individual houses (Pt VI) have been grafted:

  - Provisions designed to prevent housing which is in serious disrepair but not yet unfit from deteriorating further into actual unfitness; and

  - Provisions permitting local authorities to take action in respect of premises which—without being unfit or in serious disrepair—are nonetheless in such a condition as materially to interfere with the personal comfort of an occupying tenant.

12.08   Slum clearance

- Pt IX of the 1985 Act also concerns the clearance of areas of unfit housing by compulsory purchase and demolition.

- That Part contains additional provisions to deal with obstructive buildings, and to exempt from some of the unfitness procedures houses which are subject to improvement or redevelopment schemes by their owners.

12.09   Grants and Assistance

- Under the 1996 Act there was a scheme for renovation, common parts, disabled facilities and "HMO" (houses in multiple occupation) grants; except for disabled facilities grants, these were all discretionary.

- From July 19, 2002 the regulatory reform order introduced a new regime of "housing assistance", which will run in parallel with the 1996 Act regime for one year, after which the 1996 Act provisions will be repealed, save for the mandatory disabled facilities grants.

- Before the powers under the regulatory reform order can be used, the authority must publish a policy on how they intend to use them.

- The regulatory reform order gives authorities the power to provide "assistance for housing renewal". Assistance may be provided for:
  - Repair improvement and adaptation of housing;
  - Demolition of a dwelling and help with rebuilding costs;
  - Provision of alternative accommodation, either where this supports improvement of living conditions and the authority propose to purchase the existing accommodation or else where the provision of accommodation of alternative accommodation represents a better alternative than repair, improvement or adaptation;

- Assistance may be provided to persons directly, or through a third party and may be in any form, including grants and loans.

12.10 Renewal areas

- Local authorities may declare a renewal area when the requirements set out in the 1989 Act are met.

- Prior to declaring the area, an authority must compile a report on the circumstances justifying the declaration.

- There are publicity requirements which must be met both before and after declaration of the area.

- Once an area has been declared, the authority have additional powers to acquire land in the area and to carry out works on land they own.

12.11 Displacement of occupiers

- Many of the provisions referred to will lead to the displacement of occupiers, permanently or temporarily.

- In the case of permanent displacement, occupiers have will enjoy rights to rehousing and also to compensation, both for tenants and for owner-occupiers.

12.12   Occupier action

- Occupiers may complain to local authorities about conditions.

- The 1985 Act specifically provides for complaint about unfitness to a magistrate and—if satisfied that the complaint is well-founded—the magistrate must forward this to the local authority, who must inspect the premises concerned.

Preliminary matters

12.13   Local authorities. For the purposes of these provisions, local authorities are: (i) district councils; (ii) London Borough Councils; (iii) the Common Council of the City of London; and (iv) Welsh county or county boroughs (1985, s.1), save that in the area of a Housing Action Trust (3.252) these powers may be transferred to the Trust, additionally to or instead of the local authority (Housing Act 1988 ("1988") s.65). Although county councils have some reserve powers in relation to housing, they are powers to provide housing, not to take action under these provisions (1985, s.28). Where there is only one—unitary—authority, whether called district, county or otherwise, they will be the local authority for the purposes of these provisions (The Local Government (Changes for England) Regulations 1994, (S.I. 1994/867)).

12.14   Inspection duties. Under s.605 of the 1985 Act, the authorities mentioned above (12.13), are obliged at least once a year to consider the housing conditions in their district, with a view to deciding what action they ought to take under the provisions to be considered in this Chapter (and in Chapter 14). The Secretary of State is entitled to give the authority directions as to exercise of this duty, with which directions the authority are obliged to comply.

12.15   Housing and environmental health. The 1985 Act may be distinguished from the Environmental Protection Act 1990, considered in the next Chapter, which has as its principal objective the remedying of conditions which are so bad as to put in jeopardy the health of occupants. The provisions of the Housing Act and of the Environmental Protection Act are cumulative, not mutually exclusive: *Salford CC v McNally*, 1975.

12.16 Broadly, the Housing Act sets a higher standard than will be achieved by Environmental Protection Act action and—save in those exceptional circumstances when Environmental Protection Act action encompasses all that action which ought otherwise to have been taken under the Housing Acts or (less exceptionally) vice versa—action under one body of law is no substitute for action under the other (*McNally; R. v Kerrier DC Ex p. Guppy's (Bridport) Ltd*, 1985).

Unfitness

1. DEFINITIONS

12.17 Premises. The most common object of action under the unfitness provisions is the terraced house. The provisions apply, however, to dwelling-houses, houses in multiple occupation and buildings containing flats, purpose built or conversion. A dwelling-house includes both houses, properly so-called and flats (1985, ss.207, 183). "House in multiple occupation" is defined in the same way as for the provisions which deal specifically with such houses (14.18). A building not constructed as a house but used as such will qualify (*Ashbridge Investments v Minister of Housing and Local Government*, 1965).

12.18 Principal definition. The principal definition of unfitness for the purpose of these provisions is contained in s.604 of the 1985 Act. Under that section, a property is fit for human habitation unless it fails to meet one or more of specified requirements and, by reason of that failure, is not reasonably suitable for occupation in that condition.

12.19 The requirements are that the property:

Is structurally stable;

Is free from serious disrepair;

Is free from damp prejudicial to health;

Has adequate provision for lighting, heating and ventilation;

Has an adequate supply of wholesome water;

Has satisfactory facilities for the preparation and cooking of food (including a sink with hot and cold water);

Has a suitably located water-closet;

Has suitably located fixed baths or showers and wash-hand basins with hot and cold water; and,

Has an effective system for the draining of foul, waste and surface water.

12.20   Flats. In addition, where a flat is under consideration, unfitness may be found by reference to the condition of the building in which it is situated (1985, s.604(2)), if it (the building) or part of it fails to meet one of specified requirements and by reason of that failure the flat is not reasonably suitable for occupation.

12.21   The requirements are that the building or part:

Is structurally stable;

Is free from serious disrepair;

Is free from dampness;

Has adequate provision for ventilation; and,

Has an effective system for the draining of foul, waste and surface water.

12.22   Ordinary use. In one case, the only window in one of the bedrooms of a house had a broken sash-cord. It could only be opened at risk of injury, and the house was small enough that— without being able to open the window—it could no longer be said to be properly ventilated.

"If the state of repair of a house is such that by ordinary use damage may naturally be caused to the occupier, either in respect of personal injury to life or limb, or injury to health, then the house is not in all respects reasonably fit for human habitation." (*Morgan v Liverpool Corp*, 1927; *Summers v Salford Corp*, 1943).

2.   OUTLINE OF ACTION

12.23   Four courses of action. If a property is unfit for human habitation, then the burden of action falls on the local authority.

Once satisfied of the unfitness, the authority are bound to take action (*R. v Kerrier DC, Ex p. Guppy's (Bridport)*, 1985), which means one of four courses:

Use the repairs procedure to ensure that the premises are rendered fit again,

Serve a demolition order,

Serve a closing order, or

Serve a deferred action notice.

12.24 Most satisfactory course. In deciding whether to serve a repairs notice, a demolition order, a closing order, or a deferred action notice, the authority must choose that which is the most satisfactory course of action. This new test was introduced by the 1989 Act and replaced the previous—predominantly economic—test of whether the property was repairable at reasonable expense.

12.25 Guidance. Authorities are to make the choice taking into account the Guidance issued by the Secretary of State under s.604A of the Housing Act 1985. This Guidance is currently to be found in the Housing Renewal Guidance (Consultative Document), June 2002, Annex G, and suggests both that the individual unfit property should be looked at in the broader context of its surroundings, and that as well as economic factors, social and environmental ones should be incorporated into the assessment.

12.26 Pre-notice procedures. Under 1996, s.86, there is power for the Secretary of State to introduce a preliminary notice procedure prior to service of a repairs notice, closing or demolition order or deferred action notice, being served. This power has been exercised. Under the Housing (Fitness Enforcement Procedures) Order 1996 (SI 1996/2885), the authority must—unless they consider it necessary to take immediate action—first serve a "minded to" notice, setting out the action they are considering taking and the reasons for it, and giving the person served at least 14 days in which to make representations. The authority must consider any representation made before the action is then taken.

12.27 Charges. Authorities may make reasonable charges in order to recover their administrative and other expenses incurred in taking action to serve or renew a deferred action notice, repairs notice or make a closing or demolition order (1996, s.87). The maximum charge has been set at £300 (Housing (Maximum Charge for Enforcement Action) Order 1996 (SI 1996/2886)).

3. REPAIRS NOTICES

12.28 On whom served. A repairs notice is served on the person having control of the premises (1985, s.189) or, in the case of a flat found to be unfit because of the condition of the building in which it is situated, on the person having control of that part of the building which requires repair. Where a house in multiple occupation is unfit the notice can, alternatively, be served on the person managing the house (14.32). It must, additionally, be served on others with an interest in the premises.

12.29 Person having control. The person having control is defined in relation to a dwelling-house or house in multiple occupation as the person in receipt of not less than two-thirds of the full net annual value of the premises (often referred to as the "rack rent"), whether on his own account or as agent or trustee for another, or who would be in receipt of the rack-rent were the premises let (1985, s.207). A rack-rent means "the full amount which a landlord can reasonably be expected to get from a tenant," having regard (where relevant) to rent restrictions (*Rawlance v Croydon Corp*, 1952). If the landlord cannot be found, the notice may be served on an agent.

12.30 Where action is being taken with regard to a building (12.20) the person having control is the owner who, in the opinion of the authority, ought to execute the works specified in the notice. Owner means the freeholder or someone holding a lease of three years or more (1985, s.207).

12.31 The premises need not be tenanted: the provisions could be, though rarely are, used against owner-occupiers. Where there is a long lease of a dwelling-house, the person having control will usually be the leaseholder, rather than the freeholder.

12.32 The authority may also, but are not obliged to, serve a copy of the notice on anyone else they know to have an interest in the house, such as a freeholder or mortgagee.

12.33 Service on local authorities. Where the authority are themselves the person having control, the repairs notice procedure is inapplicable (*R. v Cardiff CC Ex p. Cross*, 1983). This is because authorities cannot serve notices on themselves, at least where there is no one else to be served with a copy of the notice.

12.34 The exemption does not stem from the authority's status as a public body. Thus, if one authority have property in the area of another authority, it is the second authority who will be obliged to serve notice under s.189, and they are free to serve such a notice on the first authority. Similarly, if the authority serving the notice happen to be the freeholders but a private landlord or housing association is the long leaseholder, the notice should still be served. But if the authority have the leasehold, then even though there may be a private freeholder, the provisions will not apply.

12.35 Contents of repairs notice. The notice must specify what works are, in the opinion of the authority, necessary to render the premises fit, and must state the opinion of the authority that once the works are carried out they will be fit (1985, s.189). The works must be specified with enough precision to enable a reasonable builder to provide an estimate (*Church of Our Lady of Hal v Camden LBC,* 1980).

12.36 Time. The notice must give the person served a minimum of 28 days within which to commence the works and a reasonable period in which to complete them.

12.37 Ancillary provisions. Unless there is an appeal (12.40), the notice will become operative 21 days from service (1985, s.189). If the person served neither appeals nor complies with the notice in the time permitted by the notice, the local authority may themselves go in and do the work in default (1985, s.193) (the expenses of which they can recover).

12.38 It is a criminal offence to fail to comply with the notice (1985, s.198A). Non-compliance means not commencing and completing within the time allowed (subject to the right to appeal: 12.40) or not making reasonable progress with works, in which latter case, however, it is a defence to both a criminal offence and a claim for recovery of works in default that reasonable progress was in fact being made.

12.39 Once the authority have served notice of their intention to execute works in default, a criminal offence may be committed by the person served by any subsequent attempt to do the works, unless he can show that it was necessary in order to obviate danger towards the occupiers.

12.40 Appeal against repairs notice. Appeal lies to the county court, at the instigation of the person served with, or anyone else aggrieved by the service of, the notice (1985, s.191). The appeal must be lodged within 21 days of service. Once the appeal has been lodged, then the notice does not become operative until the time allowed on the final determination of the appeal or 21 days after the withdrawal of an appeal (1985, s.193).

12.41 The county court has power to confirm the notice, to quash it or to vary it, *e.g.* by the addition or deletion of works. There is a specific ground of appeal applicable to repair of parts of a building containing flats which are outside the flat itself, that some other person ought to do or pay (in whole or part) for the cost of the works, in which case the court can also vary the notice, or make a cost-allocation order between those who it considers should pay for the work (1985, s.191(3A)).

12.42 It is a specific ground of appeal that a demolition order or closing order would have been a more satisfactory course of action: if the judge decides to allow the appeal on this basis, then the authority may ask him to include in his judgment a specific finding as to the most satisfactory course of action, with which request the judge is bound to comply. Failure to serve a "minded to" notice (12.26), also provides a ground of appeal.

4. CLOSING AND DEMOLITION ORDERS

12.43 Closing orders. A closing order may be made where an authority are of the opinion that it is the most satisfactory course of action (12.24) for an unfit dwelling-house, house in multiple occupation or building (1985, s.264). The order is to be served on any owner of the premises (12.30) and every mortgagee whom it is reasonably practical to ascertain (1985, s.268).

12.44 Effect of closing order. The order prohibits the use of the premises for any purpose other than a purpose approved by the local authority (1985, s.267). The order will become operative 21 days after service, unless there is an appeal (12.59), in which case the order will become operative on the final determination of the appeal (1985, s.268). Use of the premises in contravention of the closing order may constitute a criminal offence (1985, s.277).

12.45 Protection, rehousing and compensation. Tenants in premises the subject of a closing order will lose any Housing Act

1988 and Rent Act 1977 protection they may enjoy (1985, s.276), but they, as other occupiers, will gain rights to rehousing (12.142–12.148) and to compensation (12.149–12.158). The fact that statutory protection has been lifted does not mean that the landlord can recover possession without terminating the contractual tenancy (1.45–1.59; *Aslan v Murphy*, 1989).

12.46 Approved uses. No express provision is made for seeking the approval of the local authority to use the premises for a particular (non-residential) purpose (12.44): such approval may be granted on the issue of the closing order, or may be granted later. By necessary construction of the provisions, such approved use will not include use for human habitation. The authority are not unreasonably to withhold consent to a particular use (1985, s.267), and a person aggrieved by the withholding of such a consent may appeal to the county court against the refusal within 21 days of the refusal (1985, s.267).

12.47 Revocation. Application may be made for revocation of the closing order, in whole or in part, on the ground that the premises have again been rendered wholly or partially fit for human habitation (1985, s.278(1)). Refusal of revocation may be appealed (1985, s.278(2)), though not by anyone still in occupation under a tenancy of which there is less than three years to run (1985, s.278(3)), which will include a periodic tenant, such as a weekly or monthly tenant.

12.48 Substitution of demolition order. At any time after a closing order has been made on a house (but not a flat), the authority may revoke it and substitute a demolition order: this might occur if houses in a terrace have been closed individually, but not demolished because of the support they provide to houses not yet closed, but the last house has itself now been closed or ordered to be demolished, so that the need for support has gone (1985, s.279). If the authority substitute a demolition order for a closing order, then the same consequences follow as if they had imposed a demolition order in the first place (12.49–12.58), although time for appeal (12.59) will run from the date of substitution of the demolition order, not from the original imposition of the closing order.

12.49 Demolition orders. As with a closing order, a demolition order may be made where the authority are of the opinion that this is the most satisfactory course of action (12.24) for an unfit dwelling-house, house in multiple occupation or building (1985, s.265). The order is to be served on any owner of the premises (12.30) and every mortgagee whom it is reasonably practical to ascertain (1985, s.268).

12.50   Effect of demolition order. Unless there is an appeal against a demolition order (12.59), the order becomes operative 21 days after service (1985, s.268). The order will specify a time within which the building is to be vacated, which is to be not less than 28 days after the order becomes operative, and a time within which it is to be demolished, which is to be within six weeks of the premises being vacated or such longer period as the authority may specify (1985, s.267).

12.51   Notice to Occupiers. Once the order has become operative, the authority are bound to serve on any occupier in the premises a notice which states the effect of the order, specifies the date by which the building is to be vacated, and requires the occupier to quit within 28 days of service of this notice (1985, s.270).

12.52   Protection, rehousing and compensation. Once a tenant is obliged to quit, he loses any Housing Act 1988 and Rent Act protection he enjoys (1985, s.270), although he, and other occupiers, will, again (12.45), be entitled to rehousing (12.142–12.148) and to compensation (12.149–12.158).

12.53   Ancillary provisions. Entry into occupation of the premises after the order has become operative is a criminal offence (1985, s.270). Not only can the landlord seek possession of the premises from an occupier, but so also can the local authority (1985, s.270). The authority have power to cleanse the building of vermin before demolition, should it appear to be necessary (1985, s.273). If the owner does not proceed to demolish the building, the authority may themselves do so in default (1985, s.271), and recover their costs.

12.54   Substitution of closing order. If, after a demolition order has become operative, but before the house is demolished, the house becomes a listed building under the Planning (Listed Buildings and Conservation Areas) Act 1990, s.1, the authority are to substitute a closing order (1985, s.304).

12.55   Deferral and revocation. An owner, or anyone else who appears to the authority to be in a position to put such a proposal into practice, may also cause demolition to be deferred, to provide an opportunity for the premises to be reconstructed, enlarged or improved in such a way as to provide one or more dwellings fit for human habitation (1985, s.274). If the works are completed to the authority's satisfaction, the demolition order is then determined.

12.56 Purchase notice. In place of either demolition or closing order, the authority may serve a purchase notice, if it appears to them that the premises are, or can be, rendered capable of providing accommodation which is adequate for the time being (1985, s.300). They cannot purchase premises which are a listed building (1985, s.300(5), see also 12.54). These provisions cannot be used when the premises are a flat, although the authority may purchase a whole building containing flats, if an order has been made on the building itself.

12.57 Effect of purchase notice. The purchase notice becomes operative 21 days after service, unless there is an appeal (12.59), in which case it will become operative on the final determination of the appeal (1985, s.300(2)). If the owner will not agree to sell the house to the authority, the authority may, with government consent, compulsorily purchase it (1985, s.300(3)). Compensation will be available to owner-occupiers, tenants or other occupiers when they are actually moved (12.149–12.158, but see 1973, s.41), at which point they will also acquire rights to rehousing (12.142–12.148). During the intervening period, any Housing Act protection is lost (1988, s.1 and Sch.1, para.12) as is any Rent Act protection (Rent Act 1977, ss.14, 19), but it would seem that occupiers do not become secure tenants of the authority (1985, s.79 and Sch.1, para.3: 3.39(e)).

12.58 Use for time being. It is implicit in the provisions that the standard to which a property that has been purchased is to be maintained for the time being is lower than that of fitness for human habitation, and the provisions of s.8 of the Landlord and Tenant Act 1985 (11.43–11.46) are expressly stated not to apply (1985, s.302). The purpose of the power is to do no more than provide temporary accommodation: the power cannot be used to add to the authority's permanent housing stock (*Victoria Square Property Co Ltd v Southwark LBC*, 1977). The provisions of the Environmental Protection Act (Chapter 13) will, however continue to apply, and the authority must prevent the property from becoming a statutory nuisance as long as it remains in use (*Salford CC v McNally*, 1975).

12.59 Appeals. A demolition order, closing order, or purchase notice can be appealed to the county court, which has power to confirm, quash, or vary the notice or order (1985, s.269(3)). The appeal must be lodged within 21 days of service of the appropriate notice, and pending the appeal, the authority are to carry out no action in relation to the notice (1985, s.269). A tenant may not appeal if he is in occupation under a lease with less than three years to run, *e.g.* a periodic tenant (1985, s.269(2)), although in the rare circumstances when a challenge can be made on principles of administrative law (10.173), such a tenant may seek a judicial review of the authority's decision (*R. v Maldon DC Ex p. Fisher*, 1986; *R. v Woking BC Ex p. Adam*, 1995).

12.60 It is a specific ground of appeal that an alternative course of action, *i.e.* repair or demolition in the case of a closing order, and repair or closure in the case of a demolition order, would have been a more satisfactory course of action (12.24). If the judge decides to allow the appeal on this basis, then the authority may ask him to include in his judgment a specific finding as to the most satisfactory course of action, with which request the judge is bound to comply. Failure to serve a "minded to" notice (12.26), also affords a ground of appeal.

5. DEFERRED ACTION NOTICES

12.61 Content. A deferred action notice does not require any action by the person served, but notifies him of the state of the property, thus providing a period in which he may take voluntary action to remedy the position. A deferred action notice must state (1996, s.81) that the authority are of the opinion that the premises are unfit, must specify the works which are required to make them fit, and must set out the other courses of action available to the authority (repairs notice, closing or demolition order). The notice may only be served if the authority are of the opinion that deferred action is the most satisfactory course of action (12.24), although the notice does not prevent the authority from taking any other course of action in relation to the premises at any time.

12.62 Service. The notice is served on the person having control of the dwelling-house or house in multiple occupation (12.29). Where action is being taken with regard to a building (12.20) it is served on the person having control of the building (12.30).

12.63 Appeal. A deferred action notice may be appealed to the county court by a person aggrieved (1996, s.83). The appeal must be lodged within 21 days, and the grounds for and effect of appeal are the same as for repairs notices (12.40).

12.64 Review. The deferred action notice may be reviewed at any time, but must be reviewed within two years of service (1996, s.84). The review must include an inspection of the property. If the authority decide that the deferred action notice remains the most satisfactory course of action, they must renew it and serve notice of their decision. Or, the authority may decide to take one of the other courses of action open to them (as they can do without a review: above, 12.61). If other than following a review, the deferred action notice automatically ceases to the operative (1996, s.84(6)). The notice of decision on review is itself open to appeal in the same way as an initial notice (12.40).

6. ANCILLARY PROVISIONS

12.65 Powers of entry, offences and other orders. The 1985 Act contains a number of related powers:

(a) Permitting authorities to enter premises (s.319);

(b) Creating additional offences of obstruction of authorities or, in some circumstances, persons served with notice requiring works (ss.315, 320); and

(c) Granting the county court power to make orders affecting or altering the rights of persons affected, or who may be affected, by local authority action under the Act (ss.317–318).

7. SERIOUS DISREPAIR

12.66 Prevention of unfitness. Where an authority are satisfied that, although a dwelling-house or house in multiple occupation is not unfit for human habitation, substantial repairs are required to bring the property up to a reasonable standard, they may serve a repairs notice (1985, s.190(1)). Where they are satisfied that the works are necessary to bring the flat up to a reasonable standard, such a notice may also be served in relation to a building containing a flat where works are necessary to a part of the building outside the flat (1985, s.190(1A)).

12.67 The purpose of this provision is to prevent housing becoming unfit (*Hillbank Properties Ltd v Hackney LBC*, 1978). Save in respect of a house in multiple occupation and where premises are in a renewal area (12.130), such a notice cannot, however, be served unless there is an "occupying tenant," which means someone who is not an owner-occupier who is a tenant, a statutory tenant (5.24), a restricted contract occupier (6.64) or an agricultural occupier (4.52, 5.15) (1985, s.207).

12.68 The provisions relating to pre-notice procedures (12.26) and charging (12.27) governing a repairs notice on unfit property, also apply to a repairs notice under s.190.

12.69 Notice. The notice is served on the person having control of the premises, or—in the case of a house in multiple occupation—alternatively on its manager, and on others with a relevant interest in them (12.29). It must allow a minimum of 28 days for commencement of the works and a reasonable time for completion. It must specify the works required, which cannot include works of internal decorative repair. In all other respects, the provisions governing the service of such a notice are the same as those governing an unfitness repairs notice, including the power of the local authority to execute works in default and the offence of non-compliance (12.37).

12.70 Reasonable expense? Although not specified in the legis-lation, it has been held that such a notice should only be served if the works could be executed at a reasonable expense (*Hillbank Properties Ltd v Hackney LBC*, 1978). In this latter respect, however, it would seem that a county court on appeal can take a broad, social view of what constitutes reasonable expense (*Kenny v Kingston-upon-Thames Royal LBC*, 1985). As the requirement of repairability at a reasonable expense in relation to unfit premises has now been repealed, however, there must be some doubt as to whether these propositions remain good law.

8.   INTERFERENCE WITH PERSONAL COMFORT

12.71 Complaint of occupying tenant. Where an authority are satisfied that premises are in such a state of disrepair that, although not unfit, the condition is such as materially to interfere with the comfort of an "occupying tenant" (12.67), they may also serve a repairs notice (1985, s.191).

12.72 Such a notice can either be served on the authority's own initiative or on the complaint to the authority of an "occupying tenant." All of the remarks made in paragraphs (12.68–12.70) apply in relation to a personal comfort repairs notice. It is also limited in the same way and to the same extent as a serious disrepair notice (12.67), to properties where there is an occupying tenant.

9 REDEVELOPMENT AND IMPROVEMENT BY OWNERS

12.73 Proposals by owners. The Act contains provisions permitting the submission of proposals:

    (a) For the redevelopment of property; or

    (b) For the improvement of property (1985, ss.308, 310).

12.74 If accepted by the authority, a redevelopment scheme prevents any action under the provisions considered above, or under the clearance area provisions considered below. If accepted by the authority, an improvement scheme prevents action under the procedures to close, demolish or purchase the premises considered above (12.43–12.60), or the clearance area provisions considered below.

12.75 Neither set of provisions is available when a demolition order has already become operative (12.50), or if the property is in a clearance area in respect of which there is already a confirmed compulsory purchase order (12.80, (1985, s.310)). Note, however, the availability of alternative provisions in the case of an operative demolition order (12.55).

Slum Clearance

1. CLEARANCE AREAS

12.76 Decline of use. Clearance areas were once the principal means of dealing with large sections of unfit housing. Today, improvement is more probable, although clearance has recently enjoyed a resurgence to deal with areas of uneconomic housing where the private market has collapsed and properties have been left vacant.

12.77 Outline. In outline, the clearance area provisions operate by:

    (a) Declaration of clearance area;

   (b) Compulsory purchase proceedings to enable the local authority to acquire property not already in their ownership;

   (c) Demolition.

12.78 Provision is also made for temporary user pending demolition (12.86).

12.79 **Pre-conditions.** The pre-conditions for declaration of a clearance area are:

   (a) **Unfitness.** The authority are satisfied that "residential buildings," (dwelling-houses, houses in multiple occupation and buildings containing one or more flats), in the area are unfit for human habitation; or

   (b) **Bad arrangement.** The authority are satisfied that residential buildings in the area are dangerous or injurious to the health of inhabitants, by reason of their bad arrangement, or the narrowness or bad arrangement of the streets; and

   (c) **Non-residential buildings.** The authority are satisfied that any other buildings in the area are also dangerous or injurious to the health of inhabitants, for the same reasons; and

   (d) **Demolition the most satisfactory course.** The authority are satisfied that the most satisfactory course of action having regard to the Code of Guidance (see 12.25) is demolition of all the buildings in the area; and

   (e) **Representations.** The authority have considered representations made to them following the consultation they are required to carry out with those with an interest in the buildings and the occupiers of any residential buildings; and

   (f) **Alternative accommodation.** The authority are satisfied that they can provide or secure alternative accommodation for those displaced prior to demolition; and

   (g) **Resources.** The authority are satisfied that they have sufficient resources to carry out the clearance programme (1985, s.289).

12.80 **Compulsory purchase.** The principal stage in the clearance procedure is compulsory purchase (1985, s.290). The authority are entitled not only to seek to purchase the houses and other buildings in the area, but also any land (including houses and other buildings) surrounded by the area, or adjoining the area, which is necessary in order to acquire a cleared area of convenient shape, or in order satisfactorily to develop the area (1985, s.290(2)).

12.81 Own land. The authority may include in the proposals any land which they already themselves own, which qualifies either under the principal criteria (12.79) or under the "added land" provisions (1985, s.293) referred to in 12.80.

12.82 Need for confirmation. Compulsory purchase will require central government approval, which will normally mean an inquiry into the proposals. At any time before the compulsory purchase order is confirmed, application can be made for the exclusion of land from the order on the ground that the owner will himself execute the demolition and that the authority do not, in those circumstances, actually need the land for the purpose of redevelopment of the area (1985, s.292).

12.83 Protection, rehousing and compensation. Tenants and other occupiers displaced by the programme will be entitled to rehousing (12.142–12.148) and to compensation (12.149–12.158). Tenants will lose any status as assured under the 1988 Act (1988, s.1 and Sch.1, para.12) once the authority become their landlord, and any Rent Act protection, (1977, ss.14, 19) but, it would seem, will not become secure tenants of the authority (3.39(e) and 1985, s.79 and Sch.1, para.3).

12.84 Relocation grant. Unless already incorporated into their housing assistance scheme (12.98), until July 17, 2003, local authorities must, as part of their decision-making process, also consider whether to introduce a relocation grant scheme, as a part of the clearance process (1996, s.131). After that date, the relocation grant scheme will be abolished.

12.85 Demolition. Once the order has been confirmed, the authority's main obligation is to demolish all the buildings on the land, and either sell or let the land for redevelopment or themselves redevelop the land (1985, s.291).

12.86 Demolition only follows "as soon as may be," an extremely vague phrase: commonly, clearance area land is left untreated for many years. If satisfied that the houses are, or can be rendered, capable of providing accommodation "at a standard which is adequate for the time being," the authority may postpone demolition and retain the housing in use, (*cf.* 12.58; 1985, s.301). This is implicitly a standard that is lower than that of fitness for human habitation, and s.8 of the Landlord and Tenant Act 1985 (11.43–11.46) is expressly excluded. The provisions of the Environmental Protection Act will, however, continue to apply (Chapter 13), so that the authority must prevent the property from becoming a statutory nuisance so long as it remains in use (*Salford CC v McNally*, 1975).

2. OBSTRUCTIVE BUILDINGS

12.87 Dangerous or injurious to health. The local authority also enjoy powers in relation to "obstructive buildings," defined as a building which "by reason only of its contact with, or proximity to, other buildings, is dangerous or injurious to health" (1985, s.283). This power extends beyond housing to any building (13.12). The procedure is similar to that which used to lead to a demolition order; the minded to and deferred action procedures do not apply. Instead, the time-and-place procedure is retained, which results in a meeting at the property at which all its owners are entitled to be heard. Not until this has taken place can the authority proceed to a demolition order, with rights of appeal (1985, ss.284, 285). However, the proceedings cannot be used against the property of statutory undertakers (*e.g.* gas, electricity or water suppliers), nor can it be used against the property of any local authority (1985, s.283).

12.88 Ancillary provisions. Tenants lose any Housing Act 1988 and Rent Act security they may enjoy (1985, s.286), but they and other occupiers will acquire rights to rehousing (12.142–12.148) and to compensation (12.149–12.157). In addition, an owner can serve on the authority a purchase notice, requiring the authority to buy the property and carry out the demolition themselves as owners, instead of by way of requiring the owner to demolish (1985, s.287). A criminal offence may be committed by entry into occupation after the demolition order has become operative (1985, s.286).

Improvements, Grants and Housing Assistance

12.89 Improvements. "Improvements," or other works to a house, may involve application for permission under the Town and

Country Planning Act 1990, or may have to comply with the Building Regulations under the Building Act 1984 (in London, with the London Building Acts). Further, when the occupier is a leaseholder or tenant, the permission of the landlord may be necessary; and even a freeholder, or a leaseholder or tenant, may find that those in possession of neighbouring land enjoy the benefit of covenants restricting what the person wishing to carry out the improvements may do, *e.g.* if the improvements were to interfere with a right of way, or of light, or of support.

12.90 Nor does a landlord have an unfettered right to improve under the terms of lease or tenancy. Whether or not the landlord can execute improvements will depend on the terms of the tenancy. A clause that is too wide may be considered inconsistent with the covenant for quiet enjoyment (8.72), and will be construed (in the tenant's favour) narrowly so as to avoid any such conflict: *Yeomans Row Management Ltd v Bodentie-Meyrick*, 2002.

12.91 Statutory right to improve. Certain Rent Act protected tenants, Rent Act statutory tenants and Housing Act secure tenants, enjoy a qualified statutory "right to improve" their homes. It is a term of all such tenancies that the tenant will not make any improvement without the written consent of the landlord, which consent is not unreasonably to be withheld (Housing Act 1980, s.81; Housing Act 1985, ss.79–99). Although cast in a negative frame, the term substantively confers a positive entitlement to improve, where consent has been granted. A refusal of consent can be challenged in the county court (1980, s.82; 1985, s.110).

12.92 The term does not apply, however, in the case of a protected shorthold tenant (Chapter 6), or one to whom notice has been given under the mandatory grounds for possession in the Rent Act 1977 (5.123–5.142). Nor are Housing Act assured tenants under the Housing Act 1988 (see Chapter 4) included.

12.93 For these purposes, improvement includes addition or alteration to a dwelling, and external decorations (1980, s.81(5); 1985, s.97).

12.94 If the landlord does refuse consent, he is obliged to provide a written statement of reasons and in the course of any subsequent challenge by the tenant, the burden will lie on the landlord to show that the refusal was reasonable, *e.g.* because the improvement would make the dwelling, or neighbouring premises, less safe, or would cause him to incur additional expenditure, or would reduce the value of the house either for the purposes of sale or rental (1980, s.82; 1985, s.98).

12.95   Grants. The current regime under which grant-aid may be available to owners and tenants to carry out improvements is shortly to undergo a major change. Under the 1996 Act, there was a statutorily defined structure of discretionary and mandatory grants, with detailed provisions governing application, entitlement and payments. That Act also contained provision for group repair schemes and home repair assistance. The regulatory reform order (12.04, above) introduces a substantially more flexible system of "housing assistance," "both in terms of the policy tools available to [authorities], and in terms of their ability to work in partnership with others (Housing Renewal Guidance (Consultative Document) June 2002, ODPM, "the guidance").

12.96   Transitional arrangements. The regulatory reform order came into force on July 19, 2002, and from that time local authorities may move over to the provision of assistance under the order rather than the 1996 Act. The relevant provisions of the 1996 Act will, however, be repealed with effect from July 18, 2003 (for which reason they are not detailed here).

12.97   Disabled Facilities Grant. Under the 1996 Act, the only mandatory grant was that for disabled facilities. Such grants will remain available and are considered below (12.107).

1.   HOUSING ASSISTANCE

12.98   Adoption of policy. Before providing assistance under the regulatory reform order, an authority must have adopted a policy for the provision of assistance, of which they must have given public notice (regulatory reform order, art. 4). The authority must ensure that a full copy of the policy is available for inspection free of charge at their principal office at all reasonable times and that a summary document is available by post on payment of a reasonable charge. Any assistance must be provided in accordance with the policy.

12.99   Types of assistance. The purposes for which assistance may be provided are to be found in art.3 of the regulatory reform order. For the purpose of improving living conditions in their area, local authorities may provide direct or indirect assistance to a person for the purposes of enabling him (art. 3(1)):

(a) To acquire living accommodation (whether within or outside their area);

(b) To adapt or improve living accommodation (whether by alteration, conversion or enlargement);

(c) To repair living accommodation;

(d) To demolish building comprising of including living accommodation; or,

(e) Where buildings comprising or including living accommodation have been demolished, to construct buildings that comprise or include replacement living accommodation.

12.100 Living accommodation. For these purposes, "living accommodation" means a building or part of a building, or a caravan, boat or similar structure, occupied or available for occupation for residential purposes (art. 2).

12.101 Types of assistance. Assistance may be provided in any form and may be subject to conditions, including as to repayment or making a contribution towards the assisted work (art. 3(3), (4)). Examples of possible conditions, *e.g.* as to eligibility and payment, are provided in Annex B of the Guidance. Before imposing a condition as to repayment or contribution, the authority must have regard to the ability of the person to make the repayment or contribution.

12.102 The primary means of assistance will be grants or loans (see Guidance, Chapter 3), although other forms of assistance, *e.g.* discounted materials, access to tool hire schemes, may also be provided. Where a loan is given, the authority may take any form of security in respect of it (art. 3(6)). Where the security is a charge on a property, the authority may at any time reduce the priority of the charge or secure its removal (art. 3(7)).

12.103 Statements, advice and assistance. Before providing any assistance, the authority must provide the person with a statement in writing of any conditions attaching to the assistance, and satisfy themselves that the person has received appropriate advice or information about the extent and nature of any obligation (whether financial or otherwise) to which he will become subject as a consequence of the assistance (art. 3(5)).

12.104 Consent of owner. By art.5 of the regulatory reform order, assistance to adapt, improve, repair or demolish living accommodation may not be given unless the authority are satisfied that the owner of the living accommodation has consented to the works. The owner is the person entitled to receive (or would be so entitled if the accommodation was let) a rent at an annual rate of not less than two-thirds of the net annual value who is not himself liable as tenant of the accommodation to pay such a rent to a superior landlord. Where the accommodation is a caravan, boat or similar structure, the owner is the person currently entitled to dispose of it.

12.105 Provision of information and evidence. The authority may require a person to whom assistance has been provided or who has applied for assistance to provide them, within a reasonable period, with such information as they may reasonably require (art. 6). This may include information as to the person's financial circumstances. The regulatory reform order does not lay down any procedures which authorities have to adopt, but guidance is provided in Annex B of the Guidance.

12.106 Central government contributions. Contributions towards expenditure incurred in providing housing assistance may be made by the Secretary of State in England, or the National Assembly in Wales (art. 7).

2. DISABLED FACILITIES GRANT

12.107 Nature of grant. A "disabled facilities grant" is available for the provision of facilities for a disabled person in a dwelling, a qualifying houseboat or park home, or in common parts of a building (1996, s.1).

12.108 Qualifying houseboat. A qualifying house boat is a boat or similar structure designed or adapted for use as a place of permanent habitation which has its only or main mooring with the area of a single local authority, which is moored in pursuance of a right to that mooring and which is a dwelling for council tax purposes (1996, s.58).

12.109 Qualifying park home. A qualifying park home is a caravan within the meaning of the Caravan Sites and Control of Development Act 1960, Pt 1, which is stationed on land forming part of a protected site within the meaning of the Mobile Homes Act 1983, which is occupied under an agreement to which the 1983 Act applies or a gratuitous licence, and which is a dwelling for council tax purposes (1996, s.58).

12.110 Purposes of grant. A disabled facilities grant may not be approved unless the authority are satisfied that the works are necessary and appropriate to meet the needs of the disabled occupant; and that it is reasonable and practicable to carry out the works having regard to the age or the condition of the building (1996, s.24(3)). Applications should be assessed in conjunction with the social services authority.

12.111 The grant is available if it is for one or more of the following purposes:

(a) Facilitating access by the disabled occupant to and egress from the premises;

(b) Making the dwelling, qualifying houseboat or park home (12.108, 12.109) or building safe for the disabled occupant or other persons residing with him;

(c) Facilitating access by the disabled occupant to a room used or usable as the principal family room;

(d) Facilitating access to, or providing, a room used or usable for sleeping;

(e) Facilitating access to, or providing, a room in which there is a lavatory, bath, shower or wash-hand basin, or facilitating the use of such a facility;

(f) Facilitating the preparation and cooking of food;

(g) Improving any heating system in the dwelling to meet the needs of the disabled occupant, or, if there is no existing heating system or it is unsuitable, providing a suitable system;

(h) Facilitating the use by the disabled occupant of a source of power, light or heat, by altering the position of access and control or providing additional means of control;

(i) Facilitating access and movement by the disabled occupant around the dwelling in order to enable him to care for a person who is normally resident in the dwelling and is in need of such care; and,

(j) Other purposes specified by the Secretary of State (1996, s.23(1)).

12.112 Constraints on commencement of works. Works for which it is intended to apply for a disabled facilities grant should generally not have been started before approval of application, unless there is good reason and provided the works have not been completed (1996, s.29).

12.113 Pre-conditions. An application for a disabled facilities grant must be in writing and include details of the works and at least two estimates for the costs of carrying out the works (1996, s.2). The applicant must be at least 18 years old (1996, s.3).

12.114 Required interest. The applicant must have the requisite interest in the property. He must either be an owner, *i.e.* the freeholder or under a leasehold interest of at least five years, or be a tenant (1996, s.19). In the case of a qualifying houseboat or park home, he may be an occupier of the houseboat or park home.

12.115 Future use. An application for a disabled facilities grant must be accompanied by either an owner's certificate stating that the applicant has or proposes to acquire an owner's interest (12.114) and intends that the disabled occupant will live in the property as his only or main residence for five years, or a tenant's certificate stating that the applicant is a tenant and has the same intention (1996, ss.21, 22).

12.116 In the case of a qualifying houseboat or park home (12.108, 12.109), an occupier's certificate is required stating that the disabled occupier will live in the houseboat or park home as his only or main residence for five years (1996, s.22A).

12.117 The authority may in the case of any of the certificates set a shorter period of intended residence, as the health of the disabled person or other relevant circumstances permit.

12.118 Approval. Authorities must, by notice in writing, approve or refuse a grant application as soon as reasonably practicable, and in any event no later than six months after it has been made (1996, s.34).

12.119 An approval must include a statement of the works eligible for grant, the amount of expenses which in the authority's opinion are properly incurred on the eligible works, together with any preliminary or ancillary services or charges (*e.g.* the cost of having plans drawn up) and the amount of grant which will be paid.

12.120 Grant Maxima. The amount of grant will be calculated applying the means testing provisions (12.121). Maximum amounts

(1996, s.33) have been set, of £25,000 in England, and £30,000 in Wales (the Disabled Facilities and Home Repair Assistance (Maximum Amounts) Order 1996, (SI 1996/2888), as amended).

12.121 Means-testing. Where the application is by an owner-occupier or a tenant, the amount of grant is reduced in accordance with regulations which are very similar to those applied to housing benefit calculations, and which ascertain an amount which the applicant could himself finance, and by which the grant is accordingly reduced (1996, s.30).

12.122 Landlords' means test. The means-testing provisions applicable where the application is by a landlord letting or intending to let to a disabled occupier, are somewhat less proscribed. In deciding the amount of grant, the authority should have regard to the extent to which the landlord is able to charge a higher rent for the premises because of the works and such other matters as may be directed pursuant to the statute (1996, s.31). Authorities may seek the advice of rent officers (1996, s.31(4)).

12.123 Payment of grant. Once approved, an authority may only refuse to pay the grant in one or more of seven circumstances:

Where the applicant ceases to be a person entitled to the grant;

Where the authority ascertain that the amount to be paid was determined on the basis of inaccurate or incomplete information and exceeds that to which the applicant was entitled;

Where the applicant fails to complete the works satisfactorily within the time allowed (12.126);

Where the cost of the eligible works and costs incurred on preliminary or ancillary service is less than the estimated expense;

Where the authority ascertain that without their knowledge the works were not carried out by one of the contractors who submitted an estimate (1996, ss.42, 43);

Where the works are not carried out to the satisfaction of the authority; and,

Where the applicant fails to provide an acceptable invoice, demand or receipt for payment for the works or for the preliminary or ancillary services and charges (1996, s.37).

12.124 In such circumstances there are provisions, where appropriate, for the recovery of grant already paid (1996, ss.42, 43).

12.125 Stage payments. The authority may make payment in whole after completion of the works. Alternatively, they may make stage payments, as the work progresses, provided that no more than nine-tenths of the grant is paid before completion (1996, s.35). The authority may specify a delayed date for payment, up to 12 months after the date of application (1996, s.36). This is to enable authorities to stagger payments of the grant to fit into their budgets. Grants may be paid directly to the contractor provided that the applicant was informed of this prior to approval of the grant (1996, s.39).

12.126 Conditions as to completion of works. The authority may make it a condition of the grant that the works are carried out in accordance with their specifications, *e.g.* as to materials to be used. It is a mandatory condition of all grants that the works are finished within 12 months of approval, although the authority may extend this time at their discretion (1996, s.37). It is also a mandatory condition that the works are carried out by one of the two contractors from whom estimates were submitted with the application, unless the authority direct otherwise (1996, s.38). An approved contractor scheme may be centrally established, in which case it will be a condition that the contractor is a member of the scheme.

12.127 Compensation conditions. With the consent of the Secretary of State, an authority may attach a condition that the applicant takes reasonable steps to pursue any relevant insurance or legal claim which relates to the premises, *e.g.* where a grant is being sought following fire damage and an insurance claim can be made (1996, s.51).

12.128 Other conditions. Other conditions may be applied with the consent of the Secretary of State, *e.g.* as to nomination rights, insurance or maintenance (1996, s.52).

12.129 Voluntary repayment. An owner or mortgagee entitled to exercise the power of sale can repay the grant voluntarily. On such a repayment, all grant conditions cease to have effect (1996, s.55).

Renewal Areas

12.130 Area action. The provisions governing the declaration of and powers and duties in renewal areas are to be found in Local

Government and Housing Act 1989, Pt VII, as amended by the Regulatory Reform Order.

12.131 Declaration. The starting-point for the declaration of a renewal area is a "report" requested by the local housing authority, which should contain a reasoned recommendation that the renewal area should be declared (1989, s.89).

12.132 The report may include any matters which the authority consider relevant and in particular must include particulars of the following matters:

(a) **Living conditions.** The living conditions in the area concerned;

(b) **Improvement.** The ways in which conditions may be improved (whether by the declaration of a renewal area or otherwise);

(c) **Powers.** The powers available to the authority if the area is declared;

(d) **Proposals.** The authority's detailed proposals for the exercise of those powers during the period that the area will be a renewal area;

(e) **Costs.** The costs of the proposals;

(f) **Resources.** The financial resources available, or likely to be available, to the authority for implementing the proposal; and,

(g) **Representations.** Any representations (12.135) made to the authority in relation to the proposals.

12.133 Guidance. A renewal area may be declared if the authority are satisfied, on the basis of the report, that the living conditions in an area within their district which consists primarily of housing accommodation, are unsatisfactory and can most effectively be dealt with by declaring a renewal area (1989, s.89(1)). In reaching this decision or a decision to extend (12.136), the authority must have regard to the central government guidance issued (1989, s.89(5)), to be found in Housing Renewal Guidance (Consultative Document) (ODPM, June 2002), Annex H.

12.134 The guidance recommends a method known as Neighbourhood Renewal Assessment which "provides a thorough and systematic appraisal technique for considering alternative courses of action." It involves both an economic and a socio-environmental assessment of different options.

12.135 Prior publicity. Prior to declaration, the authority must take steps designed to secure that the proposals are brought to the attention of persons residing or owning property in the proposed area, and that those persons are informed of the name and address of the person to whom inquiries and representations concerning the proposals should be addressed (1989, s.89(6), (7)).

12.136 Duration and termination. It is for the authority to determine the length the renewal area is to last (1989, s.89(4)(a)). The authority may decide to extend the period (1989, s.89(4)(b)). Or, the authority may decide to bring the area to an end at an earlier date, or to exclude land from it (1989, s.95). Prior and subsequent to making such a resolution, the authority must fulfil requirements as to publicity and consideration of representations.

12.137 Duties and powers. As soon as possible after the declaration or any later extension, the authority must take steps designed to secure that their decision is brought to the attention of persons residing or owning property in the proposed area, and that those persons are informed of the name and address of the person to whom inquiries and representations concerning action to be taken should be addressed (1989, s.91). As well as the duty to publicise the declaration, the authority are under a continuing duty to bring to the attention of residents and property-owners information about the proposed and existing action in the area and assistance available for the carrying out of works (1989, s.92).

12.138 Compulsory purchase powers. Local housing authorities may by agreement or, with the consent of the Secretary of State, compulsorily acquire land in a renewal area which comprises premises consisting of or including housing accommodation. The purchase must be for one of the following objectives (1989, s.93):

(a) Improvement or repair of premises, either by the authority or by someone (*e.g.* a housing association) to whom they propose to dispose of them;

(b) Proper and effective management and use of housing accommodation, again either by the authority themselves or by another; or,

(c) The well-being of residents in the area.

12.139 The authority may also compulsorily acquire any land in the area in order to improve the amenities in the area, whether they intend to effect the improvement themselves or dispose of the land to someone else intending to do so (1989, s.93(4)).

12.140 Works. The authority have power to carry out works on any land they own in the area (whether acquired under their powers of acquisition outlined above, or not) (1989, s.93(5)). This power may be delegated to a housing association or other person.

12.141 Ancillary provisions. There are also special powers relating to extinguishing rights of ways over highways (1989, s.94) and powers of entry, together with correlative offences of obstruction, in order to survey and inspect (1989, s.97).

Rehousing and Compensation

1. REHOUSING

12.142 Relationship to homelessness. The rights to be considered under this heading are entirely separate from, and are additional to, those provided under Pt VII of the Housing Act 1996 (Chapter 10). Thus, for example, it is not necessary for a displaced occupant qualifying under these provisions also to show that he has a priority need for accommodation (10.29–10.44). Nor is rehousing under these provisions an allocation under Pt VI (10.194) (Allocation of Housing Regulations (SI 1996/2753), reg.3).

12.143 Duty to rehouse. Unless suitable alternative residential accommodation is otherwise available, on reasonable terms, a person displaced from land in consequence of a series of public actions will be entitled to rehousing from, or arranged by— usually—the local authority (in some cases, from another public body such as a Housing Action Trust, or new town corporation (Land Compensation Act 1973—"1973"—s.39).

12.144 The entitlement is not, however, to immediate permanent rehousing: the authority have do no more than their best, and if this means that the displaced occupant is provided with a series of short-life dwellings pending permanent rehousing, the authority will properly have discharged their duty (*R. v Bristol Corp Ex p. Hendy*, 1973).

12.145 Pre-conditions. The circumstances are:

(a) Displacement in consequence of compulsory purchase;

(b) Displacement in consequence of a housing order or under-taking, *i.e.* a demolition order under Pt IX of the Act (12.49–12.58), or a closing order under Pt IX (12.43–12.48) or s.368 (14.85).

(c) Displacement by an authority who have previously acquired the land, and who now decide to redevelop or improve it.

12.146 Additional conditions. For an occupier to qualify, displacement in consequence of improvement must be permanent (1973, s.39(6A)). So also must be displacement in consequence of an undertaking. An occupier claiming rehousing under (b) in the last paragraph must have been in occupation at the time the relevant order was made, undertaking accepted or notice served (1973, s.39(6)). An occupier claiming to be rehoused under (a) or (c), above, will not qualify unless he was in occupation when proceedings to purchase the land were commenced (1973, s.39(6)). Only a person in lawful occupation will qualify, not a trespasser, nor someone to whom permission has been given to use the property pending demolition or improvement, *i.e.* short-life user (1973, s.39(3)). The 1973 Act contains provisions enabling the local authority to advance money to a displaced owner-occupier (1973, s.41), and an owner-occupier who avails himself of this power, cannot also claim the right to rehousing (1973, s.39(4)).

12.147 Caravan dwellers. Analogous rehousing provision is made for caravan dwellers displaced by the same public activities (1973, s.40).

12.148 Local authority tenants. Local authority tenants may qualify under (a) or (c), but as authorities will not usually be obliged (or able) to serve a demolition or closing order on themselves (12.33), they will not normally enjoy rights to rehousing under this provision (*R. v Cardiff CC Ex p. Cross*, 1983). The authority will, however, usually be obliged to offer alternative accommodation under 1985, s.84 and Sch.2, Ground 10 (3.127), and duties under 1996, Pt VII will still apply (Chapter 10).

2. HOME LOSS PAYMENT

12.149 Availability. A home loss payment will be available in the same circumstances set out in 12.145, and also:

(a) In the event of permanent displacement of a housing association tenant on the carrying out of improvement to the dwelling or redevelopment of the land by the association, and

(b) To those evicted following an order under Ground 10 or 10A of the Housing Act 1985 (3.127) (1973, s.29(1)).

12.150 While this payment will in the circumstances set out in 12.145 normally be paid by the local authority (even where one of the other public bodies has the rehousing obligation), displacement by a housing association under this additional ground results in payment by the association. Local authority tenants who normally not qualify under 12.145(b) ought to qualify instead under 12.145(c) (*R. v Corby D.C., Ex p. McLean*, 1975).

12.151 Pre-conditions. Home loss entitlement is limited to those with a legal interest in the dwelling, (*i.e.* freeholders, leaseholders, tenants), statutory tenants, those with a restricted contract, and those with a right to occupy the dwelling under a contract of employment (1973, s.29(4)). The main limitation is that the claimant must have been in occupation of the dwelling for a minimum of one year, ending with the date of displacement (not purchase proceedings or other action, *cf.* 12.146), and that occupation was:

(a) As or with a tenant or other person entitled to payment;

(b) As an only or main residence; and

(c) Of the whole dwelling or a substantial part of it (1973, ss.29(2), 32(3)).

12.152 Additional conditions. Where the claimant has been in occupation of different rooms in the same building, *e.g.* a series of bedsitting-rooms, he is entitled to be treated as if he had remained in one room (1973, s.32(5)). Where there are two or more persons equally entitled, *e.g.* joint tenants (1.193–1.222), they each get an equal share (1973, s.32(6)). A spouse with matrimonial homes rights under the Family Law Act 1996 (9.20) may also claim (1973, s.29A).

12.153 In the case under 12.145(a), the claimant does not have to remain in occupation until required to leave by the authority:

provided his qualifying period is fulfilled, he may leave at any time after the date when the authority were given consent to make the compulsory purchase, although not before (1973, s.29(3)).

12.154 Amount. The amount of the home loss payment, which must be claimed within six years of displacement (1973, s.32(7A)), is, in the case of an owner, 10 per cent of the market value of the interest, to a maximum of £15,000. In all other cases, the amount is £1,500.

3. DISTURBANCE PAYMENT

12.155 Availability. A disturbance payment is available in the same circumstances as a home loss payment, set out at 12.145. It is available from the same body (12.143) (1973, s.37(1)). The claimant must have been in lawful possession of the land: in a case within 12.145(a) at the date when notice was first published of the intention compulsorily to purchase; within 12.145(c), when proceedings towards the purchase were begun; or, within 12.145(b), at the date when the order was made, notice was served, or undertaking accepted (1973, s.37(3)).

12.156 No payment is made if the claimant is entitled to compensation for the making of a closing or demolition order (12.158). Displacement in consequence of an undertaking, or the carrying out of improvement, must be permanent (1973, s.37(3A)). Where there is no absolute entitlement under these provisions, and no compensation under any other enactment, the local authority have a discretion to make a disturbance payment in any event (1973, s.37(5)).

12.157 Amount. The amount of the disturbance payment is "the reasonable expenses of the person entitled to the payment in removing from the land from which he is displaced" (1973, s.38(1)). These words mean more than mere removal costs, but include the costs of setting up in the new home. Many local authorities purport to fix amounts for disturbance payments, by scale, by maxima, or by limiting the matters for which payment will be made. There is no legal authority for such an approach: the amount may be small or it may be large, and each case is to be judged on its facts. A dispute may be referred to the Lands Tribunal (1973, s.38(4)), which is one of the few tribunals for which legal aid is available.

4. COMPENSATION FOR CLOSING AND DEMOLITION ORDERS

12.158 Availability and amount. Where a closing (12.43) or demolition order (12.49) is made, every owner of the premises is entitled to compensation (1989, s.584A). The amount of compensation is determined on the day the order is made and is the diminution in the compulsory purchase value of the owner's interest as a result of the order being made. If a demolition order is subsequently substituted for the closing order, then the compensation already paid is to be deducted from that paid for the demolition order. Where the demolition order is revoked to permit reconstruction of the premises (12.55), or a closing order is determined because the premises are rendered fit (12.47), the recipient must, on demand, repay the compensation to the authority (1989, s.584B). Where the closing order is determined in relation to part only of the premises, provision is made for the amount repayable to be apportioned.

Occupier Action

12.159 Taking the initiative. An occupier can specifically initiate action where there is interference with personal comfort (12.71). Of course, there is nothing to stop an occupier complaining about other conditions, or seeking other classes of action from the authority.

12.160 Judicial review. Indeed, authorities are usually obliged to act wherever their information comes from, and an authority which declined to receive or act on information, without cause, could be compelled to take action by the courts. It is not possible in this work to specify the circumstances in which an authority can be so compelled by the courts, but it should be noted that public bodies must act within the ambit of legislation, and that the courts will intervene (using their powers of judicial review), if authorities misunderstand or misapply the law, act in bad faith or otherwise fail to take relevant matters into account or disregard the irrelevant, or fail to take decisions in individual cases where they were obliged to do so. In such cases, the authority act *ultra vires* (outside their powers).

12.161 Limits of judicial review. It is imperative, however, to bear in mind that a court (other than a court given express powers on appeal) reviewing the conduct of a public body does not intervene because it disagrees with a decision entrusted by Parliament to that authority, nor because its (or the applicant's) view of what is reasonable is different from that of the authority, but because the authority have acted wrongly in one of the ways illustrated, or so unreasonably that no reasonable authority, properly approaching the matter, could have so acted (see also 10.173–10.180).

12.162   Human Rights Act. The right to "respect for the home" as required by Art.8 of the European Convention on Human Rights may be breached by a person's home being in severe disrepair (*Lee v Leeds CC*, 2002). Furthermore, in cases where there has been a severe interference, *e.g.* through environmental pollution, with an occupier's right to "respect for the home," the European Court of Human Rights has imposed a positive duty on member states to take action (*Powell and Rayner v UK* (1990); *Lopes Ostra v Spain* 1995). Thus in cases involving very poor housing conditions, a failure to act by a local authority under one of the duties set out in this Chapter may arguably be a breach of Art.8, which could be actionable under the Human Rights Act 1998, s.6.

12.163   Complaint to a J.P. The 1985 Act, however, does provide the occupier with one, express and additional recourse. He may complain to a justice of the peace (magistrate) either that an individual dwelling-house or house in multiple occupation or that a whole area is unfit for human habitation (1985, s.606).

12.164   If the magistrate is satisfied that the complaint is correct, perhaps following a visit to the premises or area, he will in turn complain to the local authority's Medical Officer of Health or, if they have none, the proper officer of the authority. It is this officer's duty then to inspect the house or area, and report to his authority (or appropriate committee). That is as far as the obligation goes. There is no sanction. The officer or committee are free to disagree with the magistrate. The procedure is, however, a useful way of making the authority inspect, and, if the inspection satisfies them of the unfitness they will be bound to take action (12.23).

CHAPTER THIRTEEN

Disrepair Under Environmental Law

Introduction

13.01 Scope. This Chapter is concerned with a series of powers now to be found principally in the Environmental Protection Act 1990 ("1990"), which consolidated much of the law formerly contained in the Public Health Act 1936 ("1936") and the Public Health (Recurring Nuisances) Act 1969. It will also briefly consider some related powers to be found in the Building Act 1984 ("1984") and in various Public Health Acts. It should be appreciated that in relation to housing the Environmental Protection Act does not amount to a comprehensive or cohesive programme or policy. The provisions are not aimed exclusively at housing. The approach of this Chapter is, accordingly, necessarily selective.

Outline

13.02 Preliminary matters

- Powers and duties to deal with environmental problems are imposed on local authorities.
- Authorities must inspect their area from time to time to detect statutory nuisances.
- Action under the Environmental Protection Act is not mutually exclusive to action under the Housing Act 1985.
- Authorities have powers of entry, which it is a criminal offence to obstruct.

13.03 Statutory nuisance

- The Environmental Protection Act 1990 applies to statutory nuisances, defined to include any premises in such a state as to be prejudicial to health or a nuisance.

- Where an authority are aware of a statutory nuisance they must serve an abatement notice on the person responsible.
- An abatement notice may be appealed to the magistrates' court.
- It is a criminal offence not to comply with an abatement notice.
- There is a special procedure for a "person aggrieved" to take action in the magistrates' court, which is available (among other circumstances) where the authority themselves are the person responsible for the nuisance.
- Notice of intention to take action must first be served on the person responsible for the nuisance.
- If the nuisance is proved the court may make an abatement or works order, impose a fine, prohibit use of the premises for human habitation, or order works in default.
- The court may award an applicant his costs, and the case may be conducted by solicitors on a conditional fee basis; the court can also award compensation.
- There is a special procedure under the Building Act 1984 for urgent statutory nuisances.

13.04   Other controls

- There is a number of other statutory controls to deal with environmental problems:
  - Dangerous buildings may be dealt with under the procedures in the Building Act 1984 (1984);
  - There is a similar procedure under the 1984 Act to deal with dilapidated buildings;
  - Some fire precaution measures are included in the Fire Precautions Act 1971 and the Building Act 1984;
  - The provision and maintenance of sanitary accommodation is also regulated by the 1984 Act, as are drains and sewers and the provision of adequate food storage;
  - Vermin can be controlled under the Public Health Act 1936;
  - Certain diseases are controlled by the Public Health (Control of Disease) Act 1984.

Preliminary matters

13.05   Local authorities. As in the last Chapter, and in the next, we are here concerned primarily with duties imposed on local authorities, rather than rights as between individuals. Local authorities for these purposes are the same authorities who have duties under the Housing Acts (12.13), save that in the area of a Housing Action Trust (3.252) some of these powers may be transferred to the Trust, additional to or instead of the local authority (Housing Act 1988, s.68).

13.06 Default powers. Where duties arise under the 1990 Act, the Secretary of State for the Environment has power to declare that an authority are in default of their duties, and may direct them to carry out actions to remedy their default, or even take over their obligations (1990, Sch.3).

13.07 Inspection. Authorities are obliged to inspect their districts with an eye to the performance of their duties in relation to statutory nuisances, the main class of action with which we shall be concerned in the present Chapter (1990, s.79).

13.08 Overlapping powers. Action under the Housing Acts and under the Environmental Protection Act is not mutually exclusive: for example, statutory nuisance procedure is no substitute for procedure under Pts VI or IX, Housing Act 1985 (12.17–12.72; *R. v Kerrier DC Ex p. Guppy's (Bridport)*, 1985) and even though an area may be declared a clearance area (12.76–12.86) under the Housing Act 1985, Pt IX, the authority will still be bound to take action under the 1990 Act if such action is called for (*Salford CC v McNally*, 1975).

13.09 Powers of entry. Whether the purpose of the entry is in order to inspect premises, or in order to carry out works which they are entitled to do, local authorities have a general power of entry into premises, which may be exercised at any reasonable hour (1990, Sch.3, para.2). At least 24 hours' notice must be given to the occupier of residential premises under this general power, although there is an additional power to apply to the magistrate's court for a warrant authorising entry, if necessary by force, which can be issued not only when entry has been sought and refused under the general power, but also when warning of a visit would defeat the purpose of the visit (1990, Sch.3, para.2(3), (4)). Authorities also have power to enter unoccupied premises in order to prevent them being or becoming a danger to public health (Local Government (Miscellaneous Provisions) Act 1982, s.29), although they are obliged to give an owner of the premises 48 hours' notice of intention of so doing.

13.10   Obstruction. Obstruction of an officer of the authority executing duties under the Acts is a criminal offence (1990, Sch.3, para.3).

Statutory Nuisance

13.11   Definition. For the purposes of this work, a statutory nuisance means "any premises in such a state as to be prejudicial to health or a nuisance" (1990, s.79(1)). The limbs are alternative, so that statutory nuisance may be established by way of either:

(a) Prejudice to health, or

(b) Nuisance.

13.12   Prejudicial to health. Prejudicial to health is, in turn, defined as meaning "injurious or likely to cause injury to health" (1990, s.79(7)). This phrase has not been much considered by the courts, though it is clear that the most common complaint—dampness, including condensation dampness—is capable of causing injury to health (*GLC v Tower Hamlets LBC*, 1983; *Dover DC v Farrar*, 1979; *Birmingham DC v Kelly*, 1985; *Birmingham DC v McMahon*, 1987; *Southwark LBC v Simpson* 1998).

13.13   Sleeplessness could amount to injury to health for the purposes of the Act (*Lewisham LBC v Fenner*, 1995). The persons best equipped to determine prejudiciality to health are doctors and environmental health officers (*O'Toole v Knowsley MBC*, 1999). Whether or not premises are injurious to health, although a question of fact, may to an extent be a technical question, so that magistrates cannot (without controverting evidence) simply substitute their own opinions for those of a qualified person, unless, of course, they disbelieve the evidence (*Patel v Mehtab*, 1981). There can be a statutory nuisance even although the landlord is not in breach (see Chapter 11) of any repairing obligation (*Birmingham City DC v Kelly*, 1985).

13.14   Nuisance. To qualify as a nuisance within the definition, it must be shown that there is what is identifiable as a nuisance at common law (*National Coal Board v Thorne*, 1976). It follows (see also 8.89) that the nuisance must emanate from one set of premises, and create an effect in another. Thus, a leaking roof may be a nuisance to the occupier of the house, but unless it is injurious to his health, it will not be a statutory nuisance. If, however, the effect of the leak spreads to the next-door property, there will be a nuisance, and as such a statutory nuisance, in the leaking premises, actionable in relation to the next door house.

13.15 In this connection, it should be noted that where what is occupied is a flat or a room, or anything less than a whole building, the common parts of the building will remain in the landlord's possession and for these purposes will constitute another set of premises, *e.g.* roof, halls, stairs, corridors. It is therefore important to define the premises which suffer the nuisance: where there was condensation throughout a block of flats, it was none the less each flat which suffered the nuisance, not the block as a whole (*Birmingham DC v McMahon*, 1987).

1. ABATEMENT PROCEEDINGS BY AUTHORITY

13.16 Whose responsibility? Once an authority are satisfied that there is a statutory nuisance, or that a nuisance is likely to recur, they are obliged to take action (1990, s.80). They must serve an abatement notice on the "person responsible" for the nuisance. This is the person to "whose act, default or sufferance" the nuisance is attributable (1990, s.79(7)). If that person cannot be found, then the authority may serve the notice on either the owner or the occupier although, if the abatement notice requires structural works, they can only serve the notice on the owner.

13.17 If it is clear that there is no fault on the part of either owner or occupier, and the authority cannot find the person responsible to serve an abatement notice on him, they may, instead of serving an abatement notice, carry out such works themselves as they consider necessary to abate the nuisance and to prevent its recurrence.

13.18 Owners. "Owner" is not defined in the 1990 Act, although under the Public Health Act 1936 it was defined in similar terms to a person having control under the Housing Acts (12.29) and that definition should still be applied (*Camden LBC v Gunby*, 1999). It is clear that in many cases this will be the authority themselves. In such a case, they cannot serve a notice on themselves (*R. v Cardiff CC Ex p. Cross*, 1983: 12.33), although the occupier will still be able to take his own proceedings against them (13.23–13.38).

13.19 Abatement notice. If the abatement can be effected without works, *e.g.* by the removal of some object causing the nuisance, the authority need do no more than require abatement of the nuisance; if works are needed, however, then the authority must specify what works they require (1990, s.80; *Kirklees MBC v Field*, 1997). The authority should allow a reasonable time for abatement, which they should state in the notice.

13.20 Appeal against abatement notice. A person who is served with an abatement notice may within 21 days appeal it to a magistrates' court (1990, s.80(3)). Appeal is by way of complaint and there is a further right of appeal to the Crown Court (1990, Sch.3). The grounds of appeal are set out in SI 1995/2644, and include that the notice was not justified, that it should have been served on another person and that the time given to comply was not long enough. On hearing the complaint, the magistrates' court may:

(a) Quash the notice; or,

(b) Vary it in favour of the appellant; or,

(c) Dismiss the appeal (SI 1995/2644, reg.3(5)).

13.21 Prosecution for non-compliance. If without reasonable excuse the abatement notice is not complied with, and any appeal is unsuccessful, the recipient may be prosecuted. If found guilty, he may be fined up to level 5 on the standard scale, and one tenth of that amount for each day the offence continues after conviction (1990, s.80(4), (5)). A nuisance is not abated just because the premises have been vacated (*Lambeth LBC v Stubbs*, 1980). Prosecution is a criminal proceeding, and does not lie within the residual civil jurisdiction of the magistrates' court: it should, accordingly, be commenced by information and summons, rather than by complaint (*R. v Newham East Justices Ex p. Hunt*, 1976).

13.22 Works in default. Where an abatement notice has not been complied with, the authority may, either additionally or instead of prosecution, abate the nuisance themselves and carry out any necessary works (1990, s.81(3)). Any expenses incurred may be recovered from the person by whose act or default the nuisance was caused (1990, s.81(4)). Where the expenses are recoverable from the owner, they become a charge on the premises, and may be repaid by instalments (1990, ss.81A and 81B).

2. PROCEEDINGS BY OCCUPIER

13.23 Person aggrieved. There is a special procedure which can be used by a private individual (1990, s.82). The individual must be a "person aggrieved" by the nuisance, *i.e.* someone suffering its effects, not—as it were—a mere busybody. A person cannot be aggrieved in relation to a whole block of flats, only in relation to the flat he occupies (*Birmingham DC v McMahon*, 1987).

13.24 Legal aid. Legal aid is not available for the prosecution of criminal offences, and is, accordingly, not available to an occupier seeking to use this provision. Initial assistance may be available under the "legal help" scheme and solicitors are permitted to enter into conditional fee arrangements to take action under s.82 on the basis of recovering their costs under s.82(12) (13.36) (Courts and Legal Services Act 1990, as amended). If the person responsible appeals to the Crown Court against any order, the person aggrieved will be entitled to legal aid (*R. v Inner London Crown Court, Ex p. Bentham*, 1988).

13.25 Local authority landlords. There are two circumstances in which an occupier is likely to want to use s.82: when the authority will not take action against a private landlord: and, more commonly, when the landlord is the authority themselves. It is well-established that s.82 permits proceedings against a local authority, even the authority who would otherwise be responsible for taking action (*R. v Epping (Waltham Abbey) Justices, Ex p. Burlinson*, 1948).

13.26 Procedure. Action is to be taken against the person responsible or the owner in the same way as with an abatement notice (13.16; 1990, s.82(4)). Prior to taking any proceedings under this section, the occupier must give 21 days notice in writing to the proposed defendant (1990, s.82(6), (7)). Proceedings are commenced by "laying an information" before the magistrates.

13.27 Powers of court. Having heard the complaint the magistrates' court may do one or more of the following:

(a) **Nuisance order.** Make a nuisance order requiring the defendant to abate the nuisance and/or execute works to prevent its recurrence (1990, s.82(2);

(b) **Fine.** Impose a fine not exceeding level five on the standard scale (1990, s.82(2));

(c) **Prohibition of use.** If the nuisance renders the premises unfit for human habitation, prohibit the use of the premises for that purpose (1990, s.82(3));

(d) **Works in default.** Where neither the person responsible for the nuisance, nor the owner or occupier can be found, direct the local authority to do anything which the court would have ordered that person to do (1990, s.82(13)).

13.28 If without reasonable excuse the nuisance order is not complied with, further proceedings may be taken against the defaulter and he may be fined, continuing on a daily basis (1990, s.82(8)).

13.29 Types of work. The works to be included in a nuisance order can include structural works (13.16). There is, indeed, no express limitation on what works can be ordered, and cases under the Public Health Act 1936 will be relevant in this regard. In one case (*Dover DC v Farrar*, 1980), a magistrates' court ordered the installation of gas heating in place of electric heating, in premises suffering severely from condensation-dampness. The Divisional Court quashed this order, because the reason the electric heating was not being used was not that it did not work but that the tenants could not afford to use it. It is quite clear from the case, however, that had the electric heating not worked, or had it been wholly unsuitable to eliminate such dampness even if fully and properly used by the tenants, that the order could have been regarded as a proper order, within the power of the magistrates.

13.30 Division of responsibility—landlord and tenant. In the *Dover* case, the landlord was held not to be responsible for the nuisance, as it was considered to be the fault of the tenants that the heating that had been provided was not being used (above, 13.16).

13.31 In another case (*GLC v Tower Hamlets LBC*, 1983), the GLC owned a corner flat situated on the ground floor of a block, but at a raised level, with three sides and the whole of its underneath open to the air, so that an exceptionally large part of the flat was exposed to the elements. Originally, the flat had an open solid fuel fire but this was subsequently blocked up and replaced with an electric heater, itself later removed. The flat suffered from severe condensation dampness. It was held that the flat was prejudicial to the health of the occupants because of dampness caused by the failure of the landlord to take necessary precautions, either by way of ventilation or insulation, or by providing any special form of heating, for a property wholly exceptionally vulnerable to condensation.

13.32 A landlord has to apply his mind to the need for ventilation, and, if need be, to insulation and heating, and must provide a combination of these factors to make a house habitable for the tenant. Once the landlord has done so, it is the tenant's responsibility to use the facilities and if the cause of continuing condensation is the tenant's unwillingness to do so, then the landlord cannot be held responsible.

13.33 A landlord will also not be held responsible, where the reason why works have not been done to abate the nuisance is refusal by the tenant to allow access (*Carr v Hackney LBC*, 1995).

13.34 Contents of order. An order should be as detailed and as specific as possible (*Salford CC v McNally*, 1975). The court has a relatively generous discretion as regards time. Thus, although the fact that Housing Act action is to be taken, *e.g.* by way of clearance (12.76–12.86), does not exclude the court's duty to make a nuisance order (13.27), it may still influence the amount of time allowed for compliance (*Nottingham Corporation v Newton*, 1974).

13.35 There is also a discretion as to extent of works: if the premises are shortly to be demolished, fewer works than otherwise may be ordered, provided what is ordered is sufficient to abate the nuisance for the period for which the property is likely to remain in use (*Lambeth LBC v Stubbs*, 1980; *Coventry CC v Doyle*, 1981). The fact that the premises are to be vacated does not, however, mean that the nuisance will be abated, for in the absence of an order prohibiting use (13.27), the premises might otherwise be used again in their current state of statutory nuisance (*Lambeth LBC v Stubbs*, 1980).

13.36 Expenses. The court has a discretion (1990, s.82(12)) to order a defendant to pay the person bringing the proceedings an amount it considers reasonably sufficient to compensate him for any expenses (including legal expenses) properly incurred in the proceedings, but only if the alleged nuisance existed at the date of making the complaint. Legal expenses can, however, only be recovered if there is a clear agreement by the person to pay the costs irrespective of outcome, but a conditional fee arrangement under the Courts and Legal Services Act 1990 is sufficient for this purpose.

13.37 When considering whether to make an order for costs, magistrates are entitled to take into account the failure of the person bringing the proceedings to allow the landlord access to the flat prior to the complaint being made and notice of intention to bring proceedings (13.26) being served (*Jones v Walsall M.BC*, 2002).

13.38 Compensation. The court can also award compensation under the Powers of Criminal Courts (Sentencing) Act 2000, s.130 (formerly the Powers of Criminal Courts Act 1973, s.35), to a statutory maximum of £5,000 (*Botross v Hammersmith & Fulham LBC*, 1994). Where proceedings are instituted by a person aggrieved compensation can only be awarded from the date of the period of the existence of the nuisance indicated in the summons, provided that date was not before whichever was the later of:

(a) The date when the statutory notice expired, and

(b) A date not more than six months before the complaint was made (*R. v Liverpool CC Ex p. Cooke*, 1996).

3. URGENT STATUTORY NUISANCES

13.39 Unreasonable delay. In view of the length of time which normal court proceedings can take, the local authority also have power to use a special, speedy procedure, when it appears to them that premises are in such a defective state as to be a statutory nuisance, and that there would be unreasonable delay were the abatement procedure to be used (1984, s.76). In one case (*Celcrest Properties Ltd v Hastings BC*, 1979), the difference between four weeks under one of the Public Health Acts, and 11–12 weeks under normal abatement procedure, was upheld as an unreasonable delay, sufficient to justify use of the speedy procedure.

13.40 Notice and counter-notice. The procedure commences with a notice of intent served by the authority on the same person as would an abatement notice be served (13.16). The notice has to state what works the authority intend to execute. The notice must be served at least nine days before commencement of works. During the seven days following service, the person served is entitled to serve on the authority a counter-notice, stating that he intends himself to remedy the defects which have been specified by the authority. The authority are then debarred from using this speedy procedure unless the person who has served the counter-notice does not commence or progress with the works within what appears to the authority to be a reasonable time.

13.41 Claim by authority. The owner's remedy against use of this procedure is to do nothing: after the works have been completed, the authority will issue civil proceedings (generally in the county court), to recover their expenses; it is a defence to such a claim to show that no unreasonable delay would have flowed from use of the abatement procedure, and, if upheld, the authority recover none of their expenditure, even though the owner will have benefited to the extent of the works executed. The owner may also defend a claim for the authority's expenses if he served a counter-notice (13.40) but the authority entered to do works on the ground of unreasonable time, by proving to the court that the time taken to start or complete the works would not have been unreasonable.

13.42 Building preservation order. The 1984 Act procedure is not available if the works would contravene a building preservation order under the Planning (Listed Buildings and Conservation Areas) Act 1990, designed for the protection of buildings of special historic or architectural interest. The 1984 Act procedure can be used, however, even though the works to be carried out could have been ordered by way of repairs notice under s.189 of the Housing Act 1985 (12.28–12.42).

4. APPEALS

13.43 Courts. Appeal lies from the magistrates' court to the Crown Court, although in certain circumstances it is possible for the appeal (on a point of jurisdiction) to lie by way of proceedings in the Divisional Court. Appeal lies from both a county court and the High Court to the Court of Appeal.

Other Controls

1. DANGEROUS BUILDINGS

13.44 Two procedures. A dangerous building is any building in such a condition, or used to carry such a load, that it is dangerous (1984, s.77). Authorities have two means of dealing with dangerous buildings:

> By normal procedure; and
>
> By urgent procedure.

13.45 Normal procedure. The normal procedure is by way of application by the authority to the magistrates' court, for an order requiring the owner (13.18), at his own election, either to carry out works to obviate the danger or to demolish the building or its dangerous part (1984, s.77).

13.46 Works to obviate the danger means something in the nature of a permanent or semi-permanent remedy, rather than shoring it up (*London CC v Jones*, 1912), or securing the doors against entry and excluding the tenants (*Holme v Crosby Corp*, 1949).

13.47 Though the court does not have to specify the exact works needed, it will need to specify a time for compliance, for no offence of non-compliance can arise until the time allowed has elapsed, nor will the authority acquire their rights to carry out the works in default (1984, s.77).

13.48 No provision is made for the removal, rehousing or compensating of tenants.

13.49 **Urgent procedure**. The urgent procedure is similar to that available in relation to urgent statutory nuisances (13.39–13.42). There is, however, no provision for counter-notice (13.40), and the authority need only serve notice of intention if it is reasonably practicable to do so (1984, s.78).

13.50 It is a defence to the authority's proceedings to recover their costs to show that the normal procedure (13.45) could reasonably have been used and, if successful, then again (*cf.* 13.41) the authority recover no part of their costs.

13.51 There is no provision for removal, rehousing or compensation of tenants.

2. DILAPIDATED BUILDINGS

13.52 **Definition**. For these purposes, a dilapidated building is one which is seriously detrimental to the amenities of the neighbourhood, (*e.g.* unsightly, health hazard), by reason of its ruinous or dilapidated condition (1984, s.79).

13.53 **Procedure**. Procedure is by way of notice requiring the owner (13.18) either to carry out works of repair or restoration or, at his own election, to demolish the building or a part of it. This procedure is subject to the special appeals and enforcement provisions contained in 1984, Pt IV, which permit the owner to challenge the notice by way of appeal on specified grounds, allow the authority to do works in default of compliance with the notice, and create offences of non-compliance.

13.54 No provision is made for removing, rehousing or compensating tenants.

3. FIRE PRECAUTIONS

13.55 Fire Precautions Act 1971. Apart from the provisions governing fire precautions in houses in multiple occupation, considered in the next Chapter (14.83–14.90), there is not much legislation in force governing fire precautions in housing. The principal enactment is the Fire Precautions Act 1971. Save in relation to a house which is used as a single dwelling, s.3 of the Fire Precaution Act 1971 could require a fire certificate from the fire authority for any other property, but this power has still not been brought into force. Some part of the Act is in force, however: s.1 makes a fire certificate mandatory for premises subject to a designated use, although the only designated use relevant to housing is use for providing sleeping accommodation (for staff or guests) in connection with a business as a hotel or a boarding house (SI 1972/238).

13.56 Building Act 1984. Local authorities enjoy a residual power to require fire precautions, but only in buildings which exceed two storeys in height and in which the floor of any upper storey is or will be 20 feet above the surface of the street or ground at any point around the building (1984, s.72). The building must, additionally, be one which is let in flats or tenements, or used as an inn, hotel, boarding-house, hospital, nursing home, boarding school, children's home or similar institution, or is used as a restaurant, shop, store or warehouse and has sleeping accommodation for employees on the upper floor.

13.57 Procedure. The authority may serve notice on the owner of the building, requiring the execution of such works or the provision of such other facilities as may be necessary to provide the building with such means of escape from fire as the authority consider necessary in respect of each of the storeys of the building above the 20–foot limit specified (1984, s.72).

13.58 Owner is defined for these purposes (1984, s.126, *cf.* 13.18), again in terms similar to the Housing Act 1985 as the person for the time being receiving the rack-rent, including an agent or trustee, or the person who would receive it if the premises were let at a rack-rent. The provisions are subject to the special appeals and enforcement procedures contained in Pt IV of the 1984 Act (13.53).

4. SANITARY ACCOMMODATION

13.59 Powers. Local authorities have a duty to serve notice on an owner (13.18) of premises, requiring the provision of closets, when a building has insufficient sanitary accommodation, or when any part of the building occupied as a separate dwelling has insufficient sanitary accommodation (1984, s.64, as amended). They also have a duty to serve a similar notice if they are satisfied that such sanitary accommodation as exists is in such a state as to be prejudicial to health or a nuisance (13.12–13.15) and cannot be rendered satisfactory without reconstruction (1984, s.64).

13.60 For the purposes of the latter provision, local authorities not only enjoy their usual powers of entry (13.09), but are also entitled to apply tests or otherwise examine the closet's condition (1936, s.48).

13.61 If, on examination, the authority come to the conclusion that the closet can be rendered satisfactory without reconstruction, they serve notice requiring the execution of such works as may be necessary (1936, s.45). Such a notice may be served on either the owner or occupier.

13.62 Finally, the authority have power to require the replacement of earth or other (non-water) closets with water closets, even if the existing closets are in all other respects satisfactory (1936, s.47). This power can, however, only be used if there is a sufficient supply of water and sewer available. In the case of such a "substitution" order, the authority must pay half the costs of the installation; the authority have a choice between ordering the owner to execute the works and paying him half the costs, and doing the work themselves and recovering half the costs from the owner (1984, s.66).

13.63 Appeals, works in default and offences. These provisions are subject to the appeals procedure contained in 1984, Pt IV (13.53), which will entitle the person served to challenge a notice by way of appeal, but which also entitle the authority to carry out works in default, and which create offences of non-compliance.

13.64 In addition, there are three specific offences related to sanitary accommodation:

- (a) **Flushing or deodorising**. Failure to keep the convenience supplied with water for flushing, or in the case of an earth closet with dry earth or other suitable deodorising material (1936, s.51);

- (b) **Injury, fouling and obstruction**. When a convenience is used by more than one family, anyone who injures or improperly fouls the convenience, or anything used in connection with the convenience, or who wilfully or negligently obstructs the drain leading from the convenience, commits an offence (1936, s.52); and

- (c) **Insanitary state**. When a convenience is used by more than one family, leaving the convenience or the approach to the convenience in an insanitary state, for want of cleaning or attention, is also an offence (1936, s.52.).

5. DRAINS AND SEWERS

13.65 Powers and procedure. Local authorities enjoy wide powers to require owners (13.18) to make satisfactory provision for drainage and sewage, *e.g.* if a drain or sewer admits subsoil water, or is prejudicial to health or is a nuisance (1984, ss.21, 59). In some circumstances, they may require remedial action by an occupier as well as, or instead of, by an owner: *e.g.* in the case of a blockage (Public Health Act 1961, s.17). In this last case, the authority can require removal of a blockage within 48 hours, in default of compliance with which they may themselves enter and carry out the works in default, recovering their expenses of so doing.

13.66 An authority may also secure repair of a drain or sewer, if they conclude:

- (a) That it is not sufficiently maintained and kept in good repair; and

- (b) That it could be repaired at a cost of less than £250 (Public Health Act 1961, s.17).

13.67 This power proceeds by way of notice of intention to carry out the works themselves, and recover the costs of so doing. There is no appeal against either of the last two classes of notice, but in each case the authority's decision can be challenged by way of defence to the claim for recovery of expenses. Local authorities have additional discretionary powers to cleanse drains, at the request and cost of an owner or occupier (Public Health Act 1961, s.22).

6. FOOD STORAGE

13.68 Powers and procedure. Local authorities have power to require the provision of sufficient and suitable accommodation for the storage of food in houses, or in parts of a building occupied as separate dwellings (1984, s.70). The power proceeds by way of notice on the owner (13.18), who may challenge it under Pt IV, 1984 Act (13.53), which also gives the authority power to execute works in default and to recover the costs of so doing.

7. VERMIN

13.69 Powers. Vermin are harboured by filth. It follows that, not uncommonly, the property most in need of repair will be verminous, for everyday experience shows how impossible it is as a matter of practice for those living in shoddy property to keep the premises clean, and how little incentive there is constantly to clean up, when the more serious problems of disrepair are never remedied. If the local authority are satisfied that premises are so filthy, or in such an unwholesome condition, as to be prejudicial to health (13.12) or verminous, they are bound to take action (1936, s.83, as amended).

13.70 Procedure. Action is by way of notice served on either the owner (13.18) or the occupier. The notice may require such steps as may be necessary to preventing the prejudice to health, or to remove and destroy the vermin, which steps can include, if necessary, the removal of wallpaper and other wall-coverings, papering or repapering, painting and distempering, at the option of the person served (1936, s.83, as amended). In the event of non-compliance, the authority may execute works in default, and seek to recover their costs from the person served, though it will be a defence to such an action to show either:

(a) That the notice was not necessary; or

(b) That as between owner and occupier, it is the other who should have been served (1936, s.83).

13.71 Gas attack. In some cases, the premises may be in such a condition that a gas attack is called for. A gas attack is carried out by, and at the cost of, the authority, who must give notice to both owner and occupier of their intention to proceed. They may require the premises (and neighbouring premises) to be vacated during the attack, in which cases they must provide alternative temporary accommodation, free of charge (1936, s.83; Public Health Act 1961, s.36). A notice requiring the premises to be vacated may be appealed, but subject to the right of appeal it is an offence not to comply with it (1936, s.83).

8. DISEASE

13.72 Classes of disease. These provisions govern notifiable diseases, and infectious diseases. A notifiable disease means cholera, plague, relapsing fever, smallpox, typhus or any other disease specified in regulations (Public Health (Control of Disease) Act 1984, ss.10, 13).

(i) *Notifiable diseases*

13.73 Classes of offences concerning notifiable disease. There are three classes of offence related to notifiable diseases.

(a) **Enquiries by new occupier.** If a person seeking to rent premises asks whether there is, or during the preceding six weeks has been, anyone in the house suffering from a notifiable disease, it is a criminal offence, committed by anyone involved in letting the house, or showing the house with a view to its being let, or anyone who has recently ceased to occupy the house, to give an answer known to be false (Public Health (Control of Disease) Act 1984, s.29).

(b) **Clearance certificates.** A person letting premises in which someone has suffered from a notifiable disease, without first securing a clearance certificate from the local authority or a registered G.P., commits an offence (Public Health (Control of Disease) Act 1984, s.29).

(c) **Departing occupiers.** If notice has been given by the local authority both to the owner (13.18) and to an occupier, informing them of their obligations in relation to notifiable diseases, anyone who ceases to occupy premises in which, to his knowledge, anyone has, within the six weeks prior to his departure, suffered from a notifiable disease, may commit one of three, further offences:

(i) Failing to have the house and any articles within it which are liable to retain infection disinfected and certified as such by an authority or a registered G.P.;

(ii) Failing to give the owner of the premises notice of the existence of the disease;

(iii) Giving a false answer to an owner who expressly asks whether anyone has been suffering from a notifiable disease during the six weeks before departure (Public Health (Control of Disease) Act 1984, s.30).

(ii) *Infectious diseases*

13.74 Cleansing of premises and property. If the Medical Officer of Health, or proper officer of the authority, certifies that premises need cleansing of infectious disease (which includes, but is not limited to the specified notifiable diseases, *cf*. 13.72), or that articles in the premises likely to retain infection require cleansing or destruction, the local authority must give notice to the occupier that they intend to enter and cleanse or destroy, unless within 24 hours the occupier notifies them that he will himself execute all works as are specified in the notice, within a time to be stated for this purpose in the body of the notice (Public Health (Control of Disease) Act 1984, s.31).

13.75 If there is no counter-notice, or if the occupier fails to comply with his counter-notice, the authority may carry out the works in default of compliance and recover their costs. If the authority form the view that the occupier would in any event be unable to comply, they may dispense with the notice, and proceed directly to the works, but they must then bear the cost themselves.

13.76 Removal and vacating. The authority enjoy additional power to remove persons from the premises, with consent or on an order of a justice of the peace, but only if the Medical Officer of Health or proper officer has certified that this is necessary (Public Health (Control of Disease) Act 1984, s.32). The authority may also order the house to be vacated for the purpose of disinfecting it. In either event, the authority may provide, free of charge, alternative, temporary accommodation.

CHAPTER FOURTEEN

Overcrowding and Houses in Multiple Occupation

Introduction

14.01 Governing legislation. Overcrowding and houses in multiple occupation (HMOs) are treated together in one Chapter because in practice the problems tend to overlap. Overcrowding is dealt with in Pt X of the Housing Act 1985, save to the extent that it concerns HMOs, the provisions governing which are to be found in Pt XI of the 1985 Act (as substantially amended by the Housing Act 1996). The overcrowding provisions HMOs will be discussed under that head rather than under overcrowding.

Outline

14.02 Preliminaries

- It is local housing authorities as defined by the Housing Act 1985, which have primary responsibility for dealing with overcrowding and houses in multiple occupation.

- Local housing authorities should inspect conditions in their area annually.

- Authorities have powers of entry for examining premises.

14.03 Overcrowding

- The overcrowding provision apply to "separate dwellings".

- There are two overcrowding tests:

    - *The room standard* is based on persons aged 10 or over, who are not husband and wife, having to sleep in the same room;

- *The space standard* works by calculating the permitted number for a dwelling based on the number and size of the rooms.

- Even where there is statutory overcrowding, it may be licensed by the authority, and it will not be unlawful if caused by family members staying temporarily or through natural growth.

- A number of offences may be committed in relation to overcrowding:
  - Rent books must contain details of the overcrowding provisions, failure to comply with which requirement is an offence;
  - A landlord who permits overcrowding commits an offence;
  - An occupier who causes or permits overcrowding commits an offence.

- Local housing authorities who have the power to prosecute these offences.

- Rent Act protection is lost in the case of illegal overcrowding.

14.04 Houses in multiple occupation (HMOs)

- A house in multiple occupation is a house (or flat) occupied by persons who do not form a single household.

- There are no fixed criteria for assessing whether there is a single household, but in general terms a single household requires a relationship between the occupiers which provides a particular reason for living in the same house.

- Action is usually taken against the person "having control" of, or "managing," the HMO; there are provisions to appeal against orders.

- There are five different types of action which a local authority may take in relation to an HMO:
  - *Overcrowding controls*—these permit authorities to permit a maximum number of occupiers and require reductions in the numbers; breach of a notice is a criminal offence; alternatively, overcrowding directions may fix the appropriate number of occupants for the HMO and, if necessary, require the landlord

not to permit the numbers in the house to increase beyond this number or replace departing occupants (in addition to or in place of carrying out works);

- *Registration schemes* may be adopted by authorities for the whole or part of their area, requiring all HMOs to be registered; where the scheme includes control provisions, the authority may refuse registration on the grounds of unsuitability of the premises or that the person having control of or managing the house is not a fit and proper person to do so; the authority may also attach works conditions to the registration; special control provisions, if adopted, allow further conditions and grounds for refusal or revocation of registration;

- *A notice requiring execution of works* may be served to ensure that there are adequate facilities, including fire escapes and other fire precautions, in the HMO for the number of occupiers;

- *The management regulations* set standards of management for HMOs, breach of which is a criminal offence; the authority may serve notice requiring works to ensure compliance with the regulations;

- *Control orders* allow the authority to take over control of the HMO; a control order may only be made where the conditions in the HMO have led to or warrant a works notice or overcrowding direction and the living conditions in the house are such that the order is necessary for the protection of the safety, welfare or health of the occupiers of the HMO; the owner is entitled to compensation, and the authority must draw up a management scheme for the HMO or else compulsorily purchase it.

Preliminary matters

14.05 Local authorities. The authorities with responsibility for all of these provisions are the same as those who have general responsibility under the 1985 Act (12.13), save that in the area of a Housing Action Trust (3.252) these powers may be transferred to the Trust, in addition to or instead of the local authority (Housing Act 1988, s.65).

14.06 Inspection. The Housing Act duties to be considered in the present Chapter are amongst those for the purposes of which the authority are bound to consider housing conditions in their districts on an annual basis (12.14; 1985, s.605).

14.07 In addition, whenever it appears to an authority that occasion has arisen for a report on overcrowding in their district, they must inspect and prepare a report for submission to the Secretary of State, including in it their proposals for dealing with the problem by way of providing new accommodation (1985, s.334). The Secretary of State has power to require them to carry out such an inspection.

14.08 Powers of entry. The authority enjoy the powers of entry referred to in connection with the unfitness provisions (12.65). In addition, there are powers to enable the authority to obtain a warrant of entry for the purpose of examining premises to decide whether powers under Pt XI (14.18–14.118), should be exercised (1985, s.397).

Overcrowding

1. DEFINITION

14.09 Use as a separate dwelling. The overcrowding provisions apply to premises used or suitable for use as a separate dwelling (1985, s.343). As much as a house could be overcrowded, or as little as a single room (see 3.18).

14.10 Alternative tests. There are alternative tests of overcrowding. If either is offended, the premises are overcrowded in law.

(a) **Room standard.** There is overcrowding whenever there are so many people in a house that any two or more of those persons, being 10 or more years old, and of opposite sexes, not being persons living together as husband and wife, have to sleep in the same room (1985, s.325). For these purposes, children under 10 may be disregarded.

A room means any room normally used in the locality as either a bedroom or a living room (1985, s.325). Kitchens used to be considered a living room, and might still so be held in this connection, at least if it is big enough to accommodate a bed (*Zaitzeff v Olmi*, 1952) as well as all the necessary kitchen utilies.

The final point to note, which reduces the impact of this test, is that there is overcrowding not when two or more people do actually sleep in the same room, as prescribed, but when the number of rooms means that they have to do so. Thus, a couple, with two children of opposite sexes and 10 years old or more, with two living rooms, are not overcrowded, because the couple could occupy separate rooms, with one each of the children (of the appropriate sex).

(b) **Space standard.** This standard works by the calculation of a permitted number for the dwelling, in one of two ways: the lower number thus calculated is the permitted number for the dwelling (1985, s.326).

One test is based on the number of living rooms in the dwelling (disregarding a room of less than 50 square feet):

> One room, two persons;
> Two rooms, three persons;
> Three rooms, five persons;
> Four rooms, seven and a half persons;
> Five rooms or more, 10 persons plus two for each room in excess of five rooms.

The other test is based on floor areas of each room size:

> Less than 50 square feet, no-one;
> 50 to less than 70 square feet, half a person;
> 70 to less than 90 square feet, one person;
> 90 to less than 110 square feet, one and a half persons;
> 110 square feet or larger, two persons.

The reference to a "half person" is because, for these purposes, a child below the age of one counts not at all, and a child from one year old but who has not yet reached 10 counts as a half.

2. PERMISSIBLE OVERCROWDING

14.11 Categories. There are four circumstances in which overcrowding, although offending the above criteria, is still permissible:

(a) **Licensed overcrowding.** On the application of an occupier, or an intending occupier, of a dwelling (but not on the application of the landlord, or of the local authority), a licence may be issued (in prescribed form), which lasts for no more than one year at a time (1985, s.330).

The licence is issued by the local authority, having regard to exceptional circumstances, expedience and, where appropriate, seasonal increases in population.

The licence must state how many people are to be permitted. A copy must be served on the landlord. It may be revoked at any time by one month's notice.

(b) **Temporary overcrowding**. There is no overcrowding if additional members of the occupier's family are staying with him temporarily (1985, s.329).

(c) **Natural growth**. Natural growth occurs when a child achieves a relevant age (14.10).

If the occupier applies to the local authority for alternative accommodation, either before the child reaches the relevant age or before any prosecution is instigated (or possession proceedings, *cf*. 14.16), there will be no illegal overcrowding until either there is an offer of suitable alternative accommodation (14.12) by the authority, which the occupier fails to accept, or the opportunity arises (after the child reaches the relevant age) of asking someone else living in the house, who is not himself a member of the occupier's family, to leave, which opportunity the occupier fails to take (1985, s.328).

An occupier need only ask someone else to leave if it is reasonably practicable for that person to do so, which is to be considered in all the circumstances, including whether or not there was suitable alternative accommodation available to him.

The exemption only continues to apply provided all the people sleeping in the house are those who were sleeping there at the date on which the child reached the relevant age, or their children.

(d) **Original overcrowding**. This refers to premises overcrowded when the overcrowding provisions themselves first applied to the house (Housing (Consequential Provisions) Act 1985, Sch.4). As the provisions have applied throughout the country since at least 1935, this exemption is unlikely to be of relevance today.

14.12 Suitable alternative accommodation. Although this phrase is used in the Rent Act 1977 (5.170) and the Housing Acts 1985 (3.120) and 1988 (4.107–4.115), the term has its own meaning in the context of overcrowding (14.11, (c), (d)).

14.13 Alternative accommodation is only suitable for these purposes if:

(a) The occupier and family can live in the house without overcrowding;

(b) The authority certify it as suitable to his needs and the needs of his family as regards security of tenure, proximity to work, means, and otherwise; and,

(c) If the house belongs to the authority, they can certify it as being suitable to his needs as regards extent of accommodation (1985, s.342).

They can only so certify extent if they provide a house with two bedrooms (*n.b.* not living rooms) for four people, three bedrooms for five, and four bedrooms for seven. It is, accordingly, a higher standard than that set by the overcrowding limits.

3. OFFENCES

14.14 Categories of offence. There are three sets of offences created by the overcrowding provisions:

(a) **Rent book offences.** Every rent book or similar document must contain:

  (i) A summary of the overcrowding offences;
  (ii) A statement of the power of the authority to licence overcrowding (14.11, (a)); and
  (iii) A statement of the permitted number of occupants (14.10, (b)), (1985, s.332).

  Either the occupier or the landlord can ask the authority for a written statement of permitted number at any time. The authority can require the occupier to produce his rent book for inspection and—provided the occupier has it—it is an offence to fail to do so (1985, s.336). It is also an offence to fail to provide the summary and statements, although it is a defence to a charge based on the insertion of an incorrect permitted number that it was number provided by the authority (1985, s.332).

(b) **Landlord's offences.** A landlord who causes or permits a dwelling to be overcrowded commits an offence (1985, s.331). This may occur when the landlord has reasonable cause to believe there might be illegal overcrowding, or by failing to make enquiries as to the number intending to occupy a dwelling, or, if the authority serve notice on the landlord that there is illegal overcrowding, by failing to take possession proceedings (14.16; 1985, s.331). Finally, unless the authority already know of the overcrowding, the landlord is obliged to notify the authority once he learns of it (1985, s.333).

(c) **Occupier's offences**. The occupier commits an offence when he causes or permits premises to be illegally overcrowded (1985, s.327).

The authority have power to seek information from the occupier as to numbers in a dwelling, failure to comply with which demand, or providing an answer which the occupier knows to be false in a material particular, is also an offence (1985, s.335).

14.15 Prosecution of offences. The local authority may themselves commit an offence under these provisions. No one but a local authority may prosecute an overcrowding offence committed by a private individual, but a private individual may prosecute an authority, albeit only with the consent of the Attorney-General (1985, s.339); this will not easily be forthcoming.

4.   POSSESSION PROCEEDINGS

14.16 Protection. Rent Act protection is lost to occupiers whose premises are illegally overcrowded (Rent Act 1977, s.101). It is, however, only illegal overcrowding that Rent Act protection, so that permissible overcrowding will allow the occupier to remain in the premises. The landlord must still determine the tenancy at common law (1.108–1.141). There is no equivalent lifting of Housing Act 1988 security for Housing Act assured tenants.

14.17 In addition, the authority may themselves bring proceedings for possession of premises illegally overcrowded, and recover their costs of doing so from the landlord (1985, s.338). The authority must serve prior notice on the occupier, giving the occupier 14 days within which to abate the overcrowding.

Houses in Multiple Occupation

14.18 Occupation of house or flat. A house in multiple occupation (HMO) is a house occupied by persons who do not form a single household (1985, s.345). The definition was extended by the Local Government and Housing Act 1989 to include parts of buildings, *i.e.* flats in multiple occupation (1985, s.345(2)).

14.19 Occupation. Occupation for these purposes includes any class of occupation (Chapter 1), not only tenants, so that a former tenant occupying pending the expiry of a suspended possession order was held still to be in occupation under these provisions (*Minford Properties v Hammersmith LBC*, 1978).

14.20 Single household. The key question is whether the occupants form a single household. There are no fixed criteria (*Simmons v Pizzey*, 1977).

14.21 In *Barnes v Sheffield CC*, 1995, the Court of Appeal considered whether a group of students living in a shared house were a single household. The Court said that although it would be wrong to suggest that there was a litmus test which could be applied to the question whether they were a separate household, the following factors were helpful indicators:

(a) Whether the persons living in the house came to it as a single group or whether they were independently recruited;

(b) What facilities were shared;

(c) Whether the occupiers were responsible for the whole house or just their particular rooms;

(d) Whether individual tenants were able to, or did, lock other occupiers out of their rooms;

(e) Whose responsibility it was to recruit new occupiers when individuals left;

(f) Who allocated rooms;

(g) The size of the property;

(h) How stable the group composition was;

(i) Whether the mode of living was communal.

14.22 On this basis, the Court of Appeal upheld the decision of the county court judge that the house was not an HMO because the group of students occupying it were a single household.

14.23 In *Islington LBC v Rogers* (1999), the occupants, young professionals, came to the property individually and stayed for dissimilar periods. It was held that the occupants could only be said to form a single household if the relationship between them provided a particular reason for them living in the same house, e.g. family, employment or longstanding friendship. That was lacking in the present case.

14.24 People living in single rooms but sharing a kitchen could still constitute a single household (*Hackney LBC v Ezedinma*, 1981).

14.25 Hostels. A house used as a hostel for women, including alcoholics and the mentally disturbed, who stayed for different lengths of time and lived in dormitories has been held to be an HMO (*Silbers v Southwark LBC*, 1977). Similarly, a Women's Aid Refuge, in which 75 people were living temporarily, was held to be an HMO even though no-one had any particular part of the house to themselves and the business of the house (eating, cooking, cleaning) was organised collectively (*Simmons v Pizzey*, 1977).

14.26 A bed-and-breakfast hotel used to accommodate the homeless can be an HMO (*R. v Hackney LBC, Ex p. Thrasyvoulou*, 1986; *R. v Hackney LBC Ex p. Evenbray*, 1987).

14.27 Classes of action. There are five classes of action which an authority may take in relation to an HMO.

14.28 They are:

    (i) Overcrowding controls;

    (ii) Registration schemes;

    (iii) Execution of works;

    (iv) Management regulations; and

    (v) Control orders.

14.29 These powers are additional to those considered in the last two Chapters. Codes of Practice on any matter arising under Pt XI of the Housing Act 1985 (1985, s.395A), may be, but have not yet been, issued. While breach of a Code does not give rise to any civil or criminal liability, a Code will be admissible in evidence in proceedings and—where relevant—must be taken into account in determining questions arising in proceedings.

14.30 Persons having control and managing. Action in relation to HMOs is generally taken against the person having control of the HMO or the person managing it.

14.31   The person having control is defined in the same way as for repairs notices (12.29).

14.32   The person managing is the owner or lessee of the house who receives—directly or through an agent or trustee—rents or other payments from persons who are tenants of parts of the premises or who are lodgers. The manager remains so even if the rents or other payments are being paid to another person, who is not the owner or lessee, whether voluntarily or in pursuance of a court order, *e.g.* to the local authority to cover arrears of rates owed by the landlord (1985, s.398(6)). "Other payments" includes the collection of meter monies from gas and electricity meters used by tenants (*Jacques v Liverpool CC*, 1996).

1.   OVERCROWDING CONTROLS

14.33   Overcrowding notice. Under 1985, s.358, a local authority may serve notice in respect of an HMO which appears to them to accommodate, or to be likely to accommodate, an excessive number of persons, specifying the maximum number who are to sleep in each room in the house. The notice may also state that some rooms are unsuitable for sleeping. The maximum stated may be age-related.

14.34   The notice is to be served on the occupier of the house, or on any person having control and management of the house.

14.35   The notice must additionally contain one of two further classes of prohibition.

(a) **Reduction of existing occupation.** The person served must not:

   (i) Knowingly permit a room to be occupied other than in accordance with the notice; or
   (ii) Allow so many people to live in the house that it is impossible for them to occupy without offending the notice, or without sleeping in parts of the house which are not rooms, or without two persons of the opposite sex and over the age of 12 (*cf.* 14.10(b)), not living together as man and wife, being obliged to sleep in the same room.

(b) **Natural wastage.** The person served must not:

   (i) Knowingly permit a room to be occupied by a new resident, other than in accordance with the notice; or

(ii) Knowingly permit a new resident to occupy any part of the premises if it is not possible so to do without offending the notice, or without sleeping in parts of the house which are not rooms, or without two persons of the opposite sex and over the age of 12, not living together as man and wife, being obliged to sleep in the same room.

14.36   Breach of either class of notice is a criminal offence.

14.37   Procedure. The authority must provide seven days' notice of intention before serving the overcrowding notice itself, to permit appeal, the effect of which will be to defer the operative date of the notice until the final determination of the appeal.

14.38   Variation and revocation. The notice may be revoked or varied by the authority at any time, on application by someone with an estate of interest in the house, and a refusal to revoke or vary may also be appealed. If the authority have served notice of class (b), above, they may revoke it and substitute a notice of class (a) at any time.

14.39   Overcrowding directions. Under 1985, s.354, the authority have an additional power to serve directions to reduce overcrowding, by fixing a limit to the number of persons, or households, or both, who may occupy the house, in order either to remedy, or to prevent the occurrence of, a state of affairs calling for a works notice (14.69–14.81).

14.40   Although the house must be in multiple occupation at the time of service of the directions, the number stated may be a larger number than is currently in occupation, so that, to this extent, it is not exclusively a direction to reduce (*Simmons v Pizzey*, 1977).

14.41   Directions do not require the owner or occupier of the house to reduce to the number set, by eviction: if there are already more people in the house than the authority have specified, the duty is not to permit the number to increase further, and not to replace departing occupants. If the number set is higher than the number in the house for the time being, the duty is not to exceed that number.

14.42   Procedure. The authority must likewise give seven days' notice of intention to issue directions (14.37), and must post a copy of this notice and, when they issue, the directions themselves, in some part of the house where it is accessible to those living there (*e.g.* entrance hall).

14.43 Variation and revocation. There is no direct right to appeal the directions themselves, but persons served may make representations to the authority between notice of intention and issue of directions, and may apply for variation or revocation of directions, on refusal of which application, an appeal may be made to the county court.

14.44 Criminal offence. It is an offence to fail to comply with the duties imposed by the directions.

14.45 Directions and works notice. An authority may, when issuing a "works notice" (14.69–14.81), instead of specifying such works as are necessary for the people presently in occupation, specify lesser works for a smaller number, and contemporaneously issue a direction under the last paragraph (1985, s.352).

14.46 Additional powers. When an overcrowding notice has, or directions have, been issued, the authority enjoy additional powers to require of any occupier information that enables them to supervise continued occupation of the premises. It is a criminal offence to fail to comply with such a request, or to reply with information known to be false in a material particular (1985, s.356).

2. REGISTRATION SCHEME

14.47 Model schemes. Local authorities enjoy power to introduce registration schemes, either for all HMOs in their area, or for all HMOs within a specified description, or within a specied area. These have no greater purpose in themselves than to record information about HMOs in their districts (1985, s.346, s.346A).

14.48 The Secretary of State may prepare model schemes, and provided that a scheme conforms to one of these models no consent is required from the Secretary of State to introduce it; otherwise, express confirmation of a scheme is required (1985, s.346B). Model schemes are available in DoE Circular 3/97.

14.49 Prior to adoption of a registration scheme, steps must be taken to publicise it and, once adopted, both the scheme and the register itself must be available for inspection (HA 1985, s.349).

14.50 A scheme may be revoked at any time by the authority (1985, s.346(3)).

14.51 Registration. Subject to any prescribed maximum, authorities must charge for registration (1985, s.346A(4), (5)). Registration is for a five year period, after which application must be made to renew it (1985, s.346A(2)).

14.52 Additional powers. The authority obtain additional powers to require information from persons with an interest, or living, in an HMO within a scheme, failure to comply with which request, or compliance through what is known to be a misstatement, constitute a criminal offence (1985, s.350).

14.53 Control provisions. Onto a registration scheme, the authority may graft "control provisions" (not to be confused with control orders: 14.101–14.118) (1985, s.347). Such provisions cannot affect occupation at the time they are imposed provided all the occupiers have been in occupation without interruption since before registration.

14.54 Scope of provisions. control provisions prevent both occupation of a house which is not registered under the scheme, and occupation in numbers greater than those for which the house is so registered (1985, s.347(1)). Control provisions may empower the authority to decline registration on the grounds of unsuitability of premises or that the person to have control (12.29) or management of the house (14.32) is not a fit and proper person to do so.

14.55 Control provisions may also empower the authority to impose a precondition on registration, by way of requiring works to make the premises suitable for the extent of use for which registration is sought, or imposing conditions as to the management of the house during the registration period.

14.56 Where there is a finding that the proposed manager is not a fit and proper person, registration should be refused. If there are doubts about the fitness of the manager conditions may be appropriate: *Brent LBC v Reynolds*, 2001.

14.57 Refusal and variation of registration. The authority are bound to give written reasons for refusal of registration or preconditions. Refusal of application for registration, or for a variation or renewal of registration, may be appealed. Even once registered, the authority may alter the number of persons for which the house is registered or revoke registration for failure to carry out works because the house has deteriorated (1985, s.348A). The authority may also subsequently revoke registration because the person having control of or managing the house is not a fit and proper person. Subsequent action may be appealed.

14.58 Special control provisions. A further layer of control may be added to a registration scheme through the adoption of special control provisions, intended to prevent HMOs—either through their existence or the behaviour of their residents—"adversely affecting the amenity or character of the area in which they are situated" (1985, s.348B(1)).

14.59 There is no model registration scheme for special control provisions (*cf.* above, 14.48), and consent to the individual scheme must be obtained (14.48).

14.60 Special control provisions may provide for the refusal or revocation of registration, reduction of the numbers of households or persons for which the house is registered, or the imposition of conditions (1985, s.348B). The conditions can relate to the management of the house or the behaviour of its occupants.

14.61 Refusal of registration and renewal. Other than houses in multiple occupation prior to the registration scheme being introduced, special control provisions may permit refusal of registration on the basis of the number of other HMOs in the vicinity (1985, s.348B(5), (6)). Nor can there be a refusal of application for renewal (14.51) unless there has been a "management failure" (1985, s.148B(5)), *i.e.* a failure on the part of the person having control of or managing the house to take such steps as are reasonably practicable to prevent the existence of the house or the behaviour of its residents from adversely affecting the amenity or character of the area in which the house is situated, or to reduce the adverse effect (1985, s.384F).

14.62 Revocation of registration. Special control provisions may (1985, s.384B(4)) permit the authority to revoke registration where there has been occupation in excess of the permitted number, or where there has been a breach of condition and in either case this is due to a "management failure" (14.61).

14.63 Written statement. A written statement must be given by the authority of reasons for any refusal, revocation or imposition of conditions (1985, s.348C(1)).

14.64   Appeal. The decision of the authority may be appealed (1985, s.348C(3)).

14.65   Occupancy directions. Where the authority revoke the registration of a house, special control provisions may provide for an occupancy direction to be served, requiring—within a minimum of 28 days—a reduction in the level of occupation to that below which registration is required (14.54)—1985, s.348D(1).

14.66   An occupancy direction can only be served if there has been a serious management failure (14.61) which has resulted in a serious adverse effect on the amenity or character of the area (1985, s.348D(2)). A written statement of reasons for serving the direction must be given and it can be appealed (1985, s.348E).

14.67   The direction is served on the person having control of (12.29) or managing the house (14.32) and requires him to take all reasonably practicable steps to reduce the level of occupancy within the specified timescale (1985, s.348D(4)). To achieve this, all assured tenants (including assured shorthold) (4.04) lose their security of tenure (the same does not, however, apply to Rent Act 1977 tenants).

14.68   Criminal Offences. Breach of any requirement of the scheme, including occupation of an unregistered house, occupation by a number in excess of those for which the house is registered, is a criminal offence, as is failure to take practical steps to comply with an occupancy direction (1985, s.348G).

3.   EXECUTION OF WORKS

14.69   Works notices. Authorities can require works to be carried out to HMOs. These powers are additional to those considered in the last two Chapters. Authorities must keep a register of any works notices (1985, s.352). Where a works notice has been complied with, a further notice may not be served in relation to the same requirement for five years, unless there has been a change in circumstances in the house.

14.70   General works. Under 1985, s.352, an authority may serve notice requiring the execution of those works considered necessary, where the premises fails to meet one or more of the prescribed requirements and because of that failure the premises are not reasonably suitable for occupation by the number of people or households for the time being accommodated on the premises. Alternatively, the notice may specify a lesser schedule of works, and be accompanied by overcrowding directions (14.39).

14.71 The requirements are (*cf.* 12.19):

(a) Satisfactory facilities for the storage and preparation and cooking of food including an adequate number of sinks with a satisfactory supply of hot and cold water (although note that in *R. v Hackney LBC Ex p. Evanbray*, 1987, it was held that no reasonable local authority could require the provision of cooking facilities in a hotel where food was available);

(b) An adequate number of suitably located water closets for the exclusive use of the occupants;

(c) An adequate number of suitably located fixed baths or showers and wash-hand basins each of which has a satisfactory supply of hot and cold water for the exclusive use of occupiers;

(d) An adequate means of escape from fire; and

(e) Adequate other fire precautions.

14.72 Preliminary notice. A preliminary notice procedure to proceed service of a works notice has been prescribed (1985, s.377A). Under the Housing (Enforcement Procedures for Houses in Multiple Occupation) Order 1997, unless the authority consider it necessary to take action immediately, the authority must first serve a "minded to" notice, setting out why they are considering serving a works notice and the proposed works, affording the person served at least 14 days in which to make representations. The authority must consider any representation made.

14.73 Service of notices. The preliminary notice is to be served on the person having control of the house (12.29), or the person managing the house (14.32) (1985, s.352). The authority must also inform any other, owner, lessee, occupier or mortgagee of the service of the notice. The same applies if the authority proceed to the works notice itself.

14.74 Compliance. The authority have power to withdraw the works notice if, after service, they are satisfied that the numbers in the house have been reduced to such an extent that the works are no longer necessary (1985, s.352). In the absence of withdrawal, however, the works must be executed within such time as the authority specify in the notice, which must be not less than 21 days after service, or such longer time as the authority may subsequently permit, even if there is an appeal: an authority will normally permit a longer time if there is an appeal (14.77), though they are not bound to do so.

14.75 Criminal offence. Appeal does, however, defer any criminal offence: it is otherwise an offence to fail to comply with the notice within the time specified, or allowed, or within such longer time as the court may allow of the final determination of an appeal (1985, s.376).

14.76 Works in default. Once there has been criminal non-compliance, or if the authority are of the opinion that reasonable progress towards compliance is not being made, the authority have power, on giving seven days' notice, to execute the works in default, and to recover their costs of so doing (1985, s.375).

14.77 Appeal. Appeal lies to the county court, and must be issued within 21 days of service of notice (1985, s.353). The court has limited powers, and there are limited grounds on which an appeal may be pursued. These include:

> That the notice was not justified having regard to conditions in the house and number of occupants;
>
> That the authority have unreasonably refused to agree an alternative schedule of works;
>
> That the works required are unreasonable in extent or character, or are unnecessary; and,
>
> That the time allowed is insufficient.

14.78 In addition, it is a ground for appeal that the authority failed to serve a "minded to" notice (14.72).

14.79 If the court is satisfied that since service the numbers in the house have been reduced, it may revoke the order, or vary the schedule of works, provided that it is also satisfied that adequate steps have been taken, (*e.g.* by the issue of directions: 14.39), to keep the numbers down.

14.80 The reference to an alternative schedule of works (14.77) as a ground of appeal underlies the essentially administrative nature of these provisions. Even after service the authority may decline to take further action, or postpone the time for compliance with the notice, to enable the person served to execute such alternative works.

14.81 Expenses. In addition to recovering the cost of works carried out in default (14.76), the authority may charge for the administrative costs of determining whether to serve a notice, identifying the works to be carried out and serving the notice (1985, s.352A). The maximum charge is £300: the Housing (Recovery of Expenses for Section 352 Notices) Order 1997.

14.82 Private law duty. Housing Act 1996, s.73 provides for a new s.353A of the 1985 Act, under which the person having control (12.29) or managing (14.32) the HMO will be under a duty to take all reasonably practicable steps to prevent the HMO falling into a state requiring the service of a works notice. If any tenant, other occupier or any other person, such as a visitor, suffers any loss, damage or personal injury because of a failure to comply with this duty, will be able to sue for damages (1985, s.353A(2)). It will also be a criminal offence to fail to comply with this duty. The section has not yet been brought into force.

14.83 Fire precautions. In the case of any house within a designated class, the otherwise discretionary powers to serve a works notice (1985, s.352 (14.70) become mandatory so far as concerns means of escape from fire and other fire precautions, *i.e.* the authority are bound to use them (1985, s.365).

14.84 The class designated is that of houses which comprise at least three storeys (excluding a storey lying wholly or mainly below the floor level of the principal entrance to the house), unless within a number of exemptions, including properties owned or managed by local authorities and registered social landlords, those with only a small number of occupiers, and those containing at least one third self-contained flats let on long leases which complied on their creation with building regulations: Housing (Fire Safety in Houses in Multiple Occupation) Order 1997.

14.85 Partial closure. In addition, if the authority conclude that—were part of the HMO not used for human habitation— existing fire precautions would be adequate, they may make a closing order on that part (1985, s.368). Alternatively, they may accept an undertaking that part is not used for human habitation.

14.86   In either event, the same general provisions as in relation to unfitness (12.43–12.48) (including as to rehousing and compensation—12.142–12.158) apply, save that the only ground on which the authority may subsequently determine the order is that there has been such a change of circumstances that the means of escape from fire would be adequate, even if the formerly closed part were again to be used.

14.87   Scope of notice. Before serving a notice, the authority are bound to consult with the fire authority either if the action is compulsory (14.84) or if it falls within regulations (1985, s.365, see the Housing (Fire Safety in Houses in Multiple Occupation) Order 1997).

14.88   The extent of precautions required can include smoke screens at the top of a flight of stairs (*Horgan v Birmingham Corp.*, 1964), and the authority can have regard to the age, character, or other requirements of the particular occupants, including whether or not there is any supervision, *e.g.* by way of a housekeeper, in the house (*Kingston-Upon-Hull DC v University of Hull*, 1979).

14.89   The notice must specify a time for completion of the works, although the authority may subsequently extend it.

14.90   If the notice is not complied with not only may a criminal offence be committed, but the authority also acquire power to execute the works in default, and recover their costs of so doing (14.76).

14.91   Cumulative provisions. These provisions are additional to those considered in the last Chapter: 13.55–13.58.

4.   MANAGEMENT REGULATIONS

14.92   Proper standards of management. Under 1985, s.369 regulations ("Management Regulations") may be issued to ensure that the person managing (14.32) an HMO observes proper standards of management (1985, s.369). The current Management Regulations are to be found in SI 1990/830.

14.93   The regulations require the manager of the house to ensure the repair, maintenance, cleansing or, as necessary the good order of:

  (a) All means of water supply and drainage in the house;

(b) Parts of the house and installations in common use;

(c) Living accommodation;

(d) Windows and other means of ventilation;

(e) Means of escape from fire, apparatus, systems, and other things provided by way of fire precautions;

(f) Outbuildings, yards, etc. in common use.

14.94 The manager must also:

(g) Make satisfactory arrangements for the disposal of refuse and litter from the house;

(h) Ensure the taking of reasonable precautions for the general safety of residents;

(i) Display in the house a notice of the name and address and telephone number, if any, of the manager;

(j) Provide specified information to the local authority about the occupancy of the house where the authority give him written notice to that effect.

14.95 Occupier duties. Duties are imposed on those living in the house to ensure that the manager can effectively carry out these requirements.

14.96 Criminal offence. Failure to comply with the regulations is a criminal offence.

14.97 Execution of works. If the authority are of the opinion that the condition of the premises is defective because of a failure to comply with the management regulations, they may first serve a preliminary "minded to" notice (14.72) and, subsequently, order the execution of works (1985, s.372). Notice is served on the manager of the house (14.32).

14.98 The works notice must specify the works to be carried out. It must specify a period of not less than 21 days for commencement and a reasonable time for completion. If there is an appeal, the notice does not take effect until such time as the court may allow from the final determination of the appeal (14.100). Once the notice takes effect, however, the authority acquire the right to carry out works in default and recover their expenses of so doing, in the same way as failure to comply with a works notice under 1985, s.352 (14.76).

14.99   Criminal offence. It is a criminal offence to fail to comply with a notice.

14.100   Appeal. An appeal against a works notice under these provisions is on similar grounds to those available against a works notice under s.352 (14.77).

5.   CONTROL ORDER

14.101   Vesting control in authority. A control order has been described as, and is, the most draconian measure which a local authority can apply to an HMO. Substantively, it involves vesting in the authority themselves "control," by which is meant management and possession, of the premises, *i.e.* the authority literally take them away from the landlord.

14.102   Conditions. The power to make a control order arises if either:

(a) A notice has been served or directions given under ss.372 (14.97), 352 (14.69–14.74), or 354 (14.39) of the 1985 Act; or

(b) It appears to the authority that action might be taken under any of these provisions (1985, s.379).

(c) It must also appear to the authority that living conditions in the house are such that, for the protection or the safety, welfare or health of people living in the house, it is necessary to make the order.

14.103   The inclusion of welfare would seem to enable the authority to take into account factors which would not necessarily qualify under any of the specified provisions, *e.g.* smells, noise, anti-social behaviour. The threat of eviction has been held a proper welfare consideration (*R. v Southwark LBC Ex p. Lewis Levy*, 1983).

14.104   Procedure. A control order comes into force as soon as it is made (1985, s.379). It is designedly peremptory, to prevent action against occupiers in retaliation for, or to remove conditions calling for, the order. As soon as practicable after making the order, the authority enter into possession of the premises and take such steps as appear to them necessary to protect the safety, welfare or health of residents. The authority must also post a copy of the order, and a notice setting out the effect of the order, in some place in the house where it is accessible to those living in it (*cf.* 14.42), and serve a copy of the order and notice on anyone the authority know to have been the manager of the premises (14.32), and anyone else with an interest in it.

14.105 Existing orders under the provisions considered hitherto come to an end on the commencement of the control order (1985, s.381).

14.106 Powers. Once the control order is in operation (14.104), the authority have power to do anything which anyone else in possession of the premises could do. They must exercise this power so as to maintain proper standards of management in the house (*cf.* the Management Regulations, 14.93), and are otherwise to take such steps as, had the control order not been imposed, they would have considered necessary by way of notice or directions (1985, s.381).

14.107 The authority may also take over responsibility for any furniture in the house which has been provided to residents (1985, s.383). The owner of any such furniture may, however, ask the authority to renounce this right, if they think fit.

14.108 The authority acquire rights to enter the house and any part of it for the purposes of survey, examination or the execution of works, and if anyone obstructs them in the exercise of this power, they may apply to the magistrates' court for an order to permit such exercise, breach of which is a criminal offence (1985, s.397).

14.109 Rights of occupation. The authority may, but need not, exclude from the effect of the order a part of the premises occupied by someone having an interest in the house, although not someone without such an interest even if he qualifies as the manager of the house (1985, s.380).

14.110 In relation to existing tenancies, Rent Act and Housing Act 1988 security will continue notwithstanding the control order (1985, s.382), although any new tenancies which the authority may create will not be protected by the Rent Acts or the Housing Act 1988 (1985, s.381), but would seem to be secure tenancies, under Housing Act 1985, at least until there is a determination of the control order, at which time they will become protected or assured.

14.111 The authority have power to grant new tenancies or other rights of occupation (*i.e.* licences), although they cannot grant a fixed-term entitlement for a period in excess of one month, or a periodic right which requires more than four weeks' notice (1985, s.381).

14.112 Management scheme. Subject to the exercise of the compulsory purchase power (14.117), the authority must draw up a "management scheme" for the house, within eight weeks of making the order (1985, s.386). If—within the same period—the authority seek to use their compulsory purchase powers, this obligation is deferred until eight weeks after a final decision on the purchase (1985, Sch.13).

14.113 The scheme is a plan for the improvement of the house, by way of a statement of what works the authority would have considered necessary under the powers considered in paras 14.69–14.100, above, or under any public health legislation (Chapter 13). The scheme must specify a maximum number of occupants, and must estimate the cost of the works to be executed.

14.114 A copy of the scheme must be served on anyone known to the authority to have an interest in the house, and anyone else on whom the control order was served (14.104), primarily for the purposes of appeal (14.118).

14.115 Provision is made for detailed accounts to be drawn up and maintained by the authority (1985, s.390), and for the payment of compensation, on a scale related to market rents, to the dispossessed proprietor (1985, s.389).

14.116 Life of order. Unless previously determined by revocation on the authority's own motion, or on application (1985, s.392), or on an appeal against imposition of the order or against a refusal to revoke (14.118), or by compulsory purchase by the authority, the control order lasts exactly five years from the date when it was made (1985, s.392).

14.117 Compulsory Purchase. The authority enjoy power to purchase, compulsorily if needs be, a house made the subject of a control order, in which case they are exempt from the obligation to draw up a management scheme (1985, s.394 and Sch.13), for the improvement of the house, provided the compulsory purchase order is made (not confirmed) within eight weeks of the control order (14.112).

14.118 Appeal. There are three classes of appeal:

(a) **Against control order.** This lies to the county court, and must be made within six weeks of the date a copy of the management scheme is served (1985, s.384).
The grounds include:

> That it was not necessary to make the order to protect the safety, welfare or health of residents;
> That conditions in the house do not call for a control order; and,
> That a part of the premises occupied by a dispossessed proprietor ought to have been excluded.

If, on an appeal, the court is minded to revoke the order, it may authorise the authority to create longer residential interests than could otherwise have been created (14.111), although only interests which will determine within six months of the proposed date for termination of the order (1985, Sch.13). The purpose of this power is to protect the occupants when the dispossessed proprietor resumes control.

(b) **Against management scheme.** An appeal also lies to the county court against the management scheme, which must likewise be brought within six weeks of service of a copy of the scheme: if there is an appeal against the order as well as the scheme, the two appeals should be heard together if possible (1985, Sch.13).
The grounds include:

> That the works proposed are unreasonable in character and extent;
> That the number of individuals specified for the house is unreasonably low; and,
> That the appellant does not accept financial factors in the scheme.

The court has power to vary or revoke the scheme, although if it decides to revoke the order itself it need not trouble with the appeal against the scheme.

(c) **Against refusal to revoke.** This also lies to the county court, and no special grounds are set out, although if the court dismisses an appeal against refusal to revoke, the appellant cannot appeal against a further refusal to revoke for another six months (1985, s.393).

INDEX